Frank Müller-Langer

Creating R&D Incentives for Medicines for Neglected Diseases

GABLER RESEARCH

Ökonomische Analyse des Rechts

Die ökonomische Analyse des Rechts untersucht Rechtsnormen auf ihre gesellschaftlichen Folgewirkungen und bedient sich dabei des methodischen Instrumentariums der Wirtschaftswissenschaften, insbesondere der Mikroökonomie, der Neuen Institutionen- und Konstitutionenökonomie. Sie ist ein interdisziplinäres Forschungsgebiet, in dem sowohl Rechtswissenschaftler als auch Wirtschaftswissenschaftler tätig sind und das zu wesentlichen neuen Erkenntnissen über Funktion und Wirkungen von Rechtsnormen geführt hat.

Die Schriftenreihe enthält Monographien zu verschiedenen Rechtsgebieten und Rechtsentwicklungen. Sie behandelt Fragestellungen aus den Bereichen Wirtschaftsrecht, Vertragsrecht, Haftungsrecht, Sachenrecht und verwaltungsrechtliche Regulierung.

Frank Müller-Langer

Creating R&D Incentives for Medicines for Neglected Diseases

An Economic Analysis of Parallel Imports, Patents, and Alternative Mechanisms to Stimulate Pharmaceutical Research

With a foreword by Prof. Dr. Hans-Bernd Schäfer

GABLER

RESEARCH

Bibliographic information published by the Deutsche Nationalbibliothek
The Deutsche Nationalbibliothek lists this publication in the Deutsche Nationalbibliografie; detailed bibliographic data are available in the Internet at http://dnb.d-nb.de.

Doctoral thesis, Hamburg University 2008

1st Edition 2009

Editorial Office: Claudia Jeske | Sabine Schöller

Gabler is part of the specialist publishing group Springer Science+Business Media.
www.gabler.de

Umschlaggestaltung: KünkelLopka Medienentwicklung, Heidelberg
Printed on acid-free paper
Printed in Germany

ISBN 978-3-8349-1730-0

Meinem Großvater Alois und in Erinnerung an Lieselotte

Foreword

This book is the revised version of a doctoral thesis written at the *Graduiertenkolleg* Law and Economics at Hamburg University. It addresses the market failure with respect to R&D for medicines for tropical diseases and the lack of access to affordable medicines in poor countries.

Tropical diseases, such as malaria or leishmaniasis, are among the main causes of death and disability in developing countries. Medical scholars have since long argued that medicines for those neglected infectious diseases either do not exist at all or badly need improvement. This neglect has two main reasons. First, tropical diseases virtually do not occur in the rich countries of the Northern Hemisphere where the bulk of new pharmaceutical inventions are made. Second, intellectual property protection in poor countries of the Southern Hemisphere, i.e. patents or copyrights, is often poorly developed. The innovator faces the risk of losing research and development (R&D) costs as imitators can offer generic drugs at marginal costs. Therefore, not much research is targeted at developing medicines for tropical diseases as the expected market returns from R&D in the private pharmaceuticals sector are too low.

Frank Müller-Langer provides a well-researched outline of the legal landscape regarding international patent protection. He focuses on the relevant provisions stated in the Agreement on Trade-Related Aspects of Intellectual Property Rights (TRIPS Agreement), which is aimed at harmonizing and strengthening intellectual property protection around the world. He then provides a sophisticated and topical survey of the economic analysis of patents, particularly focusing on patent races, the problem of fragmented patents in biomedical research and on optimal patent design. By applying game-theoretic models the author provides a convincing analysis of the complex economic effects of patents and the question of whether they are beneficial or detrimental to welfare.

In Chapter 4, the author focuses on the effects of intellectual property right extension to poor countries. He shows that the extension of patent protection from an IP-exporting developed country in the Northern Hemisphere to an IP-importing developing country in the Southern Hemisphere is likely to increase welfare in the IP-exporting country but may decrease welfare in the IP-importing country. It follows an up-to-date overview of the empirical evidence regarding the investment in R&D for medicines for tropical diseases showing that there is still insufficient research. R&D efforts to fight malaria have however slightly increased during the last two decades.

In Chapter 5, Frank Müller-Langer provides an excellent and original contribution to the formal literature on the welfare effects of parallel imports. Frank Müller-Langer develops an innovative double-marginalization model with complete information, in which an original manufacturer of a pharmaceutical product faces potential competition from parallel imports by a foreign distributor. The model suggests that parallel imports will never occur in the sub-game perfect Nash equilibrium, as it will always be profitable for the manufacturer to monopolize the home country by undercutting the price of the re-imported pharmaceutical product. But the credible threat of parallel imports reduces the profit of the manufacturer and thus diminishes his incentive to invest in R&D in the first place. Parallel imports undermine patent protection. Therefore, if the unique social objective were to stimulate research, innovators should be entitled to prevent parallel imports. Furthermore, Frank Müller-Langer argues that cross-country price discrimination is beneficial to low-income countries for the following reasons: Low-income countries typically have a relatively high price elasticity of demand for medicine. Thus, they are likely to have access to cheaper medicines when the innovator can successfully engage in international price discrimination. Therefore, parallel trade freedom that makes cross-country price discrimination unfeasible is likely to reduce welfare in low-income countries. Hence, Frank Müller-Langer concludes that a global regime of banning parallel imports from low-income countries to high-income countries is desirable from a developing country's perspective. However, the net effect of parallel imports on global welfare is ambiguous.

This work also provides a comprehensive analysis of mechanisms to stimulate R&D for pharmaceutical products beyond patent protection. Frank Müller-Langer analyzes push mechanisms that typically subsidize research inputs, i.e. publicly-funded research institutions and targeted R&D tax credits. Furthermore, he analyzes the efficacy of pull mechanisms such as advanced purchase commitments and patent buyouts that link payment to successful development of a desired innovation. He concludes that push mechanisms are more suitable than pull mechanisms for stimulating basic research. However, pull mechanisms, such as legally-binding and enforceable advanced purchase commitments, may be better to stimulate research into neglected infectious diseases, and may help mitigate the problem of those consumers in low-income countries who lack access to affordable medicines.

This publication makes a valuable contribution on how to understand and overcome the problem of underinvestment for medicines for tropical diseases. The book also provides an insightful and well-researched analysis of the ambiguous welfare effects of parallel trade freedom.

Prof. Dr. Hans-Bernd Schäfer

Acknowledgments

I wrote this thesis as a doctoral student at the Doctoral College for Law and Economics in Hamburg. In July 2008 it was accepted as a doctoral thesis by the Faculty of Economics at Hamburg University. Since then I have revised the book to include more recent developments, most importantly I have updated the pharmaceutical market figures as well as the global burden of disease figures as soon as new data have become available.

This thesis has accompanied and challenged me from my first scientific steps as a research associate at the Institute of Law and Economics in Hamburg and the Alfred-Weber-Institute for Economics in Heidelberg. It has also enriched my life throughout visiting scholarships at UC Berkeley in 2007 and at Columbia University in 2008 until I finally took up a post-doctoral position at the Max Planck Institute for Intellectual Property, Competition and Tax Law.

First and foremost I would like to take this opportunity to thank my parents, my sister and Nathalie Jorzik for their loving support, kind words, patience and encouragement. I am especially grateful to Prof. Hans-Bernd Schäfer who supervised the thesis. Hans-Bernd Schäfer allowed me to benefit from his comments, advice and generous support. I also owe special thanks to Prof. Martin Nell for acting as a second reviewer, to the chairman of the disputation, Prof. Wolfgang Maennig and to the editors of the scientific series *Economic Analysis of Law* Prof. Peter Behrens, Prof. Thomas Eger, Prof. Manfred Holler and Prof. Claus Ott. Furthermore, I would like to thank Professors Jürgen Eichberger, Eberhard Feess, Keith E. Maskus, Pranab Bardhan, Reto M. Hilty, Monika Schnitzer, Klaus Schmidt, Dietmar Harhoff, Josef Drexl, Alan V. Deardorff, Thomas S. Ulen, Doctors Stephen M. Maurer, Florens Sauerbruch, Henning Grosse Ruse-Kahn and Martina Samwer, along with Andrea Wechsler and Jan Peter Sasse as well as two anonymous reviewers for their helpful comments. I also greatly benefited from the comments and support of my student assistants, colleagues and friends at Hamburg University, Heidelberg University, LMU Munich and the Max Planck Institute for Intellectual Property, Competition and Tax Law. I also wish to thank conference participants in Bologna, Copenhagen, Toulouse and Zagreb as well as seminar participants in Hamburg, Munich and Heidelberg for their valuable comments.

I would particularly like to thank Prof. Robert D. Cooter, Prof. Andrew T. Guzman, Prof. Daniel L. Rubinfeld and Prof. Avery W. Katz for their kind hospitality in Berkeley and New York City, respectively. Special thanks also go to Dr. Ido Baum and Dr. Ohad Soudry for their organization of an invaluable summer school experience at the Universities of Haifa and Tel Aviv in 2005. I also extend a cordial thank you to my students in the European Master Program in Law and Economics who taught me how to teach and to the doctoral students of the International Max Planck Research School for Competition and Innovation.

This thesis owes a great debt to several institutions. The Max Planck Institute for Intellectual Property, Competition and Tax Law financially supported the printing.

Furthermore, the Institute of Law and Economics and the German Research Foundation (DFG) financially supported my research both in Germany and the United States with generous research grants. Needless to say, I also owe a special thank you to my parents who always supported my career aspirations for an even more generous research grant from 1978 to 2003.
Finally, Katherine Walker, Edward Einsiedler, Jesse Jacob, Gabi Rauscher as well as Ute and Steve Saunders kindly agreed to read the manuscript, eliminating errors and providing helpful comments along the way.

Dr. Frank Müller-Langer

Summary Contents

Detailed Contents

List of Abbreviations

AIDS/HIV:	Acquired Immune Deficiency Syndrome/Human Immunodeficiency
AIPLA:	American Intellectual Property Law Association
AMG:	Arzneimittelgesetz (German Drug Law)
BfArM:	Bundesinstitut für Arzneimittel und Medizinprodukte (Federal Institute for Drugs and Medical Devices)
CERGE-EI:	Center for Economic Research and Graduate Education Economic Institute
CRADAs:	Cooperative Research and Development Agreements
CRIPS:	Computer Retrieval of Information on Scientific Projects
DALYs:	Disability Adjusted Life Years
DGP:	Development Guide Plan
DND:	Drugs for Neglected Diseases
Doha Declaration:	Declaration on the TRIPS Agreement and Public Health
DSB:	Dispute Settlement Body
DSU:	Uruguay Round Understanding on Rules and Procedures Governing the Settlement of Disputes
DWL:	Deadweight Loss
ECJ:	European Court of Justice
EMEA:	European Agency for the Evaluation of Medical Products
FDA:	Food and Drug Administration
GATT:	General Agreement on Tariffs and Trade
GDP:	Gross Domestic Product
ICTSD:	International Centre for Trade and Sustainable Development
IFPMA:	International Federation of Pharmaceutical Manufacturers Associations
IUATLD:	International Union Against Tuberculosis and Lung Disease
IP:	Intellectual Property
IPRs:	Intellectual Property Rights
JPO:	Japan Patent Office
LDC:	Least-Developed Country
MMV:	Medicines for Malaria Venture
MSF:	Médecines Sans Frontières
NERA:	National Economic Research Associates
NIAID:	National Institute of Allergy & Infectious Diseases

NIH:	National Institutes of Health
NSAP:	Brazilian National STD/AIDS Programme
OECD:	Organisation for Economic Cooperation and Development
PCR:	Polymerase Chain Reaction
PhRMA:	Pharmaceutical Research and Manufacturers of America
PRISM:	Unit for Policy Research in Science and Medicine
R&D:	Research and Development
SBIR:	Small Business Innovation Research
STD:	Sexually Transmitted Diseases
TB Alliance:	Global Alliance for Tuberculosis Drug Development
TB:	Tuberculosis
TDR:	UNICEF/UNDP/World Bank/WHO Special Programme for Research and Training in Tropical Diseases
TRIPS Agreement:	Agreement on Trade-Related Aspects of Intellectual Property Rights
UN:	United Nations
UNCTAD:	United Nations Conference on Trade and Development
UNDP:	United Nations Development Programme
UNICEF:	United Nations Children's Fund
URA:	Urban Redevelopment Authority of Singapore
USAID:	U.S. Agency for International Development
USPTO:	United States Patent and Trademark Office
WHO:	World Health Organization
WIPO:	World Intellectual Property Organization
WTO:	World Trade Organization

List of Figures and Tables

1. Introduction

"Today, in what is now a globalizing market economy, a growing injustice confronts us. More than 90% of all death and suffering from infectious diseases occurs in the developing world. Some of the reasons that people die from diseases like AIDS, TB, sleeping sickness and other tropical diseases are that lifesaving essential medicines are either too expensive, are not available because they are not seen as financially viable, or because there is virtually no new research and development for priority tropical diseases. This market failure is our next challenge."[1]

Moreover, 98 percent of children who die before their fifth birthday live in the developing world as do all but a few thousand of the millions who die prematurely of TB, malaria, tetanus or measles.[2]

We shall analyze the market failure mentioned above with respect to R&D for medicines for neglected infectious and tropical diseases and the lack of short-term access to affordable medicines in low-income countries.

In recent years several disease-based initiatives supported by governments and private foundations have been set up in order to solve the problem of underinvestment in R&D for pharmaceuticals and insufficient access to medicines in developing countries. Examples include the Medicines for Malaria Venture ("MMV") which accounts for most of today's antimalarial drug development projects,[3] the Global Alliance for TB Drug Development ("TB Alliance")[4] and the Special Programme for Research and Training in Tropical Diseases ("TDR") set up by UNICEF, UNDP, World Bank and WHO.[5] The MVV and TB Alliance's main objective is to convert drug candidates into registered entities. Moreover, they are managed as non-for-profit ventures and employ a social venture capital model that is funded by the public sector.[6] Usually, they collaborate with partners from the pharmaceutical industry, academia and development agencies and rely on business drug development models.[7] Newer sources of funding like the Bill & Melinda Gates Foundation[8] play a significant role in securing short and medium term budgets.[9]

Despite the programs mentioned above the world's poorest regions are still suffering from death and disability from infectious diseases for which vaccines either exist but

---

1 Orbinski, J. (1999), Nobel Prize acceptance speech, Oslo, December 1999.
2 See Sachs (1999) on p. 17.
3 See Ridley et al. (1999).
4 See http://www.tballiance.org/home/home.php (last visited March 24, 2009).
5 See http://www.who.int/tdr/ (last visited March 24, 2009).
6 See also Trouiller et al. (2002) on p. 2192.
7 For instance, see Trouiller et al. (2002) on p. 2192.
8 See http://www.gatesfoundation.org/GlobalHealth/Pri_Diseases/ (last visited March 24, 2009).
9 See Lister (2005).

need improvement or do not exist at all.[10] In fact, deaths caused by infectious diseases contribute most to the health disparity between rich and poor countries (comparative life expectancy at birth being 77 and 52 years respectively).[11] Furthermore, infectious diseases kill 14 million people worldwide every year predominantly amongst poor populations in the developing world.[12]

We shall focus our analysis on infectious diseases such as malaria, trachoma, and dengue as well as on tropical diseases such as lymphatic filariasis, leishmaniasis, and schistosomiasis that predominantly plague poor nations.[13] Despite substantial advances in molecular biology with regard to the biology of the parasites that cause leishmania, African trypanosomiasis or malaria virtually no new chemical entities for these diseases have been developed and marketed so far. Adequate and sufficient R&D for new medicines against these diseases does not exist. For instance, R&D for HIV/AIDS per fatal case is at least 80 times higher than for malaria.[14]

Table 1 shows 20 diseases for which 98 percent of the global burden fell on developing countries.[15] For all these diseases, virtually no R&D efforts are aimed at producing appropriate treatments because potential consumers are too poor to generate sufficient demand which would allow pharmaceutical producers to cover their R&D costs.[16] With respect to the potential incentives for R&D through patent protection the analysis will not consider HIV/AIDS as it is a different disease in the sense that there are strong incentives for pharmaceutical companies in the Northern Hemispehre to develop drugs and treatments for patients in high-income economies.[17] As these incentives have already spurred the development of effective pharmaceutical products and treatments, the debate concerning HIV/AIDS has shifted to how these medicines can be transferred to patients in poor countries.[18]

10 See World Health Organization (2003b). See also Economist (2008) on p. 90ff with respect to the problem of malarial drug resistance. See also McNeil (2008).

11 See Widdus (2001).

12 See World Health Organization (2001b) on p. 144. See also Scholing (2000) on p. 7ff.

13 See Murray et al. (2001) on p. 490ff.

14 See Anderson et al. (1996).

15 See **Appendix 1** for a detailed list of the developing countries with regard to different levels of child and adult mortality. See also Murray and Lopez (1996) and Lanjouw (2002b).

16 For instance, see Trouiller et al. (2002). See also Kremer and Glennerster (2004) on p. 6ff.

17 See Chin and Grossman (1990) and Diwan and Rodrik (1991) on IPRs in the North-South trade context. See also Hestermeyer (2007) on p. 37ff and Grossman and Lai (2004) on p. 1641ff.

18 See Ganslandt et al. (2005) on p. 207ff.

Table 1 *Infectious and Parasitic Diseases for which 98 Percent or More of the Global Burden Fell on Developing Countries*

Disease	Disease DALYs[19] (Thousands, 2004)	Total Deaths (Thousands, 2004)
Syphilis	2,846	99
Diarrhoeal diseases	72,777	2,163
Pertussis	9,882	254
Diphtheria	174	5
Measles	14,853	424
Tetanus	5,283	163
Malaria	33,976	889
Trypanosomiasis	1,673	52
Chagas disease	430	11
Schistosomiasis	1,707	41
Leishmaniasis	1,974	47
Lymphatic filariasis	5,941	0
Onchocerciasis	389	0
Leprosy	194	5
Dengue	670	18
Japanese encephalitis	681	11
Trachoma	1,334	0
Ascariasis	1,851	2
Trichuriasis	1,012	2
Hookworm disease	1,092	0

Source: World Health Organization (2008b)

Trouiller et al. (2002) analyze quantitatively and qualitatively the global drug development output over a period from 1975 to 1999 and conclude that there is an underinvestment in R&D for pharmaceutical products for the diseases mentioned above. In particular, they examined the registration of new chemical entities for tropical diseases that represent a substantial burden in the developing world.[20] They find that although these diseases together account for 11.4 percent of the global disease burden only 1 percent of the 1393 new entities marketed between 1975 and 1999 were registered for them.[21]

Based on the results of Trouiller et al. (2002) it is pertinent to question the effectiveness of the worldwide introduction of patent protection under the TRIPS Agreement and whether it has substantially increased willingness to invest in R&D for pharmaceuticals for tropical diseases.

19 DALYs estimate years of life lost or lived with a disability [Lanjouw (2002b), Table 1 and World Health Organization (2003c) on p. 160].

20 See Trouiller et al. (2002) on p. 2189ff.

21 See Trouiller et al. (2002) on p. 2189, Table 1.

1.1. The Malaria Case

The dearth of R&D for tropical infectious diseases may be further illustrated by the case of malaria, a disease responsible for up to 889,000 deaths and 33,976,000 Disability Adjusted Life Years (DALYs)[22] each year that also contributes to many additional deaths because of comorbidity with other illnesses.[23] **Figure 1** illustrates the distribution of the global burden of malaria and tropical diseases such as trypanosomiasis, chagas disease, schistosomiasis, leishmaniasis, lymphatic filariasis, and onchocerciasis.[24]

Figure 1: *Global Burden of Malaria and Tropical Diseases*

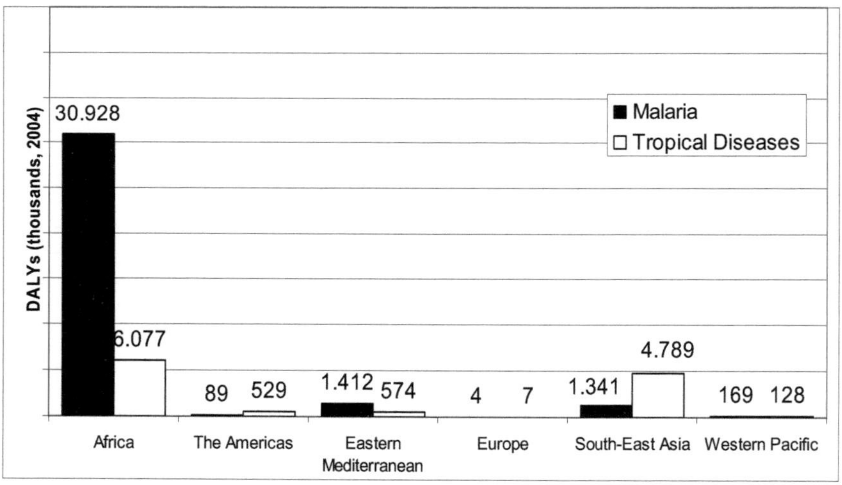

Source: World Health Organization (2008b)

Although recent advances in the biotechnology industry suggest that the development of a malaria vaccine is scientifically feasible its development is not high on the agenda of private pharmaceutical firms. For instance, a report by the National Academy of Science concluded that the development of a malaria vaccine is scientifically

22 According to the WHO DALYs are defined as "the sum of years of potential life lost due to premature mortality and the years of productive life lost due to disability". See World Health Organization (2003c) on p. 160.

23 See World Health Organization (2008b) on p. 54ff. See also World Health Organization (2005); http://rbm.who.int/wmr2005/html/toc.htm (last visited March 24, 2009). See also Breman et al. (2004) and Chima et al. (2003).

24 See also Trouiller et al. (2002) on p. 2189.

feasible.[25] However, scientist and investors doubt that malaria research will be financially rewarding. As potential consumers are too poor to afford new and expensive medicines in sufficient quantities the pharmaceutical firms cannot cover their high costs of R&D for new pharmaceutical products.[26] Furthermore, the phenomenon of fast-developing resistance to existing treatments of malaria makes the situation even more difficult and only constant R&D efforts can ensure a continuous output of new medicines.[27] Another important issue with respect to pharmaceutical products needed to combat malaria is the fact that children and pregnant women are most susceptible to malaria. They represent the majority of more than 3 billion people that live under the threat of malaria.[28] Thus, medicines with specific formulations and clinical studies are required to meet the needs of the most vulnerable population.[29]
From the author's point of view it is therefore of vital importance to examine the following questions:

1. Can stronger patent rights for pharmaceuticals in developing countries – as required by the TRIPS Agreement – ease the problem of underinvestment in R&D for medicines for neglected infectious and tropical diseases?

2. Which incentive programs will provide adequate mechanisms to secure short-term access to affordable medicines in low-income countries?

Addressing the questions mentioned above, the remainder of this thesis is organized as follows.
In Chapter 2, we outline the legal landscape regarding patent protection with respect to medicines for neglected diseases.
Chapter 3 provides a survey of the economic analysis of patents – i.e. the fundamental trade-off of patent protection, patent races, optimal patent design and the problem of fragmented patents in biomedical research – as well as the economics of drug development and pricing.
In Chapter 4, we focus on the microeconomic theory and empirical evidence with respect to patent protection in the developing world. More specifically, we elaborate on the empirical evidence regarding the investment in R&D for medicines for tropical diseases in order to analyze the question as to whether stronger patent protection in the

25 See National Academy of Sciences (1996). See also Morthy et al. (2004) and Kremer and Glennerster (2004) on p. 27. As to the good prospects for schistosomiasis vaccine development, see also Bergquist (2004).
26 See Sachs (1999) on p. 17. See also Médecins Sans Frontières (2003).
27 See http://www.who.int/csr/resources/publications/drugresist/malaria.pdf (last visited March 24, 2009). See also Ridley (2002), Zumla and Grange (2001), and Bloland (2001);
28 See the World Health Organization (2005); http://rbm.who.int/wmr2005/html/toc.htm (last visited March 24, 2009). See also World Health Organization (2008a) on tuberculosis drug resistance. See also World Health Organization (2003a); http://www.rbm.who.int/amd2003/amr2003/amr_toc.htm (last visited March 24, 2009).
29 See Bremen (2001). See International Federation of Pharmaceutical Manufacturers Associations (2004); https://www.who.int/intellectualproperty/topics/research/en/IFPMA.R&D.pdf (last visited March 24, 2009).

developing world – as required in the TRIPS Agreement – spurs R&D for medicines for neglected infectious and tropical diseases.

Chapter 5 focuses on the economic rationale behind parallel imports and their impact on drug pricing in the pharmaceutical industry. In particular, we develop a double marginalization model with complete information, in which an original manufacturer of a pharmaceutical product faces potential competition from parallel imports by a foreign exclusive distributor.

In Chapter 6, we focus on additional mechanisms to encourage R&D for pharmaceutical products alongside patent protection, i.e. prizes, purchase commitments and patent buyouts.

2. The TRIPS Agreement and Access to Patented Medicines

2.1. Introduction

The Agreement on Trade-Related Aspects of Intellectual Property Rights (henceforth, TRIPS Agreement) is to date the broadest multilateral agreement on intellectual property (IP).[30] In particular, the TRIPS Agreement is a result of the negotiations of the Uruguay Round (1986-1994), which finalized the General Agreement on Tariffs and Trade (GATT) by creating the World Trade Organization (WTO) on January 1, 1995.[31]

Before the TRIPS Agreement came into force the main international IPR covenants were the Paris Convention[32] and the Berne Convention.[33] The last revision on substance of both conventions took place at the Stockholm Conference on July 14, 1967 that established the World Intellectual Property Organization (WIPO).[34]

A perceived weakness of the international IPR system prior to the TRIPS Agreement was that membership was far from universal as developing countries in particular were reluctant to ratify the Paris Convention.[35] Furthermore, it has been argued that – prior to the TRIPS Agreement – the international IPR system lacked both a harmonization of national patent laws as well as a binding enforcement and settlement mechanism.[36] More specifically, before 1995, national IP laws were mainly unregulated within the GATT system and the details of patent protection were for the most part left to national discretion.[37] The TRIPS Agreement addresses the perceived weaknesses mentioned above.

---

30 More specifically, the Agreement on Trade-Related Aspects of Intellectual Property Rights is Annex 1C of the Marrakesh Agreement Establishing the World Trade Organization which was signed in Marrakesh on April, 15 1994. See also http://www.wto.org/english/docs_e/legal_e/04-wto.doc (last visited March 24, 2009). See also Gervais (2003) on p. 3 and Hestermeyer (2007) on p. 51ff.

31 For instance, see Hestermeyer (2007) on p. 44ff and Gervais (2003) on p. 10ff.

32 Paris Convention for the Protection of Industrial Property signed on March 20, 1883. See also http://www.wipo.int/export/sites/www/treaties/en/ip/paris/pdf/trtdocs_wo020.pdf (last visited March 24, 2009).

33 Berne Convention for the Protection of Literary and Artistic Works signed on September 9, 1886. For instance, see http://www.wipo.int/export/sites/www/treaties/en/ip/berne/pdf/trtdocs_wo001.pdf (last visited March 24, 2009).

34 See Bettcher et al. (2000). See also Gervais (2003) on p. 9 and Hestermeyer (2007) on p. 34ff. See also http://www.wipo.int/export/sites/www/treaties/en/convention/pdf/trtdocs_wo029.pdf (last visited March 24, 2009).

35 See also Hestermeyer (2007) on p. 36.

36 See Bettcher et al. (2000). See also Gervais (2003) on p. 3, Hestermeyer (2007) on p. 37 and Dreier (1996).

37 See Sykes (2002) on p. 49ff.

Nevertheless, there is still a huge difference between the developed countries in the North and the developing countries in the South with regard to the scope of international IPRs.[38] The industrialized countries in the Northern Hemisphere that have higher levels of education and technical capabilities tend to generate the bulk of new inventions.[39] Furthermore, they provide a high degree of patent protection under national law in order to protect inventors and to strengthen R&D incentives.[40] By contrast, countries in the developing world often lack a strong patent protection under national law.[41] These different levels of patent protection have been the source of many fierce controversies between developed and developing countries which continue today.[42] For instance, the United States unilaterally initiated various trade cases under Section 301 of the Trade Act of 1974 against developing countries such as Brazil, Argentina, India, China, and Thailand that did not adequately protect U.S. intellectual property.[43]

With regard to the different levels of IP protection around the world the TRIPS Agreement is aimed at strengthening the status of IP protection and establishing minimum standards for IPRs.[44] The ratification and implementation of TRIPS is obligatory for the member countries of the WTO but the exact date for full implementation depends on the level of economic development.[45] For instance, developing countries and transition countries were allowed to delay the implementation of the TRIPS Agreement until January 1, 2000. Furthermore, countries on the United Nations list of least developed countries (LDCs)[46] were allowed to delay the implementation of the TRIPS Agreement until July 1, 2013.[47] In addition, LDCs that did not provide patent protection for pharmaceutical products before the TRIPS Agreement came into force have until January 1, 2016 to afford patent protection for pharmaceuticals.[48]

In particular, the TRIPS Agreement covers the following areas of IP: copyright, trademarks, industrial designs, the layout-designs of integrated circuits, undisclosed information, and patents.[49]

---

38 For instance, see Chin and Grossman (1990) and Diwan and Rodrik (1991) on IPRs in the North-South trade context. See also Hestermeyer (2007) on p. 37ff, Grinols and Lin (2006), Grossman and Lai (2004) on p. 1641ff, Lai and Qiu (2003), and Yang (1998).

39 See Maskus (2000a) on p. 33ff. See also http://www.who.int/trade/glossary/story073/en/index.html (last visited March 24, 2009).

40 See Cooter and Schäfer (2008) on p. 55. See also Hestermeyer (2007) on p. 37ff.

41 For instance, see Cooter and Schäfer (2008) on p. 56 and Maskus (2000a) on p. 33ff. See also Castro Bernieri (2006) for an excellent treatment of IPRs and access to medicines in the context of bilateral investment treaties.

42 See Sell (2003). See also Hestermeyer (2007) on p. 37ff.

43 See Sykes (1992) on p. 307ff for a comprehensive overview of these cases and their outcomes.

44 See Maskus (2000a) on p. 21ff. See also Hestermeyer (2007) on p. 51ff.

45 See Gervais (2003) on p. 27.

46 For instance, see http://www.un.org/special-rep/ohrlls/ldc/list.htm (last visited March 24, 2009).

47 See http://www.wto.org/english/news_e/pres05_e/pr424_e.htm (last visited April 7, 2009). See Michaelis and Jessen (2005) on p. 167. See also Gervais (2003) on p.27.

48 See Gervais (2003) on p. 27. See http://www.wto.org/english/tratop_e/trips_e/tripfq_e.htm (last visited April 7, 2009).

49 For instance, see Maskus (2000a) on p. 17ff. See also Gervais (2003) on p. 73ff and Hestermeyer (2007) on p. 44ff.

The remainder of this chapter is organized as follows. The first part outlines the section of the TRIPS Agreement that sets out minimum standards of protection with respect to patents, trademarks and copyright. In particular, we focus on the most pertinent articles of the TRIPS Agreement with regard to patent protection and elaborate two central but controversial TRIPS Agreement flexibilities: compulsory licenses and parallel imports.

In the second part of this chapter, we outline the most pertinent provisions of the TRIPS Agreement with respect to the enforcement of IPRs: specifically civil judicial procedures and remedies as well as criminal procedures.

Lastly, the third part of this chapter provides a brief overview of the relevant provisions of the TRIPS Agreement with respect to dispute settlement issues.

2.2. Standards

With respect to the main areas of intellectual property such as patents, industrial design, trademarks, trade secrets and copyright, the standards section of the TRIPS Agreement sets out the minimum standards of protection to be implemented in each member country.[50] In particular, it defines the subject-matter to be protected and the minimum duration of protection.[51] It also defines the rights to be conferred and permissible exceptions to those rights.[52]

The TRIPS Agreement requires that WTO member countries comply with the substantive obligations of the Paris Convention for the Protection of Industrial Property and the Berne Convention for the Protection of Literary and Artistic Works.[53] However, the TRIPS Agreement enacts additional obligations on issues where these earlier conventions were seen as being inadequate.[54]

In terms of patent protection for pharmaceuticals the TRIPS Agreement establishes minimum international standards of protection.[55] Furthermore, it attempts to solve the trade-off between providing access to affordable life-saving medicines in the short-term and providing incentives to the pharmaceutical companies for R&D of new pharmaceutical products in the long-term.[56]

In the following sections the most relevant provisions of the TRIPS Agreement in terms of patent protection for pharmaceuticals are described in more detail.

50 See Maskus (2000a) on p. 17ff. See also Gervais (2003) on p. 123ff.
51 See Gervais (2003) on p. 123ff.
52 See Gervais (2003) on p. 123ff.
53 For instance, see Gervais (2003) on p. 9ff for an overview of the WIPO-administered agreements.
54 See also http://www.wto.org/english/tratop_e/trips_e/intel2_e.htm (last visited March 24, 2009).
55 See Mercurio (2004) on p. 217ff.
56 See Mercurio (2004) on p. 217ff.

2.2.1. *Patent Protection under the TRIPS Agreement*

The most pertinent articles with regard to patent protection are Articles 27-34 of the TRIPS Agreement.[57] Unless stated otherwise, references are to articles of the TRIPS Agreement in this chapter. Articles 27-34 require that WTO member countries provide a minimal standard of protection for inventions for twenty years.[58] They also require member countries to make patent protection available for both innovative products as well as innovative processes.[59]

2.2.1.1. *Patentable Products and Processes*

Article 27(1) requires that WTO member countries make patents available in all fields of technology[60] without discrimination, based on the three criteria; novelty,[61] inventiveness, and industrial applicability.[62] Furthermore, Article 27(1) explicitly includes both product inventions as well as process inventions.[63] For instance, patents have to be made available for pharmaceutical products such as new molecules and compound substances as well as chemical processes to produce a new compound.[64] However, laws of nature and already existing discoveries are not patentable.[65]

Another important element is that Article 27(1) requires that patent rights are enjoyable without discrimination as to the place of production, the place of invention and the field of technology.[66] For instance, the exclusion of pharmaceutical products or processes from patentability is impermissible because it would constitute a discrimination as to the field of technology.[67]

However, Article 27(2) and Article 27(3) establish the option to foresee three exceptions to the central rule on patentability.[68] First, new products or processes that are contrary to *ordre public* or morality may be excluded from patentability, i.e. in case it is necessary to prevent their commercial exploitation in order protect the *ordre public*.[69] This can include both inventions dangerous to human, animal or plant life or health and inventions that are seriously prejudicial to the environment. Nevertheless,

---

57 See http://www.wto.org/english/tratop_e/trips_e/t_agm3_e.htm for the exact wording of Articles 27-34 (last visited March 24, 2009). See Sykes (2002) on p. 49ff, Maskus (2000a) on p. 20ff and Gervais (2003) on p. 217ff.

58 See Maskus (2000a) on p. 20ff. See also Mercurio (2004) on p. 218.

59 See http://www.wto.org/english/tratop_e/trips_e/trips_e.htm (last visited March 24, 2009). See also Mercurio (2004) on p. 218.

60 See Sykes (2002) on p. 50ff.

61 See Correa (2000b) on p. 57ff for on overview of the requirements of protection under the TRIPS Agreement. See also Maskus (2000a) on p. 20ff.

62 See *Canada – Term of Patent Protection*, WT/DS170/AB/R (2000) paragraphs 65 and 66. See also Gervais (2003) on p. 220ff.

63 See Gervais (2003) on p. 217ff.

64 See Hestermeyer (2007) on p. 55 and on p. 64.

65 For instance, see Correa (2000b) on p. 51ff. See also Hestermeyer (2007) on p. 54.

66 See Gervais (2003) on p. 221.

67 See Hestermeyer (2007) on p. 59.

68 See Michaelis and Bender (2005) on p. 455. See also Gervais (2003) on p. 222ff.

69 For instance, see Hestermeyer (2007) on p. 56. See also Gervais (2003) on p. 223.

pharmaceuticals cannot be excluded from patentability under Article 27(2),[70] although several authors have supported the opposite view.[71] The main argument of the advocates of the exclusion of pharmaceuticals from patentability is that they should be excluded in order to protect the *ordre public* since the high price of these products impedes access to medicines for poor people. This, they believe, is detrimental to the *ordre public* and human health.[72] However, this view disregards the fact that Article 27(2) explicitly requires that the prevention of the commercial exploitation of the innovative product or process must be *necessary* to protect the *ordre public*.[73] In general, a WTO Member's measure cannot be *necessary* within the meaning of Article XX(d) of the GATT "if an alternative measure which it could reasonably be expected to employ and which is not inconsistent with other GATT provisions is available to it."[74] In the case of innovative pharmaceutical products, the risk to the *ordre public* does not stem from the commercial exploitation of the product but rather from the alleged patent rents.[75] As an *alternative measure* to tackle this problem countries often open their market for the commercial exploitation of generics.[76] Consequently, the prevention of the commercial exploitation of pharmaceutical products is not *necessary* to protect the *ordre public* under WTO jurisprudence on Article XX(d) of the GATT. Thus, pharmaceutical products cannot be excluded from patentability under Article 27(2) of the TRIPS Agreement.

2.2.1.2. Disclosure

Article 29(1) establishes a precise test that is imposed on an applicant for the patent regarding the description of the invention.[77] One condition to pass the test is that an invention must be described in such a way as to allow a "person skilled in the art"[78] to carry out the invention. This so-called disclosure requirement is a key principle of patent law and provides the following essential justification of patents.[79] Disclosure ensures that the scientific knowledge contained in the patent enters the public domain after the expiration of the patent.[80] For instance, the scientific knowledge contained in a patent for a pharmaceutical product can be used to develop a better product with a reduced amount of negative side effects.[81] In other words, patents are valuable to society because they promote the diffusion of scientific knowledge and foster

70 See Hestermeyer (2007) on p. 56.
71 See Wojahn (2001/2002) on p. 479ff. See also Ford (2000) on p. 965.
72 See Hestermeyer (2007) on p. 56.
73 See Gervais (2003) on p. 223 and Hestermeyer (2007) on p. 56.
74 See *Dominican Republic – Measures Affecting the Importation and Internal Sale of Cigarettes*, WT/DS302/AB/R (2005) paragraph 67. See also Hestermeyer (2007) on p. 56, footnote 252, and Gervais (2003) on p. 223.
75 For instance, see Hestermeyer (2007) on p. 56ff for a comprehensive treatment of this issue.
76 See Hestermeyer (2007) on p. 57.
77 See Gervais (2003) on p. 239.
78 See Article 29(1). See also Gervais (2003) on p. 237ff.
79 See Scotchmer (2006) on p. 82ff. See also Hestermeyer (2007) on p. 67.
80 See Michaelis and Bender (2005) on p. 454. See also Gervais (2003) on p. 239ff.
81 For instance, see Scotchmer (2006) on p. 127ff on cumulative innovations.

technological progress.[82] We will elaborate on further benefits of patents, i.e. the stimulating impact of patents on pharmaceutical R&D, comprehensively in Chapter 3.

2.2.1.3. Rights Conferred

If a product or process fulfills the conditions of patentability such as novelty, industrial applicability, inventiveness and disclosure, national patent offices such as the USPTO and the JPO have to provide the patent applicant with a patent.[83]
According to Article 28(1), a product patent must confer exclusive rights of "making, using, offering for sale, selling, or importing for these purposes".[84] For instance, a patent on a pharmaceutical product confers on the patentee the right to exclude other pharmaceutical companies from competing with him so that the he can fully exploit its value.[85]
However, the TRIPS Agreement also provides WTO member countries with some flexibilities that potentially limit the exclusive rights of the patent holder as we will see in the following.[86]

2.2.1.4. Compulsory Licenses and Parallel Imports

In this section we briefly outline two central but controversial exceptions to the exclusive rights of the owner of a patent which are particularly important in the pharmaceutical sector: compulsory licenses and parallel imports.

2.2.1.4.1. Compulsory Licenses

Article 31 permits WTO member countries to approve compulsory licenses for patented products and processes under certain circumstances.[87] Consider the following

---

82 See Lévêque and Ménière (2004) on p. 9ff.

83 See Hestermeyer (2007) on p. 67ff. See also http://www.trilateral.net/ for further information on the trilateral cooperation between the EPO, JPO and USTPO, i.e. the annual trilateral statistical reports on worldwide patenting activities (last visited March 24, 2009). See also Michaelis and Bender (2005) on p. 456.

84 Note, however, that – according to Article 30 – WTO member countries may also provide exceptions to exclusive patent rights provided that they "do not unreasonably conflict with a normal exploitation of the patent" and provided that they do not "unreasonably prejudice the legitimate interests of the patent owner". See also Gervais (2003) on p. 242ff and Hestermeyer (2007) on p. 234ff.

85 See Hestermeyer (2007) on p. 68. See also Michaelis and Bender (2005) on p. 456.

86 See Hestermeyer (2007) on p. 229. See also Gervais (2003) on p. 244ff and Michaelis and Bender (2005) on p. 456ff.

87 Note that Art. 5(b) of the Doha Declararion on the TRIPS Agreement and Public Health prescribes that "*(e)ach Member has the right to grant compulsory licences and the freedom to determine the grounds upon which such licences are granted.*" See Mercurio (2004) on p. 218, Maskus (2000a) on p. 178ff, World Trade Organization and World Health Organization (2002) on p. 45ff and Abbott (2005) on p. 338ff. See also Hestermeyer (2007) on p. 239ff, Ridder (2004) and Cottier (2003).

example: subject to conditions explained later, the government of a developing country can – without the consent of the holder of a pharmaceutical patent – permit another pharmaceutical company or a government agency to produce the patented pharmaceutical product.[88] For instance, the government may grant a compulsory license in case of a national emergency such as an epidemic,[89] or to guarantee domestic supply of low-cost generic substitutes of the patented pharmaceutical product where the patent holder fails to place the product on the market.[90] Moreover, a compulsory license can be granted in order to "remedy a practice determined after judicial or administrative process to be anti-competitive".[91]
However, the mere threat of a compulsory license and the threat of competition from generic substitutes may induce the holder of a patent to supply the market with the patented pharmaceutical product at a lower price.[92] In other words, compulsory licenses may provide developing countries with a means to reduce prices of essential medicines and to promote affordable access to medicines for poor people.[93] For instance, the Brazilian National STD/AIDS Programme (NSAP)[94] has – among other things – established the threat of compulsory licensing as a means to negotiate with pharmaceutical companies in order to promote low-price access to AIDS drugs.[95]
In order to avoid abuse, compulsory licenses can only be granted under certain conditions as we shall see in the following.

2.2.1.4.1.1. Prior Negotiations with the Right Holder

The issuance of a compulsory license is only permitted if the proposed user has carried on negotiations with the rights holder in order to obtain "authorization on reasonable commercial terms".[96] More specifically, a compulsory license can only be granted if these negotiations "have not been successful within a reasonable period of time".[97] For instance, suppose that a holder of a patent on a new medicine deliberately delays negotiations with the proposed user of a compulsory license by making unduly

See also http://www.wto.org/english/tratop_e/trips_e/factsheet_pharm02_e.htm#compulsorylicensing (last visited March 24, 2009). See also Garrison (2006) on p. 72ff, Chien (2003) on p. 869ff and Gervais (2003) on p. 244ff.

88 See World Health Organization (2002) on p. 18. See also Hestermeyer (2007) on p. 260ff and Gervais (2003) on p. 47.

89 See Article 31(b). See also World Health Organization (2002) on p. 18.

90 See Mercurio (2004) on p. 218ff. See also Curci and Vittori (2004). For instance, Article 5A(2) of the Paris Convention for the Protection of Industrial Property prescribes that: "*Each country of the Union shall have the right to take legislative measures providing for the grant of compulsory licenses to prevent the abuses which might result from the exercise of the exclusive rights conferred by the patent, for example, failure to work.*" See also Gervais (2003) on p. 250ff.

91 See Article 31(c). For instance, see Gervais (2003) on p. 244.

92 See Hestermeyer (2007) on p. 241. See also Watal (2000) on p. 742ff.

93 See Commission on Intellectual Property Rights (2002) on p. 42ff.

94 See http://www.aids.gov.br/data/Pages/LUMISACC5B55EENIE.htm (last visited March 24, 2009).

95 See Commission on Intellectual Property Rights (2002) on p. 42ff. See also Benson (2005).

96 See Article 31(b). See also Mercurio (2004) on p. 220ff and Sykes (2002) on p. 52.

97 See Article 31(b). See also Gervais (2003) on p. 250ff.

burdensome demands in order to prevent the granting of a compulsory license.[98] In this case, the "reasonable period of time" ends.[99]

2.2.1.4.1.2. Adequate Remuneration for the Right Holder

The right holder must be paid an "adequate remuneration in the circumstances of each case, taking into account the economic value of the authorization".[100]

However, the question as to which level of remuneration is adequate is particularly important with respect to the access to medicines through compulsory licenses.[101] Suppose that the remuneration that a proposed user of a compulsory license has to pay the right holder exceeds the expected profits that he can generate by manufacturing under a compulsory license. In this case, the proposed user of the compulsory license will choose not to produce and thus affordable access to essential medicines could not be promoted through compulsory licensing.[102]

Nevertheless, the adequacy of the remuneration also depends on the economic circumstances of the country where the compulsory license is granted and on the public's right to access to medicines in that country.[103] For instance, where a developing country issues a compulsory license in order to control a national epidemic a relatively low level of remuneration may be adequate.[104] To give a real life example, the government of Zambia – facing an AIDS crisis – issued a compulsory license for a triple-drug AIDS treatment to the Italian company PHARCO LTD, incorporated in Zambia, in September 2004 in order to provide a legal mechanism for obtaining generic AIDS drugs.[105] Clearly the Zambian government's objective was to bring final drug prices closer to manufacturing costs in order to fight the AIDS crisis. As to the remuneration of the right holders, the Zambian government determined that the royalty rate to be paid to the owners of the patent rights "shall not exceed 2.5 % of the total turnover of the mentioned products at the end of each financial year of PHARCO LTD."[106]

Another important limitation to the admissible scope of compulsory licenses in addition to the requirement of adequate remuneration is the territoriality requirement discussed in the next section.

---

98 See Hestermeyer (2007) on p. 245ff.

99 See Article 31(b). See Hestermeyer (2007) on p. 246.

100 See Article 13(h). See also Mercurio (2004) on p. 220ff, Gervais (2003) on p. 252 and Hestermeyer (2007) on p. 247ff.

101 See Hestermeyer (2007) on p. 248.

102 See also Subramanian (2001).

103 See Vaughan (2001). See also Hestermeyer (2007) on p. 248ff.

104 See Hestermeyer (2007) on p. 249 and Ridder (2004) on p. 106. See also Love (2001) paragraphs 35-40 for a general treatment regarding the determination of compensation in the context of compulsory licensing.

105 See http://www.cptech.org/ip/health/c/zambia/zcl.html (last visited March 24, 2009).

106 See *Compulsory License No. CL 01/2004*, MCT1/104/1/1c issued by the Republic of Zambia Ministry of Commerce, Trade and Industry (September 21, 2004). See also Hestermeyer (2007) on p. 249.

2.2.1.4.1.3. Predominant Supply for the Domestic Market

The requirement that WTO member countries shall grant a compulsory license only if it is used "predominantly for the supply of the domestic market of the Member authorizing such use" is prescribed in Article 31(f).[107]

In particular, this provision restricts the possibility of a domestic manufacturer proposed for producing generics under a compulsory license to export surplus production to another country.[108] Consequently, if the domestic market is not sufficiently large to enable a manufacturer of generics to generate a profit, the manufacturer will not be willing to manufacture generics under a compulsory license.[109]

As to the access to medicines in the context of compulsory licensing, Article 31(f) implies that the domestic pharmaceutical industry in the country where the compulsory license is to be issued must have the technical and non-technical manufacturing capabilities to produce medicines.[110]

To illustrate this consider the case where least-developed country *B* faces a severe health crisis but lacks sufficient domestic pharmaceutical manufacturing capabilities. In this case, the medicines to address the public health problem in country *B* would have to be manufactured under a compulsory license granted by another country *A* and then exported to country *B*. This approach, however, is not permissible under Article 31(f) if the drugs manufactured are not predominantly consumed in country *A* where they are made.[111]

The Declaration on the TRIPS Agreement and Public Health (hereafter, Doha Declaration) sets out a mandate to address this problem.[112] In particular, Paragraph 6 of the Doha Declaration prescribes:

"*We recognize that WTO Members with insufficient or no manufacturing capacities in the pharmaceutical sector could face difficulties in making effective use of compulsory licensing under the TRIPS Agreement. We instruct the Council for TRIPS to find an expeditious solution to this problem and to report to the General Council before the end of 2002.*"[113]

In response to this requirement the General Council established the so-called "Paragraph 6 system" in its decision on the Implementation of Paragraph 6 of the

---

107 See also Article 31(k). In particular, Article 31(k) provides that Article 31(f) is not applicable in case that a compulsory license is granted to remedy an anti-competitive practice. See Gervais (2003) on p. 252 and Hestermeyer (2007) on p. 250ff.

108 See Gervais (2003) on p. 252. See also Hestermeyer (2007) on p. 251.

109 See Hestermeyer (2007) on p. 251.

110 See Correa (2002) on p. 19ff for an overview of the levels of development of the pharmaceutical industry in 190 countries. See also Ballance et al. (1992). See also World Trade Organization (2002) paragraph 4 and Hestermeyer (2007) on p. 251ff.

111 See Hestermeyer (2007) on p. 251ff.

112 See http://www.wto.org/english/thewto_e/minist_e/min01_e/mindecl_trips_e.htm (last visited March 24, 2009) for the exact wording of the *Declaration on the TRIPS Agreement and Public Health*, Ministerial Conference, Doha, 9 - 14 November 2001, WT/MIN(01)/DEC/2 (November 20, 2001). See also Hestermeyer (2007) on p. 255ff, 't Hoen (2002), Lévêque and Ménière (2004) on p. 46ff, Abbott (2002) and Abbott (2005).

113 See also Gervais (2003) on p. 46ff and Hestermeyer (2007) on p. 256ff.

Doha Declaration on the TRIPS Agreement and Public Health.[114] This provides that for least-developed countries which cannot make effective use of compulsory licensing (by importing generics from a country where they are produced under a compulsory license), the requirement to grant a compulsory license "predominantly for the supply of the domestic market" as prescribed in Article 31(f) can be waived under the following conditions.[115]

The least-developed country has to notify the Council for TRIPS about "the names and expected quantities of the product(s) needed"[116] and it has to confirm "that, where a pharmaceutical product is patented in its territory, it has granted or intends to grant a compulsory license".[117]

Additionally, the exporting country must fulfill following requirements.[118]

First, "only the amount necessary to meet the needs"[119] of the least-developed country can be manufactured under the compulsory license.

Second, the products manufactured under the compulsory license shall be clearly identified as being produced under the Paragraph 6 system "through specific labeling or marketing".[120]

Finally, the exporting country has to notify the Council for TRIPS of the grant of the compulsory license.[121] Furthermore, it has to post on its website both the quantities supplied to each destination as well as the distinguishing features of the products.[122]

The Paragraph 6 system was heavily debated during the negotiations prior to the Decision of 30 August 2003.[123] Its adoption was praised by various developing countries as an effective means of addressing the problem of access to medicines in the developing world.[124] It remains to be seen whether the Paragraph 6 system will

---

114 See http://www.wto.org/english/tratop_e/trips_e/implem_para6_e.htm (last visited March 24, 2009) for the exact wording of the *Implementation of Paragraph 6 of the Doha Declaration on the TRIPS Agreement and Public Health*, Decision of the General Council of August 30, 2003, WT/L/540 (September 1, 2003). See also *Amendment of the TRIPS Agreement*, Decision of the General Council of December 6, 2005, WT/L/641 (December 8, 2005).

115 Note that the Decision of the General Council of December, 6 2005 transformed the August, 30 2003 "waiver" into a permanent amendment of the TRIPS Agreement. See also Hestermeyer (2007) on p. 264ff. See also the Annex of the Decision of the General Council of August 30, 2003, WT/L/540 (September 1, 2003). Note that also countries other than a least-developed country can make use of the Paragraph 6 system. In this case, the conditions to be fulfilled in order to benefit from the Paragraph 6 system are more restrictive. However, this issue is beyond the scope of this thesis.

116 See Paragraph 2a(i) of the Decision of the General Council of August 30, 2003, WT/L/540 (September 1, 2003). See also Hestermeyer (2007) on p. 267.

117 See Paragraph 2a(iii) of the Decision of the General Council of August 30, 2003. See also Hestermeyer (2007) on p. 267.

118 See Hestermeyer (2007) on p. 267.

119 See Paragraph 2b(i) of the Decision of the General Council of August 30, 2003. See also Hestermeyer (2007) on p. 267.

120 See Paragraph 2b(ii) of the Decision of the General Council of August 30, 2003. See also Hestermeyer (2007) on p. 267.

121 See Paragraph 2c of the Decision of the General Council of August 30, 2003.

122 See Paragraph 2b(iii) of the Decision of the General Council of August 30, 2003. See also Hestermeyer (2007) on p. 268.

123 For instance, see Hestermeyer (2007) on p. 262ff for an excellent treatment of the negotiation history of the Decision of 30 August 2003.

124 See the *Minutes of the Meeting,* held in the Centre William Rappard on 25, 26 and 30 August 2003, General Council, WT/GC/M/82 (November 13, 2003), paragraphs 36, 40, 44, 50, 72 and 84.

become an effective and widely used means of addressing the problem of access to affordable medicines in the developing world. The first and only country so far to use it was Rwanda on July 19, 2007.[125]

We now consider another highly debated issue in the global trading system additional to the Paragraph 6 system: the doctrine of exhaustion of intellectual property rights and parallel imports.

2.2.1.4.2. Exhaustion of IPRs and Parallel Imports

Patents confer on the patentee the right to prevent others from taking certain actions such as making, selling, and using a patented product.[126] However, patents do not confer on the patentee the right to control the product after the product has been placed on the market either by himself or with his consent.[127] The patent holder looses his privileges to control further commercial distribution after the first distribution of the patented product.[128] Put differently, the exclusive rights conferred by a patent "exhaust" as soon as the patented product has been brought to the market by the patent holder or his licensee.[129] This doctrine is also known as the doctrine of exhaustion[130] or the "first-sale doctrine" in the U.S..[131] There are two main approaches to exhaustion of intellectual property rights:[132] national and international exhaustion of intellectual property rights.[133]

2.2.1.4.2.1. National Exhaustion of IPRs

Under a system of national exhaustion of intellectual property rights, patent rights "exhaust" upon first sale within the country in which the patent holder or his licensee launches the patented product.[134] In other words, the launch of a patented product leads to the exhaustion of the property rights to control further commercial distribution only in the country where the product was launched.[135] Subsequent acts of resale, rental or lending by third parties cannot be controlled or opposed by the patent holder

---

125 See *Notification under Paragraph 2(a) of the Decision of 30 August 2003 on the Implementation of Paragraph 6 of the Doha Declaration on the TRIPS Agreement and Public Health, Rwanda*, Council for Trade-Related Aspects of Intellectual Property Rights IP/N/9/RWA/1 (19 July 2007).

126 See also Hestermeyer (2007) on p. 230.

127 See Nauta (2004). See also Hestermeyer (2007) on p. 230.

128 See Fink (2005) on p.171.

129 For instance, see Hestermeyer (2007) on p. 230.

130 See Kobak (2005) on p. 4ff. See also Hestermeyer (2007) on p. 68, Gervais (2003) on p. 111ff and Maskus (2000a) on p. 208ff.

131 See U.S. Supreme Court case *Bobbs-Merrill Co. vs. Straus*, 210 U.S. 339 (1908). The "first-sale doctrine" was later codified in section 109(a) of the Copyright Act of 1976. See also Maskus (2000a) on p. 210.

132 A third rule of exhaustion is regional or community exhaustion. We will elaborate on this issue in section 5.2.2 in Chapter 5.

133 See Yusuf and Moncayo von Hase (1992) on p. 127 and Maskus (2000a) on p. 208ff.

134 See Maskus (2000b) on p. 1272ff. See also Michaelis and Bender (2005) on p. 445ff.

135 See Maskus (2000a) on p. 208ff.

in the domestic market but can continue to be controlled in international markets.[136] To give an example, consider a world with two countries *A* and *B* and one manufacturer of a patented pharmaceutical product. Suppose that the manufacturer (or his licensee) launches the product in country *A* as well as in country *B*. Under a system of national exhaustion in both countries, the patent holder cannot control subsequent acts of resale, rental or lending by third parties in either country *A* or *B*: his exclusive rights are exhausted nationally. However, his rights are not exhausted internationally and he can prevent a third party purchasing the patented product in country *B* and reselling it in country *A*.

2.2.1.4.2.2. International Exhaustion of IPRs

Under a system of international exhaustion of intellectual property rights, patent rights exhaust upon first sale anywhere.[137] Specifically, once a patented product is launched by the patentee (or with his consent) anywhere in the world the property rights of commercial exploitation of the product are exhausted.[138] Subsequent acts of resale, rental or lending by third parties on any market can no longer be controlled or opposed by the patent holder.[139] Consider again our example mentioned above. Under a system of international exhaustion in both countries, the patent holder cannot control subsequent acts of resale, rental or lending by third parties either in country *A* or *B* nor can he prevent third parties purchasing the product in country *B* and reselling it in country *A*. Nevertheless, it is important to note that the question of whether the patent holder can prevent third parties reselling the product in country *A* depends only on the exhaustion regime in country *A* where the resale takes place. For instance, assume that country *B* adopts a rule of international exhaustion whereas country *A* adopts a rule of national exhaustion. In this case, the patent holder can prevent third parties purchasing the product in country *B* and reselling it in country *A* even though the product was first placed on the market in country *B* that adopts a rule of international exhaustion. Stated differently, the rule of international exhaustion in country *B* does not have any impact on the question of whether or not rights are exhausted in country *A*.[140] It should be noted that WTO member countries are free to choose whether or not they adopt a rule of international exhaustion of intellectual property rights.[141]

---

136 See Michaelis and Bender (2005) on p. 445ff.

137 See Michaelis and Bender (2005) on p. 445ff. See also Stack (1998) and Maskus (2000a) on p. 208.

138 For instance, see Maskus (2000a) on p. 208.

139 See Szymanski (1999) for a discussion of the economic aspects of international exhaustion. See also Gervais (2003) on p. 112f.

140 This is due to the general principle of territoriality in international IP law whereas national IP laws are only relevant for acts taking place within their jurisdiction. For example, a patent granted under the U.S. Patent Act can only be infringed by acts conducted with a sufficient link to U.S. territory. Furthermore, a copyright granted under the Indian Copyright Act can only be infringed by acts conducted with a sufficient link to the Indian territory.

141 See Article 6 of the TRIPS Agreement. For an extensive treatment of this issue see Gervais (2003) on p. 11ff. See also Maskus (2001) on p. 4, Yusuf and Moncayo von Hase (1992), Gallus (2005) on p. 77ff, Hestermeyer (2007) on p. 233, Correa (2000b) and Slotboom (2003).

2.2.1.4.2.3. International Exhaustion of IPRs and Parallel Imports

An important and highly debated difference between national and international exhaustion of intellectual property rights is the following.[142] On the one hand, the patent holder is awarded the right to prevent re-imports – also known as parallel imports in WTO parlance[143] – from other countries under a rule of national exhaustion of IPRs as the rights exhaust only nationally but not internationally.[144] On the other hand, the patent holder cannot prevent parallel imports under the rule of international exhaustion as patent rights exhaust upon first sale anywhere.[145]

To understand the concept of parallel imports more precisely, consider the following example.[146] Suppose that the manufacturer of a patented pharmaceutical product sells the product in a least-developed country at a relatively low price. Then, parallel imports occur when a buyer exports this pharmaceutical product through channels other than those used by the patent holder to another country, e.g. a highly-industrialized country, where the patent holder charges a higher price for the same pharmaceutical product.[147] This means that, under a regime of international exhaustion of IPRs, a higher price in one market will attract parallel imports whenever the price difference is more than the additional cost due to exportation, i.e. tariffs or transportation cost.[148] Moreover, there is typically no contract between the patent holder and the parallel importing firm. Thus, parallel-imported goods are often referred to as "grey-market imports".[149]

Because of these problems the regulation of parallel imports in the field of pharmaceuticals has become a critical issue in the global trading system.[150] Advocates of strong patent rights for new pharmaceutical products support a global policy of banning parallel imports arguing that they reduce the profits of pharmaceutical companies and thus reduce the incentive to invest in R&D for new pharmaceutical products.[151] By contrast, policy makers in many developing countries support an open regime of permitting parallel imports.[152] They place a greater emphasis on the affordability of pharmaceuticals than on promoting R&D in the highly-industrialized

142 See Abbott (1998). See also Maskus (2000a) on p. 21. See also Correa (2000a) on p. 71ff, Rott (2002), Bale (1998) and Jehoram (1996).
143 See http://www.wto.org/english/tratop_e/trips_e/factsheet_pharm02_e.htm#parallelimports (last visited March 24, 2009). See also Sykes (2002).
144 See Michaelis and Bender (2005) on p. 446 and Maskus (2000a) on p. 208.
145 See Maskus (2000a) on p. 208.
146 See also Ganslandt and Maskus (2004), Maskus (2000b) and Sykes (2002) on p. 53.
147 For instance, see Sykes (2002) on p. 63ff.
148 See Ganslandt and Maskus (2004) and Maskus (2000a) on p. 212. We will come back to this issue in the analysis of parallel trade and the pricing of pharmaceutical products section 5.2.4 in Chapter 5.
149 See Maskus (2000b) on p. 1269. See also Heath (1999).
150 For instance, see Abbott (1998), Bale (1998), Kanavos et al. (2004), Rey (2003) and York Health Economics Consortium (2003). See also Maskus (2000a) on p. 211ff.
151 See also Danzon (1998) who argues that – provided that parallel imports are not allowed – a segmented equilibrium with a price-discriminating monopolist can be optimal from a welfare perspective. See also Barfield and Groombridge (1998), Barfield and Groombridge (1999) and Bale (1998).
152 See Abbott (1998). See also Maskus (2000a) on p. 211ff.

countries, arguing that it is important to be able to purchase pharmaceuticals from the cheapest sources possible.[153]
We will discuss these issues more extensively in Chapter 5.[154] In particular, we will contribute to the existing game-theoretic literature on parallel imports by setting up our own model in order to analyze the impact of parallel imports on the pricing decision of pharmaceutical producers.[155]

2.3. Enforcement of IPRs under the TRIPS Agreement

The provisions on enforcement are covered in Part III of the TRIPS Agreement which is divided into five Sections.

2.3.1. General Provisions regarding Enforcement Procedures under the TRIPS Agreement

The first section of Part III of the TRIPS Agreement sets out some general principles that can be applied to all IPRs enforcement procedures. These principles are particularly aimed at ensuring the effectiveness of the enforcement procedures.[156]
Art. 41(1) prescribes some general principles relating to the effectiveness of action to be taken in the light of any acts of infringement of IPRs, and the availability of expeditious remedies in order to prevent infringements, i.e. seizure and damages.[157]
Art. 41(2) deals with enforcement procedures and requires that they "shall be fair and equitable".[158] Furthermore, Art. 41(2) requires that they shall not be "unnecessarily complicated" or involve unreasonable time limits in order to guarantee due process.[159]
Finally, Art. 41(5) requires that the provisions for enforcement do not create any obligation to establish additional judicial apparatus for the enforcement of IPRs distinct from the existing judicial system for the enforcement of law in general.[160]

2.3.2. Civil Judicial Procedures and Remedies under the TRIPS Agreement

The second section of Part III of the TRIPS Agreement deals with civil and administrative procedures and remedies. More specifically, it requires that civil judicial

153 See Sykes (2002) on p. 53. See also Commission on Intellectual Property Rights (2002) on p. 41ff.
154 See Maskus and Chen (2004) and Danzon and Towes (2003). See also Maskus (2001) and Ganslandt and Maskus (2004) on p. 1036ff.
155 See also Müller-Langer (2007).
156 See Michaelis and Bender (2005) on p. 460. See also Gervais (2003) on p. 287ff and Maskus (2000a) on p. 24ff.
157 See Bently and Sherman (2004) on p. 1086ff, Gervais (2003) on p. 287 and Blair and Cotter (2005).
158 See also Gervais (2003) on p. 288.
159 See http://www.wto.org/english/tratop_e/trips_e/intel2b_e.htm#enforcement (last visited March 24, 2009). Note, however, that also Art. 41(3) and Art. 41(4) aim at guaranteeing due process. See also Gervais (2003) on p. 288.
160 See Gervais (2003) on p. 289.

procedures shall be available with respect to the enforcement of the IPRs covered by the TRIPS Agreement.[161]

For instance, Art. 42 provides certain principles that are aimed at ensuring due process, i.e. the entitlement of the defendant to written and sufficiently specified notice of the claims and the right to be represented by independent legal counsel.[162]

Furthermore, Art. 43 deals with the application of the rules on evidence. For instance, Art. 43(1) requires that the judicial authority must be empowered to oblige the parties to a proceeding to provide relevant evidence.[163]

The second section of Part III of the TRIPS Agreement also contains provisions on remedies such as injunctions, damages, and the destruction of counterfeit products.

Art. 44 prescribes that the judicial authorities shall be empowered to order injunctions.[164] For instance, they shall be authorized to order a party to a proceeding to desist from an infringement and to prevent counterfeit products entering domestic channels.[165]

With regard to damages, Art. 45(1) requires that the courts must have the authority to order the infringer to pay the right holder adequate damages.[166] Moreover, they shall be empowered to order the infringer to pay the expenses of the right holder, e.g. "appropriate attorney's fees".[167]

Art. 46 aims at creating "an effective deterrent to infringement".[168] In particular, Art. 46 provides that the courts shall be authorized to order the destruction of counterfeit or pirated goods, unless destruction would be constitutionally impossible.[169] Where the destruction of counterfeit goods is "contrary to existing constitutional requirements",[170] the judicial authorities shall be empowered to order the infringing party to dispose those goods outside the domestic channels of distribution. However, the judicial authorities must also take into consideration the rule of proportionality with respect to the gravity of the infringement and the remedies ordered.[171]

In order to help the right holder find the source of infringing products, Art. 47 prescribes that the courts must have the authority to order the infringing party to notify the right holder about other parties involved in the production and distribution process.[172]

The second section of Part III of the TRIPS Agreement also contains certain safeguards against the use of enforcement procedures in good faith against innocent defendants or the abuse of enforcement procedures, e.g. to create barriers to legitimate trade.[173] For instance, Art. 48 prescribes that the courts shall be authorized to order a

161 See Art. 42. See also Michaelis and Bender (2005) on p. 460. See also Gervais (2003) on p. 290ff.
162 See Gervais (2003) on p. 291ff.
163 See Gervais (2003) on p. 293ff.
164 See Michaelis and Bender (2005) on p. 460. See also Gervais (2003) on p. 295ff.
165 See Art. 44. See also Gervais (2003) on p. 295ff.
166 See Gervais (2003) on p. 298 and Michaelis and Bender (2005) on p. 460.
167 See Art. 45(2). See also Gervais (2003) on p. 298ff.
168 See Art. 46. See also Gervais (2003) on p. 299.
169 See Gervais (2003) on p. 299ff.
170 See Art. 46.
171 See Art. 46. See also Gervais (2003) on p. 300.
172 See Michaelis and Bender (2005) on p. 460 and Gervais (2003) on p. 301.
173 See Gervais (2003) on p. 302ff.

plaintiff who has abused the enforcement procedure to pay "adequate compensation"[174] to a defendant who has wrongfully been restrained.[175]

Art. 49 deals with "administrative procedures on the merits of a case"[176] that result in ordering a civil remedy. In particular, Art. 49 prescribes that such procedures "shall conform to principles equivalent in substance of those set forth" in Arts. 42 to 48.

2.3.3. Provisional Measures under the TRIPS Agreement

Art. 50 of the TRIPS Agreement deals with provisional measures.[177] As professional infringers rarely remain available to pay the right holder damages or to cover his expenses provisional measures often are the only effective means of combating counterfeiting and piracy.[178] Therefore, the judicial authority shall be authorized "to order prompt and effective provisional measures".[179]

According to Art. 50(1), these measures must be available with respect to any IPR in order to prevent an infringement occurring or infringing products entering the domestic channels of distribution.[180]

Art. 50(2) prescribes that judicial authorities shall be empowered to take action without prior hearing of the defendant and without prior notice to the defendant "where appropriate".[181] For instance, this action might be appropriate where otherwise the measures would be ineffective as any delay could result in evidence being destroyed causing irreparable harm to the right holder.[182]

Moreover, the courts shall be authorized to order the plaintiff to provide them with any reasonably available and relevant evidence to show that he is the right holder and that his right is being infringed (Art. 50(3)).[183]

However, Art. 50 (4) contains a safeguard where actions have been taken without prior notice to the defendant.[184] For instance, Art. 50 (4) prescribes that the defendant must "be given notice, without delay after the execution of the measures at the latest". Furthermore, the defendant has the right to review, "within a reasonable period of time after the notification of the measures",[185] whether the measures adopted shall be revoked, confirmed or modified.[186]

Art. 50(5) provides that the plaintiff may be required to supply additional information in order to identify "the goods concerned by the authority that will execute the provisional measures."[187]

---

174 See Art. 48(1).
175 See Gervais (2003) on p. 302ff.
176 See Art. 49. See also Michaelis and Bender (2005) on p. 460.See also Gervais (2003) on p. 304.
177 For instance, see Gervais (2003) on p. 305ff.
178 See Gervais (2003) on p. 307ff.
179 See Art. 50(1).
180 For instance, see Hestermeyer (2007) on p. 69. See also Gervais (2003) on p. 304ff.
181 See Art. 50(2).
182 See Gervais (2003) on p. 308.
183 See Gervais (2003) on p. 308ff.
184 See Gervais (2003) on p. 309.
185 See Art. 50(4).
186 See Gervais (2003) on p. 309.
187 See Art. 50(5). See also Gervais (2003) on p. 309.

However, with regard to safeguards against abuse of provisional measures Art. 50(6) prescribes that provisional measures shall be revoked, if the plaintiff fails to initiate proceedings within a reasonable period, i.e. 30 working days.[188]
Moreover, the courts must have the authority to order the plaintiff to provide the defendant "appropriate compensation"[189] where the provisional measures are revoked or when it is subsequently discovered that there has not been any infringement of an IPR.[190]

2.3.4. Border Measures under the TRIPS Agreement

Articles 51-60 of the TRIPS Agreement lay down special requirements related to border measures to authorize the right holder to obtain the cooperation of customs administration and to prevent the release of infringing goods into free circulation.[191]
For instance, Art. 51 provides that – if a right holder has valid grounds for suspecting that the importation of infringing goods may take place[192] – he shall be authorized to initiate a procedure and to apply for suspension of the release of the goods.[193]
Art. 52 contains additional information with regard to the application for suspension. For instance, the right holder shall supply adequate evidence of a *prima facie* infringement.[194] Furthermore, he must provide "a sufficiently detailed description of the goods"[195] to enable customs authorities to recognize the infringing goods.[196]
As to the safeguards against abuse of border measures, the judicial or administrative authorities may require the plaintiff to provide a security to protect the defendant (Art. 53(1)).[197] Furthermore, Art. 54 requires that the importer shall be immediately "notified of the suspension of the release of goods".[198]
According to Art. 55, the duration of suspension should not exceed 10 working days when the right holder fails to initiate "proceedings leading to a decision on the merits of the case".[199]
Art. 56 provides an additional safeguard with regard to wrongful detention and prescribes that the plaintiff may be required "to pay the importer, the consignee and the owner of the goods appropriate compensation for any injury caused to them through wrongful detention of goods."[200]

188 See Gervais (2003) on p. 309ff.
189 See Art. 50(7).
190 See Art. 50(7). See also Gervais (2003) on p. 305ff.
191 For instance, see Gervais (2003) on p. 310ff.
192 See Gervais (2003) on p. 312ff.
193 See Gervais (2003) on p. 310ff.
194 See Gervais (2003) on p. 314.
195 See Art. 52.
196 See Gervais (2003) on p. 314.
197 See Gervais (2003) on p. 315ff.
198 See Gervais (2003) on p. 315ff.
199 See Art. 55. See also Gervais (2003) on p. 318ff.
200 See Art. 56. See also Gervais (2003) on p. 320.

2.3.5. Criminal Procedures under the TRIPS Agreement

The fifth section of Part III of the TRIPS Agreement deals with criminal procedures in cases of copyright piracy and willful trademark counterfeiting on a commercial scale. More specifically, Art. 61 prescribes that criminal measures, including monetary fines and/or imprisonment shall be available for cases of organised infringement in order to provide a deterrent.[201]

2.4. Dispute Settlement

Patent protection for pharmaceutical products has featured prominently in dispute settlement cases within the TRIPS framework so far.[202]

The first TRIPS case to go through the entire WTO dispute resolution process was *India – Patent Protection for Pharmaceutical and Agricultural Chemical Products* (WT/DS50) in which the U.S. requested consultations with India as to the absence of patent protection for pharmaceutical and agricultural chemical products in India.[203] In particular, the U.S. claimed that India failed to meet its intermediary obligations under the Articles 27, 63, and 70 of the TRIPS Agreement.[204]

In *Canada – Patent Protection of Pharmaceutical Products* (WT/DS114), the EC requested consultations with Canada on December 19, 1997.[205] It alleged that Canada's Patent Act was not compatible with its obligations under Articles 27(1), 28 and 33 of the TRIPS Agreement, because it did not provide for the full protection of patented pharmaceutical inventions for the entire term of protection.[206]

In *Brazil – Measures Affecting Patent Protection* (WT/DS199), the U.S. requested consultations with Brazil on May 30, 2000.[207] In particular, the U.S. complained that Brazil's 1996 industrial property law[208] discriminates the enjoyability of patent rights on the grounds of whether products are locally produced or imported.[209]

Additional WTO dispute settlement cases involving patent protection for pharmaceutical products are *Pakistan – Patent Protection for Pharmaceutical and*

201 See Gervais (2003) on p. 326ff.

202 See http://www.wto.org/english/tratop_e/dispu_e/find_dispu_cases_e.htm#results (last visited March 24, 2009). See also Hestermeyer (2007) on p. 56ff. See Delich (2002) with respect to developing countries and the WTO dispute settlement system.

203 See Gervais (2003) on p. 89ff and Hestermeyer (2007) on p. 73ff.

204 See Gervais (2003) on p. 89ff.

205 For instance, see Gervais (2003) on p. 226ff.

206 See Gervais (2003) on p. 226ff.

207 See document WT/DS199/1. See also Hestermeyer (2007) on p. 243ff.

208 Law No. 9.279 of May 14, 1996, to Regulate Rights and. Obligations Relating to Industrial Property. For instance, see http://www.cptech.org/ip/health/cl/brazil1.html (last visited March 24, 2009).

209 See http://www.wto.org/english/news_e/news01_e/dsb_1feb01_e.htm (last visited March 24, 2009). See also Champ and Attaran (2002) and Hestermeyer (2007) on p. 242ff on "local working requirements".

Agricultural Chemical Products[210] and *Argentina – Patent Protection for Pharmaceuticals and Test Data Protection for Agricultural Chemicals.*[211]

For a better understanding of the dispute settlement mechanism within the TRIPS framework we now examine in more detail the relevant provisions of the TRIPS Agreement and the "Understanding on Rules and Procedures Governing the Settlement of Disputes" (henceforth, DSU)[212].

Disputes concerning TRIPS obligations between WTO member countries are subject to the WTO's dispute settlement procedures.[213]

In particular, Art. 64 of the TRIPS Agreement contains the provisions on dispute settlement. Art. 64(1) of the TRIPS Agreement confirms the application of the dispute settlement mechanism that was negotiated in the Uruguay Round and that is a combination of the provisions of Articles XXII and XXIII of GATT 1994 and the DSU.[214]

If a member country of the WTO requests consultation with another member country Art. 4(3) of the DSU requires the latter to enter into consultations in good faith within a period of 30 days "with a view to reaching a mutually satisfactory solution".[215]

According to Art. 6(1) of the DSU, a panel may be established if either a dispute is not settled through consultation within 60 days or if a member country refuses to consult.[216] Where one or more of the parties is a developing country Art. 12(10) of the DSU prescribes that parties to the dispute may agree to extend the periods established in Art. 4 of the DSU.[217]

Moreover, Art. 7 of the DSU sets out specific rules with regard to the terms of reference of panels.[218] Furthermore, it sets out specific rules with regard to the composition of panels.[219]

Normally, the panel consists of three persons that satisfy specific criteria prescribed by Art. 8(1) of the DSU. For instance, a panel could consist of representatives of a WTO member country and/or persons that have already served on a panel.[220]

---

210 See document WT/DS36/4.

211 See document WT/DS/171/3.

212 See Annex 2 to the Marrakesh Agreement Establishing the World Trade Organization. See also http://www.wto.org/English/thewto_e/whatis_e/tif_e/disp1_e.htm (last visited March 24, 2009). See also Hestermeyer (2007) on p. 212ff and Gervais (2003) on p. 340ff. See also Koopman and Straubhaar (2006) on p. 6ff.

213 See Gervais (2003) on p. 337ff. See also Samuelson (1999) for a treatment of the policy issues involved in dispute resolution. See also Hestermeyer (2007) on p. 212ff.

214 See Hestermeyer (2007) on p. 212ff and Gervais (2003) on p. 340ff.

215 See Art. 4(3) of the DSU.

216 See http://www.wto.org/English/thewto_e/whatis_e/tif_e/disp1_e.htm (last visited March 24, 2009). See also http://www.wto.org/English/docs_e/legal_e/ursum_e.htm#Understanding (last visited March 24, 2009). See also Gervais (2003) on p. 481.

217 See Gervais (2003) on p. 485.

218 See http://www.wto.org/English/docs_e/legal_e/ursum_e.htm#Understanding (last visited March 24, 2009). See also Hestermeyer (2007) on p. 216ff. and Gervais (2003) on p. 481.

219 See http://www.wto.org/English/docs_e/legal_e/ursum_e.htm#Understanding (last visited March 24, 2009). See also Hestermeyer (2007) on p. 216ff. and Gervais (2003) on p. 481.

220 See Art. 8(1) of the DSU. See also Gervais (2003) on p. 482ff.

Furthermore, specific panel procedures are set out in the DSU. Art. 12(8) of the DSU provides that the panellists shall conduct their examination and issue their report to the parties within six months or, in cases of urgency, within three months.[221]

With regard to the adoption of panel reports Art. 16(1) of the DSU prescribes that 20 days after the panel reports have been circulated to the parties they shall be considered for adoption by the "Dispute Settlement Body" (DSB) that essentially is the WTO General Council.[222]

With regard to appeals from panel cases, Art. 17(1) of the DSU provides that the DSB shall establish an Appellate Body that shall hear these appeals.[223]

Furthermore, Art. 17(5) of the DSU prescribes that "the proceedings shall not exceed 60 days from the date a party to the dispute formally notifies its decision to appeal."[224]

According to Art. 17(14) of the DSU, the Appellate Body report shall be accepted by the parties to dispute and adopted by the DSB within 30 days from the date of its circulation.[225]

Art. 21(3) of the DSU provides that – once the panel report or the Appellate Body report is adopted by the DSB – the WTO member country concerned shall notify the DSB if it will implement the DSB's rulings and follow its recommendations.[226]

According to Art. 22(2) of the DSU, if a WTO member country fails to comply with the rulings of the DSB "within a reasonable period of time determined pursuant to paragraph 3 of Article 21",[227] it shall enter into negotiations with the complaining party.[228]

The DSU also contains certain provisions with regard to procedures involving least-developed countries and takes their specific interests into account.[229] For instance, Art. 24(1) of the DSU provides that WTO member countries "shall exercise due restraint"[230] in applying the rules and procedures of the DSU when a LDC is involved. Moreover, complaining parties shall also "exercise due restraint in asking for compensation" in dispute settlement cases involving a LDC.[231]

According to Art. 24(2) of the DSU, where consultations did not result in a mutually agreeable solution, LDCs shall also have the right to request assistance from the Director-General or the Chairman of the DSB to settle the dispute.[232]

---

221 See http://www.wto.org/English/docs_e/legal_e/ursum_e.htm#Understanding (last visited March 24, 2009). See Art. 12(8) of the DSU. See also Gervais (2003) on p. 484ff.

222 See Gervais (2003) on p. 343.

223 See Gervais (2003) on p. 342 and on p. 487.

224 See http://www.wto.org/English/docs_e/legal_e/ursum_e.htm#Understanding (last visited March 24, 2009). See Art. 17(5) of the DSU. See also Gervais (2003) on p. 488.

225 See http://www.wto.org/English/docs_e/legal_e/ursum_e.htm#Understanding (last visited March 24, 2009). See also Gervais (2003) on p. 342.

226 See http://www.wto.org/English/docs_e/legal_e/ursum_e.htm#Understanding (last visited March 24, 2009). See Grosse Ruse-Khan (2008) on p. 340ff for an excellent overview on the provisions of Art. 22 of the DSU. See also Gervais (2003) on p. 342.

227 See Art. 22(2) of the DSU.

228 See Art. 22(2) of the DSU.

229 See http://www.wto.org/English/docs_e/legal_e/ursum_e.htm#Understanding (last visited March 24, 2009). See also Gervais (2003) on p. 495ff.

230 See Art. 24(1) of the DSU.

231 See Gervais (2003) on p. 495ff.

232 See Gervais (2003) on p. 495ff.

To sum up, in this chapter, we have briefly outlined the most pertinent provisions of the TRIPS Agreement with respect to patent protection, the enforcement of IPRs and the WTO dispute settlement system. Having dealt with the legal aspects of international patent protection the next chapter focusses on the microeconomic analysis of patents.

3. Economic Analysis of Patents

3.1. Introduction

In the first part of this chapter, we will review the underlying economic theory as to patent protection and R&D incentives.[233] More specifically, we will focus on patent races, the deadweight loss on monopolistic markets associated with patents, and the tragedy of the anticommons. In particular, we will contribute to the formal literature on the tragedy of the anticommons by generalizing the model originally formulated by Schulz et al. (2002).

The second part of the chapter provides a survey of the economic literature on optimal patent design. More specifically, we will focus on optimal duration, breadth and depth of patents.

In the third part of this chapter, we shall elaborate on private enforcement of patents and remedies for patent infringement. More specifically, a patent only has value if the exclusive use of the patented innovation can be enforced effectively.[234] However, it is generally left to the holder of a patent to scrutinize and discover patent infringements and to bring the infringement case to court.[235] In particular, we will consider money damages and injunctions that courts typically utilize to punish the infringer of a patent.[236]

The fourth part of this chapter provides a brief survey of the literature on patent litigation and out-of-court settlement of patent cases.

Finally, in the fifth part of this chapter, we shall discuss the specifics of the market for pharmaceuticals, i.e. the economics of drug development and drug pricing.

---

233 See also Dam (1994) on p. 283ff. In general, see Ott and Schäfer (1994) for a comprehensive treatment of innovations from a Law and Economics perspective.

234 See Lévêque and Ménière (2004) on p. 16ff. See also Scotchmer (2006) on p. 72ff.

235 See Becker and Stigler (1974) for a general treatment of law enforcement. See also Landes and Posner (1975) and Friedman (1984) who particularly focus on the private enforcement of law.

236 See Scotchmer (2006) on p. 72. See also Menell and Scotchmer (2007). For a general treatment of the *ex post* efficiency of damages and injunctions see Calabresi and Melamed (1972), Polinsky (1980) and Kaplow and Shavell (1996). See also Blair and Cotter (1998) who provide an analysis of the *ex post* efficiency of damages rules in IP law. For an analysis of the *ex ante* effects of damages and injunctions in the IP context, see Schankerman and Scotchmer (2001). See also Conley (1987) and Anton and Yao (2007).

3.2. Underlying Economic Theory

3.2.1. The Economics of Patents

Before we focus on the economic theory of patents, let us first have a quick look at the legal notion of patents.
A patent confers on its owner the sole right to exploit economically an invention for a limited period of time.[237] According to the priority principle, patents are assigned to the first person to file for a patent on the invention.[238] To be patentable, an invention must be accurately described and published in order to permit a person skilled in the particular field of the invention to carry it out. The patentee who has revealed the secret of her invention in return has the right to compensatory damages when another person infringes the patent.[239] Furthermore, patentable inventions must satisfy particular requirements, i.e. they must be new, must involve a considerable advance in knowledge, and must be capable of industrial application.[240]

3.2.1.1. The Monopoly/Innovation Tradeoff: Deadweight Losses vs. Incentives for R&D

Innovative products or processes, henceforth innovations, that typically embody new scientific knowledge, are non-excludable and non-rival – attributes that are specific to public goods.[241] For instance, – without intellectual property rights – once the information inherent in the innovation is public, competitors of the innovator cannot be prevented from making use of it. Furthermore, the use of knowledge by one person does not reduce the availability of the knowledge to others.[242]
In particular, Arrow (1962) suggests that, without appropriate legal measures, the market system will not handle new knowledge properly and will result in a market failure.[243]
The intuition behind this is the following: Without appropriate legal measures, competitors of the initial innovators have the incentive to free-ride on the efforts made by the initial innovator who incurs all R&D costs. The initial innovator, however, anticipates that – once the R&D costs are sunk and the innovation made – he will not make sufficient profit to recover his costs.[244] Hence, if the market for innovations is perfectly competitive and the information inherent in the innovation is publicly

---

237 Typically, the maximum duration of a patent in European countries is 20 years from the date of the application to the designated patent office. See Menell and Scotchmer (2007) for an excellent survey of the literature on the economic analysis of intellectual property. See also Merges and Duffy (2007) for a comprehensive treatment of U.S. patent law.
238 See Schäfer and Ott (2005) on p. 450. See also Kitch (1998) and Silbertson (1998).
239 See Scotchmer (2006) on p. 72ff.
240 See Hestermeyer (2007) on p. 54ff and on p. 65ff. See also Hilf and Oeter (2005) on p. 454ff.
241 See Langinier and Moschini (2002) on p. 31ff.
242 See Lévêque and Ménière (2004) on p. 4ff.
243 See also Arrow (1959).
244 See Arrow (1959) on p. 11ff.

available, the potential innovator will not be willing to incur the risks and costs involved in the innovative process. Consequently, – given that innovations are socially desirable – the level of innovations will be sub-optimal if innovations remain unprotected.

However, patents are a legal means to address this market failure. More specifically, the key purpose of patents is to provide potential innovators with sufficient incentives to stimulate innovations.[245]

Nevertheless, by giving the holder of the patent an exclusive right to the commercial exploitation of the patented good, patents with a finite length create a temporary monopoly situation.[246]

Furthermore, standard economic theory tells us that a monopoly creates a deadweight loss to society as the monopolist charges a price for the patented product that is typically higher than the manufacturing costs and higher than the price that would prevail under perfect competition.[247] Furthermore, the total quantity demanded in the monopoly situation will typically be lower than the quantity demanded under perfect competition as some consumers will not be willing to pay the full monopoly price.[248] This typically results in a loss of consumer surplus that is higher than the additional producer surplus generated by the monopolist.[249] In economic parlance, this net welfare loss is referred to as deadweight loss.[250]

To sum up, the fundamental trade-off of patent protection is to strike a balance between the benefits of patent protection due to higher R&D incentives and a higher level of innovation on the one hand and the deadweight loss to society resulting from patent protection on the other.[251]

Nevertheless, another benefit of patents is that they make the scientific information that is inherent in the patented innovation available to the public as the patent document is typically published by the patent office.[252] For instance, without patent protection, the innovators could alternatively resort to trade secrets to protect their innovation.[253]

However, there is a huge variety of additional benefits and costs of patent protection – i.e. positive effects on follow-up innovations, on the one hand, and wasteful duplication of costs in patent races and the anticommons problem in the biomedical industry, on the other hand – which we will elaborate upon in the following sections.

---

245 See Mazzoleni and Nelson (1998) for a comprehensive treatment of the benefits and costs of strong patents.

246 See Fink (2005) on p. 174ff. See also Langinier and Moschini (2002) on p. 33.

247 For an early formal analysis of the trade-off between encouraging innovation through patents and deadweight losses associated with patent protection, see Nordhaus (1969). See also Scherer (1972) and Kaplow (1984).

248 See also Shavell and Van Ypersele (2001) on p. 529ff.

249 See Scherer (1980) on p. 14ff.

250 See Harberger (1954). See also Tirole (1988) on p. 66ff.

251 See Kremer and Glennerster (2004) on p. 33. See also Langinier and Moschini (2002) on p. 34. For an early treatment of the patent controversy see Machlup and Penrose (1950).

252 See Langinier and Moschini (2002) on p. 35.

253 For instance, see Friedman et al. (1991).

3.2.1.2. Patent Races

As already mentioned above, there is an additional source for deadweight losses due to the monopoly situation associated with patent protection.[254] The prospects of monopoly rents associated with patent protection may encourage too many potential innovators to invest in R&D in order to make the innovation and to obtain the patent. Eventually, in this so-called patent race, the combined R&D investments of all potential innovators will be higher than the optimal investment effort that would be sufficient to produce the innovation.[255] Put differently, patent races result in a situation where the social return of an innovation – with the social return being the difference between the expected profits of an innovation and its cost – is not maximized.[256]

Another characteristic of a patent race is that research firms create negative externalities on their opponents in a sense that each firm's profit will depend on the research efforts of its opponent.[257] Therefore, it is straightforward to see that the interaction of profit functions suggests a game-theoretic approach.[258]

The classic model of a non-cooperative patent race game was pioneered by Loury (1979). In his equilibrium model of R&D investment, Loury (1979) predicts that, given a fixed market structure, competing firms invest more in R&D than would be socially optimal as they do not take into account the negative externalities that their efforts create on their opponents. Also Reinganum (1981) comes to the conclusion that – in the equilibrium – firms do not choose the socially optimal rates of investment in R&D.[259]

However, whereas Loury (1979) focuses on the role of fixed costs in the R&D technology, Lee and Wilde (1980) emphasize the importance of variable costs in R&D technology. Nevertheless, both studies come to identical welfare conclusions. Moreover, they suggest that firms will vigorously compete with each other until the patent is obtained and thus the patent race is over. Whereas Loury (1979) and Lee and Wilde (1980) predict continuous competition, Dasgupta and Stiglitz (1980) come to the opposite conclusion that a monopolist can persist by engaging in sufficiently fast R&D in order to deter market entry from potentially competing innovators.[260]

The studies mentioned above have in common that they restrict attention to R&D technologies in which a firm's past expenditures in R&D do not have an impact on its current likelihood of discovery.[261] This strong assumption has a considerable impact on the patent race as it is impossible for a firm that is losing to its opponent in the patent race to pull ahead. Therefore, we shall elaborate on a model by Fudenberg et al.

254 For a discussion on races and tournaments that lead to excessive investments by the competitors see Schäfer and Ott (2005) on p. 621. See also Aoki (1991).

255 For instance, see Lévêque and Ménière (2004) on p. 24ff.

256 See Lévêque and Ménière (2004) on p. 25.

257 See Kremer (1998) on p. 1140.

258 See Reinganum (1981) on p. 21ff. See also Dasgupta and Stiglitz (1980), Lee and Wilde (1980) and Loury (1979). See also Reinganum (1984) for a review of patent races.

259 See also Reinganum (1982).

260 See Dasgupta and Stiglitz (1980) on p. 26.

261 See Fudenberg et al. (1983) on p. 4. See also Tirole (1988) on p. 394ff as to "memoryless" patent races.

(1983) where a firm's current chances of discovery depend on the stock of past expenditures in R&D.

The remainder of this section is organized as follows.

First, we shall explain briefly the most important features of a patent race. In game-theoretic parlance, a patent race is a timing game where each player's or firm's choice is when to choose the action "stop investment in R&D". More specifically, a patent race is a "war of attrition" or a "game of chicken".[262]

Second, we shall describe the dynamic two-player patent race model set up by Fudenberg et al. (1983) in which accelerated R&D programs are not possible and the early entrant can successfully block the entry of the later entrant.

Third, we shall describe the multi-stage version of the model originally formulated by Fudenberg et al. (1983, p. 10ff) in which accelerated R&D programs are possible in order to explain how vigorous competition in a patent race may arise.

3.2.1.2.1. The Game of Chicken

The game of chicken is a game in which two players choose actions that will result in serious harm unless one player backs down. Hence, the principle of the game is to create pressure until one player backs down.

The classic game of chicken is played by two drivers that head toward each other in their cars. The first driver to swerve out of the way to avoid the crash loses and is humiliated as the coward or – in colloquial language – as the "chicken".[263] The game of chicken is represented in the payoff matrix in **Table 2**.

Table 2 *Payoff Matrix of the Game of Chicken*

		Player 2 Swerve	Drive straight
Player 1	Swerve	(0, 0)	(–1, +1)
	Drive straight	(+1, –1)	(–100, –100)

Players 1 and 2 each have two strategies, 'Swerve' or 'Drive straight'. If both choose to drive straight the cars collide and each player has a payoff of –100; if both choose to swerve each receives a payoff of 0 assuming that they swerve in different directions; but if one chooses 'Swerve' and the other 'Drive straight' then the "chicken" receives the payoff –1 and the other player receives the payoff +1.

Let us first find out if the game of chicken has one or several Pareto efficient outcomes. It is straightforward to see that (Swerve, Swerve), (Drive straight, Swerve), and

262 For the classic example of the "war of attrition" see Maynard Smith (1974). See also the Hawk-Dove game in biological game theory that was originally formulated by Maynard Smith (1982).

263 See Fudenberg and Tirole (1996) on p. 119, footnote 7.

(Swerve, Drive straight) are Pareto efficient outcomes as it is impossible to make one player better off without the other player being made worse off.[264]

Let us now find out if the game has a unique Nash equilibrium or several Nash equilibria.[265] Note that the game is symmetrical. Hence, both players will do precisely the same calculations to find their optimal strategies.

First, consider which strategy Player 1 should choose when Player 2 chooses to swerve. If Player 1 swerves too, he will yield a payoff of 0. If he drives straight when Player 2 swerves he could gain a higher payoff of +1. Thus, if Player 2 swerves, the best thing for Player 1 to do is to drive straight. As Player 1 has an incentive to deviate from (Swerve, Swerve), it is not a Nash equilibrium.

Second, what should Player 1 do when Player 2 chooses to drive straight? If he chooses to swerve, he will generate a payoff of –1, and a payoff of –100 if he drives straight. Clearly the best strategy for Player 1 is to swerve given that Player 2 drives straight. Hence, given that Player 2 drives straight Player 1 has no incentive to deviate from the strategy "Swerve". Therefore, (Swerve, Drive straight) is a Nash equilibrium. As the game is symmetrical, the same logic applies to the second Nash equilibrium in pure strategies (Drive straight, Swerve). Obviously, (Drive straight, Drive straight) is not a Nash equilibrium as Player 1 has an incentive to deviate given that Player 2 drives straight as he could generate a payoff of –1 instead of –100.

This game also has a Nash equilibrium in mixed strategies:[266] both players choose "Swerve" with a probability of 0.99 and "Drive straight" with a probability of 0.01.[267] We can check that if Player 1 uses this strategy, Player 2 cannot do better in terms of expected payoffs with any other strategy, and vice versa. The outcome is random, and both players will have an expected payoff of –0.01.[268]

Note also that there is no dominant strategy as the individually optimal choice depends on the opponent's choice: Given that the opponent plays "Drive straight", it is optimal for the other player to swerve. Moreover, given that the opponent plays "Swerve", it is optimal for the other player to drive straight.

---

264 See Schäfer and Ott (2004) on p. 23.

265 See Kreps (1990) on p. 409 for a proof that every game has at least one Nash equilibrium in pure or mixed strategies when the number of players, and the number of actions are finite. See also the reprint of John Nash's PhD thesis in Kuhn and Nasar (2002) on p. 51ff.

266 A mixed strategy is a strategy in which the drivers randomize their strategies. That is, the drivers assign a probability to each of the two possible strategies "Swerve" and "Drive straight" and play their choices according to those probabilities. Furthermore, a Nash equilibrium in mixed strategies refers to an equilibrium in which each driver chooses the optimal frequency with which to play his strategies given the frequency choices of the other driver.

267 See Pindyck and Rubinfeld (2005) on p. 483. See also Varian (1996) on p. 484.

268 To check that no player has an incentive to deviate from this situation suppose that Player 1 randomizes, letting p be the probability of "Swerve" and $(1–p)$ the probability of "Drive straight". Because Player 2 is using probabilities of 0.99 for "Swerve" and 0.01 for "Drive straight", the probability that both will choose "Swerve" is $0.99p$, and the probability that both will choose "Drive straight" is $0.01(1–p)$. Thus, Player 1's expected payoff is $0.99(1–p)–0.01p–100*0.01(1–p)=0.99–0.99p–0.01p–1+p= –0.01$. This payoff is independent of p, so player 1 cannot do better in terms of expected payoff no matter what he chooses. As the game is symmetrical, the same logic applies to the choice of Player 2.

To sum up, the game of chicken has two Nash equilibria in pure strategies that generate Pareto efficient outcomes: (Drive straight, Swerve), and (Swerve, Drive straight).
Nevertheless, suppose now that the two players mentioned above are not drivers but two pharmaceutical companies that are both engaged in research into the same drug yet to be developed. Furthermore, assume that only the first firm to invent the drug can obtain a patent on the drug that enables him to generate monopoly profits.
In order to analyze the strategic interaction between two rival pharmaceutical companies, let us now turn to a more sophisticated dynamic model of a patent race.

3.2.1.2.2. Blocked Entry in a Dynamic Patent Race Model without Leapfrogging

In this section, we shall consider the dynamic patent race game originally formulated by Fudenberg et al. (1983) in which the first firm to enter the race can successfully block the entry of the opponent resulting in a R&D monopoly situation.
The crucial assumption in this section is that the late entrant cannot undertake an accelerated R&D program and leapfrog the early entrant in the accumulation of knowledge that determines the success probability. Put differently, the probability of discovery is always greater for the firm with more experience.

3.2.1.2.2.1. Dynamic Patent Race Model

Consider a continuous-time version of a timing game with two pharmaceutical producers (Firm 1 and 2) where R&D competition takes on the characteristics of a race, as only the first firm to make a patentable discovery "wins" and realizes monopoly profits assuming that "inventing around the patent" is not possible.[269] If Firm i has not stopped investing in R&D at any $\tau<t$, Firm i's action set at t is

$$A_i(t) = \{\text{stop R\&D investment, keep on investing in R\&D}\}$$

where stopping means abandoning the race. The following analysis applies backward induction and is restricted to the subgame-perfect equilibria of the patent race.[270]
The basic idea of backward induction is to solve firstly the optimal choice of the last player of a multistage game for each possible situation she might face, and then work backward to solve for the optimal choice of the penultimate player, the antepenultimate player and so on until the first stage of the game is reached.
However, in games where several players choose simultaneously at several stages, including the last stage, simple backward induction is not applicable. Remarkably, the German economist Reinhard Selten from the University of Bonn extended the concept

269 See Fudenberg and Tirole (1996) on p. 121ff. See also Fudenberg et al. (1983). However, Denicolò (1996) provides a game-theoretic analysis of a patent race where the "winner takes all" assumption may not hold. Moreover, Reinganum (1982) has introduced a loser's prize in her analysis of a single stage patent race and has shown that increasing payoffs to losers result in decreasing R&D efforts.
270 See Fudenberg and Tirole (1996) on p. 122ff.

of backward induction to extensive games where players move simultaneously in several periods.[271] Furthermore, Selten has shown that some Nash equilibria are based on non-credible threats and are therefore not valid. Selten originally formulated the concept of subgame perfection in order to eliminate those Nash equilibria that are based on non-credible threats.

A subgame-perfect Nash equilibrium is defined as an equilibrium in which the players' strategies constitute a Nash equilibrium in every subgame of the original game.[272] Normally, the subgame-perfect Nash equilibrium is found by backward induction. In the course of backward induction branches of the game that involve any player making a non-credible choice are eliminated so that subgame perfect Nash equilibria do not involve non-credible threats.[273]

Nevertheless, the fact that players cannot be fooled by non-credible threats also has a considerable impact on the analysis of a patent race. For instance, a pharmaceutical producer could try to preempt the opponent using an empty threat to invest in R&D forever no matter what the opponent does. However, the constraint of subgame perfection prevents the opponent from being fooled by this threat. Hence, the analysis can focus on circumstances in which preemption is credible.

First, we shall analyze the last subgame of the patent race where one firm has already stopped its R&D investment.[274] The maximization problem of the remaining firm is then easily solved.

Second, subgames in which both firms invest in R&D shall be analyzed.

Note that the payoffs of the firms can be expressed as functions of time.[275] In the following, the payoffs of the firms will be described using the payoff functions F_i, K_i and B_i:

If only Firm i stops at t and the opponent j does not stop, Firm i receives the payoff $F_i(t)$. Furthermore, if only Firm j stops at t and Firm i does not stop, Firm i receives a payoff $K_i(t)$. If both firms stop simultaneously at t, the payoffs are $B_1(t)$ and $B_2(t)$.[276]

The last step in describing the patent race is to specify the strategy spaces. The pure strategies are simply maps from times t to {stop R&D investment, keep on investing in R&D}.

Let us now turn to the conditions that a two-player patent race satisfies as formulated by Fudenberg and Tirole (1996, p. 121ff).

More specifically, the continuous-time version of a two-player patent race satisfies the following eight conditions for all firms i and all dates t:

$$K_i(t) \geq K_i(\tau) \text{ for } \tau > t, \quad (1)$$

271 See Selten (1965).

272 See Selten (1965).

273 We will come back to non-credible threats in the context of parallel trade of pharmaceutical products in section 5.2.4 in Chapter 5.

274 See Fudenberg and Tirole (1996) on p. 124ff.

275 See Fudenberg and Tirole (1996) on p. 121ff.

276 Note that the notations $Ki(\cdot)$ and $Fi(\cdot)$ express "*K*eep on investing in R&D" and "*F*irst to stop investing in R&D", respectively. The notation $Bi(\cdot)$ expresses that "*B*oth firms stop simultaneously".

where $K_i(\cdot)$ denotes the payoff of Firm *i* when the opponent stops first and Firm *i* keeps on investing in R&D. Condition (1) states that if Firm *i*'s opponent is going to stop first in the subgame starting at *t*, then Firm *i* prefers the opponent to stop immediately. Furthermore,

$$K_i(t) \geq F_i(\tau) \text{ for } \tau > t, \tag{2}$$

where $F_i(\cdot)$ denotes the payoff of Firm *i* when it is the first to stop investing in R&D.[277] Condition (2) says that each firm prefers his opponent to stop first at any time *t* to any outcome where Firm *i* stops first at some $\tau > t$.

$$K_i(t+1) > F_i(t) \text{ for all } i \text{ and } t.^{278} \tag{3}$$

Condition (3) asserts that fighting (keep on investing in R&D) for one period is worthwhile if successful in the sense that the opponent stops investing.
Moreover, Fudenberg and Tirole (1996, p. 122ff) assume that

$$F_i(t) = B_i(t), \tag{4}$$

where $B_i(\cdot)$ denotes the payoff of Firm *i* when both firms stop investing in R&D at the same time. This condition states that when Firm *i* stops, it does not matter if the other firm stops investing or continues investing in R&D.
Furthermore,

$$F_i(0) > F_i(+\infty).^{279} \tag{5}$$

More specifically, condition (5) asserts that fighting forever is costly. Moreover, Fudenberg and Tirole (1996, p. 122) assume that each player would rather quit immediately than fight forever:

$$F_i(+\infty) = K_i(+\infty). \tag{6}$$

Assuming that players discount their bounded payoffs condition (7) is always satisfied.

$$\text{For all } i \text{, there exists } T_i > 0 \text{ such that } F_i(t) > F_i(+\infty) \text{ for } t < T_i \text{ and } F_i(t) < F_i(+\infty) \text{ for } t > T_i. \tag{7}$$

Condition (7) says that even though at the beginning of the game it is better to stop investing in R&D than to invest forever, things get better later on so that – ignoring past sunk costs – the pharmaceutical firms would rather continue investing than stop investing in R&D.[280]
Furthermore, Fudenberg and Tirole (1996, p. 122) assume that

277 See Fudenberg and Tirole (1996) on p. 122, assumption (ii).
278 See Fudenberg and Tirole (1996) on p. 122, assumption (ii').
279 See Fudenberg and Tirole (1996) on p. 122, assumption (iv).
280 See Fudenberg and Tirole (1996) on p. 122.

$$\text{for all } i, \text{there exists } \overline{T}_i \text{ such that } F_i(\cdot) \text{is strictly decreasing before } \overline{T}_i \text{ and increasing after} \overline{T}_i . \quad (8)$$

Condition (8) states that $F_i(\cdot)$ has a single minimum. Furthermore, the conditions (7) and (8) correspond to the market growing or the research technology improving over time, i.e. because of learning by doing.[281]
Now assume that the medicinal product to be invented can be patented. Furthermore, let the value of the patent be denoted by v.[282] If the pharmaceutical company has not stopped investing in R&D before date t, it pays $c_i\, dt$ and successfully invents the medicinal product with probability $x_i(t)dt$ between t and $t+dt$. Consequently, the instantaneous flow profit is given by $[x_i(t)v-c_i]dt$.[283]
Suppose that $dx_i/dt>0$ due to learning by doing and the accumulation of experience over time.
Furthermore,

$$F_i(t) = \int_0^t [x_i(\tau)v - c_i]\exp\left(-\int_0^\tau [x_1(s)+x_2(s)]ds\right)\exp(-r\tau)d\tau . \quad (9)$$ [284]

Note that the rate of interest is denoted by r. The probability that no pharmaceutical company has invented the medicinal product at date τ conditional on both firms having continued to invest in R&D [see (9)] is

$$\exp\left(-\int_0^\tau [x_1(s)+x_2(s)]ds\right). \quad (10)$$ [285]

Moreover, Fudenberg and Tirole (1996, p. 123) assume that a R&D monopoly is viable at date 0:

$$0 < \int_0^\infty [x_i(\tau)v - c_i]\exp\left(\int_0^\tau x_i(s)ds\right)\exp(-r\tau)d\tau = K_i(0), \quad (11)$$

and that a R&D duopoly is not viable at date 0, that is, $F_i(\infty)<0$ where $F_i(\infty)$ is the date-0 payoff if neither pharmaceutical company ever stops investing in R&D. Moreover, Fudenberg and Tirole (1996, p. 123) state that – due to the fact that $x_i(\cdot)$ increases because of learning by doing and the accumulation of knowledge – if a monopoly is viable at date 0 then it is also viable from any date $t>0$ on. Consequently, it is optimal for each pharmaceutical company to continue investing in R&D until discovery once his opponent has stopped investing. Hence, the payoff of Firm i when it keeps on investing in R&D is given by[286]

281 See Fudenberg and Tirole (1996) on p. 122.
282 For instance, see Mansfield (1986) for an analysis of the importance of patents in various industries. More specifically, Mansfield (1986) suggests that the pharmaceutical industry relies heavily on patents. Furthermore, see Hall et al. (2005) for an analysis of the usefulness of patent citations to measure the market value of patents. See also Harhoff et al. (2003) and Reitzig (2003).
283 See Fudenberg and Tirole (1996) on p. 123.
284 See Fudenberg and Tirole (1996) on p. 123.
285 See Fudenberg and Tirole (1996) on p. 123. See also Scotchmer (2006) on p. 59.
286 See Fudenberg and Tirole (1996) on p. 123.

$$K_i(t)=\int_0^t [x_i(\tau)v-c_i]\exp\left(-\int_0^\tau [x_1(s)+x_2(s)]ds\right)\exp(-r\tau)d\tau$$
$$+\int_t^\infty [x_i(\tau)v-c_i]\exp\left[-\left(\int_0^\tau x_i(s)ds+\int_0^t x_j(s)ds\right)\right]\exp(-r\tau)d\tau. \tag{12}$$

The payoff of the pharmaceutical firm *i* in the continuous-time patent race when it keeps on investing in R&D after the opponent has stopped investing as well as the payoff of pharmaceutical firm *i* when it is the first to stop investing in R&D is depicted in **Figure 2**.

Figure 2 *Payoffs in a Continuous-Time Patent Race*

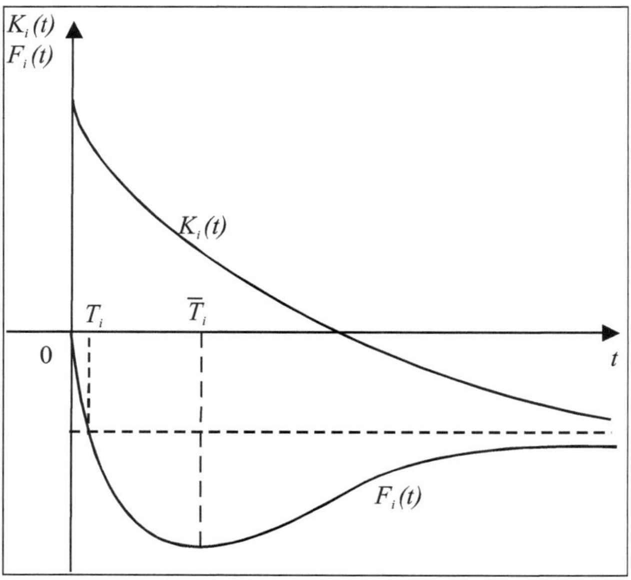

Figure 2 shows that $K_i(t)$ always lies above $F_i(t)$ as pharmaceutical firm *i* always prefers his opponent to stop first to any outcome where pharmaceutical firm *i* stops first.[287] As implied by Condition (6), in the very long run, $K_i(t)$ and $F_i(t)$ converge to a certain level depicted by the dotted horizontal line. One can also see that between 0 and T_i it would be better for pharmaceutical firm *i* to stop investing in R&D than to invest forever as $F_i(t)>F_i(+\infty)$.

Nevertheless, for $t>T_i$ pharmaceutical firm *i* prefers to continue investing in R&D than to stop investing.

Let us now turn to a more specific description of $F_i(t)$ in particular with regard to $\overline{T}_i$. One can see that $F_i(t)$ first decreases, has its single minimum at date $\overline{T}_i$, and then

287 See Fudenberg and Tirole (1996) on p. 124, Figure 4.4.

increases. To understand this curve progression, we have got to analyze $\overline{T}_i$. $\overline{T}_i$ is the date where $x_i(\overline{T}_i)v = c_i$.[288] Furthermore, as $x_i(\cdot)$ increases $x_i(t)v > c_i$ for $t > \overline{T}_i$ which explains the fact that $F_i(t)$ increases after $\overline{T}_i$.
Let us now analyze the game elaborated above to analyze the question as to whether it has a unique subgame perfect Nash equilibrium or several subgame-perfect Nash equilibria.

3.2.1.2.2.2. Analysis of the Continuous-time Patent Race

Condition (7) guarantees that the pharmaceutical firm *i* never stops investing in R&D after T_i. By stopping investment in R&D at date $t > T_i$ pharmaceutical firm *i* receives

$$F_i(t) < F_i(+\infty) = K_i(+\infty) \leq K_i(\tau) \qquad (13)$$

for all τ.[289] Hence, the pharmaceutical firm *i* always receives more by never stopping investment after T_i. Therefore, ceasing to invest in R&D is a (conditionally) strictly dominated strategy at date $t > T_i$.[290]
Furthermore, Fudenberg and Tirole (1996, p. 124) assume that the times (T_1, T_2) defined in condition (7) satisfy $T_1 + 1 < T_2$. That is, the pharmaceutical firm 1 prefers to invest in R&D forever than to stop investing at an earlier date than pharmaceutical firm 2. For instance, this is the case when the intervals between two dates are small and the pharmaceutical firms have different cost structures and research technologies and thus different probabilities of discovery. The following proposition asserts that a marginally earlier entry in the patent race is sufficient to guarantee a monopoly position in R&D.[291]

Proposition 1

Assume:

R&D is viable for a monopolist [*inequality* (11)];[292]

288 For instance, see Nerkar (2003) for an empirical analysis of the value of new knowledge using patent data from the pharmaceutical industry. See also Fudenberg and Tirole (1996) on p. 123, footnote 9.
289 See Fudenberg and Tirole (1996) on p. 124.
290 See Fudenberg and Tirole (1996) on p. 124.
291 See Fudenberg et al. (1983) on p. 8, Proposition 1. See also Fudenberg and Tirole (1996) on p. 124.
292 Note that – in a different version of the model – assumption (1) could be more specifically analyzed with regard to R&D for neglected infectious and tropical diseases. In the case of neglected infectious and tropical diseases, a R&D monopoly may not be viable at all for various reasons. For instance, the value of the patent *v* might be too small relative to the cost of R&D investment. In particular, several authors argue that introduction of patent protection in the developing world alone is not sufficient for solving the problem of underinvestment in R&D for neglected infectious and tropical diseases that are prevalent in low-income countries. See for instance, see Maurer (2005) on p. 10 and

A R&D duopoly in which both firms always engage in R&D is not profitable [$F_i(\infty)<0$];
Pharmaceutical firm 1 has a small advantage in the sense that it enters the patent race $k \geq 2$ *periods before pharmaceutical firm 2. It then follows – with regard to Condition* (7) – *that* $T_1+1<T_2$ *if both firms have the same technology* ($x_2(t)=x_1(t-k)$ *and* $c_1=c_2$).

With these assumptions, a unique subgame perfect equilibrium exists in which pharmaceutical firm 1 engages in R&D and pharmaceutical firm 2 quits at date 0. Thus, no patent race occurs.

Fudenberg and Tirole (1996, p. 124ff) prove uniqueness by backward induction. At date T_1+1, if both pharmaceutical firms are still investing in R&D, pharmaceutical firm 2 anticipates that pharmaceutical firm 1 will never stop investing in R&D.
Because $T_1+1<T_2$,

$$F_2(T_1+1) > F_2(+\infty), \tag{14}$$

as depicted in **Figure 3** by the corresponding thin-dotted horizontal line.

Figure 3 *Payoff for Firm 2 when Firm 1 enters the patent race* $k \geq 2$ *periods before Firm 2 and Firm 2 is the first to stop investing in R&D*

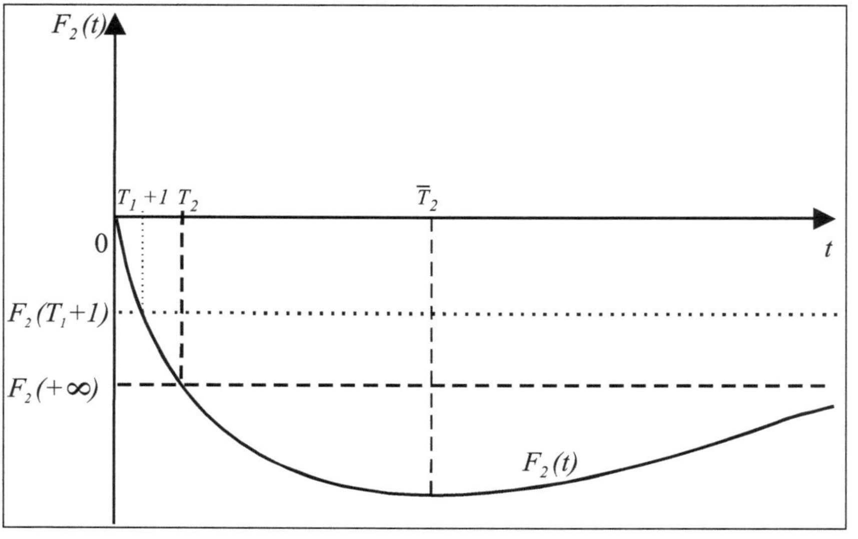

Kettler (2002) on p. 667ff. See also Lanjouw (2003) on p. 100ff, Lanjouw and Cockburn (2001), Kremer (2001a), Kremer (2001b), Kremer (2002), Attaran and Gillespie-White (2001) and Attaran (2004). We will come back to this issue in the sections 6.1 and 6.2 in Chapter 6.

Furthermore, because $F_2(\cdot)$ has a single minimum (Condition (8)),

$$F_2(T_1+1) > F_2(t) \qquad (15)$$

for all $t>T_1+1$ which is also depicted in **Figure 3.**[293] Consequently, it is optimal for pharmaceutical firm 2 to stop investing in R&D at T_1+1.
Working backwards, Fudenberg and Tirole (1996, p. 125ff) consider now date T_1. As $K_1(T_1+1)>F_1(T_1)$ which follows from Condition (3), pharmaceutical firm 1 does not stop investing in R&D. Analogous to (15), it follows that

$$F_2(T_1) > F_2(t) \qquad (16)$$

for all $t>T_1$.[294] Therefore, pharmaceutical firm 2 stops investing in R&D at T_1 if both firms have not yet stopped investing in R&D at that date. The same reasoning shows that pharmaceutical firm 2 stops investing in R&D and pharmaceutical firm 1 keeps on investing at any date $t<T_1$. Hence, a unique subgame-perfect Nash equilibrium exists in which pharmaceutical firm 1 invests in R&D and pharmaceutical firm 2 stays out of the market.

3.2.1.2.2.3. Conclusion as to the Continuous-Time Patent Race

Pharmaceutical firm 1 that starts investing in R&D before his opponent can successfully preempt him even though the advantage due to the early entrant is only very small.
Consequently, pharmaceutical firm 1 is the winner without a fight and no patent race occurs. Put differently, this game exhibits "ε-preemption", as a small advantage proves decisive.[295]
Furthermore, a deadweight loss due to a patent race between the two competing firms does not occur but it may occur due to the monopoly power of the early entrant.
Nevertheless, this result is based on the strong assumption that the late entrant cannot undertake an accelerated R&D program and leapfrog the early entrant in the accumulation of knowledge.
In the following section, we shall describe the multi-stage patent race with random discovery originally formulated by Fudenberg et al. (1983, p. 10ff) in which leapfrogging by the late entrant (pharmaceutical firm 2) is possible and where the competitors engage in a patent race under certain circumstances.

293 See Fudenberg and Tirole (1996) on p. 124ff.
294 See Fudenberg and Tirole (1996) on p. 125.
295 See also Dasgupta and Stiglitz (1980), Fudenberg and Tirole (1996) on p. 125, Harris and Vickers (1985) and Hendricks et al. (1988).

3.2.1.2.3. Vigorous Competition in a Multi-Stage Patent Race with Accelerated R&D Programs

3.2.1.2.3.1. Introduction

In the patent race game in the previous section, discovery was stochastic. Nevertheless, the probability of discovery $x_i(t)$ – as $dx_i/dt>0$ due to learning and accumulation of experience – was always greater for pharmaceutical firm 1 that started to invest in R&D earlier than his opponent. Put differently, pharmaceutical firm 2 did not have the possibility to undertake an accelerated R&D program and to overtake pharmaceutical firm 1 in the previous model.[296]
However, the model set up by Fudenberg et al. (1983, p. 10ff) to be elaborated in this section is different in the sense that it more specifically analyzes the link between the investment in R&D and the accumulation of experience.
Indeed, randomness in the link between the R&D investment and the accumulation of experience is introduced so that a firm that starts to invest in R&D at a later stage than the opponent could still get ahead of the rival firm. Another difference between the two models is that R&D takes place in two stages.[297]
In the first stage, a preliminary invention must be made. The first stage is completed by pharmaceutical firm i when it makes the preliminary invention which immediately becomes public knowledge. For instance, the preliminary invention with regard to R&D for a new pharmaceutical product could be the invention of a set of new molecules that succeeded in preclinical testing.[298]
However, the second stage entails the progress toward a patentable design, i.e. through clinical trials and the approval by the regulator. As in the previous model the first firm to get the patent is the winner of the race and yields the corresponding rewards.

3.2.1.2.3.2. Multi-Stage Patent Race

Assume that pharmaceutical firm 1 enters the race at $t=0$ and k periods of time ahead of pharmaceutical firm 2 that enters the race at a time t_k. Furthermore, assume that the later entrant (pharmaceutical firm 2) makes an expected loss if both firms engage in R&D over the two stages until one of them wins the patent.[299]
Nevertheless, pharmaceutical firm 2 has a chance to pass the first stage before his opponent and may induce him to stop investing in R&D if it makes the preliminary discovery before a certain point of time as we will see in the following.

296 See Fudenberg et al. (1983) on p. 10.
297 See Roberts and Weitzman (1981). See also Fudenberg et al. (1983) on p. 10.
298 More specifically, the R&D process for new medicines from discovery to approval of medicines covers several complex, expensive, and risky stages. For instance, see PhRMA (2005). We will come back to this issue in section 3.2.5.2.2 in this chapter.
299 See Fudenberg et al. (1983) on p. 10.

In the first stage, the invention of new molecules that succeeded in preclinical testing generates costs c_1 per period of time. Moreover, pharmaceutical firm i makes the preliminary discovery with probability

$$x(e_i^1(t)) \tag{17}$$

where $e_i^1(t)$ denotes pharmaceutical firm i's total experience at date t relevant to the preliminary invention in the first stage.[300] Fudenberg et al. (1983, p. 10) define experience as the total time that pharmaceutical firm i has engaged in R&D. More specifically, the investment in R&D over one period of time generates one unit of experience, the investment in R&D over two periods of time generates two units of experience and so on. Hence, total experience can be expressed in periods of time investing in R&D.

Similarly, second-stage R&D generates costs c_2 per period of time, and the probability of obtaining the patent is

$$z(e_i^2(t)) \tag{18}$$

where $e_i^2(t)$ denotes pharmaceutical firm i's experience relevant in the second stage.[301] Furthermore, pharmaceutical firm i has got to complete the first stage before it can accumulate second-stage experience. To understand how pharmaceutical firm 2 could overtake pharmaceutical firm 1 suppose that both firms are in the first stage and that the early entrant pharmaceutical firm 1 has accumulated a higher stock of relevant experience than pharmaceutical firm 2, that is $e_1^1(t) > e_2^1(t)$ at t.

However, with probability $x(e_2^1(t))$ pharmaceutical firm 2 will make the preliminary discovery and complete the first stage ahead of pharmaceutical firm 1.

Moreover, as soon as pharmaceutical firm 2 completes the first stage its probability of making the second-stage invention and obtaining the patent discontinuously jumps to $z(0)$. More specifically, the zero in $z(0)$ expresses that pharmaceutical firm 2 has not yet made any the relevant stage-two experience.

Nevertheless, this probability will exceed pharmaceutical firm 1's probability of obtaining the patent if pharmaceutical firm 1 is still in the first stage. Although pharmaceutical firm 2 had the disadvantage of starting to invest in R&D later than pharmaceutical firm 1 the possibility of an accelerated R&D program may still enable pharmaceutical firm 2 to be the first to make the preliminary invention.

In order to illustrate how a firm may pull ahead in the patent race, Fudenberg et al. (1983, p. 11) assume that the probability of making the preliminary discovery in the first stage increases with experience and that the probability of success in the second stage is constant and equal for both firms. Furthermore, the authors assume that pharmaceutical firm 1 is leading in the first stage and pharmaceutical firm 2 is the follower. This yields the following *Proposition 2*.[302]

---

300 See Fudenberg et al. (1983) on p. 10.
301 See Fudenberg et al. (1983) on p. 10.
302 See Fudenberg et al. (1983) on p. 11, Proposition 2.

Proposition 2

When the probability of making the preliminary discovery increases with experience in the first stage and the probability of obtaining the patent in the second stage is constant – thus does not depend on experience and is equal for both firms in the second stage – a unique subgame perfect equilibrium exists.
Pharmaceutical firm 1 that is leading in the first stage always invests in R&D unless pharmaceutical firm 2 invests in R&D and makes the first-stage discovery before a specified time $\overline{e}^1$.[303] *Depending on the values of the parameters, such as the expected profit of pharmaceutical firm 2 at a certain date and the time at which either pharmaceutical firm 1 or 2 makes the preliminary discovery, pharmaceutical firm 2 either*

(i) *does not enter the patent race,*
(ii) *invests in R&D until $\overline{e}^1$, or*
(iii) *always does R&D unless the leader passes the first stage before $\left(\overline{e}^1 + t_k\right)$.*

The decision points that are interesting in the course of the analysis occur when only one firm has made the preliminary discovery, or when both firms remain in the first stage.[304]
Let us first consider the decision problem of the leading pharmaceutical firm 1 when pharmaceutical firm 2 is the first to make the preliminary invention and passes the first stage. The decision points are depicted in **Figure 4**.

Figure 4 *Decision points for Pharmaceutical Firm 1 when Pharmaceutical Firm 2 is the first to complete the first stage*

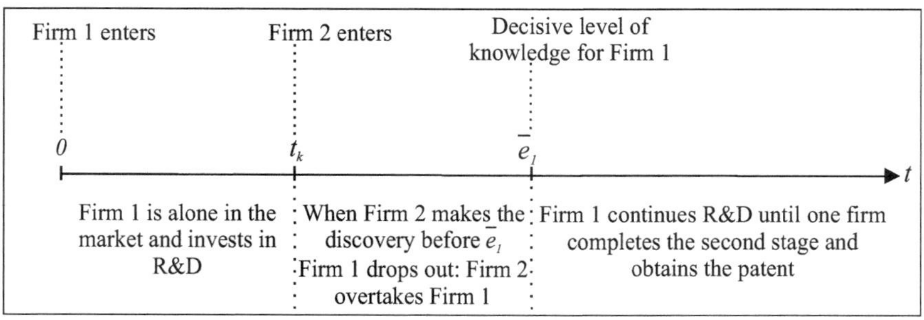

Let $\overline{e}^1$ denote the level of first-stage experience such that pharmaceutical firm 1 with experience less than $\overline{e}^1$ drops out when pharmaceutical firm 2 has completed the first stage.[305]

---

303 Recall that a firm's total experience is just the total time that it has invested in R&D.
304 See Fudenberg et al. (1983) on p. 12ff for the proof of Proposition 2.
305 See Fudenberg et al. (1983) on p. 12.

Nevertheless, in case that pharmaceutical firm 2 has made the preliminary discovery at some time $t \geq \overline{e}^1$, pharmaceutical firm 1 stays in and continues R&D until one of the firms wins the patent race in the second stage.[306] In other words, one may also refer to $\overline{e}^1$ as the decisive level of experience or knowledge for pharmaceutical firm 1.
Let us now consider the decision problem of pharmaceutical firm 2 that is – by assumption – behind in the race as depicted in **Figure 5**.

Figure 5 *Decision points for Pharmaceutical Firm 2 when Pharmaceutical Firm 1 is the first to complete the first stage*

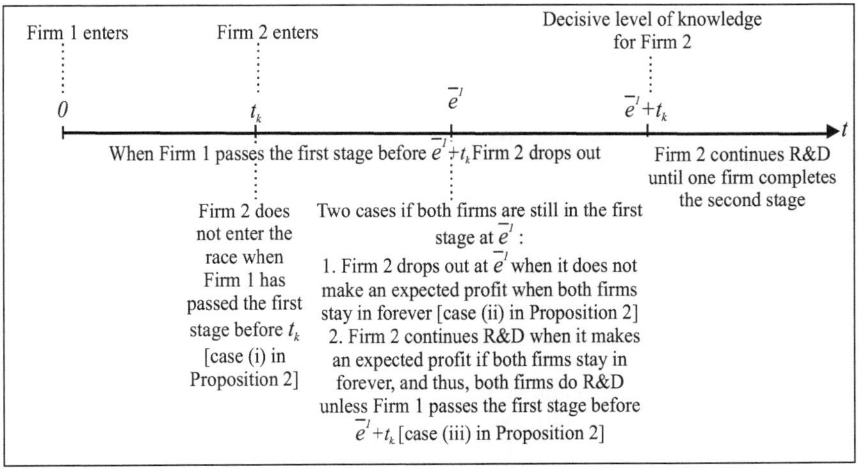

As before, one may refer to $(\overline{e}^1 + t_k)$ as the decisive level of first-stage experience or knowledge for pharmaceutical firm 2 expressed in units of time such that pharmaceutical firm 2 with experience less than $(\overline{e}^1 + t_k)$ drops out of the race when pharmaceutical firm 1 has completed the first stage.
However, in case that pharmaceutical firm 1 has made the preliminary discovery at some time $t \geq \overline{e}^1 + t_k$, pharmaceutical firm 2 does not drop out of the race and continues to invest in R&D.[307]
Consider now the case that neither firm has passed the first stage at time $\overline{e}^1$. In this case, we know that pharmaceutical firm 1 will continue to invest in R&D until one firm wins the patent.
Nevertheless, pharmaceutical firm 2's decision depends on its expected profit at $\overline{e}^1$. If pharmaceutical firm 2 does not make a positive expected profit when both firms

306 Recall the assumption that pharmaceutical firm 2 makes an expected loss if both firms engage in R&D over the two stages until one of them obtains the patent and therefore that a perpetual duopoly is not viable. Hence, $\overline{e}^1$ and thus $(\overline{e}^1 + t_k)$ cannot be zero.

307 See Fudenberg et al. (1983) on p. 12ff.

continue to invest in R&D forever, the race from $t=\overline{e}^1$ on is a natural monopoly in which pharmaceutical firm 2 stops investing in R&D and drops out of the race at $\overline{e}^1$.[308] This is case (ii) in *Proposition 2*.
However, when pharmaceutical firm 2 makes a positive expected profit when both firms continue to invest in R&D forever, both firms continue to invest in R&D, unless pharmaceutical firm 1 passes the first stage before $\left(\overline{e}^1+t_k\right)$.[309] This is case (iii) in *Proposition 2*.
However, also ε-preemption – as in the previous model without leapfrogging – may occur when pharmaceutical firm 1 passes the first stage before t_k.

3.2.1.2.3.3. Conclusion and Ideas for Further Research

The question as to whether both firms continue competing although they cannot earn positive profits if they continue investing in R&D forever depends on the expected profit of pharmaceutical firm 2 at a certain date as well as on the time at which either firm makes the preliminary discovery.
In particular, as case (iii) of *Proposition 2* suggests, the patent race could result in a waste of resources and a deadweight loss provided that pharmaceutical firm 1 does not pass the first stage before $\left(\overline{e}^1+t_k\right)$.
More specifically, the firm that is behind in the first stage may continue investing in R&D because it still could be the first to make the preliminary discovery and thus overtake the leading opponent.
Nevertheless, a basic assumption in the two models elaborated above is that R&D is a viable activity for a monopolist because he can obtain a patent on the medicinal product.[310] However, this assumption may not hold if we take into consideration research into medicines for neglected infectious and tropical diseases. More specifically, the expected returns to research into these diseases may be too low to spur research.[311] We will come back to this issue in Chapter 6.
However, in the following sections, we will focus on the tragedy of the anticommons. In particular, we will contribute to the existing anticommons model set up by Schulz et al. (2002) by formulating a more general set-up.

3.2.1.3. Property Rights and the Tragedy of the Anticommons

In this section, we shall firstly give a short review of property ownership and property rights including an outline of the tragedy of the commons.
In the second part, we shall describe the tragedy of the anticommons in more detail providing a formal model of the anticommons fragmentation in property with regard to the problem of underinvestment in R&D for tropical diseases.

308 See Fudenberg et al. (1983) on p. 12ff.
309 See Fudenberg et al. (1983) on p. 12ff.
310 For instance, see Proposition 1 and inequality (11).
311 See Maurer (2005) on p. 10. See also Lanjouw (2003) on p. 100ff, Kremer (2002), Attaran and Gillespie-White (2001) and Attaran (2004).

3.2.1.3.1. A Review of Property Rights and Property Ownership

In general, property rights are those socially accepted legal rules that relate to the ownership and use of scarce resources and commodities.[312] The basic idea is that property rights are an instrument of society as the owner of property rights possesses the consent of the other members of society to act in particular ways in order to derive utility from ownership and use of resources and commodities.[313] Furthermore, the owner of property rights expects the community to prevent others from interfering with his actions, provided that these actions are within the boundaries of the rights referred.[314]

Property rights are inseparably linked to economic concepts, such as the concepts of externalities, Pareto-efficiency and transaction costs. For instance, Demsetz (1967) argued that a primary function of well-specified property rights is that of providing and guiding incentives to achieve a greater internalization of external benefits and costs and thus to achieve an efficient allocation of resources.[315]

Most notably, the Coase theorem, attributed to the Nobel-Laureate in Economics Ronald H. Coase, relates to the Pareto-efficient allocation of resources.[316] In essence, the Coase theorem states that – provided that parties can bargain to their mutual advantage in the absence of transaction cost, and when property rights are well specified and transferable – the resulting outcome will be Pareto-efficient regardless of the original allocation of property rights.[317] Put differently, when transaction costs are zero, resources will find their highest value use regardless of the original allocation of property rights.[318]

In general, there are three basic forms of property ownership: state property, private property and commons property.

State property, on the one hand, has been defined as a property regime in which material resources are aimed at satisfying the needs and purposes of society as a whole rather than maintaining individual interests.[319]

In a private property regime, on the other hand, an individual is the sole owner of a bundle of rights over resources. Moreover, it can exercise control over the resources and is protected from interference by others.[320]

Lastly, commons property has been defined as a property regime in which every individual has free access to a resource and no individual has the right to exclude someone else from using the object of property. Hence, there are no exclusionary

---

312 See Schäfer and Ott (2004) on p. 84ff. See also Demsetz (1998) on p. 144ff and Pejovich (1997).

313 See Demsetz (1967) on the economic theory of property rights.

314 See Demsetz (1998) on p. 144.

315 See Furubotn and Pejovich (1972). See also Pejovich (1997) and Sim et al. (2002) on p. 459ff. See also Pindyck and Rubinfeld (2005) on p. 659.

316 See Coase (1960). See also Schäfer and Ott (2005) on p. 100ff.

317 Interestingly, Coase (1988) on p. 174 made the following remark with regard to the multiple misinterpretations of his theory: "*The world of zero transaction costs has often been described as a Coasian world. Nothing could be further from the truth. It is the world of modern economic theory, one which I was hoping to persuade economists to leave.*"

318 See Schäfer and Ott (2004) on p. 87ff and Cooter and Ulen (2004) on p. 85ff.

319 For instance, see Waldron (1988).

320 See Penner (1997).

rights.[321] For instance, air and water are two common examples for common property resources.[322]
However, apart from the three basic types there are several hybrid types of property ownership such as the anticommons or the so-called limited commons hybrids.[323] Notably, Heller (1998) elaborated in detail on the concept of anticommons that was coined by Michelman (1982).
Nevertheless, a substantial part of the literature on property rights focused on private and commons property whereas very little has been written on the anticommons property.
In the next section, we shall elaborate upon the concept of anticommons by Heller (1998) and provide a simple game-theoretic model including a personal contribution and extension of the model by Schulz et al. (2002). Beforehand, we shall give a short review of the tragedy of the commons.

3.2.1.3.2. The Tragedy of the Commons

Hardin (1968) extended and popularized the term of the tragedy of the commons that originally derives from a work on population control by Lloyd (1833). Hardin (1968) used this term to describe the negative effects of freedom of use in a commons and to explain overpopulation and the overexploitation of certain resources, i.e. air pollution.[324]
In essence, people often overuse commonly owned scarce resources because they individually internalize the benefits of the usage, while the external costs of the individual action are distributed between all users of the commonly owned resource.
Hardin (1968) illustrated the main problem with a hypothetical example of a pasture commonly shared by local herders.[325] Assume that the rational herder is profit-maximizing and consequently tends to increase the size of his herd as long as marginal revenue exceeds marginal costs. The crucial point is that the herder fully internalizes the proceeds from the sale of additional cattle but that the disadvantage due to the effects of overgrazing created by the additional cattle is shared between all herders using the pasture.[326]
Tragically, as long as the individual gain from additional cattle exceeds the distributed cost, all herders add extra cattle resulting in overgrazing and, in the limit, in the complete degradation of the pasture.[327] The same logic applies to fishing grounds, oil

321 See Michelman (1982) on p. 5ff.
322 See Pindyck and Rubinfeld (2005) on p. 662.
323 See Rose (2000).
324 See Bell (1986). See also Heller and Eisenberg (1998) on p. 698ff and Sim et al. (2002) on p. 460ff.
325 See Pindyck and Rubinfeld (2005) on p. 662ff for an example of the problem of overutilization of fishing grounds.
326 See Hardin (1968) on p. 1244.
327 See Hardin (1968) on p. 1244.

pools, hunting territories and the growth of human population, with the resources on earth being a general commons.[328]

However, from a game-theoretic perspective the tragedy of the commons can be seen as a collective prisoner's dilemma.[329] The herders can either cooperate with the group and graze a certain socially efficient number of animals in order to jointly avoid the degradation of the pasture or they defect from the group and graze a number of cattle that maximizes individual profit.

In essence, game theory shows that individuals benefit from defecting in a prisoner's dilemma situation. Nevertheless, they would be better off if everybody cooperated.

In the following section, we shall elaborate on the theory of anticommons property popularized by Heller (1998) that can be seen as a "mirror image of commons property".[330]

3.2.1.3.3. Tragedy of the Anticommons

First, we shall review the theory of anticommons property and the classic example originally formulated by Heller (1998).

Second, we will set up a game-theoretic model to analyze a potential tragedy of the anticommons in the pharmaceutical and biotechnology industries, in particular with regard to research into a potential malaria vaccine.

The author's contribution to the literature is the extension of the models originally formulated by Buchanan and Yoon (2000) and Schulz et al. (2002) to a generalized set up with regard to the biotechnology industry.

3.2.1.3.3.1. Introduction

The term "anticommons" originally derives from Michelman (1982) and has been popularized and explained in detail by Heller (1998) and Heller (1999).

In essence, the tragedy of the anticommons occurs when rationally and separately acting individuals collectively under-utilize and thus partly waste a given scarce resource.[331]

In theory, individuals under-utilize a scarce resource when too many individuals hold effective rights of exclusion in the given scarce resource.[332] Heller (1998, p. 633ff) provides empirical explanations and examples to illustrate the tragedy of the anticommons, such as the phenomenon that in post-1990 Moscow many stores remained empty while numerous open air kiosks popped up in the streets.[333]

---

328 See Buchanan and Yoon (2000) on p. 2ff, Sim et al. (2002) on p. 459ff, and Heller and Eisenberg (1998) on p. 698ff.

329 See Luce and Raiffa (1957) on p. 95 for a typical example of the prisoner's dilemma. See also Schäfer and Ott (2005) on p. 92ff.

330 See Heller and Eisenberg (1998) on p. 698. See also Michelman (1982).

331 See Heller and Eisenberg (1998) on p. 698 and Lévêque and Ménière (2004) on p. 17ff.

332 See Heller (1998) on p. 668.

333 See also Sim et al. (2002) on p. 460ff.

Heller (1998, p. 635ff) found out that many different private parties and agencies such as private enterprises, local, regional, and federal governments and worker's collectives held effective rights over usage of store space.
Hence, as new entrepreneurs had to secure the agreement or permission of several owners it was difficult or even impossible for them to successfully negotiate for the usage of store space.[334] Each owner could simply exercise his right of exclusion and withhold the permission of use.[335]
Thus, the distribution of fragmented rights to various owners with competing interests, i.e. different objectives for facility development, led to an under-utilization of store space even though each owner was losing money with the empty stores.[336]
In a paper on the effects of the redevelopment program by the Singaporean Urban Redevelopment Authority (URA) in order to provide more land for private housing in land-scarce Singapore, Sim et al. (2002) found out that en bloc sales of land to release prime land for higher density redevelopment may have resulted in a tragedy of anticommons.
In response to the development guide plans by the URA (1991) and URA (1993) and the Land Titles (Strata) (Amendment) Act (1999), property owners in Singapore tended to pool their fragmented interests and to band together to collectively sell combined sites for redevelopment aiming at generating higher profits.[337]
Nevertheless, as differing interests were involved, i.e. with regard to the sale price, many en bloc sales failed although they would have been collectively profitable.
Thus, Sim et al. (2002, p. 468ff) conclude that the disagreements of owners with effective rights of exclusion in the scarce resource land led to an under-utilization of land and to a tragedy of the anticommons.
Of course, in a hypothetical world with zero transaction costs, individuals could always avoid the tragedy of the commons as well as the tragedy of the anticommons.[338] In practice, however, as people have to overcome transaction costs and strategic behavior of trading partners, such tragedies are likely to occur, in particular when trading partners are hostile strangers and do not interact repeatedly.[339]

3.2.1.3.3.2. The Tragedy of Anticommons in the Pharmaceutical and Biotechnology Industries from a Game-Theoretic Perspective

In the first part of this section, we shall describe the problem of fragmented patents in the pharmaceutical industry. Then follows a simple formal model to show how the

334 See Sim et al. (2002) on p. 459ff.
335 See Dagan and Heller (2001). See also Sim et al. (2002) on p. 460.
336 See Heller (1998) on p. 633ff.
337 See The Land Titles (Strata) (Amendment) Act (1999), Singapore. See also The Land Titles (Strata) Act (Chapter 158) (1988), Singapore; http://statutes.agc.gov.sg/non_version/cgi-bin/cgi_retrieve.pl?&actno=Reved-158&date=latest&method=part (last visited March 24, 2009). See also http://www.ura.gov.sg/legal/legal-partA.htm for further information on the URA (last visited March 24, 2009). See Sim et al. (2002) on p. 458.
338 See Coase (1960).
339 See Heller and Eisenberg (1998) on p. 698.

fragmentation of patents in the pharmaceutical sector may result in an "anticommons deadweight-loss".

3.2.1.3.3.2.1. Fragmented Patents in Biomedical Research

Firstly, we shall describe the business environment in which upstream research in biomedical sciences takes place. Secondly, we shall explain in detail how the problem of anticommons may arise in biomedical sciences.

3.2.1.3.3.2.1.1. Biomedical Business Environment

Nowadays, most of upstream research in the biomedical sector is carried out in pharmaceutical companies, commercial biotechnology companies, supported by private funds and privately appropriated through patents or trade secrecy.[340]

Moreover, academic laboratories and public research institutions and their technology transfer offices increasingly tend to patent and license their inventions.[341] Due to the privatization of biomedical research upstream discoveries are less likely to be made freely available in the public domain as the rights holder can either restrict or prohibit the use of patented technologies or even demand a prohibitively high license fee.[342] In particular, Heller and Eisenberg (1998, p. 698) suggest that in such a business environment – when property rights are fragmented in a sense that too many owners hold rights in previous discoveries – the privatization of biomedical research potentially constitutes obstacles to future research.[343]

Of course, as we have already mentioned before, patents for upstream discoveries and the conferred monopolies in discoveries are means to motivate high-risk R&D for new medicines resulting in inefficiently high prices and deadweight losses.[344] Nevertheless, the tragedy of the anticommons refers to an additional problem that is inherent in any patent system, in particular with regard to the biomedical sciences.[345]

When a potential inventor needs multiple licenses for the use of several patented inputs, i.e. genetic diagnosis tests or receptors that are required to create a new pharmaceutical product, each owner of an upstream patent is in a strong bargaining position when negotiating with the potential inventor.[346] For instance, each owner of a

---

340 See Heller and Eisenberg (1998) on p. 698ff. See also Correa (1991).

341 See Eisenberg (1996). See also Heller and Eisenberg (1998) on p. 698. See also Kenney (1986) and Kitch (2003). See also Epstein and Kuhlik (2004) for a critical comment with respect to the anticommons problem in the biomedical industry. See also Scotchmer (2006) on p. 127ff on cumulative innovations.

342 See Heller and Eisenberg (1998) on p. 698.

343 See Merton (1973). See also Walsh et al. (2003) who find evidence that there has been a recent increase in patents on research tools in drug discovery. However, the authors come to the conclusion that the increase in patents on research tools has not significantly impeded drug discovery. See also Scotchmer (2006) on p. 143, footnote 7.

344 See Scotchmer (2006) on p. 127ff on cumulative innovations and on p. 34ff on IPRs and deadweight losses.

345 See Heller and Eisenberg (1998).

346 See Scotchmer (2006) on p. 132ff. See also Vanneste et al. (2006) on the tragedy of the anticommons and opportunistic behavior.

patent could charge a prohibitively high license fee for the use of his technology resulting in increasing cost for product development and decelerated downstream biomedical innovation.[347]

3.2.1.3.3.2.1.2. Anticommons Problem in Biomedical Sciences

In the following, we shall describe in more detail how a tragedy of anticommons may arise in biomedical sciences according to Heller and Eisenberg (1998).
Basically, a tragedy of anticommons may arise when the government permits the creation of too many concurrent fragments of IPRs in potential new medicinal products and permits too many reach-through licensing agreements that confer upstream patent owners rights in subsequent downstream discoveries resulting in royalties or exclusive licenses on future innovations.[348]

3.2.1.3.3.2.1.2.1. "Concurrent Fragment" Anticommons

First, an anticommons problem due to the creation of too many concurrent fragments may arise when property rights are conferred on isolated gene fragments.[349] For instance, most of the genetic diagnosis tests and therapeutic proteins require the use of multiple gene fragments.[350] Thus, an increasing number of patents on gene fragments held by multiple owners will result in increasing transaction costs of bundling the licenses that are required to develop the corresponding products.[351] Obviously, this may have a negative impact on the willingness of a potential investor in the course of the bargaining process to invest in R&D.[352]
Second, a tragedy of anticommons due to concurrent fragments in biomedical innovation may occur when patents are conferred on receptors that – at the preclinical stage – are useful for screening potential medicines to analyze their therapeutic effects and side effects.[353] As in the first case of concurrent fragments mentioned above, when the number of owners of patented receptors increases, the transaction costs of collecting the required licenses also increase.
Nevertheless, increasing the transaction costs of research projects involving multiple recaptors potentially hampers or even destroys any R&D incentives.[354] Instead, research firms may prefer to invest in projects that may be less promising but also less vulnerable to licensing obstacles.[355]

347 See Heller and Eisenberg (1998) on p. 698ff.
348 See Heller and Eisenberg (1998) on p. 699ff. See also Scotchmer (2006) on p. 142ff and Green and Scotchmer (1995) on strategic licensing. See also Scotchmer (2006) on p. 142ff.
349 See Heller and Eisenberg (1998) on p. 699. See also Eisenberg (1990).
350 See Heller and Eisenberg (1998) on p. 699.
351 See also Merges and Nelson (1990) on p. 860ff on blocking patents. See also Adelman (2005) for a critique of the anticommons model in biotechnology patenting.
352 See Merges and Nelson (1990).
353 See El Feki (2005) on p. 5ff on preclinical testing and screening. See also Heller and Eisenberg (1998) on p. 699.
354 See Heller and Eisenberg (1998) on p. 698ff.
355 See Heller and Eisenberg (1998) on p. 699.

3.2.1.3.3.2.1.2.2. Reach-Through Licensing Agreements on Patented Research Tools

A tragedy of the anticommons through reach-through licensing agreements may occur when several upstream patent owners of research tools such as the basic technology of bioengineering (Cohen-Boyer patent) and the polymerase chain reaction (PCR) charge inefficiently high license fees or royalties from potential downstream innovators in the course of the bargaining process.[356] High fees or royalties result in higher costs for the potential downstream inventor and may decrease his incentives to invest in R&D.[357]
Furthermore, the anticommons problem may be more severe in the pharmaceutical and biotechnology industries than in other industries for several reasons.[358]
First, patents play a more significant role in the pharmaceutical and biotechnology industries than in any other industry due to higher costs and risks of research projects in these industries.[359]
Second, some inventions lack adequate substitutes, i.e. receptors and patented genes.[360] Therefore, the holdup problem in the course of the bargaining process may aggravate and may result in higher bargaining costs of collecting required licenses for research tools in the pharmaceutical industry compared to other industries.
Furthermore, patent pools that could help to overcome the anticommons problem are less likely to occur in these industries as pharmaceutical and biotechnology firms are less likely to be willing to give up the significantly high gains from exclusivity.[361]
Heller and Eisenberg (1998, p. 699ff) suggest that there are the following major concerns as to the tragedy of the anticommons in biomedical innovation: High transaction costs of bundling IPRs in biomedical research, heterogeneity of interests of upstream patent owners, and cognitive biases among upstream patent owners.[362]

3.2.1.3.3.2.1.2.3. High Transaction Costs

First, high transaction costs may hamper the bundling of IPRs as they occur in the course of the bargaining process for licenses.[363] More specifically, they occur at the very beginning of the whole R&D process, when the outcome of an investment in R&D is still uncertain and the potential value of a future product rather speculative.[364]
For instance, for every 10,000 molecules screened in the first stage of drug development, an average of 250 candidates enter the next stage of preclinical testing.[365]
Moreover, just ten molecules make it to the next stage of clinical trials, and only one is

356 See Scotchmer (2006) on p. 142ff. See also Heller and Eisenberg (1998) on p. 699ff.
357 See Heller and Eisenberg (1998) on p. 699.
358 See Heller and Eisenberg (1998) on p. 699ff.
359 See Mansfield (1986) on p. 175. See also DiMasi et al. (1991), DiMasi et al. (2003) and Heller and Eisenberg (1998) on p. 699ff.
360 See Heller and Eisenberg (1998) on p. 699.
361 See Levin et al. (1987). See also Heller and Eisenberg (1998) on p. 700. See also Lerner and Tirole (2004) on patent pools.
362 See Heller and Eisenberg (1998) on p. 699ff.
363 See Heller and Eisenberg (1998) on p. 700.
364 See Heller and Eisenberg (1998) on p. 700.
365 For instance, see PhRMA (2005) for an overview of the different stages of biomedical innovation.

approved by the legal authorities.[366] Under these conditions, investors may be less willing to pay for a bundle of licenses required for their research project in order to overcome the anticommons problem.

3.2.1.3.3.2.1.2.4. Heterogeneity of Interests among Public and Private Patent Owners

Second, the bundling of IPRs may require case-by-case negotiations as heterogeneous interests among public and private patent owners with conflicting goals are likely to complicate the development of standard license terms or even make their emergence impossible.[367]

For instance, a public upstream patent owner such as a government agency, on the one hand, may have the objective to ensure widespread access to affordable new medicines. Private pharmaceutical firms, on the other hand, may follow the conflicting objective to use their IPRs to maintain an exclusive and lucrative monopoly and thus to use their rights to block the strategies of the other – public – upstream patent owners.[368] Heller and Eisenberg (1998, p. 700) suggest that – under these conditions – it may be impossible to find "an agreement that leaves enough private value for downstream developers."[369]

3.2.1.3.3.2.1.2.5. Cognitive Biases and the Value of Inventions

Another major concern with regard to a biomedical anticommons tragedy are cognitive biases among upstream patent owners.[370] Tversky and Kahneman (1992) found out that individuals tend to consistently overestimate the likelihood that events with high payoffs but very low likelihood, i.e. lotteries, occur. Heller and Eisenberg (1998, p. 701) suspect that a similar bias may cause upstream patent owners to overvalue the importance of their innovation in downstream product development and that they, therefore, are likely to charge a license fee for the use of their discoveries that exceeds their real value. In particular, the more upstream owners of patented research tools are cognitively biased and overestimate the value of their innovations, the bigger may be the gap between the aggregate license fees and the input value of patented research tools. Consequently, it is more likely that the downstream developer refuses the offers resulting in a potentially useful new product not being developed.[371]

Nevertheless, in the following section, we shall theoretically analyze the question how an anticommons problem may arise in the biomedical industry.

---

366 See El Feki (2005) on p. 5ff.

367 See Heller and Eisenberg (1998) on p. 700.

368 See also Kremer and Glennerster (2004) on p. 40ff as to the difference between private returns and social returns to pharmaceutical innovation. See also Nadiri (1993) and Heller and Eisenberg (1998) on p. 700.

369 See Heller and Eisenberg (1998) on p. 700.

370 See Heller and Eisenberg (1998) on p. 701.

371 See Heller and Eisenberg (1998) on p. 701.

3.2.1.3.3.2.2. The Tragedy of the Anticommons in the Biomedical Industry from a Game-Theoretic Perspective

In this section, we shall first elaborate on the anticommons model set up by Buchanan and Yoon (2000) to illustrate the tragedy of the anticommons in the biomedical industry in the context of research into a malaria vaccine.
In the second part of this section, we shall contribute to the existing model originally formulated by Schulz et al. (2002) and set up an extended version to illustrate the case with multiple patent owners.

3.2.1.3.3.2.2.1. The Tragedy of the Anticommons in a Game with two Patent Owners

In the light of the problem of fragmented patents mentioned above let us now consider the following model of the tragedy of the anticommons in the biomedical industry.[372]
Suppose that two pharmaceutical companies hold a patent for particular technologies required to do research for a potential malaria vaccine.[373] In price-theoretic parlance, the two technologies are fully complementary goods provided by two monopolists.[374]
For instance, Firm A holds a patent for a newly identified gene fragment of the malaria parasite.[375] Firm B holds a patent for a receptor useful for screening a potential malaria vaccine. Furthermore, suppose that any third firm that wishes to use the gene fragment and the receptor needs to obtain access to both patents.[376] There is a continuum of third-party firms. Furthermore, each firm is characterized by its willingness to pay for the licenses to use the gene fragment and the receptor.[377] Let w denote the willingness to pay. Moreover, w is uniformly distributed across [0,1]. Let p_i, $i \in \{A,B\}$, denote the price of Firm i that it charges for the use of its patented research tool.
Thus, a third-party firm has to pay a total price P of p_A+p_B.[378] It is straightforward to see that a third-party firm will be willing to pay total price P in order to use both patented technologies if it is smaller than his willingness to pay w.[379] If the demand for patents is $Q=1-(p_A+p_B)$, Firm A generates a profit of

372 See Buchanan and Yoon (2000).
373 For a general stylized example see also Schulz et al. (2002) on p. 600ff and Buchanan and Yoon (2000) on p. 4ff.
374 See Buchanan and Yoon (2000) on p. 5, footnote 5.
375 Note that recent biotechnology advances in mapping the genome of the malaria parasite point to a possible malaria vaccine. Nevertheless, the development of a malaria vaccine is not high on the agenda of private pharmaceutical firms as Sachs (1999) noted on p. 17. The model elaborated in this section may, in part, explain why the anticommons fragmentation in property of gene fragments and receptors may hamper the development of a malaria vaccine. However, the main reason for the underinvestment in R&D for medicines for neglected infectious and tropical diseases is the insufficient expected market size for those medicines. For instance, see Kremer and Glennerster (2004) on p. 55ff and Acemoglu and Linn (2004).
376 See Schulz et al. (2002) on p. 600ff, example 4.
377 See Schulz et al. (2002) on p. 600.
378 See Schulz et al. (2002) on p. 600.
379 See Schulz et al. (2002) on p. 601.

$$\pi^A(p_A, p_B) = p_A(1-(p_A + p_B)).^{380} \tag{19}$$

Analogously, Firm *B*'s profit function is given by

$$\pi^B(p_B, p_A) = p_B(1-(p_A + p_B)). \tag{20}$$

Assume that both firms choose the prices for the licenses simultaneously, each taking the price of the other firm as given.[381] In this simultaneous-move game, we can therefore use the Nash equilibrium concept to determine the profit-maximizing prices.[382]

$$\max_{p_A} \pi^A(p_A, p_B) = p_A - p_A^2 - p_A p_B$$

$$\frac{\partial \pi^A}{\partial p_A} = 1 - 2p_A - p_B = 0$$

$$\Leftrightarrow p_A^*(p_B) = \frac{1}{2}(1-p_B).^{383} \tag{21}$$

Firm *A*'s reaction curve given by (21) expresses Firm *A*'s profit-maximizing price as a function of Firm *B*'s price. Furthermore, for Firm *B* we obtain:

$$p_B^*(p_A) = \frac{1}{2}(1-p_A). \tag{22}$$

The Nash equilibrium is the intersection of the two reaction curves. In order to determine the profit-maximizing price for Firm *A* substitute p_B in (21) with p_B^* given by (22). By rearranging (21), we then obtain:

$$p_A = \frac{1}{2}(1 - \frac{1}{2}(1-p_A))$$

$$\Leftrightarrow p_A^* = \frac{1}{3}.^{384} \tag{23}$$

And for Firm *B*:

$$p_B^* = \frac{1}{3}.^{385} \tag{24}$$

It follows that the total equilibrium price *P* for both licenses is 2/3.

---

380 See Buchanan and Yoon (2000) on p. 9. See also Schulz et al. (2002) on p. 601.
381 See Buchanan and Yoon (2000) on p. 9ff.
382 For instance, see Mas-Colell et al. (1995) on p. 384ff and Pindyck and Rubinfeld (2005) on p. 441ff for an overview of oligopolistic markets. See also Kuhn and Nasar (2002) on p. 51ff for a facsimile of John Nash's Ph.D. thesis on non-cooperative games.
383 See Schulz et al. (2002) on p. 601.
384 See Buchanan and Yoon (2000) on p. 10.
385 See Buchanan and Yoon (2000) on p. 10. See also Schulz et al. (2002) on p. 601.

Moreover, we can determine the demand for patents by substituting P=2/3 into the general demand function. Thus, total demand is 1/3. Moreover, the total rent is given by:

$$TR = PQ = \frac{2}{3}\frac{1}{3} = \frac{2}{9}.^{386} \tag{25}$$

As a benchmark, Schulz et al. (2002, p. 601) derive the profit-maximizing price P for a license for the use of both patented technologies if a single firm were the owner of both patents. The profit of the single firm is given by:

$$\pi(P) = P(1-P). \tag{26}$$

By differentiating (26), it follows for the profit-maximizing price P^*:

$$\frac{\partial \pi(P)}{\partial P} = 1 - 2P = 0$$
$$\Leftrightarrow P^* = \frac{1}{2}.^{387} \tag{27}$$

Consequently, the total rent is given by:

$$TR = \frac{1}{4}. \tag{28}$$

Hence, the fragmentation of patents results in a higher price for both licenses. Furthermore, the total rent of the two patent holders is lower than that of a monopoly patent holder as $1/4 = 2/8 > 2/9$ [(25) and (28)].

To sum up, the fragmentation of patents has two main effects.

First, assume that future profits can be accurately foreseen and that the maximum amount that a potential innovator is willing to invest in R&D is equal to the profit that he can generate from an innovation.[388] Under these reasonable assumptions, the fragmentation of patents results in lower incentives to invest in R&D for the two innovations in the first place as the total profit under fragmented patents is lower than that of a monopoly patent holder.

Second, recall that there is a continuum of third-party firms whose willingness to pay is uniformly distributed across [0,1]. As the fragmentation of patents increases the price for both licenses, less third-party firms are willing to employ the patented technologies.

Nevertheless, one may argue that the results elaborated in this section are not robust on the grounds that the assumptions on the demand function are very specific.[389]

386 See Buchanan and Yoon (2000) on p. 10.

387 See Schulz et al. (2002) on p. 601. See also Buchanan and Yoon (2000) on p. 8ff.

388 See also Deardorff (1992).

389 We thank Hans-Bernd Schäfer for his comment in this respect.

However, **Appendix 2** shows that we obtain qualitatively identical results for a more generalized set-up.

3.2.1.3.3.2.2.2. The Tragedy of the Anticommons in a Game with Multiple Patent Owners

Consider now the case of more than two patent owners. Let $N=\{1,...,n\}$ denote the finite number of owners of patented technologies that are required to do malaria research.[390]

Furthermore, let p_i denote the price that the owner of a patented technology firm i charges for a license to use the technology.[391] Let the vector $p_{-i}=\{p_1,...,p_{i-1},p_{i+1},...p_n\}$ describe the prices of all firms other than firm i. Moreover, demand is given by

$$Q=1-(p_i+\sum_{j\in N/\{i\}} p_j). \tag{29}$$

Furthermore, firm i generates a profit of

$$\pi^i(p_i,p_{-i})=p_i(1-(p_i+\sum_{j\in N/\{i\}} p_j) \quad \forall i\in N. \tag{30}$$

Assume that firms choose the prices for their licenses simultaneously, each taking the price of the other firms as given. In this simultaneous-move game, we can therefore again use the Nash equilibrium concept to determine the profit maximizing prices:

$$\max_{p_i} \pi^i(p_i,p_{-i})=p_i-p_i^2-p_i\sum_{j\in N/\{i\}} p_j$$

$$\frac{\partial\pi^i}{\partial p_i}=1-2p_i-\sum_{j\in N/\{i\}} p_j=0$$

$$\Leftrightarrow p_i^*(p_{-i})=\frac{1}{2}(1-\sum_{j\in N/\{i\}} p_j). \tag{31}$$

At this point, we cannot directly solve this maximization problem and derive p_i^* as we cannot further rearrange (31). First, we have to show that $p_i^*=p_j^*\,\forall i,j\in N$.

Proposition 3:

To show: $p_i^*=p_j^*\ \forall i,j\in N.$

---

390 See Buchanan and Yoon (2000) on p. 10.

391 See Schulz et al. (2002) on p. 601.

Recall that in the previous case with $n=2$ and $i=A$ and $j=B$

$$p_A^* = \frac{1}{2}(1-p_B) = \frac{1}{2}\left(1-\frac{1}{2}(1-p_A)\right) \Leftrightarrow p_A^* = \frac{1}{3}$$
$$p_B^* = \frac{1}{2}(1-p_A) = \frac{1}{2}\left(1-\frac{1}{2}(1-p_B)\right) \Leftrightarrow p_B^* = \frac{1}{3}.$$

Hence, in this case, we know from (23) and (24) that

$$p_A^* = p_B^* . \qquad (32)$$

Let us now apply the same logic to the general case with n patent owners with $N = \{1,...,n\}$ in order to show that the following holds:

$$p_i^* = p_j^* \ \forall i,j \in N . \qquad (33)$$

We know that

$$p_i^* = \frac{1}{2}(1 - \sum_{k \in N/\{i\}} p_k) \qquad (34)$$

and that

$$p_j^* = \frac{1}{2}(1 - \sum_{k \in N/\{j\}} p_k) \ \forall i,j \in N. \qquad (35)$$

Let us now derive p_j^*. First, we have to reformulate p_j^*. Then, we plug in $p_i^* = \frac{1}{2}(1 - \sum_{k \in N/\{i\}} p_k)$. Finally, we get the general equation for p_j^* after some simple reformulations:[392]

$$p_j^* = \frac{1}{3} - \frac{1}{3} \sum_{k \in N/\{i,j\}} p_k . \qquad (36)$$

Similarly, we obtain for p_i^*:[393]

$$p_i^* = \frac{1}{3} - \frac{1}{3} \sum_{k \in N/\{i,j\}} p_k . \qquad (37)$$

Finally, we can see from (36) and (37) that

---

392 See **Appendix 3**.
393 See **Appendix 4**.

$$p_i^* = p_j^* \ \ \forall i, j \in N \text{. q.e.d.} \tag{38}$$

Therefore, the maximization problem is identical for each patent owner, and each will set the same price p_i^* in the equilibrium. Algebraically, we have

$$\sum_{j \in N/\{i\}} p_j = (n-1)\, p_i. \tag{39}$$

By substituting $\sum_{j \in N/\{i\}} p_j$ in (31) with $\sum_{j \in N/\{i\}} p_j$ given by (39) we obtain:

$$p_i(n) = \frac{1}{2}(1-(n-1)p_i(n))$$

$$\Leftrightarrow p_i^*(n) = \frac{1}{(n+1)}. \tag{40}$$

Consequently, the equilibrium price $P^*(n)$ for n licenses is $P^*(n) = n/(n+1)$. P^* increases in n as

$$\frac{\partial P(n)}{\partial n} = \frac{(n+1)-n}{(n+1)^2} = \frac{1}{(n+1)^2} > 0. \tag{41}$$

Put differently, as the number of licenses required increases, the total price P that third-party firms have to pay increases. To illustrate, suppose that n tends towards infinity. In this case, the total price for n licenses, $P^*(n) = n/(n+1)$, tends toward unity. Recall that there is a continuum of third-party firms, each characterized by its willingness to pay. The willingness to pay w is uniformly distributed across [0,1]. Consequently, in the limit, no third-party firm will be willing to employ the patented technologies if n tends toward infinity.
Moreover, we can determine the demand for patents by substituting P into the general demand function $Q=1-P$. Thus, total demand is

$$Q(n) = 1 - \frac{n}{(n+1)} = \frac{n+1-n}{(n+1)} = \frac{1}{(n+1)}.\text{[394]} \tag{42}$$

Furthermore, the total rent is given by

$$TR(n) = P(n)Q(n) = \frac{n}{(n+1)}\frac{1}{(n+1)} = \frac{n}{(n+1)^2}.\text{[395]} \tag{43}$$

We can see from (42) that total demand decreases in n as

394 See Buchanan and Yoon (2000) on p. 10.
395 See Buchanan and Yoon (2000) on p. 10.

$$\frac{\partial Q(n)}{\partial n} = -\frac{1}{(n+1)^2} < 0. \tag{44}$$

Furthermore, we can see from (43) that total revenue decreases in n as

$$\frac{\partial TR(n)}{\partial n} = \frac{1}{(n+1)^2} - \frac{2n}{(n+1)^3}$$
$$\Leftrightarrow \frac{\partial TR(n)}{\partial n} = \frac{n+1-2n}{(n+1)^3} = \frac{1-n}{(n+1)^3} < 0 \quad \forall n \geq 2. \tag{45}$$

Put differently, when the number of licenses for the use of patented products required to do R&D for a potential malaria vaccine increases, total demand and total revenue decrease. Furthermore, under the assumption that the maximum amount that the innovating firm is willing to invest in malaria research is equal to the total revenue, R&D incentives decrease when the number of licenses for the use of patented research tools increases.
Finally, we can see from (42) and (43) that, in the limit,

$$\lim_{n\to\infty} Q(n) = \lim_{n\to\infty} \frac{1}{n+1} = 0 \tag{46}$$

and that

$$\lim_{n\to\infty} TR(n) = \lim_{n\to\infty} \frac{n}{(n+1)^2} = 0. \tag{47}$$

Hence, total revenue generated by the patent holders and quantity demanded exhibit the following features. If n increases, the values of $Q(n)$ and $TR(n)$ approach to zero. Furthermore, fewer third-party firms are willing to employ the patented technologies. Put differently, the level of underutilization of patented research tools increases if n increases.
Furthermore, the fragmentation of patents reduces the incentives to invest in R&D for new technologies by potential innovators in the first place. To illustrate, we can see from (43) that the total revenue of a monopoly patent holder, $TR(1)$, is equal to 1/4. We can also see that $TR(1) > TR(n)$ as $1/4 > n/(n+1)^2$.[396] Put differently, the total revenue becomes lower than that of a monopoly patent holder if patents are fragmented. Assume again that future revenues can be accurately foreseen and that the maximum amount that a potential innovator is willing to invest in R&D is equal to the profit that he can generate from an innovation.[397] Under these assumptions, the fragmentation of patents results in lower incentives to invest in R&D for the innovations in the first place as the total profit under fragmented patents is lower than that of a monopoly patent holder.

396 See **Appendix 5**.
397 See also Deardorff (1992).

To sum up, the fragmentation of patents reduces the incentives to invest in R&D for new technologies.
Second, fewer third-party firms are willing to employ the patented technologies if patents are fragmented.
Finally, the infinite fragmentation of patents would result in a complete waste of the potential value of the patented technologies.[398]
We have so far elaborated on potentially negative features of patent protection such as wasteful patent races, the deadweight loss on monopolistic markets associated with patents, and the tragedy of the anticommons in the biomedical sector associated with the fragmentation of patents.
However, let us now turn to the question of how patents should be optimally designed in the following section. In particular, we will focus on optimal duration, breadth and depth of patents.

3.2.2. Optimal Patent Design: Duration, Breadth and Depth of Patents

3.2.2.1. Duration of Patents

The duration, length or term of a patent usually refers to the number of years either between the filing date of application of the patent and its expiration or between the date of grant of the patent and its expiration.[399]
However, the implementation of the TRIPS Agreement provided a significant international harmonization of the term of protection of a patent.[400] Therefore, in most patent laws the duration of a patent is 20 years from the filing date of the application.[401]
Nevertheless, taking into account that extending the duration of a patent generates both social benefits and social costs the question arises as to which is the optimal duration of a patent.
In the following section, we shall outline the analytical framework set up by Nordhaus (1969) in order to analyze the question of whether the optimal patent duration is finite or infinite.

3.2.2.1.1. Optimal Patent Duration

Intuitively, a first justification for a finite duration of patents is that the discount rate sets a limit on the efficiency of infinitely lasting patents as the inventive power of profits that occur in periods long way off in the future is gradually weakened.[402] In economic terms, the discounted value of a patent depends negatively on the discount

398 See Buchanan and Yoon (2000) on p. 10.
399 See Cooter and Ulen (2004) on p. 124. See also Gervais (2003) on p. 168.
400 For instance, see Grossman and Lai (2004) on p. 1635.
401 See also Art. 33 of the TRIPS Agreement.
402 See Lévêque and Ménière (2004) on p. 26ff.

rate.[403] Put differently, the higher the discount rate the smaller the present value of future profits and thus the incentive power for the innovator.[404]
Furthermore, as already noted before, extending the duration of a patent generates both benefits and costs to society.
On the one hand, a longer duration of a patent increases the likelihood that innovators engage in R&D for investment-intensive but socially desirable innovations.[405] On the other hand, the longer the duration of a patent the higher the loss associated with the extension of the existing monopoly.[406] Hence, the optimal duration of a patent strikes the best balance between encouraging R&D and reducing the deadweight loss from monopoly pricing.[407] In the following section, we shall describe the pioneering model by Nordhaus (1969) who originally formulated this tradeoff in order to calculate the finite optimal duration of a patent.

3.2.2.1.2. The Nordhaus-Model

In order to determine the optimal duration of a patent, Nordhaus (1969, p. 70ff) analyzes the strategic interaction between innovating firms that license their cost-reducing patented techniques and producing firms that have to pay a royalty to employ the cost-reducing techniques of the inventors.[408] More specifically, innovating firms invest in R&D for new cost-saving production processes and are assumed to license their inventions to the producers of a final product.
Furthermore, the innovating firms maximize profits, profits being discounted royalties less costs.[409] Licenses are sold at a royalty rate y per unit of output. Moreover, Nordhaus (1969, p. 71) assumes that inventions are undertaken under conditions of certainty. The manufacturer of the final product can choose between the fully available competitive process and the cost-saving patented process to produce the final product.[410] The constant costs of production of the final good are denoted by c_0 when the competitive process is chosen and c_1 when the patented process is chosen, respect-tively, with $c_0 > c_1$. The demand for output of the final product, X, is given by a conventional demand function of the price p of the final product.[411] Nordhaus (1969, p. 71) assumes that inventions are completely appropriable for T years. More specifically, T denotes the duration of the patent.

403 For instance, see Lévêque and Ménière (2004) on p. 27.
404 For a formal treatment of the present value of future profits see Varian (1996) on p. 189ff. See also Blair and Cotter (2005) on p. 189.
405 See Lévêque and Ménière (2004) on p. 27.
406 See Lévêque and Ménière (2004) on p. 27.
407 See Cooter and Ulen (2004) on p. 128.
408 See also Scherer (1972), Nordhaus (1972), Kamien and Schwartz (1974), Tandon (1982), DeBrock (1985), and Klemperer (1990).
409 See Lévêque and Ménière (2004) on p. 28ff. See also Nordhaus (1969) on p. 70.
410 See Lévêque and Ménière (2004) on p. 28ff and Nordhaus (1969) on p. 71.
411 See Nordhaus (1969) on p. 71.

3.2.2.1.2.1. The Profit-Maximizing Royalty

First, Nordhaus (1969, p. 72ff) determines the profit-maximizing royalty for a given invention by finding the derived demand for patent licenses.[412] In particular, the derived demand for licenses is determined by the maximum that the producer is willing to pay for a license. In order to understand the concept, let us have a look at **Figure 6.**[413] The demand for the final product is given by a conventional demand function denoted by D_p. The constant costs of production of the final good when the producing firm does not employ the patented technique are denoted by c_0. Furthermore, c_1 denotes the constant costs of production when the producer employs the patented technique (given by EFC in **Figure 6**).[414]
The competitive price before the invention will be c_0.[415] The corresponding demand will be X_0. If y is the royalty rate per unit of output, the competitive price after the invention will be c_1+y. Note that c_1+y can never be higher than c_0, since firms are always free to use the non-patented production process.[416]
We can see from **Figure 6** that the maximum royalty that the producer is willing to pay for given level of output is simply the difference between ABCD and EFC.[417] From this difference we obtain the derived demand for licenses denoted by D_L.

412 See also McGee (1966) on p. 143ff and Arrow (1962) on p. 619ff.
413 See Nordhaus (1969) on p. 71, Figure 5.1.
414 See also Lévêque and Ménière (2004) on p. 28.
415 For instance, see Arrow (1962) on p. 620.
416 See Arrow (1962) on p. 620.
417 See Nordhaus (1969) on p. 72.

Figure 6 *Optimal Patent Royalty*

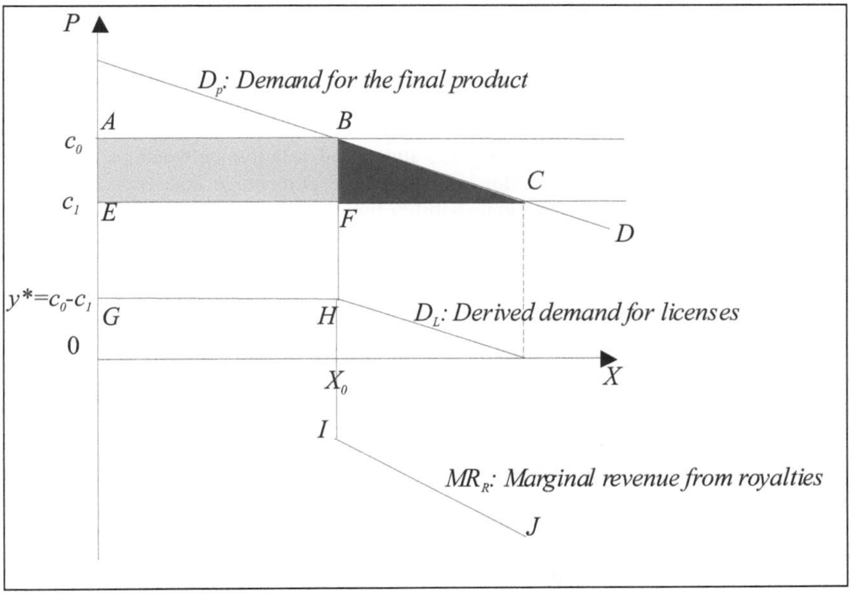

Nordhaus (1969, p. 72) now determines the optimal royalty. The optimal royalty is given by the point where marginal revenue of a license from royalties denoted by GHIJ equals marginal cost of a license where – by assumption – marginal cost of a license is zero.[418] Consequently, the optimal royalty is given by:

$$y^* = c_0 - c_1. \tag{48}$$

We can see from (48) that the optimal royalty rate equals the total cost reduction.[419] Moreover, the total revenue, *TR*, to an inventor of a patented process equals $(c_0 - c_1)X_0$ and is given by the grey-shaded rectangle ABEF in **Figure 6.**

3.2.2.1.2.2. The Optimal Level of Research

Furthermore, Nordhaus (1969, p. 72ff) analyzes the level of R&D inputs devoted to inventive activities by innovators. As already noted before, the justification for giving a monopoly to innovators is that it increases the incentive to invest in R&D and thus results in a greater amount of new knowledge.[420] In particular, the duration of a patent

---

418 See Nordhaus (1969) on p. 72.
419 See Nordhaus (1969) on p. 72.
420 See Lévêque and Ménière (2004) on p. 5ff. See also Nordhaus (1969) on p. 72.

is the most direct way for the legislator to control the scope of rights granted to innovating firms.[421]

Moreover, extending the duration of a patent provides additional profits to innovating firms and thus potentially stimulates a greater amount of invention.[422]

Therefore, let us assume that the size and the number of innovations will increase as the profits to innovators increase. In order to capture this idea Nordhaus (1969, p. 73) introduced the so-called "invention possibility function". More specifically the "invention possibility function" shows the functional relation between the level of R&D inputs R, measured in inventor-hours, and the percentage cost reduction as a result of the invention. The invention possibility function, B, is given by

$$B(R)=\frac{c_0-c_1}{c_0}.^{423} \tag{49}$$

Nordhaus (1969, p. 73) assumes that the invention possibility function is a concave function of the level of R&D inputs R. Furthermore, the author assumes that an increase in the level of R&D inputs will increase the potential cost reduction of the invention. In particular, there is a functional relation between c_1 and R. If R increases c_1 will decrease and thus – for an exogenously given c_0 – the size of the invention will increase.[424]

It is straightforward to see that the relationship between profits and R&D inputs on the one hand and the inventive output on the other hand is essential for determining the optimal duration of a patent: Without such a relationship the optimal patent duration would always be zero.[425]

Nordhaus (1969, p. 74) formulates the innovator's decision as follows. The innovator's maximization problem is given by

$$V=\int_0^T yXe^{-rt}dt-sR \tag{50}$$

where V denotes the discounted total profits and T the duration of the patent.[426] Furthermore, y denotes the royalty rate per unit output, X is the level of output, r is the interest rate, s is the per unit cost of inventive inputs, and R is the level of inventive inputs.[427] Note that – as time is continuous – $\int_0^T e^{-rt}dt$ represents discounted time from

421 See Lévêque and Ménière (2004) on p. 25.
422 See Nordhaus (1969) on p. 72ff.
423 See Nordhaus (1969) on p. 73.
424 Hence, one may also express (49) as $B(R)=(c_0-c_1(R))/c_0$ with $B'(R)>0$ and $B''(R)<0$.
425 See Nordhaus (1969) on p. 74.
426 See Nordhaus (1969) on p. 74.
427 Nordhaus (1969) differentiates between s and R for mathematical reasons. For instance, see the inventor's equilibrium given by (55) which shows that R decreases when the per unit cost of research s increase. One may also refer to s as the price of research inputs.

the present until the expiration of the patent right at T.[428] Putting (48) and (49) into (50), and normalizing by setting $c_0=1$, we obtain

$$V = \int_0^T B(R)X_0 e^{-rt}dt - sR \tag{51}$$

as $y = 1 - c_1 = B(R)$.[429] X_0 denotes the original level of output. By differentiating Nordhaus (1969, p. 74) obtains the first-order maximization condition

$$\frac{\partial V}{\partial R} = \int_0^T B'(R)X_0 e^{-rt}dt - s = 0. \tag{52}$$

Furthermore, by integrating and setting $1 - e^{-rT} = \varphi$, Nordhaus (1969, p. 74) obtains

$$\begin{aligned}
&\left[-\frac{1}{r}B'(R)X_0 e^{-rt}\right]_0^T = s \\
&\Leftrightarrow -\frac{1}{r}B'(R)X_0 e^{-rT} + \frac{1}{r}B'(R)X_0 = s \\
&\Leftrightarrow B'(R)X_0\left(1 - e^{-rT}\right) = rs \\
&\Leftrightarrow B'(R)X_0\varphi = rs.
\end{aligned} \tag{53}$$

In order to facilitate the algebra and to make the result clearer, Nordhaus (1969, p. 74) assumes that

$$B(R) = \beta R^{\alpha} \tag{54}$$

where α denotes the elasticity of output with respect to research and β measures the "ease" of invention in the sense that – ceteris paribus – easier inventions will attract a larger amount of research inputs.
Consequently, (53) becomes

$$\begin{aligned}
&\alpha\beta R^{\alpha-1}X_0\varphi = rs \\
&\Leftrightarrow R = \left(\frac{X_0\varphi\alpha\beta}{rs}\right)^{\frac{1}{1-\alpha}}.
\end{aligned} \tag{55}$$

[430]

Equation (55), henceforth the inventor's equilibrium, shows that – recalling that $\varphi = 1 - e^{-rT}$ – the level of research R increases in output and in patent duration.[431]

428 See also Scotchmer (2006) on p. 59.
429 See Nordhaus (1969) on p. 74.
430 See Nordhaus (1969) on p. 74.
431 See Lévêque and Ménière (2004) on p. 28. See also Nordhaus (1969) on p. 74.

Furthermore, R decreases when the interest rate r increases and when the per unit cost of research s increase.[432]
Putting (55) into (54), Nordhaus (1969, p. 75) obtains the size of the invention

$$B = \beta\left(\frac{X_0 \varphi \alpha \beta}{rs}\right)^{\left(\frac{1}{1-\alpha}\right)^{\alpha}}$$

$$\Leftrightarrow B = \beta\left(\frac{X_0 \varphi \alpha \beta}{rs}\right)^{\frac{\alpha}{1-\alpha}}. \tag{56}$$

As we can see from (56), the size of the invention increases in X_0 and decreases in r and s. Furthermore, recalling that $\varphi = 1 - e^{-rT}$, the size of the invention is an increasing function of the duration of the patent, T.[433]

3.2.2.1.2.3. The Optimal Patent Duration

Nordhaus (1969, p. 76ff) uses the analytical framework elaborated in the previous section to calculate the optimal duration of a patent at which benefits and costs for society generated by extending the duration of a patent balance at the margin.
On the one hand, a longer duration of a patent increases the investment in R&D and thus the amount of output for a given level of inputs.[434] On the other hand, extending the duration of a patent prolongs the monopoly on information and thus increases the deadweight loss due to monopoly pricing.
Consider again **Figure 6**. By assumption, there would be no innovation without patents.[435] Thus, the price would be equal to c_0. After the introduction of a patent a certain amount of resources, sR, is invested in R&D, lowering costs from c_0 to c_1.
However, the price remains at the level of c_0. Consequently, there is no gain in consumer surplus associated with patent protection for the duration of the patent. Instead, there is a gain in producer surplus for T years given by the rectangle ABEF in **Figure 6**. After T years the patent expires and the price falls from c_0 to c_1. Thus, there are now gains in consumer surplus illustrated by the rectangle ABEF plus the triangle BCF.
However, it remains to be seen which is the optimal duration of a patent. We shall elaborate on this issue in the following section.
In order to determine the optimal duration of a patent, Nordhaus (1969, p. 76ff) maximizes the following social welfare function measured by consumer surplus plus producer surplus less R&D cost with respect to the duration of the patent:

---

432 See also Lévêque and Ménière (2004) on p. 26ff for an explanation why the value of a patent decreases when the interest rate increases.
433 See Nordhaus (1969) on p. 75, footnote 8. By differentiating the log of (56) with respect to T we obtain $d \log B / dT = \alpha r / (1-\alpha)(e^{rT} - 1) > 0$.
434 See Nordhaus (1969) on p. 76.
435 See Nordhaus (1969) on p. 76.

$$W = \int_0^\infty B(R)X_0 e^{-\rho v}dv + \int_T^\infty \frac{1}{2}(X_1 - X_0)B(R)e^{-\rho v}dv - sR. \tag{57}$$

The first term on the right-hand side of (57) represents both the gains in producer surplus in the interval $[0,T]$ as well as the (equivalent) gains in consumer surplus available from T to ∞.[436] The second term represents the gains in consumer surplus due to a lower price and a higher output available from T to ∞ [see triangle BCF in **Figure 6**]. Furthermore, X_0 denotes the original output, X_1 the final output and ρ the social discount rate which is assumed to be equal to the individual discount rate r.[437] The last term on the right-hand side of (57) represents the resource cost of R&D. Moreover, the demand for the good is given by the demand function

$$X = a - bp \tag{58}$$

where a is the intercept of the demand function and b is the elasticity of demand. a is assumed to be positive and smaller than one. Furthermore, note from (58) that

$$X_1 - X_0 = a - bp_1 - (a - bp_0) = b(p_0 - p_1) = bB(R).\text{[438]} \tag{59}$$

Integrating (57), noting (59), and recalling that $\varphi = 1 - e^{-rt}$, Nordhaus (1969, p. 77) obtains

$$W = \frac{B(R)X_0}{\rho} + \frac{B(R)^2 b(1-\varphi)}{2\rho} - sR. \tag{60}$$

The objective of a social planner is to maximize W taking into account the constraint that relates research to patent life as given by (53).[439] Hence, the Lagrange-type objective function is

$$L = \frac{B(R)X_0}{\rho} + \frac{bB(R)^2(1-\varphi)}{2\rho} - sR + \lambda\left(B'(R)\varphi X_0 - rs\right) \tag{61}$$

where λ is the Lagrange multiplier. By differentiating (61) with respect to φ Nordhaus (1969, p. 77) obtains

$$\frac{\partial L}{\partial \varphi} = -\frac{bB(R)^2}{2\rho} + \lambda B'(R)X_0 = 0. \tag{62}$$

Furthermore, by differentiating (61) with respect to R Nordhaus (1969, p. 77) obtains

436 See Nordhaus (1969) on p. 77.
437 See Nordhaus (1969) on p. 77, footnote 12.
438 See Nordhaus (1969) on p. 77.
439 See Menell and Scotchmer (2007) on p. 1487ff. See also Nordhaus (1969) on p. 77.

$$\frac{\partial L}{\partial R}=\frac{B'(R)X_0}{\rho}+\frac{bB'(R)B(R)(1-\varphi)}{\rho}-s+\lambda B''(R)\varphi X_0=0. \tag{63}$$

By separating λ in both (62) and (63) it follows that

$$\frac{bB(R)^2}{2\rho B'(R)X_0}=-\frac{B'(R)X_0+bB'(R)B(R)(1-\varphi)-s\rho}{\rho B''(R)\varphi X_0}.\text{[440]} \tag{64}$$

By reformulating (64) Nordhaus (1969, p. 77) obtains

$$\begin{aligned}&\frac{bB(R)^2}{2B'(R)}=-\frac{B'(R)X_0+bB'(R)B(R)(1-\varphi)-s\rho}{B''(R)\varphi}\\&\Leftrightarrow -B''(R)\varphi bB(R)^2=2B'(R)^2\left(X_0+bB(R)(1-\varphi)-\frac{s\rho}{B'(R)}\right).\end{aligned} \tag{65}$$

Recalling from (53) that $B'(R)X_0\varphi=rs$ and recalling that $r=\rho$ we obtain from (65)

$$\begin{aligned}&-B''(R)\varphi bB(R)^2=2B'(R)^2\left(X_0+bB(R)(1-\varphi)-\varphi X_0\right)\\&\Leftrightarrow \varphi\left(2B'(R)^2\left(bB(R)+X_0\right)-B''(R)bB(R)^2\right)=2B'(R)^2\left(bB(R)+X_0\right)\\&\Leftrightarrow \varphi=\frac{2B'(R)^2\left(bB(R)+X_0\right)}{2B'(R)^2\left(bB(R)+X_0\right)-B''(R)bB(R)^2}.\text{[441]}\end{aligned} \tag{66}$$

Nordhaus (1969, p. 78) now normalizes the demand function by setting $p_0=X_0=1$ and converts *b* into the arc elasticity of demand at p_0. Furthermore, he defines

$$\kappa=-\frac{B''(R)B(R)}{B'(R)^2}. \tag{67}$$

κ denotes the elasticity of $B'(R)$ with respect to *B*. Finally, it follows from (66) that

$$\begin{aligned}&\varphi=\frac{bB(R)+1}{bB(R)+1-\frac{bB(R)}{2}\frac{B''(R)B(R)}{B'(R)^2}}\\&\Leftrightarrow \varphi=\frac{bB(R)+1}{bB(R)+1+bB(R)\frac{\kappa}{2}}\\&\Leftrightarrow \varphi=\frac{bB(R)+1}{bB(R)\left(1+\frac{\kappa}{2}\right)+1}.\text{[442]}\end{aligned} \tag{68}$$

---

440 See Nordhaus (1969) on p. 77.
441 See Nordhaus (1969) on p. 78.

Furthermore, the optimal life is given by

$$T = -\frac{1}{\rho} log\left(1-\varphi\right).$$ [443] (69)

According to Nordhaus (1969, p. 78ff), (68) and (69) describe the policy maker's equilibrium, whereas (53) is the inventor's equilibrium. Note that the inventor's equilibrium can also be obtained from (61) by setting $\partial L / \partial \lambda = 0$.[444]
Consequently, the optimal duration of a patent is given by the solution of the inventor's equilibrium and the policy maker's equilibrium.[445] In particular, by setting the equation for the inventor's equilibrium equal to the equation for the policy maker's equilibrium – while treating b, κ and ρ as economic parameters – Nordhaus (1969, p. 78) determines the equilibrium levels of φ and B. For instance, **Figure 7** shows the equilibrium – denoted by φ^* and B^* – for two hypothetical curves. In particular, we can see from **Figure 7** that, under normal circumstances, there will always exist a unique optimal life of a patent given by the intercept of the inventor's equilibrium and the policy maker's equilibrium.[446]

Figure 7 *Optimal Patent Duration*

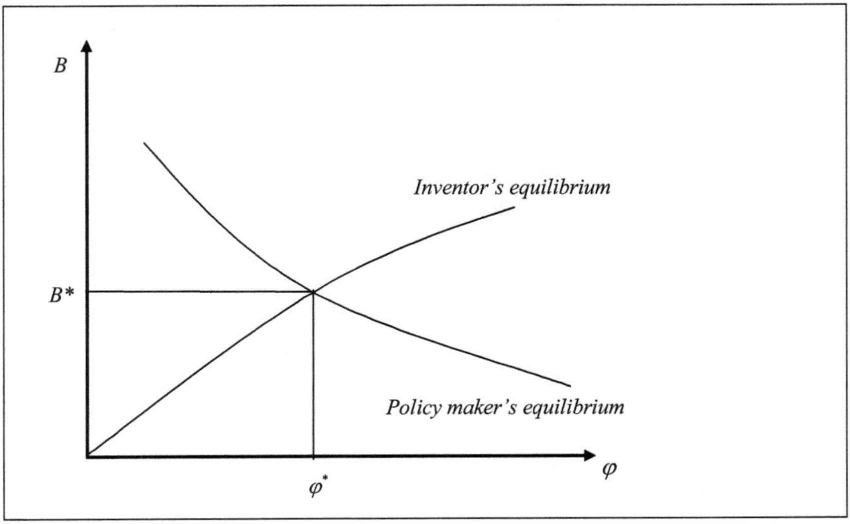

442 See Nordhaus (1969) on p. 78.
443 See Menell and Scotchmer (2007) on p. 1487ff. See also Nordhaus (1969) on p. 78.
444 See Nordhaus (1969) on p. 78.
445 See Nordhaus (1969) on p. 78.
446 See Nordhaus (1969) on p. 78, Figure 5.4.

To sum up, the pioneering analysis by Nordhaus (1969) underpins the arguments usually made about the optimal duration of patents.
First, the optimal duration of a patent is always finite.[447]
Second, the lower the elasticity of demand of a product, the higher the optimal duration of the patent for that product. We can see that from **Figure 7**, where – according to (68) – a lower elasticity of demand b shifts the policy maker's equilibrium curve to the right, resulting in – ceteris paribus – a longer optimal life of a patent.[448] The intuition behind this argument is the following: The deadweight loss in the first T years is lower the lower the elasticity of demand. Put differently, suppose that the elasticity of demand tends toward zero. In this extreme case, there is no deadweight loss and the optimal life of a patent would be infinite.[449]
Another crucial result of the analysis by Nordhaus (1969) that we shall elaborate upon in the following is the effect of the "ease" of invention – as expressed by β in the invention possibility function $B(R) = \beta R^{\alpha}$ – on the optimal duration of a patent. It is a well known fact that different industries have different technological climates.[450] In some industries it is thought that invention is easier in the sense that – for a given level of research – a larger $B(R)$ is produced.[451] In order to understand the effect of different invention possibility functions and the "ease" of invention on the optimal life of a patent, consider again (53) and (68). In the case of "easier" invention, that is, β is higher, we can see that the inventor's equilibrium as given by (53) shifts up[452] and the policy maker's equilibrium as given by (68) shifts to the left.[453] In particular, Nordhaus (1969, p. 79) suggests that patents for industries that have "easier" inventions should be shorter.
To sum up, patents for industries having easier invention should be shorter.[454] More specifically, one may also argue that the optimal duration of a patent in the pharmaceutical industry is likely to be longer than in industries with "easier" inventions because of the relatively high risks and costs of pharmaceutical innovation.[455]
However, as we shall see in the following section, Gilbert and Shapiro (1990) come to a different conclusion with respect to the optimal patent duration.

447 See also Lévêque and Ménière (2004) on p. 26ff.
448 See Nordhaus (1969) on p. 79.
449 See Nordhaus (1969) on p. 79.
450 See Mansfield (1986). See also Nordhaus (1969) on p. 79.
451 See Nordhaus (1969) on p. 79.
452 For instance, note that $\partial B'(R)/\partial\beta = \alpha R^{\alpha-1} > 0$ as $\alpha > 0$. Hence, all other things being equal, φ in (53) decreases if β increases.
453 For instance, note that φ as given in (68) decreases if β increases as $\partial B(R)/\partial\beta = R^{\alpha} > 0$ and $bB(R)(1+(\kappa/2))+1 > bB(R)+1$ as $bB(R)(\kappa/2) > 0$.
454 See Nordhaus (1969) on p. 79.
455 For instance, see Grabowski and Vernon (2000a) and Grabowski et al. (2002).

3.2.2.2. Breadth of Patents

In this section, we shall outline the link between the breadth of a patent and the legal notion of a patent as well as the following three core economic concepts of patent breadth.
The first concept is originally formulated by Gilbert and Shapiro (1990). In particular, Gilbert and Shapiro (1990) explore the breadth of a patent in terms of the market power it confers to the holder of the patent by protecting him against patent infringement.
Second, Gallini (1992) interprets the breadth of a patent in terms of the R&D cost that a competing innovator incurs to "invent around the patent", that is, to imitate the patented innovation without infringing the patent.[456]
Third, Maurer and Scotchmer (2002) analyze the breadth of a patent in the context of license agreements between the holder of the patent and potential competitors. In particular, the objective of these license agreements is typically to deter the investment in alternative technologies and maintaining the control of the market.
However, before we consider the three concepts of patent breadth in more detail, let us first have a quick look at the relationship between the economic concept of patent breadth and the legal notion of a patent.

3.2.2.2.1. Patent Breadth and the Legal Notion of Patents[457]

Although patent laws vary widely across countries, there are certain common features, in particular associated with the broad worldwide enactment of the TRIPS Agreement in 1994.[458] A patent can be granted to an inventor or the first person to file for a patent.[459] Furthermore, a patent can be obtained for both products[460] as well as processes "provided that they are new, involve an inventive step and are capable of industrial application."[461]
Typically, a patent application consists of two parts.[462] First, the patent application discloses the invention to the patent office by providing a clear and detailed description of the invention in a manner that it can "be carried out by a person skilled in the art".[463] Second, the patent application provides a list of claims precisely specifying the technology invented by the applicant that shall be protected by the patent.[464] Typically,

---

456 See Lévêque and Ménière (2004) on p. 33. See also Merges and Nelson (1990).
457 See Scotchmer (2006) on p. 64ff and on p. 103. See also Chisum (2001) for a general treatment of patents. See also Lévêque and Ménière (2004) on p. 30.
458 See Hestermeyer (2007) on p. 19ff. See also Scotchmer (2006) on p. 65ff.
459 For instance, the majority of countries adopt a first-to-file priority system. However, the U.S. is one of the few notable exceptions that operate a first-to-invent priority system. See Scotchmer and Green (1990) for a discussion of the importance of the difference between the first-to-file priority system and the first-to-invent priority system in the context of cumulative invention. See also Macedo (1990).
460 For instance, see Waterson (1990) for an economic analysis of product patents and their effects on social welfare.
461 See Art. 27 of the TRIPS Agreement.
462 See Lévêque and Ménière (2004) on p. 30. See also Hestermeyer (2007) on p. 19ff.
463 See Art. 29 of the TRIPS Agreement.
464 See Hestermeyer (2007) on p. 19. See also Schwartz (2006).

the patent office – provided that the patent application fulfills the national requirements for patentability – then publishes the application.[465]
Nevertheless, a product patent grants the patent holder a temporary legal monopoly in the sense that it gives him the right to sue for infringement if someone – without having the patent holder's consent – tries to make, use, offer for sale, sell, or import for these purposes the patented product.[466] Similarly, a process patent gives the holder of the patent the right to sue for infringement if someone – without having the patent holder's consent – tries to use the patented process or to use, offer for sale, sell, or import "for these purposes at least the product obtained directly by that process."[467]
Nevertheless, infringement must be established on the basis of one of the claims listed in the patent document that specifically define the protection granted by the patent.[468] More specifically, an accused product only infringes if it embodies each element of at least one claim listed in the patent application.[469]
However, it is straightforward to see that a product patent would be worthless if only a negligibly small change allowed potential competitors to benefit from the patented invention without paying royalties. Indeed, many patent disputes revolve around the question of how different an accused product must be in order not to infringe.[470]
Most notably, the U.S. "doctrine of equivalents"[471] provides the courts with a means to hold a third party liable for the infringement of a patent even though the accused product does not embody each element of a patent claim, but is basically equivalent to the patented product.
However, from an economic perspective, the question of how different an accused product must be in order not to infringe is interesting for the following reason. A patent will be more profitable for the patent holder if it is broader in the sense that another product must be significantly different from the patented product in order not to infringe.[472] In other words, the value of a patent is higher when the range of substitutes of the patented product that can be excluded from the market is broader.[473]
In particular, Klemperer (1990) originally set up an analytical framework of spatial product differentiation in order to analyze the trade-off between the duration of a patent and its scope of coverage. In Klemperer's analysis, increasing the breadth of a patent corresponds to widening the coverage of the product space protected by the patent. In other words, the broader the patent the higher is the number of substitute products that infringe.[474] However, Gilbert and Shapiro (1990) elaborate on a somewhat different notion of patent breadth as we shall see in the following.

---

465 See Hestermeyer (2007) on p. 19.
466 See Art. 28(1) of the TRIPS Agreement. See also Hestermeyer (2007) on p. 19ff.
467 See Art. 28(1) of the TRIPS Agreement. See also Hestermeyer (2007) on p. 19.
468 See Hestermeyer (2007) on p. 19ff.
469 See Scotchmer (2006) on p. 69.
470 See Scotchmer (2006) on p. 103.
471 The "doctrine of equivalents" was established by the U.S. Supreme Court in *Graver Tank & MFG Co. v. Linde Air Products Co.* 339 U.S. 605 (1950). See also *Warner Jenkinson Co., Inc. v. Hilton Davis Chemical Co.* (95-728), 520 U.S. 17 (1997). See also Scotchmer (2006) on p. 69 and Menell and Scotchmer (2007) on p. 1490.
472 See Scotchmer (2006) on p. 103.
473 See Scotchmer (2006) on p. 103.
474 See also Menell and Scotchmer (2007) on p. 1490.

3.2.2.2.2. Patent Breadth and Market Power

Under the assumption that a broad patent strengthens the innovator's market power by providing better protection against infringement, Gilbert and Shapiro (1990) explore the question as to what is the optimal combination of patent duration and patent breadth as policy instruments in order to achieve a given reward level in order to spur innovation.[475] Hence, in contrast to Nordhaus (1969) who analyzes the duration of a patent as a policy instrument, Gilbert and Shapiro (1990) extend the scope of patent policy and include also the breadth of a patent in their analysis. In particular, the authors define the breadth of a patent as "the flow rate of profit available to the patentee while the patent is in force".[476] In other words, Gilbert and Shapiro (1990) interpret patent breadth as the ability of the holder of the patent to raise the price for the patented product. However, the main argument brought forward by Gilbert and Shapiro (1990) goes as follows.

On the one hand, increasing the breadth of a patent reinforces the patent holder's market power and is increasingly costly in terms of deadweight loss.[477] For instance, Gilbert and Shapiro (1990, p. 108ff) show that patent breadth is indeed increasingly costly in terms of deadweight loss for the conventional case of a single patented product with downward-sloping demand and marginal revenue curves and an upward-sloping marginal cost curve.

On the other hand, increasing the duration of a patent extends the market power over time but the market power and the deadweight loss it creates – at any given point of time – remain constant.[478]

In particular, Gilbert and Shapiro (1990) show that – provided that the deadweight loss increases at a faster rate with breadth than with length – the optimal combination of patent breadth and length as policy instruments calls for patents with infinite duration.

To sum up, in contrast to Nordhaus (1969) who concluded that the optimal duration of a patent is always a finite, positive number of years, Gilbert and Shapiro (1990) come to the conclusion that – with both patent breadth and patent duration as policy instruments – the optimal patent duration may easily be infinite.[479] More specifically, they conclude that a narrow patent with infinite duration is preferable to a short-lived broad patent to achieve a given reward level in order to spur innovation.

However, Gilbert and Shapiro (1990) do not explicitly consider the effect of the breadth of a patent on the research efforts of potential competitors. For instance, they assume that imitation by competing innovators is costless and that imitation is therefore always a threat to the holder of the patent.[480] Nevertheless, as we shall see in the following section, Gallini (1992) takes into consideration the impact of the breadth of a patent on the research efforts of competing innovators and extends the theory of optimal patent design by elaborating on the cost of "inventing around a patent" that are

475 See also Lévêque and Ménière (2004) on p. 30ff.
476 See Gilbert and Shapiro (1990) on p. 106.
477 See Gilbert and Shapiro (1990) on p. 107, proposition 1.
478 See Gilbert and Shapiro (1990) on p. 107ff.
479 See also Tandon (1982) for an analysis of infinite optimal patents when both patent duration and a royalty rate for compulsory licensing are taken into consideration.
480 See also Lévêque and Ménière (2004) on p. 32ff.

neither zero – as implicitly assumed in Gilbert and Shapiro (1990) – nor prohibitively high so that imitation would never be a threat to the holder of the patent.[481]

3.2.2.2.3. Patent Breadth and the Cost of Inventing around a Patent

This section addresses the question as to how the breadth of a patent influences the decision of other innovators that compete with the patentee to invest in R&D for non-infringing imitations of the patented product.[482] More specifically, a patent leaves room for competing innovators to legally enter the protected market by using technologies that differ from the technology adopted by the patentee in such a way that their products cannot be considered infringing imitations.[483] Put differently, by using different technologies competing innovators may "invent around" the patent and offer products that can be substituted for the original innovation.[484]

In particular, Gallini (1992) proposes the definition of the breadth of a patent in terms of the R&D cost required to imitate a patented innovation without infringing the patent. Hence, by elaborating on how costly it is to develop a non-infringing substitute for the patented product, Gallini (1992) analyzes the breadth of a patent in the context of process innovation rather than in the context of product space defining how close a substitute product must be so that it can be excluded from the market.[485] However, we shall consider the main arguments brought forward by Gallini (1992) in the following.

The broader a patent, the more costly it will be for other innovators to invent around a patent.[486] In other words, a narrower patent results in lower costs of market entry and thus will lead to a lower market price as the number of competing non-infringing imitations increases.[487] Moreover, Gallini (1992, p. 53ff) argues that, with costly imitation, the decision of a competitor of the patentee to invent around a patent depends on the duration of patent protection awarded to the patentee. Put differently, the longer the duration of a patent, the higher the incentives for competing innovators to invest in R&D for non-infringing imitations and to invent around the patented product.[488] Consequently, the longer the duration of the patent, the higher the competition that arises from non-infringing substitute products will be.[489] Therefore, on the one hand, extending the duration of a patent may not increase the incentives of the innovator of the proprietary product to invest in R&D or to patent the innovation as it encourages imitation.[490] On the other hand, a broader patent deters market entry by

481 See Gallini (1992) on p. 52. See also Levin et al. (1987) and Menell and Scotchmer (2007) on p. 1490ff.

482 See also Eger et al. (1990) for a game-theorectic analysis of patents and imitation.

483 See Lévêque and Ménière (2004) on p. 33.

484 See Gallini (1992) on p. 52. See also Levin et al. (1987).

485 See Klemperer (1990). See also Menell and Scotchmer (2007) on p. 1490ff.

486 See also Lévêque and Ménière (2004) on p. 34.

487 See Gallini (1992) on p. 53ff. See also Menell and Scotchmer (2007) on 1491.

488 See also Lévêque and Ménière (2004) on p. 33ff.

489 See Gallini (1992) on p. 54ff.

490 See Gallini (1992) on p. 54ff.

competing imitators and *ex ante* provides higher R&D incentives for potential patentees.[491]
However, Gallini (1992) comes to the conclusion that – with both duration and breadth of a patent as policy instruments – the optimal patent design is given by a broad patent and a sufficiently short duration in order to discourage all imitation. More specifically, Gallini (1992) reaches the opposite conclusion to Gilbert and Shapiro (1990), by showing that a short but broad patent is superior to a narrow but long patent to achieve a given reward level in order to spur innovation.[492]
However, as we shall see in the following section, Maurer and Scotchmer (2002) – by analyzing patent breadth in the context of licensing agreements between the patentee and potentially imitating competitors – address this discrepancy between the arguments brought forward by Gilbert and Shapiro (1990) and Gallini (1992), respectively.[493]

3.2.2.2.4. Patent Breadth and Licensing

Neither Gilbert and Shapiro (1990) nor Gallini (1992) take into consideration that the patentee may strategically grant licenses to potentially imitating competitors in order to deter their investment in alternative technologies and their unlicensed market entry.[494] In other words, the patentee may have an incentive to voluntarily share the market when threatened by imitating competitors "instead of tolerating their entry through duplicative costs."[495]
Before we explore the analytical framework originally formulated by Maurer and Scotchmer (2002) who elaborate on these issues, let us first consider the following example that addresses the question as to why licensing might actually be a worthwhile business activity for the holder of a patent when he is threatened by imitation.
Consider a simple game played between a patentee and n firms that can enter the market by inventing around the patent.[496] Assume that the cost of entry, that is the costs of inventing around a patent, are F.[497] In this case, provided that F is known to the patentee as well as to the competitors, the maximum (fixed) license fee that the patentee may ask from each licensee is equal to F.[498] Note that the market entrants would generate the same profit in both scenarios with and without a licensing offer by the patentee.[499] Consequently, licensing would result in the same number of entrants and thus in the same market price as in the alternative scenario where the patentee does not offer licensing.[500]

491 See also Lerner (1994) who finds that the breadth of a patent has a significant impact on the value of the firm that holds the patent.
492 See Denicoló (1996) who analyzes the robustness of the arguments brought forward by Klemperer (1990), Gilbert and Shapiro (1990) and Gallini (1992). See also Lévêque and Ménière (2004) on p. 34.
493 See Maurer and Scotchmer (2002) on p. 542. See also Menell and Scotchmer (2007) on p. 1493ff.
494 See Lévêque and Ménière (2004) on p. 36. See also Gallini (1984).
495 See Scotchmer (2006) on p. 107. See also Menell and Scotchmer (2007) on p. 1493ff.
496 See Scotchmer (2006) on p. 107.
497 See Scotchmer (2006) on p. 107.
498 See Scotchmer (2006) on p. 107.
499 See Scotchmer (2006) on p. 107.
500 See Maurer and Scotchmer (2002). See also Scotchmer (2006) on p. 107.

The patentee, however, would be better off in the first scenario with licensing as he would generate a profit of nF through the license fee.[501] Nevertheless, the patentee would typically be better off if he was not threatened by duplication, that is n=0, since then he would be able to generate the monopoly profit.
However, let us now consider the framework set up by Maurer and Scotchmer (2002) who argue that the holder of a patent threatened by imitation has the incentive to license potential competitors and thus to voluntarily share the market in order to avoid imitation.
First of all, the question arises as to why the patentee may have the incentive to tolerate new licensed competitors on the market as this will reduce his market power and thus his profit.[502] The rationale behind the licensing strategy is the following:
Although standard economic theory tells us that the patentee's profit will decrease when other firms enter the market, the patentee can skim the profit of the competitors through the license fee. For instance, Maurer and Scotchmer (2002) – under the assumption that the number of potential licensees and imitators is unlimited – argue that the patentee can appropriate the whole profit of the licensees as he can dictate the respective licensing terms that the licensee will accept for the following reason.
Given that the number of potential licensees is unlimited and that market entry is a credible threat, i.e. the cost of imitation is not prohibitively high, the patentee will strategically grant licenses until the market price is so low that market entry without having a license is not profitable.[503] In other words, the lower market price due to licensed market entry deters potential imitators as they cannot recover their R&D costs of imitation.[504] Hence, a licensee will never be better off by refusing the licensing term dictated by the patentee as his profit is zero in both scenarios with and without a license.[505]
However, it is straightforward to see that the breadth of a patent and the cost of imitation play a key role in the analysis conducted by Maurer and Scotchmer (2002) for the following reason.
The narrower the patent, the lower the cost of imitation, the lower the market price must be in order to deter unlicensed market entry and thus the lower the expected profit of the patentee. Hence, the question arises as to whether the expected profit of the patentee is sufficiently high in order to encourage the innovation in the first place.[506]
In particular, Maurer and Scotchmer (2002, p. 540) show that the first innovator will generate an expected profit that is sufficiently high to encourage the first innovation if the costs of an imitation are not lower than half of the costs of the first innovation.[507]
To sum up, Maurer and Scotchmer (2002, p. 535) argue that licensing – although it has a profit-eroding effect – is the patent holder's best option when he is credibly threatened by imitation.

501 See Menell and Scotchmer (2007) on p. 1493. See also Scotchmer (2006) on p. 107.
502 See Menell and Scotchmer (2007) on p. 1493ff and Maurer and Scotchmer (2002) on p. 535ff.
503 See Scotchmer (2006) on p. 107. See also Maurer and Scotchmer (2002) on p. 536ff.
504 See Maurer and Scotchmer (2002) on p. 536ff.
505 See Maurer and Scotchmer (2002) on p. 537.
506 See Lévêque and Ménière (2004) on p. 36.
507 See Menell and Scotchmer (2007) on p. 1494ff.

Second, licensing generates a social benefit as the patentee limits his own market power by voluntarily sharing the market resulting in a lower price of the patented product.[508]

Third, there is another social benefit stemming from licensing as we shall see in the following. Provided that the patentee has the incentive to license his innovation in order to discourage imitation, licensing agreements make patent races less attractive and therefore have the potential to lower socially wasteful investments stemming from the patent race.[509]

Finally, Maurer and Scotchmer (2002) come to the following conclusion with respect to the optimal design of a patent. A patent shall be sufficiently narrow for a relatively long time to encourage licensing that leads to higher competition and a lower market price and thus minimizing both discounted deadweight loss[510] as well as socially wasteful investments stemming from imitation.[511]

Nevertheless, neither Gilbert and Shapiro (1990) nor Gallini (1992) nor Maurer and Scotchmer (2002) take into consideration that a patentee may not only be threatened by imitation but rather by innovations that are an improvement on the original innovation. We will elaborate on this issue in the following section.

3.2.2.3. Patents and Cumulative Innovation

As already mentioned, one purpose of patents is to disclose to the public the scientific knowledge included in the patented innovation.[512] Hence, other researchers may benefit from the initial innovation, i.e. by applying the initial innovation as a tool to develop a second-generation innovation.[513] Those innovations that result from prior innovations are often referred to as "cumulative innovations".[514] Prominent examples of cumulative technologies are biotechnology as well as information technology.[515] Before we address the questions of whether cumulative innovations should be patentable and whether follow-on innovations should be regarded as infringements, let us first have a look at the various forms of cumulative innovations.

3.2.2.3.1. Forms of Cumulative Innovations

Scotchmer (2006, p. 132ff) identifies three different forms of cumulative innovations. The first category of cumulative innovations consists of innovations that cannot be made without a single initial innovation, i.e. when the initial innovation is basic research, such as a gene target, whereas the second-stage innovation is applied

508 See Maurer and Scotchmer (2002) on p. 545.

509 See Maurer and Scotchmer (2002) on p. 535. See also Lévêque and Ménière (2004) on p. 36.

510 See Gilbert and Shapiro (1990).

511 See Gallini (1992). See also Menell and Scotchmer (2007) on p. 1493ff.

512 See Lévêque and Ménière (2004) on p. 22.

513 See Scotchmer (2006) on p. 132ff.

514 See Menell and Scotchmer (2007) on p. 1499ff. See also Chang (1995).

515 For instance, see Bessen and Hunt (2003) and Bessen and Maskin (2006).

research such as a new pharmaceutical product.[516] Typically, in basic research, a single initial innovation leads to various follow-on applications.[517]
The second category consists of second-generation innovations that require the input of various first-stage innovations, i.e. research tools such as the basic technology of bioengineering or the polymerase chain reaction in molecular biology.[518]
The third type of cumulative innovation is innovations that successively improve prior innovations.[519]
However, the main questions that arise in the context of cumulative innovations are the following:
First, should follow-on innovations be patentable and non-infringing or should the initial innovator be given the rights to all follow-on innovations?[520]
Second, how should the profits of cumulative innovations be shared in order to set sufficient R&D incentives for the initial innovator and the follow-on innovators to invest in R&D?
The purpose of the following section is to address these questions.

3.2.2.3.2. Cumulative Innovations, R&D Incentives and Licensing

Consider the following example. The development of a pharmaceutical product involves both fundamental research in the first-stage conducted by the initial innovator as well as applied research in the second stage conducted by the follow-on innovator.[521]
Let the cost of the development of the initial innovation be denoted by c_1.[522] Furthermore, assume that the initial innovation – as a stand-alone product – has no commercial value. Hence, the initial innovator can only generate profit through licensing.[523]
Moreover, the development of the follow-on innovation generates costs of c_2 and has a positive commercial value of y.
Assume that it is socially desirable that both innovations are made because of the high value of the follow-on innovation, i.e. $y - c_1 - c_2 > 0$.[524] For instance, assume that the initial innovation is a particular biological drug target specific to a particular disease condition and the follow-on innovation is the development and commercial exploitation of a new pharmaceutical product. Given that the development of both innovations is socially desirable, the question arises as to how patenting should be used to achieve that both innovations are made. More specifically, how should the initial innovator be compensated in order to stimulate fundamental research?

516 See Scotchmer (2006) on p. 132. See also Lévêque and Ménière (2004) on p. 38.
517 See Scotchmer (2006) on p. 132, Figure 5.1.
518 See Scotchmer (2006) on p. 142.
519 See O'Donoghue et al. (1998). See also Hunt (2004).
520 See also Lévêque and Ménière (2004) on p. 37ff.
521 See Green and Scotchmer (1995) and Scotchmer (2006) on p. 135ff. See also Lévêque and Ménière (2004) on p. 38ff.
522 See Scotchmer (2006) on p. 136ff and Lévêque and Ménière (2004) on p. 38.
523 See Scotchmer (2006) on p. 137.
524 See Lévêque and Ménière (2004) on p. 39.

Consider the following scenario in which both innovators have blocking patents on the follow-on innovation.[525] More specifically, the pharmaceutical product is patentable but infringes the patent for the initial innovation. Hence, both patentees can prevent the market entry of the pharmaceutical product.[526]
Note that – provided that licensing agreements are absent that would allow the initial innovator to benefit from the commercial exploitation of the pharmaceutical product – the initial innovator will not make the fundamental research as it has no commercial value as a stand-alone innovation. Consequently, neither the drug target nor the pharmaceutical product will be made, resulting in a socially non-desirable outcome.[527]
However, this problem can be solved if the two innovators can resolve the blocking patents by making license agreements that transfer enough of the commercial value of the follow-on innovation to the initial innovator and that provide the follow-on innovator with enough profit to encourage the development of the pharmaceutical product.[528]
Nevertheless, the question arises as to whether they should make the license agreement *ex ante*, that is after the initial innovation has been made but prior to the investment of the follow-on innovator, or *ex post*, that is after the follow-on innovation has been made.[529] For simplicity, suppose that both innovators prefer the *ex ante* agreement to the *ex post* agreement for the following reason.
Ex post arises a typical hold-up situation as the follow-on innovator will have to accept the licensing terms offered by the initial innovator that typically would not allow him to recover his (sunk) investment in R&D.[530] From the author's perspective this is a reasonable assumption as high R&D costs are specific to the pharmaceutical industry.
However, the follow-on innovator will anticipate that he will not be able to recover his investment and thus will not make the follow-on innovation.[531] Working backwards to the first-stage, the initial innovator will not innovate either as the initial innovation – as a stand-alone product – does not have any commercial value. To sum up, if the innovators make the licensing agreement *ex post*, both firms will end up with zero profit.
Nevertheless, the bargaining surplus to be generated by signing an *ex ante* license agreement is the following:[532] The initial innovator may credibly commit to a licensing fee lower than the fee he would charge *ex post* in order to encourage the development of the pharmaceutical product. Hence, provided that the fee is high enough to encourage the initial innovation without discouraging the follow-on innovation, both innovators can benefit from signing an *ex ante* licensing agreement.[533]

---

525 See Green and Scotchmer (1995). See also Scotchmer (2006) on p. 137 and Merges (1994).
526 Note that some authors – in the case of cumulative innovations – refer to patents which cover subsequent innovations as "deep" patents. For instance, see Lévêque and Ménière (2004) on p. 40. See also Kitch (1977) who elaborates on the idea that a (deep) patent enables the patentee to organize follow-on innovations efficiently.
527 See Lévêque and Ménière (2004) on p. 39.
528 See Scotchmer (2006) on p. 136ff.
529 See Scotchmer (2006) on p. 137.
530 See Lévêque and Ménière (2004) on p. 38 and Menell and Scotchmer (2007) on p. 1502ff.
531 See Scotchmer (2006) on p. 137.
532 See Scotchmer (2006) on p. 137ff.
533 See also Scotchmer (2006) on p. 136ff and Green and Scotchmer (1995) on p. 23ff.

However, several conclusions emerge from this admittedly highly-stylized example following Scotchmer (2006, p. 135ff) and Green and Scotchmer (1995).
First, the initial innovator must be given the opportunity to benefit from the profit generated through the commercial exploitation of the follow-on innovation in order to encourage basic research in the first place.[534] In this case, Scotchmer (2006, p. 156) suggests that the appropriate instrument of intellectual property law should allow the initial innovator to participate in the commercial exploitation of the follow-on innovation through licensing. Hence, the initial innovation should be patentable and the follow-on innovation should be infringing.[535] More specifically, the breadth of the patent on the initial innovation determines whether the follow-on innovation infringes or not.[536] Hence, in the context of cumulative innovations, the role of patent breadth is to structure the division of the joint profit between the initial innovator and the follow-on innovator in order to provide both innovators with sufficient R&D incentives.[537]
Second, if antitrust policy requires that the innovators can only sign the license agreement *ex post*, a hold-up situation might arise that discourages the follow-on innovation.[538] More specifically, Green and Scotchmer (1995, p. 31) conclude that *ex ante* licensing agreements should be legal when innovations are cumulative and the follow-on innovation is an application of the initial innovation.[539]
Third, Green and Scotchmer (1995, p. 21) suggest, that – in the case of cumulative innovations – the length of a patent determines the total profit that the initial innovator and the follow-on innovator generate jointly. Furthermore, Green and Scotchmer (1995) suggest that the duration of a patent should be longer if the innovations are made by several innovators than if they are made by only one innovator. The intuition behind this is the following. If one innovator makes both innovations, the duration of the patent should be just long enough so that the innovator can recover the total R&D costs he incurs.[540] In other words, the optimally short patent would provide the innovator with zero total profit. If, however, two innovators are involved in the cumulative innovation, the division of profit – given such a short patent and zero total profit – does not necessarily provide sufficient incentives to encourage the initial innovation.[541] More specifically, Green and Scotchmer (1995) show that – given a short patent that provides only zero total profit – the follow-on innovator would always make a positive profit and the initial innovator would not have enough

534 See also Scotchmer (2006) on p. 156ff.
535 See Scotchmer (2006) on p. 156.
536 See Green and Scotchmer (1995) on p. 21.
537 However, see also Bessen and Maskin (2006) who argue that patents should not be afforded in the case of cumulative innovations. More specifically, the authors argue that – in particular in the context of the software industry, i.e. Open Source software – the long-term gain due to the access to non-patented technologies exceeds the loss in profit due to increased competition. See also Bessen and Hunt (2003) and Hunt (2006). However, it is noteworthy that the approach of Open Source software is very specific to the software industry and may not easily be applied to other industries. See also Lévêque and Ménière (2004) on p. 41 and Scotchmer (2006) on p. 156.
538 See also Lévêque and Ménière (2004) on p. 39.
539 See also Scotchmer (2006) on p. 132ff.
540 See also Scotchmer (2006) on p. 156.
541 See Scotchmer (2006) on p. 136ff.

incentives to innovate. Therefore, a patent has to be longer if cumulative innovations are made by several innovators in order to encourage their R&D investments.[542]
Nevertheless, so far we have implicitly assumed that the patent holder can easily monitor and detect patent infringement and that he can effectively enforce the exclusive use of the patented product or process. However, as we will see in the following section, the enforcement of a patent is a complex and costly issue.

3.2.3. Private Enforcement of Patents and Remedies for Infringement

A patent only has value if the exclusive use of the patented innovation can be enforced.[543] However, it is generally left to the patentee to scrutinize and discover patent infringements.[544] Furthermore, the role of the state is basically limited to providing rules and a court system.[545] For instance, when a patent holder detects a patent infringement, the dispute between the patent holder and the infringer can be brought to court.[546] The main tools that (common law) courts typically utilize in order to punish the infringer of a patent are money damages and injunctions.[547]
Damages are a sum of money paid by the infringer of a patent to the infringed patentee that compensates the patentee for the loss suffered.[548] Damages basically serve two alternative purposes: compensation and deterrence. First, compensatory money damages aim at providing the innovator *ex ante* with sufficient incentives to invest in R&D even though patent infringement may occur *ex post*.[549] Alternatively, money damages can *a priori* deter the infringement if the likelihood of being caught multiplied with the damages that the infringer has to pay exceed the benefit that the infringer derives from the infringement.[550]
Nevertheless, in common law, there have been two main measures to determine the amount of money to be paid by the infringer:[551] lost profits and unjust enrichment.
First, under the lost-profit doctrine, the infringer of a patent must reimburse the infringed patentee's lost profits, i.e. lost royalties.[552]

---

542 See Green and Scotchmer (1995) on p. 31.
543 See Lévêque and Ménière (2004) on p. 16ff. See also Scotchmer (2006) on p. 72ff.
544 See Becker and Stigler (1974) for a general treatment of law enforcement. See also Landes and Posner (1975) and Friedman (1984) who particularly focus on the private enforcement of law.
545 See Landes and Posner (1975) on p. 1.
546 See Scotchmer (2006) on p. 73.
547 See Scotchmer (2006) on p. 72. See also Menell and Scotchmer (2007) on p. 1479ff. For a general treatment of the *ex post* efficiency of damages and injunctions see Calabresi and Melamed (1972), Polinsky (1980), and Kaplow and Shavell (1996). See also Blair and Cotter (1998) who provide an analysis of the *ex post* efficiency of damages rules in IP law. For an analysis of the *ex ante* effects of damages and injunctions in the IP context, see Schankerman and Scotchmer (2001). See also Conley (1987) and Anton and Yao (2007).
548 See Cooter and Ulen (2004) on p. 100 and Scotchmer (2006) on p. 206. See also Dari-Mattiacci and Schäfer (2007).
549 See Menell and Scotchmer (2007) on p. 1496ff.
550 See Becker (1968) for the general framework of the economic theory of crime. See also Polinsky and Shavell (1998) and Cooter (1982) for a treatment of punitive damages in addition to compensatory money damages.
551 See Scotchmer (2006) on p. 73ff and p. 206ff.

Second, under the unjust enrichment doctrine, the infringer of the patent "must disgorge his unjust enrichment"[553] which leaves him zero profit.
Furthermore, courts can impose punitive damages on the infringer of a patent in addition to compensatory damages, i.e. when the infringer acted deliberately.[554] In particular, the difference between compensatory money damages and punitive damages is that punitive damages aim at punishing the infringer whereas compensatory money damages aim at compensating the patentee.[555]
However, as already mentioned above, another remedy for patent infringement is injunctive relief.[556] More specifically, injunctions are orders by the court directing the infringer to refrain from using or selling the infringing product or process.[557] For instance, courts typically grant injunctions when the patentee would otherwise have to give up his business, damages are uncertain or there is a high probability that damages are late.[558] Moreover, if the infringer fails to abide by an injunction and continues to use or sell the infringing product or process, he can be held in contempt of court.[559]
Note, however, that it is a complex task for the holder of a patent to identify and pursue an alleged infringer and thus that patent infringement is difficult to establish in the first place.[560] For instance, it may be difficult for the patentee to prove liability as he must show that the accused product includes every element of at least one claim specified in the patent document.[561] Second, alleged infringers – as a consequence of the complaint of infringement – typically defend themselves by claiming that the patented invention was obvious and thus that the patent is invalid.[562]
However, on the one hand, uncompensated patent infringement is likely to have a negative impact on the value of a patent and thus on the incentives to innovate.[563] On the other hand, costly patent litigation may also have a negative impact on the value of a patent and on the incentive to innovate.[564] Therefore, we will elaborate on the cost and efficacy of patent enforcement and on the evidence on patent litigation in the next section.

552 See Schankerman and Scotchmer (2001) on p. 199ff. See also Schankerman and Scotchmer (2001) and Anton and Yao (2007).
553 See Scotchmer (2006) on p. 206.
554 See Polinsky and Shavell (1998) and Cooter (1982) for a treatment of punitive damages in addition to compensatory money damages.
555 See Menell and Scotchmer (2007) on p. 1496ff.
556 See Scotchmer (2006) on p. 72ff.
557 See Scotchmer (2006) on p. 206.
558 See also Scotchmer (2006) on p. 73 who elaborates on the difference between preliminary and permanent injunctions in the U.S. See also Lanjouw and Lerner (2001) for an analysis of the economic role of preliminary injunctions as a strategic means in legal disputes.
559 See Cooter and Ulen (2004) on p. 100.
560 See Menell and Scotchmer (2007) on p. 1496ff. See also Lévêque and Ménière (2004) on p. 16.
561 See Scotchmer (2006) on p. 197.
562 See Scotchmer (2006) on p. 198.
563 See Lévêque and Ménière (2004) on p. 16.
564 See Scotchmer (2006) on p. 200ff.

3.2.4. Enforcement of Patents and Patent Litigation

First of all, the vast majority of patent disputes are settled out of court.[565] For instance, joint ventures, mergers and patent pools[566] as well as licensing and cross licensing are forms of patent settlements.[567] More specifically, in a patent settlement, the patentee agrees to withdraw the complaint of patent infringement in return for licensing provisions or money payments.[568] Furthermore, the alleged infringer may agree to withdraw the counterclaim of patent invalidity in return for certain payments.[569]
However, it is straightforward to see that this mechanism only works if both parties can benefit from the settlement. In particular, high litigation costs provide a strong incentive to settle.[570] For instance, in the U.S., a patent litigation can cost each party between \$ 1 million and \$ 3 million per lawsuit[571] which exceeds the value of most patents according to Scotchmer (2006, p. 268ff).
Note, however, that patent settlements can also be anticompetitive and illegal under antitrust law, i.e. when the patent would have been found invalid by the court so that the (alleged) infringer would not have been an infringer but a regular competitor.[572]
As to the likelihood of patent litigation, roughly 2 percent of all patents are litigated resulting in a reduction of the value of a patent.[573] More specifically, Lanjouw and Schankerman (2001) find that the litigation risk is higher for high-value patents, i.e. pharmaceutical patents, and that the litigation risk can reduce the incentive to innovate provided by a high-value patent.[574] In other words, high risk and cost of litigation make patents a less effective incentive mechanism.[575] Furthermore, Lanjouw and Schankerman (2001) and Lanjouw and Schankerman (2004) find that the number of patent litigations increased from 1978 to 1999. More specifically, the authors find that patent litigations in the biotechnology, pharmaceutical and computer industry increased as a percentage of total patent grants.[576]
Nevertheless, as previously mentioned, patents play an important role in the pharmaceutical industry, in particular because of the high R&D costs involved in the development of a new pharmaceutical product. Therefore, we will elaborate on this issue and on other peculiarities of the pharmaceutical sector in the following section.

565 See Lanjouw and Schankerman (2002) and Scotchmer (2006) on p. 199.
566 See Lerner and Tirole (2004).
567 See Shapiro (2003).
568 See Scotchmer (2006) on p. 200.
569 See Scotchmer (2006) on p. 200.
570 For instance, see Crampes and Langinier (2002).
571 See Graham et al. (2003). See also Scotchmer (2006) on p. 200 and Burpee (1999).
572 See Shapiro (2003). See also Scotchmer (2006) on p. 200.
573 See Lanjouw and Schankerman (2001) and Lanjouw and Schankerman (2004). See Lerner (1994) for an estimation of the likelihood of patent litigation in the biotechnology industry. See also Lemley (2001) and Menell and Scotchmer (2007) on p. 1519ff, and Ziedonis (2003).
574 See also Levin et al. (1987), Cohen et al. (2000), Lanjouw and Schankerman (2004), and Menell and Scotchmer (2007) on p. 1519.
575 See Scotchmer (2006) on p. 201.
576 See also Menell and Scotchmer (2007) on p. 1519ff.

3.2.5. The Pharmaceutical Market

In this section we will give a brief overview of the pharmaceutical industry and specific issues as to the economics of drug development and distribution.[577]

3.2.5.1. Overview of the Pharmaceutical Industry

The vast majority of new inventions in the world have been and are generated by pharmaceutical companies in developed nations as they are endowed with the important technical and non-technical input factors required for innovation.[578] This can be further illustrated by the fact that the big multinational pharmaceutical companies in terms of world market sales are all based either in Europe or in the U.S as **Table 3** shows.[579]

Table 3 *Top 15 Pharmaceutical Companies as Measured by World Market Sales*

Company	**Pharmaceutical sales, in billion dollars (2007)**	**Based in**
Pfizer	44.4	USA
GlaxoSmithKline	38.2	UK, USA
Sanofi-Aventis	36.9	France
Novartis	32.2	Switzerland
AstraZeneca	28.7	UK
Johnson&Johnson	24.9	USA
Merck	24.2	USA
Roche	20.3	Switzerland
Wyeth	18.6	USA
Eli Lilly	17.6	USA
Bristol-Myers Squibb	15.6	USA
Bayer	15.0	Germany
Abbott	14.6	USA
Amgen	14.3	USA
Boehringer-Ingelheim	12.6	Germany

Sources: IMS Health (2007), Pharmaceutical Executive (2008)

Furthermore, according to WHO estimates the global market for pharmaceuticals is worth US$300 billion a year and is "expected to rise to US$400 billion within three years".[580] In particular, the 10 largest pharmaceutical companies control over one-third of the market for pharmaceuticals.

---

577 See also Scherer (2000) for an extensive treatment of the pharmaceutical industry.

578 See Sykes (2002) on p. 47.

579 See also Malik (2008) and http://www.medicinesaustralia.com.au/pages/page77.asp (last visited March 25, 2009). See also Scherer (2000) on p. 1303ff.

580 See http://www.who.int/trade/glossary/story073/en/index.html (last visited March 24, 2009).

However, the global pharmaceutical industry is highly competitive for the following reasons:
First, there are thousands of small and specialized pharmaceutical companies beneath the top level of major pharmaceutical companies.[581]
Second, until the TRIPS Agreement is fully implemented worldwide patents may not be recognized in various markets.[582] In this case the producers of patented pharmaceuticals compete with generic producing competitors.[583] Consequently, the patent holder cannot charge monopoly prices in those markets where the patent is not recognized.
Third, substitute products may be widely available for most of the patented drugs as the vast majority of pharmaceutical companies produce imitative varieties of the patented drug or substitutes under their own brand names.[584]
Finally, as the duration of the patent is limited, i.e. 20 years, all companies are free to launch their own product versions after the expiry of the patent and thus increase competition significantly.[585]

3.2.5.2. The Economics of Drug Development and Pricing

In this section we will give a brief overview of the economics of drug development and monopolistic pricing. In particular, we shall focus on the substantially high cost of drug development, the economic costs of epidemics, the price elasticity of demand, and its impact on the optimal output decision of a profit-maximizing producer of a patented medicine.

3.2.5.2.1. Welfare Considerations

From a welfare point of view, effective pharmaceutical products are of value to the individual as well as to society as a whole.[586] First of all, effective medicines increase the utility of the individual as they either help to end a disease or to treat the symptoms of a disease.[587] Furthermore, effective medicines are of value to society as a whole as they create a positive externality in a sense that they reduce the risk for healthy individuals to contract an infectious disease.[588]
However, where effective medicines do not exist, i.e. in the case of neglected infectious and tropical diseases, are not affordable or not accessible, epidemics of disease have large-scale negative economic consequences.[589]

---

581 See El Feki (2005).
582 See Gervais (2003) on p. 350ff as to the extension of the transitional periods for least-developed countries with respect to pharmaceuticals until January 1, 2016.
583 See also Reiffen and Ward (2005) for an analysis of the generic drug industry. See also Scott Morton (1999) and Scott Morton (2000). See also Scherer (2000) on p. 1321ff.
584 See Scherer (2000) on p. 1320. See also Lu and Comanor (1998).
585 See Nordhaus (1969) on p. 76ff.
586 See Ganslandt et al. (2005) on p. 214ff. See also Kremer and Glennerster (2004).
587 See Kremer and Glennerster (2004).
588 See Kremer and Glennerster (2004) on p. 29. See also Kremer (2001a) on p. 45.
589 See World Health Organization (2004) on p. 8ff.

First, diseases generate a loss of income and cause direct costs of medical expenditures.[590] Furthermore, diseases have negative consequences for long-term economic growth.[591] Several country-based economic studies and estimates suggest that HIV/AIDS epidemics result in a reduction of GDP of around 1 percent.[592] For instance, Arndt and Lewis (2000) have suggested that HIV/AIDS epidemics in South Africa result in a reduction of GDP of between 0.8 and 1.0 percent whereas Bonnel (2000) – applying a cross-country regression for 47 countries – suggests that the impact of HIV/AIDS on GDP per-capita growth is –0.7 percent.

Furthermore, the results of a cross-country regression study across 30 Sub-Saharan African countries conducted by Over (1992) suggest that HIV/AIDS epidemics could lead to a reduction of annual GDP of between 0.56 and 1.08 percent between 1990 and 2025.

Nevertheless, Bell et al. (2003) criticize that the studies mentioned above significantly underestimate the macroeconomic costs of epidemics. They argue that the modest estimates of the macroeconomic costs of HIV/AIDS in those studies are based on the assumption that HIV/AIDS epidemics in fact lead to an increase of the productivity of labor as the main effect of increased mortality induced by HIV/AIDS epidemics is to reduce pressure on existing land and capital.[593] Thus, the negative impact on GDP growth of HIV/AIDS epidemics leading to a reallocation of expenditures towards medical care and to a decline in savings and investment is diminished by the countervailing effect of increased labor productivity.[594] Therefore, according to Bell et al. (2003), the studies mentioned above suggest a relatively modest negative impact from HIV/AIDS epidemics on GDP growth.

In contrast to the studies by Arndt and Lewis (2000), Over (1992), and Bonnel (2000), Bell et al. (2003, p. 7) place emphasis on the importance of human capital and mechanisms through which abilities and knowledge are transmitted across generations. Adopting an overlapping generations (OLG) model, Bell et al. (2003) come to the conclusion that as the outbreak of AIDS not only destroys existing human capital but also – by killing mostly young adults – weakens the transmission mechanisms for knowledge and abilities to future generations the negative impact of HIV/AIDS epidemics on GDP growth is certainly higher than a modest 1 percent reduction. In fact, Bell et al. (2003, p. 3) suggest that a collapse of human capital and productivity at a sufficiently high level of prevalence of the disease may even result in a complete economic collapse within three generations if nothing is done to combat the epidemic.

However, in order to analyze the question of why there is an underinvestment in R&D for some diseases despite the fact that – from a welfare point of view – effective medicines are of value to the individual and to society as a whole, we must also take into consideration the profit-maximization problem of pharmaceutical companies. More specifically, let us now explore the cost of drug development and pricing strategies for patented goods in the following sections.

590 See World Health Organization (2004) on p. 8ff.

591 See Mutangadura et al. (2000).

592 See Bell et al. (2003) on p. 7, Table 1.

593 See Bell et al. (2003) on p. 7.

594 See Bell et al. (2003) on p. 7.

3.2.5.2.2. Cost of Drug Development

Sachs, Kremer, and Hamoudi (1999, p. 8) estimate the average cost for a new drug to be US$300 million that are mainly fixed and sunk cost once the drug is developed.[595] Moreover, they predict that developing vaccines for some diseases such as malaria, tuberculosis, or HIV potentially costs several times as much as US$300 million due to the significant scientific challenges involved.[596] Let us now consider the R&D process in detail for a better understanding of the risks and costs involved.
The R&D process for new medicines from discovery to approval of medicines covers several complex, expensive, and risky stages.[597]

3.2.5.2.2.1. Screening

In the first stage of drug discovery, researchers identify molecules believed to affect a certain disease.[598] Then, thousands of compounds are screened in order to identify potential medicines. However, for every 10,000 molecules screened, an average of 250 enter the second stage of preclinical testing.[599] In the stage of preclinical testing, potential medicines from the first stage receive 1 to 3 years of testing in order to assess safety and biological activity against a disease. Moreover, chemistry and manufacturing tests and pharmaceutical development studies explore the chemical purity and stability of a compound, determine what is required for large-scale production of the new medicine, and explore further issues with regard to dosing, formulation, and packaging.

3.2.5.2.2.2. Application for the Review of a New Medicine and Preclinical Testing

In the next stage, prior to the clinical testing in patients, the pharmaceutical producer must apply for the review of on investigational new drug conducted by the government authorities responsible.[600]
For instance in the U.S., the Food and Drug Administration (FDA) requires precise information about the plans for clinical testing in patients as well as manufacturing procedures, and toxicology studies on animals prior to allowing a pharmaceutical producer to initiate clinical testing in patients.[601]
In Germany, the Federal Institute for Drugs and Medical Devices (Bundesinstitut für Arzneimittel und Medizinprodukte) is responsible for reviewing safety, efficacy, and pharmaceutical quality of new medicines in the course of licensing and registration procedures on the basis of the German Drug Law (Arzneimittelgesetz).[602]

595 See also DiMasi et al. (1991), DiMasi et al. (2003), Giaccotto et al. (2005), and Grabowski and Vernon (2000a).
596 See Sachs et al. (1999) on p. 8.
597 See PhRMA (2005).
598 See also Scherer (2000) on p. 1305ff.
599 See El Feki (2005).
600 See PhRMA (2005) on p. 3ff.
601 See PhRMA (2005) on p. 4.
602 See http://www.bfarm.de (last visited May 21, 2009).

However, on average, from the 250 drug candidates that enter the second stage of pre-clinical testing ten drug candidates make it through to the following stage of clinical trials.[603]

3.2.5.2.2.3. Clinical Trials

The stage of clinical trials is aimed at testing drug candidates in patients in order to explore the question of whether the drug candidates are effective and safe.[604] This stage contains three different phases and can take up to 10 years.[605]

In the first phase, researchers test a new medicine for safe dose range, mechanisms of action, and safety in a relatively small group of up to 100 healthy volunteers.[606] The second phase contains placebo-controlled trials with up to 500 volunteers suffering from a certain disease in order to find out whether the new medicine allows an effective treatment of the disease, to look for side effects, and to determine the optimal dose strength. In the third phase, researchers test the new medicine in large trials with up to 5,000 patients in hospitals and clinics.[607] This phase is aimed at exploring the effectiveness of a new medicine and identifying its side effects. Nevertheless, parallel to these three stages researchers also continue conducting toxicity tests, planning for full-scale production, and preparing the application for approval in the next stage.[608]

The procedure of a new medicine's approval for patient use in the U.S. typically takes up to 10 months.[609] Therein, scientists and advisory committees of the responsible governmental authorities review the pharmaceutical producer's application and all clinical trial results in order to decide whether the relevant data and results justify an approval for patient use. On average, from the ten drug candidates that make it through to the stage of clinical testing only one is approved by the regulator.[610]

However, once a new medicine is launched pharmaceutical producers continue to monitor the approved medicine for safety and generate more data about how the new drug affects particular groups of patients.[611] Furthermore, the pharmaceutical companies are required to regularly report the results of their tests and studies to the regulator.[612]

To sum up, the R&D process for new medicines that takes an average of 12 years is time consuming, risky and expensive. Furthermore, since the mid-1990s, average success rates have declined at the later stages of clinical testing resulting in higher risks and costs of R&D.[613]

---

603 See PhRMA (2005) on p. 4.
604 See El Feki (2005).
605 See PhRMA (2005) on p. 4. See also DiMasi et al. (2003) on p. 177ff.
606 See PhRMA (2005) on p. 4.
607 See El Feki (2005).
608 See PhRMA (2005) on p. 4.
609 See PhRMA (2005) on p. 4.
610 See El Feki (2005) on p. 6.
611 See PhRMA (2005) on p. 4.
612 See El Feki (2005).
613 See DiMasi et al. (1991) and DiMasi et al. (2003) on the determinants of pharmaceutical R&D expenditures.

However, the marginal costs of pharmaceutical production are typically fairly low compared to the substantially high cost of drug development.[614] Let us now turn to the impact of R&D costs and marginal costs of production on the pricing strategies of a monopolistic producer of a patented pharmaceutical product.

3.2.5.2.3. Pricing Strategies of Patent Holders

As already mentioned, a patent for a particular medicine reduces competition as it blocks the entry of competitive products supplied by companies other than the patent holder.[615] Indeed, a patent may even protect the patent holder from any competition for a sustained period of time, i.e. twenty years, and allow the patent holder to exercise some market power and therefore to charge a price that exceeds his marginal cost of production during the life of the patent.[616] Put differently, a patent offers a kind of limited monopoly.[617] Nevertheless, the extent of protection from competition and thus the ability to charge a non-competitive price depends on various factors.

First, it depends on the availability of substitute products.[618] Furthermore, it depends on the extent to which the medicine is unique and desired by consumers and on the extent to which consumers are able to shift their demand to alternative non-patented products.[619] For instance, generic drug prices are significantly lower than brand-name prices, and a considerable share of the market is taken by generic drugs.[620]

However, assuming that patents allow the patent holder to charge a non-competitive price for a medicine the following questions may arise: what is the profit-maximizing optimal price? On which factors does the optimal price depend? These questions shall be explored in the following sections.

3.2.5.2.3.1. Price Elasticity of Demand and Optimal Prices

In the following, we shall explain why the optimal price is likely to vary across countries with different levels of income.[621] Moreover, we shall analyze the impact on optimal prices in local markets when the price elasticity of demand varies across these markets.[622]

As we have already mentioned above, a monopolist typically charges a price that exceeds the competitive price, and restricts output to a point where consumers are willing to pay more for an additional unit of output than it costs to produce it.[623]

---

614 See Kremer and Glennerster (2004) on p. 31ff.

615 See Lévêque and Ménière (2004) on p. 9ff.

616 See Scherer (2000) on p. 1301ff.

617 See Varian (1996) on p. 415.

618 See also Lévêque and Ménière (2004) on p. 89 for a definition of substitute products.

619 See Abbott (2001) on p. 38.

620 See Nogués (1990) on p. 95. See also Reiffen and Ward (2005), Scott Morton (1999), and Scott Morton (2000).

621 See Ganslandt et al. (2005) on p. 215ff.

622 See Case and Fair (1999) on p. 109ff. See also Varian (1999) on p. 266ff, and Abbott (2001) on p. 38.

623 See Varian (1999) on p. 434.

However, the monopolist does not produce the additional output because this would result in a decline of the uniform price he gets for all of its output and thus in a decline of profit.[624]

Nevertheless, if the monopolist could engage in price discrimination and sell different units at different prices this would enable him to capture more of the market's consumer surplus and increase his profits.[625] Following the classic taxonomy of price discrimination according to Pigou (1932), there are three different types of price discrimination; first-degree, second-degree, and third-degree price discrimination.[626]

In the following, we shall focus on third-degree price discrimination and only briefly outline the other two types of price discrimination for various reasons.

First, third-degree price discrimination is the most common form of price discrimination.[627] Second, the idealized concept of first-degree price discrimination is interesting from a theoretical point of view. However, there are only very few real-life examples for first-degree price discrimination.[628] In contrast, third-degree price discrimination is particularly relevant for the analysis of the pricing decision of a producer of a patented pharmaceutical product sold in several national markets as we shall see in the following.

In first-degree price discrimination, sometimes also called perfect price discrimination, the monopolist charges different prices for different units of output and these prices may vary from consumer to consumer.[629] Thus, first-degree price discrimination enables the monopolist to sell each unit of output to each consumer at her reservation price for that unit and thus yields the maximum possible profit.[630] Hence, no consumers' surplus is generated in a market with perfect price discrimination as the monopolist captures all surplus in this market.[631]

In second-degree price discrimination, the monopolist sells different units of output at different prices, but these prices do not differ across consumers who buy the same amount of the good.[632] Thus, the price per unit of output is not constant and depends on the quantity of output that a consumer purchases.[633] For instance, common real-life examples for second-degree price discrimination are prices per unit of electricity, water, or heating fuel that depend on the quantity bought by the consumer.[634]

---

624 For instance, see Varian (1999) on p. 434ff.

625 See Varian (1999) on p. 434ff.

626 With respect to first-degree price discrimination, see Oi (1971), Willig (1978), Schmalensee (1981a), and Hoerger (1993). Regarding second-degree price discrimination, see Spence (1977), Maskin and Riley (1984), Goldman et al. (1984), and Gal-Or (1988). With respect to third-degree price discrimination see Varian (1985), Schwartz (1990), and Layson (1994). See also Ekelund (1970) and Norman (1999).

627 See Varian (1999) on p. 440.

628 For instance, see Varian (1999) on p. 434ff.

629 See Varian (1988) on p. 601ff.

630 For instance, see Pindyck and Rubinfeld (2005) on p. 382ff.

631 See Varian (1988) on p. 601.

632 See Varian (1988) on p. 611ff.

633 See Varian (1988) on p. 611.

634 See also Varian (1988) on p. 611ff.

3.2.5.2.3.2. Third-Degree Price Discrimination

In third-degree price discrimination, the monopolist sells output to different people or segmented markets at different prices, but individuals in the same segmented market or group pay the same price per unit of output.[635] For instance, different admission prices for students or senior citizens in cinemas, theaters, amusement parks etc. are typical examples of third-degree price discrimination.[636]

The effect on social welfare of third-degree price discrimination was originally analyzed by Robinson (1933) and reexamined by Schmalensee (1981b). Schmalensee (1981b) established the result that third-degree price discrimination raises social welfare defined as the sum of consumers' surplus and producers' surplus under such specific conditions as constant marginal costs, dependent (deterministic) demand, and increasing total output associated with price discrimination as compared to uniform pricing.

Furthermore, Varian (1985) showed that third-degree price discrimination increases welfare under much more general conditions such as increasing marginal costs and independent (probabilistic) demand.

Moreover, Hausman and MacKie-Mason (1988) explore the impact of third-degree price discrimination on static and dynamic welfare. In particular, they focus on dynamic welfare benefits of encouraging innovation and on negative static welfare effects associated with monopoly misallocations and potential positive static welfare effects due to scale economies and learning effects. Hausman and MacKie-Mason (1988) conclude that third-degree price discrimination by patent holders is not only beneficial for the patent holder but that it may also raise static social welfare under two specific conditions.

First, third-degree price discrimination enables the monopolist to serve some markets that may not be served under uniform pricing.[637]

Second, when declining marginal costs are possible with increasing output due to economies of scale and learning effects, the opportunity to serve new markets because of third-degree price discrimination results in static welfare gains.[638] Hence, opening markets and achieving scale economies increase static welfare, thereby increasing the likelihood that third-degree price discrimination for patented goods will yield static welfare gains.[639]

635 Importantly, see Danzon and Towes (2003) for an excellent treatment of differential pricing, based on Ramsey pricing, for pharmaceuticals. Note that pharmaceutical companies typically use Ramsey pricing to set prices internationally. See also Varian (1988) on p. 617ff and Varian (1999) on p. 434ff.

636 See also Varian (1988) on p. 604ff.

637 See Hausman and MacKie-Mason (1988) on p. 264.

638 See Hausman and MacKie-Mason (1988) on p. 264.

639 See Hausman and MacKie-Mason (1988) on p. 264. Furthermore, Danzon (1998) shows that monopolies engaging in price-discrimination in segmented markets can be optimal from a welfare perspective.

3.2.5.2.3.2.1. Price Elasticity of Demand and Revenue

Let us now consider the monopolist's profit-maximization problem, in particular with regard to the impact of the price elasticity of demand on the optimal choice of output.[640] Let y denote output, $p(y)$ the inverse demand function, and $c(y)$ the cost function.[641] Algebraically, profit π is the difference between revenue $r(y)=p(y)y$ and cost $c(y)$. Then, the monopolist's profit-maximization problem is given by

$$\max_{y} \pi(y) = r(y) - c(y).^{642} \tag{70}$$

First, set the incremental profit equal to zero:

$$\frac{\delta \pi(y)}{\delta y} = \frac{\delta r(y)}{\delta y} - \frac{\delta c(y)}{\delta y} = 0$$
$$\Leftrightarrow \frac{\delta r(y)}{\delta y} = \frac{\delta c(y)}{\delta y}. \tag{71}$$

Thus, the profit-maximizing condition is that marginal revenue $MR(y)$ equals marginal cost $MC(y)$. Consider now the term on the left-hand side of (71). More specifically, marginal revenue is

$$MR(y) = \frac{\delta r(y)}{\delta y} = \frac{\delta p(y)y}{\delta y} = p(y) + \frac{\delta p(y)}{\delta y} y.^{643} \tag{72}$$

Multiplying and dividing the last term on the right-hand side of (72) by $p(y)$ it follows that

$$MR(y) = p(y) + p(y)\left(\frac{\delta p(y)}{\delta y}\right)\left(\frac{y}{p(y)}\right). \tag{73}$$

However, the price elasticity of demand for a competitive market is typically defined as $E_D = \frac{p}{q}\frac{\delta q}{\delta p}$ where q denotes the market demand.[644]

The concept of price elasticity of demand also applies to monopolistic markets. However, the main difference is that, on a competitive market, the output decision of a single firm does not have any impact on the market price. Put differently, a single firm on a competitive market is a price taker.[645] In contrast, as the sole seller of a product,

640 See Pindyck and Rubinfeld (2005) on p. 344ff and Varian (1996) on p. 406ff.

641 The inverse demand function $p(y)$ measures what the market price for a good would have to be for y units of output of it to be demanded. See Varian (1996) on p. 263.

642 See Pindyck and Rubinfeld (2005) on p. 344ff and Varian (1996) on p. 406ff.

643 For instance, see Varian (1988) on p. 617ff.

644 For instance, see Varian (1999) on p. 266ff.

645 For instance, see Pindyck and Rubinfeld (2005) and Varian (1996).

the monopolist completely controls the amount of output y offered for sale.[646] Hence, market demand is just total demand for the good the monopolist sells. Therefore, the price elasticity of demand on a monopolistic market can be expressed as

$$E_D = \frac{p}{y}\frac{\delta y}{\delta p}.^{647} \tag{74}$$

Hence, we can express marginal revenue given by (73) in terms of price elasticity of demand as

$$MR(y) = p(y)\left(1+\left(\frac{\delta p(y)}{\delta y}\right)\left(\frac{y}{p(y)}\right)\right)$$

$$\Leftrightarrow MR(y) = p(y)\left(1+\frac{1}{E_D(y)}\right) = p(y)\left(1-\frac{1}{|E_D(y)|}\right).^{648} \tag{75}$$

It is now straightforward to see that, if the price elasticity of demand is –1, then marginal revenue is zero. We will now apply this rule of thumb for monopolistic pricing to a monopolist's output decision in a model of third-degree price discrimination on an international level.

3.2.5.2.3.3. Model of Third-Degree Price Discrimination on an International Level

In the following section, we shall analyze the pricing decision of a monopolistic pharmaceutical company that holds a patent for a new medicine.

Suppose that the monopolist sells the new medicine on the national markets of two countries with different levels of income per capita. Country 1 is an industrialized country with a high average income per capita. Country 2 is a developing country with a low average income per capita.[649] Furthermore, suppose that the monopolist can engage in third-degree price discrimination and thus can sell the medicine to each market at a different price. Let $p_i(y_i)$ denote the inverse demand curve in Country i with $i=\{1,2\}$, and y_i the sales in Country i, respectively. Furthermore, let $c(y_T)$ denote the total cost of producing $y_T = y_1 + y_2$.[650] The following assumptions are crucially important in the course of the analysis in this section.

Assumption 1: Demand for the medicine in Country 1 is less elastic than in Country 2 at any given positive price. That is,

$$|E_D^1(y_1)| < |E_D^2(y_2)|. \tag{76}$$

646 For instance, see Pindyck and Rubinfeld (2005) and Varian (1996).
647 See Varian (1996).
648 See Varian (1988) on p. 618ff. See also Varian (1996).
649 See Varian (1999) on p. 440ff for a general model of third-degree price discrimination.
650 See Varian (1999).

Different levels of average income per capita lead to different demand curves for the two different countries and different levels of price elasticity of demand.[651] In particular, the demand in countries with low average income per capita is likely to be more elastic than demand in countries with high average income per capita.

Assumption 2: Arbitrage is not possible. More specifically, neither individual consumers nor importing firms are permitted to buy the medicine at a potentially lower price in one market and resell it in the other market at a higher price.[652] This assumption is crucially important with regard to third-degree price discrimination as arbitrage through parallel imports would make it impossible for the monopolist to charge different prices in different markets.[653]

Total profit of the pharmaceuticals producer is given by

$$\pi(y_1, y_2) = p_1(y_1)y_1 + p_2(y_2)y_2 - c(y_1 + y_2).^{654} \tag{77}$$

First, we set incremental profit for sales in Country 1 equal to zero:[655]

$$\begin{aligned} &\frac{\delta\pi(y_1, y_2)}{\delta y_1} = \frac{\delta\left(p_1(y_1)y_1\right)}{\delta y_1} - \frac{\delta c(y_1 + y_2)}{\delta y_1} = 0 \\ &\Leftrightarrow \frac{\delta\left(p_1(y_1)y_1\right)}{\delta y_1} = \frac{\delta c(y_1 + y_2)}{\delta y_1} \\ &\Leftrightarrow p_1(y_1) + \frac{\delta p_1(y_1)}{\delta y_1} y_1 = \frac{\delta c(y_1 + y_2)}{\delta y_1}.^{656} \end{aligned} \tag{78}$$

The term on the left-hand side of (78) is the incremental revenue from an extra unit of sales to consumers in Country 1. The term on the right-hand side is the incremental cost of producing this extra unit. Therefore, we have

$$MR_1(y_1) = MC(y_1 + y_2). \tag{79}$$

Similarly, for sales to consumers in Country 2, we obtain

$$MR_2(y_2) = MC(y_1 + y_2).^{657} \tag{80}$$

---

651 See Scherer and Watal (2002b) on p. 925ff. See also Ganslandt and Maskus (2001) on p. 5, footnote 3.
652 We will relax this assumption in our model of parallel trade in section 5.2.4 in Chapter 5.
653 See Ganslandt and Maskus (2004) on p. 1042ff.
654 See Varian (1988) on p. 617ff. See also Varian (1999).
655 Note that – in contrast to a firm on a competitive market – the monopolist is not a price-taker. More specifically, the monopolist has to take into consideration two effects of his output decision on profit. First, producing one extra unit at price p generates revenue p. Second, one extra unit of output results in a drop of p. Hence, the monopolist gets a lower price on all units of output sold.
656 See Varian (1999).
657 See Varian (1999).

We can see from (79) and (80) that, in each market, the cost of producing an additional unit of the new medicine must be equal to the marginal revenue.[658] Moreover, we can see that marginal cost is the same in each market and thus that

$$MR_1(y_1) = MR_2(y_2).^{659} \tag{81}$$

Using the standard elasticity formula for marginal revenue given by (75) we can write (81) as

$$p_1(y_1)\left[1-\frac{1}{\left|E_D^1(y_1)\right|}\right] = p_2(y_2)\left[1-\frac{1}{\left|E_D^2(y_2)\right|}\right] \tag{82}$$

where $E_D^1(y_1)$ and $E_D^2(y_2)$ represent the price elasticities of demand in Country 1 and Country 2, evaluated at the profit-maximizing choices of output. Recall that we have assumed that $\left|E_D^1(y_1)\right| < \left|E_D^2(y_2)\right|$ [Assumption 1]. Hence, the factor in brackets on the right-hand side of (82) is greater than the factor in brackets on the left-hand side of (82). Therefore, it follows that

$$p_1(y_1) > p_2(y_2) \tag{83}$$

for the profit-maximizing monopolist engaging in third-degree price discrimination.[660] Hence, from a theoretical point of view, it is optimal for the monopolist to charge a higher price in Country 1 than in Country 2 as the price elasticity of demand for medicines is lower in Country 1 than in Country 2.[661]

However, as we shall explore in more detail in section 5.2.4 in Chapter 5, optimal prices in segmented markets not only depend on the price elasticity of demand but also on the potential for arbitrage between markets.[662] Put differently, the value of a patent depends on the scope for price discrimination which critically depends on the existence of barriers to parallel trade.[663] Therefore, we shall elaborate on the potential arbitrage between markets when parallel imports are possible. In particular, we focus on the impact of parallel imports on the patent holder's ability to engage in third-degree price discrimination in section 5.2.4 in Chapter 5.

However, in the following chapter, we will first elaborate on theory and evidence as to patent protection in the developing world.

658 See Varian (1999).

659 See Varian (1999).

660 See Varian (1988) on p. 619.

661 So far we have implicitly assumed that patients in both countries demand the same medicines. However, the problem that patients in the developing world demand medicines that differ from those demanded by patients in the richer industrialized countries shall be addressed in section 4.2.2 in Chapter 4. See also Varian (1988) on p. 619.

662 See Fink (2005) on p. 172ff.

663 See Ganslandt and Maskus (2004) on p. 1036.

4. Patent Protection in the Developing World: Theory and Evidence

4.1. Introduction

In the first part of this chapter, we shall provide a survey of the formal microeconomic literature on the introduction of patent protection in the developing world.
In particular, we will focus on the analysis of Deardorff (1992) of global patent protection and its impact on national and global welfare. Deardorff (1992) suggests that the extension of patent protection from innovating countries where the bulk of inventions are made, i.e. the U.S. or Japan, to countries that import inventions made abroad is likely to increase welfare in the innovating countries but may decrease welfare in the importing countries. However, the overall effect of extending patent protection to IPR importing countries on global welfare is not unambiguous. More specifically, Deardorff (1992) concludes that – as patent protection is extended to more and more countries – the potentially negative impact of extending patent protection on welfare in IPR importing countries may more than outweigh the positive impact of extending patent protection on welfare in innovating countries.
Furthermore, we shall briefly outline the idea brought forward by Diwan and Rodrik (1991) that IPR developing industrialized countries from the Northern Hemisphere and IPR importing developing countries from the Southern have different technological needs and thus compete with each other for scarce R&D resources for their preferred technologies.
Finally, we elaborate on the game-theoretic model with ongoing innovation in two heterogeneous countries in terms of market size and capacity for innovation set up by Grossman and Lai (2004). In particular, Grossman and Lai (2004) suggest that the international harmonization of patents is likely to benefit industrialized northern countries at the expense of developing countries in the Southern Hemisphere.
The second part of this chapter provides a survey of the empirical literature on the underinvestment in R&D for medicines for neglected infectious and tropical diseases.
More specifically, we shall focus on the empirical papers by Lanjouw and Cockburn (2001), Trouiller et al. (2002), and Lanjouw and MacLeod (2005) that address the question as to whether stronger patent protection in the developing world – as stipulated in the TRIPS Agreement – has led to more research into medicines for neglected infectious and tropical diseases that are rampant in the developing world. In particular, Lanjouw and Cockburn (2001), Trouiller et al. (2002), and Lanjouw and MacLeod (2005) come to the conclusion that the level of pharmaceutical research into neglected infectious and tropical diseases remains extremely low relative to overall

pharmaceutical R&D. However, there may have been a slight upward trend in malaria-related pharmaceutical research between 1975 and 2002.[664]

Moreover, we shall briefly outline the paper by Chaudhuri et al. (2006) who analyze the impact of the enforcement of patents for pharmaceutical products on prices and welfare in India. More specifically, Chaudhuri et al. (2006) estimate that – for a particular subsegment of broad-spectrum antibiotics – the enforcement of patent protection in India would result in a significant welfare loss. The range of the welfare loss, however, depends on the degree to which foreign pharmaceutical producers respond to stronger patent protection in India as well as the extent of national price regulation.

Finally, we elaborate on the paper by McCalman (2001) who analyzes the potentially negative redistributive consequences of international patent harmonization for technology-importing developing countries. In particular, McCalman (2001) estimates that patent harmonization associated with the TRIPS Agreement is likely to generate large transfers of income with the U.S. being the major beneficiary.

4.2. Microeconomic Theory as to Patent Protection in the Developing World

4.2.1. Global Patent Protection and its Impact on Economic Welfare

Many authors have analyzed the likely welfare effects of the international harmonization of patent protection.[665] In particular, the question as to whether extending patent protection to the developing world has positive or negative welfare effects is often analyzed in a North-South trade framework.[666] More specifically, the predominant view in the theoretical literature regarding patent protection in the developing world is that technology-importing developing countries in the Southern Hemisphere are likely to lose from the introduction of patent protection.[667]

The intuition behind this is the following: Extending patent protection to the developing world provides the innovating firms that are predominantly located in the Northern Hemisphere with a temporary monopoly throughout the duration of the patent. Furthermore, losses in consumer surplus from monopoly pricing are – under plausible circumstances – found to be higher than the extra surplus from additional innovations stimulated by strengthened patent protection in the South. In particular, in a two-country model, Deardorff (1992) analyzes the impact of the extension of patent protection – from an inventing country to a technology-importing country – on

664 See Lanjouw and MacLeod (2005) on p. 4240.

665 For instance, see McCalman (2005) and Rapp and Rozek (1990). See also Lanjouw (1998), Watal (2000), and Scherer (2004) that focus on pharmaceutical product patents and their impact on welfare in developing countries. See also Correa (2000b) on p. 25ff, Penrose (1973), Primo Braga (1989), Nogués (1990), Subramanian (1990), and Deardorff (1990).

666 For instance, see Chin and Grossman (1990) on IPRs in the North-South trade context. See also Hestermeyer (2007) on p. 37ff, Grinols and Lin (2006), Lai and Qiu (2003), and Yang (1998).

667 See Chen and Puttitanun (2005) on p. 474ff. See also Chin and Grossman (1990).

national and global welfare. Deardorff (1992) convincingly shows that the welfare of an industrialized country in the Northern Hemisphere where the majority of inventions originate increases when patent protection is extended to a technology-importing country.
However, the extension of patent protection to the second country which imports but does not invent new products is likely to decrease welfare in this country in spite of the fact that it will benefit from increased inventive activities stimulated through the extension of patent protection.
Furthermore, Deardorff (1992) comes to the following conclusion with respect to the question as to whether global welfare increases or decreases with the extension of patent protection. If all innovations are made in the Northern Hemisphere, then the extension of patent protection to more and more countries has the positive effect that the inventors earn monopoly profits in a larger group of countries and thus have higher incentives to invest in R&D.
There are, however, diminishing returns to this effect for the following reason. As more and more countries afford patent protection, the extra market that can be covered becomes smaller as well as the extra invention that can be stimulated by the extension of patent protection.[668] Therefore, Deardorff (1992, p. 48ff) concludes that at some point the costs resulting from extending patent protection associated with monopoly pricing to existing innovations come to outweigh the benefits of making new innovations resulting from extending patent protection.
For a better understanding of the main results mentioned above, we have to look at the original model in more detail. In the following sections, we shall therefore comprehensively describe the basic framework originally formulated by Deardorff (1992).

4.2.1.1. Innovation in a Closed Economy

4.2.1.1.1. Single Invention in a Single Country

First, Deardorff (1992, p. 36ff) considers the case of a single invention in a single country as a benchmark. For instance, suppose that one specific pharmaceutical product for a specific disease is developed in a single country.
In particular, Deardorff (1992) compares the different levels of corporate profit, consumer surplus and welfare under both competitive production without patent protection as well as monopolized production with patent protection.
The research costs of the innovating firm are denoted by R.[669] According to Deardorff (1992, p. 36), the marginal costs of production are assumed to be constant and denoted by c.
For mathematical convenience, however, we will set marginal cost of production equal to zero in the following sections. Note that this is a common assumption in models that deal with the strategic decisions of pharmaceutical companies, as the marginal costs of

668 See Deardorff (1992) on p. 49.
669 See Deardorff (1992) on p. 36.

production are negligibly small compared to the cost of research and development.[670] This simplification does not, however, have any impact on the quality of the results of the model to be elaborated in the following.
The inverse demand for a new pharmaceutical product of an individual consumer is given by

$$p = a - bq. \tag{84}$$

There are n identical consumers.[671] Therefore, the inverse market demand function is given by

$$p = a - \frac{b}{n}q.^{672} \tag{85}$$

Put differently, for any given price, the market demand is n times the individual demand, that is $q = n\left(\left(a/b\right)-\left(p/b\right)\right)$.

4.2.1.1.1.1. Competitive Production of a Single Invention

First, Deardorff (1992, p. 36ff) analyzes the output as well as the consumer surplus under competitive production without patent protection. More specifically, under the assumption that patent protection is absent and that a new pharmaceutical product has already been invented, each competitor of the original manufacturer can produce the new product so that perfect competition will be established. By setting (85) equal to the marginal cost of zero, Deardorff (1992, p. 36) obtains the output under *competitive* market conditions without patent protection

$$\begin{aligned} 0 &= a - \frac{b}{n}q \\ \Leftrightarrow q^c &= n\frac{a}{b}. \end{aligned} \tag{86}$$

Graphically, the consumer surplus is the area between the inverse market demand function given by (85) and the competitive price which is equal to zero because marginal costs are assumed to be zero.[673] Formally, the *optimal* consumer surplus under competitive production is given by

$$s^o = \int_0^{q^c} a - \frac{b}{n}q \, \mathrm{d}q = \left[aq - \frac{1}{2}\frac{b}{n}q^2\right]_0^{n\frac{a}{b}} = n\frac{a^2}{b} - \frac{1}{2}n\frac{a^2}{b}$$

670 For instance, see Ganslandt and Maskus (2001) on p. 6.
671 See Deardorff (1992) on p. 36.
672 See Deardorff (1992) on p. 36.
673 For instance, see Varian (1996) on p. 248 and Tirole (1988) on p. 67.

$$\Leftrightarrow s^o = \frac{1}{2} n \frac{a^2}{b}.$$ [674] (87)

As the manufacturers of the new pharmaceutical product make a profit of zero under competitive production, it is straightforward to see that the total benefit to society under competitive production is equal to the consumer surplus given by (87).[675] Furthermore, (87) denotes the optimal consumer surplus as – under the assumption that a new product has already been invented – no deadweight loss occurs and the total benefit to society is maximized under competitive production.

4.2.1.1.1.2. Monopolized Production of a Single Invention

Consider now the opposite case in which a patent is granted to the original manufacturer of a new pharmaceutical product.[676] Standard economic theory tells us that the original manufacturer will be able to charge the monopoly price which maximizes monopoly profit given by

$$\pi = pq = \left(a - \frac{b}{n} q \right) q.$$ [677] (88)

Note that p in (88) is given by (85). By differentiating (88) Deardorff (1992, p. 37) obtains the following first-order condition

$$\frac{\partial \pi}{\partial q} = a - 2\frac{b}{n} q = 0$$

$$\Leftrightarrow q^m = \frac{1}{2} n \frac{a}{b}. \qquad (89)$$

By comparing (89) and (86) it becomes apparent that the monopoly output of the patented pharmaceutical product is just 50 percent of the competitive output without patent protection. Furthermore, by substituting q in (85) with q^m given by (89) Deardorff (1992, p. 37) obtains the monopoly price

$$p^m = \frac{a}{2}. \qquad (90)$$

By multiplying (89) and (90) – and keeping in mind the consumer surplus given by (87) – we obtain for the monopoly profit

---

674 See Deardorff (1992) on p. 36.
675 See Deardorff (1992) on p. 37.
676 See Deardorff (1992) on p. 37.
677 See Deardorff (1992) on p. 37.

$$\pi^m = \frac{1}{4} n \frac{a^2}{b} = \frac{1}{2} s^o . \text{[678]} \tag{91}$$

We can see from (91) and (87) that the monopoly profit is just half of the consumer surplus under competitive production. Nevertheless, it is important to keep in mind that the monopoly profit can be expressed in terms of the optimal consumer surplus as we will come back to this result at a later stage of the analysis.
However, let us now consider the consumer surplus under monopolized production.[679] Graphically, the consumer surplus under monopolized production is the area between the inverse market demand function given by (85) and the monopoly price given by (90).[680] Formally, taking into consideration the optimal consumer surplus given by (87), the consumer surplus under monopolized production is given by

$$s^m = \int_0^{q^m} a - \frac{b}{n} q - \frac{a}{2} \mathrm{d}q = \left[\frac{1}{2} aq - \frac{1}{2} \frac{b}{n} q^2 \right]_0^{\frac{1}{2} n \frac{a}{b}}$$

$$\Leftrightarrow s^m = \frac{1}{4} n \frac{a^2}{b} - \frac{1}{8} n \frac{a^2}{b}$$

$$\Leftrightarrow s^m = \frac{1}{8} n \frac{a^2}{b} = \frac{1}{4} s^o . \text{[681]} \tag{92}$$

Put differently, Deardorff (1992, p. 38) finds that the consumer surplus under monopolized production is just 25 percent of the consumer surplus under competitive production.
Notably, consumer surplus under monopolized production can be expressed in terms of the optimal consumer surplus. We will come back to this result at a later stage of the analysis. Nevertheless, by adding (91) and (92), Deardorff (1992, p. 38) obtains the benefit to society under monopolized production

$$b^m = \pi^m + s^m = \frac{3}{4} s^o . \tag{93}$$

Recall that the total benefit to society under competitive production is equal to the (optimal) consumer surplus, s^o, given by (87). Hence, the deadweight loss resulting from monopolized production is equal to 25 percent of the optimal consumer surplus.[682]
However, the advantage of patent protection is that the patent holder generates a monopoly profit that may compensate him for his innovative activities and thus provide him with an ex ante incentive to invest in R&D.[683] In order to explicitly explore the impact of patent protection on the level of invention that the original

678 See Deardorff (1992) on p. 37.
679 See Deardorff (1992) on p. 38.
680 See Tirole (1988) on p. 67. See also Menell and Scotchmer (2007) on p. 1492, Figure 1.
681 See Deardorff (1992) on p. 38ff.
682 See Deardorff (1992) on p. 38.
683 We will come back to this issue in our double marginalization model in section 5.2.4 in Chapter 5.

manufacturer will choose, Deardorff (1992, p. 38ff) extends his analysis and explicitly analyzes multiple inventions to be elaborated in the following section.

4.2.1.1.2. Multiple Inventions in a Single Country

Suppose now that multiple pharmaceutical products for various diseases are developed in a single country.

More specifically, Deardorff (1992, p. 38ff) considers a continuum of inventions in order to analyze explicitly the impact of patent protection on the incentive to invest in R&D. This approach enables the author to avoid the discontinuities that indivisible individual inventions imply and thus provides him with a convenient mathematical tool. Furthermore, according to Deardorff (1992, p. 38), this approach has only a negligible impact on the results of the analysis under the assumption that the number of inventions is very large.

Deardorff (1992, p. 38) then supposes that inventions are indexed by z with $z \geq 0$. Furthermore, the demand parameters are denoted by $a(z)$ and $b(z)$. The research costs are denoted by $R(z)$. Analogous to (87) in the previous section, $s^o(z)$ denotes the (optimal) consumer surplus under competitive production without patent protection. More specifically,

$$s^o(z) = \frac{n}{2}\frac{a(z)^2}{b(z)} \Big/ R(z).\text{[684]} \qquad (94)$$

Note, however, that $s^o(z)$ is now expressed per unit of $R(z)$. Moreover, Deardorff (1992, p. 39) orders the inventions so that

$$\bar{z} > \underline{z} \Rightarrow s^o(\bar{z}) \leq s^o(\underline{z}). \qquad (95)$$

Put differently, the invention that is indexed with $\underline{z}$ yields an (optimal) consumer surplus per dollar of research that is equal to or greater than that of the invention indexed with $\bar{z}$. Hence, z is a convenient mathematical tool to rank inventions by optimal consumer surplus per dollar of research.

For instance, suppose that, on the one hand, $\underline{z}$ represents pharmaceutical products for common diseases or conditions that are widespread in a single country, i.e. drugs against heart diseases or cancer.[685] On the other hand, let $\bar{z}$ represent pharmaceutical products for rare diseases or conditions such as Lou Gehrig's disease or the Tourette syndrome.[686]

Furthermore, the ordering of z by (optimal) consumer surplus under competitive production without patents given by (95) is of crucial importance for the following

684 See Deardorff (1992) on p. 38.
685 See Diwan and Rodrik (1991) on p. 28.
686 See Morris et al. (2005) on p. 15. See also Haffner (1999) on p. 565ff.

reason. As demand and costs are assumed to be linear, this ordering will also be the ordering of inventions by monopoly profit.[687] That is, if $\bar{z} > \underline{z}$ it follows that $\pi^m(\bar{z}) \leq \pi^m(\underline{z})$. More specifically, the inventions that will be made will always be those with the lowest indices. For instance, pharmaceutical manufacturers will generate a higher monopoly profit with medicines for common diseases than with medicines for rare diseases.[688]

However, Deardorff (1992, p. 39) measures the level of invention by the total costs of invention denoted by *I*. In particular, if all inventions from $z = 0$ to $z = \hat{z}$ are made, the total costs of inventions will be

$$I(\hat{z}) = \int_0^{\hat{z}} R(z)\,\mathrm{d}z.^{689} \tag{96}$$

More specifically, the marginal invention is the invention with the highest index, $\hat{z}$, that will just be made.

Nevertheless, the function given by (96) is monotonic and can – according to Deardorff (1992, p. 39) – be inverted as $\mathrm{d}I(\hat{z})/\mathrm{d}\hat{z} = R(\hat{z}) > 0$. Hence, the optimal consumer surplus of the marginal invention under competitive production, $s^o(\hat{z})$, can now be expressed in terms of the total cost of invention

$$s^o(I) = s^o\left[I^{-1}(I)\right].^{690} \tag{97}$$

By looking at (95) and (96), it becomes apparent that $s^o(I)$ (weakly monotonically) decreases if *I* increases. More specifically, $s^o(I)$ is the (optimal) consumer surplus under competitive production per unit of research cost, *R*, "obtainable from the marginal dollar of research, given that *I* dollars have already been spent on all inventions yielding a greater surplus per dollar".[691]

Taking into consideration (95), (96), (97) and the previous analysis of a single invention in a single country, it follows that the monopoly profit of the innovator, per unit of research cost, from the marginal invention, $\pi^m(I)$, and the consumer surplus, per unit of research cost, from the marginal invention, $s^m(I)$, under monopolistic production and multiple inventions can be found from $s^o(I)$.[692] In particular, it follows from (91) that

$$\pi^m(I) = \frac{1}{2}s^o(I). \tag{98}$$

687 See also (87) and (91).
688 We will come back to this issue in section 6.4.3 on orphan drugs in Chapter 6.
689 See Deardorff (1992) on p. 39.
690 See Deardorff (1992) on p. 39.
691 See Deardorff (1992) on p. 39.
692 See Deardorff (1992) on p. 39.

Furthermore, it follows from (92) that

$$s^m(I) = \frac{1}{4} s^o(I).^{693} \tag{99}$$

As already mentioned, Deardorff (1992) assumes that the number of inventions is large so that (97), (98) and (99) can be approximated as continuous.
Furthermore, Deardorff (1992) assumes that these functions are linear. In particular, the linear (optimal) consumer surplus of the marginal invention under competitive production is represented by

$$s^o(I) = n(f - gI).^{694} \tag{100}$$

Deardorff (1992) assumes that *f* and *g* are positive numbers. More specifically, *g* is the slope parameter indicating how fast the returns to invention diminish.[695] Furthermore, the number of consumers in the single country is denoted by *n*. Consequently, $f - gI$ represents the (optimal) consumer surplus per unit of research cost per consumer.[696]
Furthermore, let $z = 0$ be the highest priority invention. By definition, there is no other invention that yields a greater optimal consumer surplus per dollar of research (and monopoly profit per dollar of research). Then follows from the definition of $s^o(I)$ mentioned above that, for $z = 0$, $I = 0$ have already been spent on other inventions. Taking into account (87) and the optimal consumer surplus, per unit of research cost, per consumer, $f - gI$, it then becomes apparent that $f = a(z)^2 / 2b(z)$ for the highest priority invention $z = 0$.
However, let us now have a look at the analysis of the levels of invention, profit, consumer surplus, and welfare under competitive, optimal and monopolized invention in a single country.

4.2.1.1.2.1. Competitive Invention in a Single Country

Under competitive invention without patent protection, potential innovators cannot recover their cost of research because they do not generate any profit. Consequently, total consumer surplus, monopoly profit and total costs of invention will be zero.[697] More specifically,

---

693 See Deardorff (1992) on p. 39.
694 See Deardorff (1992) on p. 39.
695 See also Grabowski et al. (2002) for an analysis of the returns to R&D for drugs marketed in the U.S. from 1990 to 1994.
696 See Deardorff (1992) on p. 39.
697 For instance, see Mansfield (1986) for an empirical analysis of patents and innovation. Mansfield (1986) suggests that the pharmaceutical sector relies heavily on patents. More specifically, the author analyzes information obtained from a random sample of U.S. firms through interviews, correspondence, and detailed questionnaires, and finds that 65 percent of all marketed pharmaceutical products, from 1981-1983, would not have been marketed if patent protection would not have been available (Mansfield (1986) on p. 175, Table 1). See also Schmookler (1966) for an early analysis of

$$I^c = S^c = \Pi^c = 0.$$[698] (101)

Consequently, the net gain to society from competitive invention without patent protection is zero. It is, however, noteworthy that an inventor of a nonpatentable invention could still establish trade secret protection in order to prevent competitors from using or duplicating the invention.[699] Hence, one may argue that the level of invention is likely to be higher than zero even if inventions may not be patentable. Although this idea is beyond the scope of the Deardorff (1992) paper, it is certainly a very interesting idea for further research.[700]

Nevertheless, as a benchmark it is interesting to know what would be the optimal level of invention as well as the consumer surplus and the net gain to society under optimal invention.

Therefore, we will consider the optimal invention in the following section. Then follows the analysis of equilibrium levels of invention, consumer surplus, and net gain to society under monopolized invention.

4.2.1.1.2.2. Optimal Invention in a Single Country

According to Deardorff (1992, p. 40), the optimal level of invention, I^o, includes all inventions that generate an optimal consumer surplus that exceeds their cost of research.[701]

Put differently, I^o includes all inventions whose (optimal) consumer surplus per dollar of research exceeds one.[702] In order to calculate the optimal invention in a single country, note that the inverse of the function $s^o(I) = n(f - gI)$ is given by $s^{o\,-1}(I) = (nf - I)/ng$. In order to see that this is true recall that $s^o(s^{o\,-1}(I)) = n(f - g(nf - I)/ng) \Leftrightarrow s^o(s^{o\,-1}(I)) = I$. It then follows from (100) and from the definition of the inverse function mentioned above that

$$I^o = s^{o-1}(1) = \frac{nf - 1}{ng}.$$[703] (102)

the impact of market size on innovation. See also Scott Morton (1999), Grabowski and Vernon (2000b), and Acemoglu and Linn (2004).

698 See Deardorff (1992) on p. 40.

699 For instance, see Friedman et al. (1991) for an early approach to the economics of trade secret law.

700 We thank Hans-Bernd Schäfer for his comments in this respect.

701 See also Mansfield et al. (1977) and Nadiri (1993). More specifically, Mansfield et al. (1977) and Nadiri (1993) estimate that the social returns to innovations are typically twice as large as the private returns to innovations. See also Kremer and Glennerster (2004) on p. 40, Bernstein and Nadiri (1988), Bernstein and Nadiri (1989), and Lichtenberg (1992).

702 See Deardorff (1992) on p. 40.

703 Alternatively, we obtain (102) by setting $s(I^o) = n(f - gI^o) = 1$ and reformulating until we have $ngI^o = nf - 1 \Leftrightarrow I^o = (nf - 1)/ng$. See also Deardorff (1992) on p. 40.

Of course, the optimal consumer surplus can only be achieved if the price of the product is the price under perfect competition. Therefore, the monopoly profit in case of an optimal level of invention in a single country must be zero. Formally,

$$\Pi^o = 0.^{704} \tag{103}$$

Because of the assumed continuity of $s^o(I)$, the total consumer surplus, S^o, can now be obtained by integration. In particular, it is given by

$$S^o = \int_0^{I^o} s^o(I)\,\mathrm{d}I = \int_0^{(nf-1)/ng} n(f-gI)\,\mathrm{d}I$$

$$\Leftrightarrow S^o = \left[nfI - \frac{1}{2}ngI^2 \right]_0^{(nf-1)/ng}$$

$$\Leftrightarrow S^o = \frac{(nf)^2-1}{2ng}.^{705} \tag{104}$$

We can see from (104) that the total (optimal) consumer surplus decreases if g increases. More specifically, the total optimal consumer surplus decreases if the returns to invention diminish at a faster rate. This is due to the fact that – ceteris paribus – the level of invention I^o, given by (102), decreases if the returns to invention diminish at a faster rate.

Nevertheless, Deardorff (1992, p. 40) calculates the net gain to society from the optimal level of invention, N^o, which is simply the total consumer surplus (plus zero monopoly profit) minus the total cost of research. More specifically, taking into account (102), (103) and (104), N^o is given by

$$N^o = S^o + \Pi^o - I^o = \frac{(nf)^2-1}{2ng} - \frac{nf-1}{ng} = \frac{(nf)^2-1-2nf+2}{2ng}$$

$$\Leftrightarrow N^o = \frac{(nf-1)^2}{2ng}.^{706} \tag{105}$$

Let us now consider the case of monopolized invention in a single country.

4.2.1.1.2.3. Monopolized Invention in a Single Country

Under the assumption that innovating firms choose the monopoly output when their product is patented, Deardorff (1992, p. 40ff) first analyzes the level of invention under monopolistic conditions, I^m. Intuitively, inventors are willing to make all

704 See Deardorff (1992) on p. 40.
705 See Deardorff (1992) on p. 40.
706 See Deardorff (1992) on p. 40.

inventions that generate a monopoly profit that is higher than their research cost.[707] Put differently, they are willing to make all inventions whose monopoly profit per dollar of research is equal to or greater than one.

Consequently, the level of invention under monopolistic conditions, I^m, is the level for which the monopoly profit from the marginal invention is equal to the research cost of the marginal invention.[708] Put differently, I^m is the level of invention for which the monopoly profit of the innovator, per unit of research cost, from the marginal invention is equal to one, that is $\pi^m(I^m)=1$.

Taking into consideration that $2\pi^m(I)=s^o(I)$ from (98) and that $s^o(I^m)=2$ for $\pi^m(I^m)=1$, Deardorff (1992, p. 40) obtains

$$I^m = s^{m\,-1}(1) = s^{o\,-1}(2) = \frac{nf-2}{ng}. \tag{106}$$

By looking at (102) and (106), it becomes apparent that $I^o > I^m$ as $2>1$. Put differently, patent protection fails to stimulate all worthwhile inventions.[709]

However, taking into consideration (100), we have to integrate the profit function given by (98) in order to calculate the monopoly profit. More specifically, the monopoly profit is given by

$$\Pi^m = \int_0^{I^m} \frac{1}{2} s^o(I)\mathrm{d}I = \int_0^{(nf-2)/ng} \frac{1}{2} n(f-gI)\mathrm{d}I$$

$$\Leftrightarrow \Pi^m = \left[\frac{1}{2}nfI - \frac{1}{4}ngI^2\right]_0^{(nf-2)/ng}$$

$$\Leftrightarrow \Pi^m = \frac{(nf)^2-4}{4ng}.^{710} \tag{107}$$

Furthermore, Deardorff (1992, p. 41) obtains the level of consumer surplus by integrating (99)

$$S^m = \int_0^{I^m} \frac{1}{4} s^o(I)\mathrm{d}I = \int_0^{(nf-2)/ng} \frac{1}{4} n(f-gI)\mathrm{d}I = \frac{1}{4}\left(\frac{nf(nf-2)}{ng} - \frac{1}{2}\frac{ng(nf-2)^2}{n^2g^2}\right)$$

$$\Leftrightarrow S^m = \frac{nf-2}{8ng}(2nf-(nf-2))$$

$$\Leftrightarrow S^m = \frac{(nf)^2-4}{8ng}. \tag{108}$$

707 We will come back to this issue in our analysis of parallel imports in section 5.2.4 in Chapter 5. More specifically, we will analyze the negative impact of parallel trade on the profit of a monopolistic manufacturer of pharmaceuticals.

708 See Deardorff (1992) on p. 40.

709 See also Lévêque and Ménière (2004) on p. 20ff.

710 See Deardorff (1992) on p. 40.

By comparing (107) and (108), it becomes apparent that – as indicated by (98) and (99) – the consumer surplus under monopolized production, S^m, is one half of the monopoly profit, Π^m. Finally, the net gain to society from monopolized invention is the sum of (107) and (108) minus (106). More specifically, the net gain to society under patent protection is given by

$$N^m = S^m + \Pi^m - I^m = \frac{(nf)^2 - 4}{8ng} + \frac{(nf)^2 - 4}{4ng} - \frac{nf - 2}{ng}$$

$$\Leftrightarrow N^m = \frac{(nf)^2 - 4 + 2(nf)^2 - 8 - 8nf + 16}{8ng}$$

$$\Leftrightarrow N^m = \frac{(nf - 2)(3nf - 2)}{8ng}. \quad (109)$$

[711]

The deadweight loss associated with monopolized invention is given by the difference between the net gain to society from the optimal level of invention given by (105) and the net gain to society from invention under patent protection given by (109).[712] More specifically, according to Deardorff (1992, p. 42), the deadweight loss from patent rights, L^m, is given by

$$L^m = N^o - N^m = \frac{(nf - 1)^2}{2ng} - \frac{(nf - 2)(3nf - 2)}{8ng}$$

$$\Leftrightarrow L^m = \frac{4(nf)^2 - 8nf + 4 - 3(nf)^2 + 8nf - 4}{8ng}$$

$$\Leftrightarrow L^m = \frac{nf^2}{8g}. \quad (110)$$

By looking at (101), (109) and (110) it becomes apparent that the trade-off between, on the one hand, permitting the innovating firms to generate monopoly profits and thus stimulating R&D and, on the other hand, the deadweight loss resulting from monopoly pricing justifies the use of patent protection as long as the net gain to society under patent protection given by (109) is positive.

However, as already mentioned above, patent protection is not a perfect method of stimulating R&D for two reasons: First, patents fail to stimulate all worthwhile inventions as $I^o > I^m$. Second, patents lead to monopoly pricing and a deadweight loss to society as given by (110).

711 See Deardorff (1992) on p. 41.

712 See Deardorff (1992) on p. 42.

4.2.1.2. Multiple Inventions in an Open Economy with two Countries

This section addresses the question as to how the extension of patent protection from one country to another country influences the incentives of a manufacturer of pharmaceuticals to innovate.[713]

Nevertheless, the analysis of the closed economy case in the previous sections is of crucial importance in order to be able to understand the two-country case.

In particular, Deardorff (1992, p. 42ff) convincingly shows that the worldwide extension of patent protection makes consumers and producers in the inventing country better off whereas the impact on welfare in the other country – being a country that does not have an innovating domestic industry – is likely to be negative. More specifically, all inventions are made by innovating firms in country *A*.[714]

However, Deardorff (1992, p. 42) assumes that, once the new product has been invented, the production process is known. Furthermore, once the production process is known the product can be manufactured in country *A* as well as in country *B* unless it is legally prohibited by patent rights. Deardorff (1992, p. 42) assumes that consumers in country *A* and country *B* have identical demand functions. Furthermore, the world's population is given by *n*. In particular,

$$n = n^A + n^B \tag{111}$$

where the population in country *A* is denoted by n^A and the population in country *B* is denoted by n^B. Furthermore,

$$\xi = \frac{n^A}{n} \tag{112}$$

denotes the fraction of the worldwide population that lives in country *A*.[715] For instance, ξ tends toward zero if country *A* is very small in terms of population relative to the rest of the world – the rest of the world being country *B*.[716]

However, an alternative interpretation of ξ could be the following. Let n^A denote the number of individuals living in country *A* that suffer from a particular disease. Furthermore, let n^B denote the number of individuals living in country *B* that suffer from the same disease. Put differently, one could interpret ξ as a measure for country *A*'s share of the global burden of a specific disease.[717] As to this alternative interpretation, if ξ tends toward zero, this would mean that the vast majority of patients live in country *B*. We will come back to this alternative interpretation later on. Nevertheless, we can derive from (112) that $1-\xi = n^B / n$ and thus $n^B = (1-\xi)n$. The inverse market demand function in country *J* is given by

---

713 See also Chaudhuri et al. (2006) on p. 1478, footnote 1 and Deardorff (1992) on p. 42ff.

714 See Deardorff (1992) on p. 42.

715 See Deardorff (1992) on p. 42.

716 For instance, see Grinols and Lin (2006) on p. 207.

717 For instance, see Murray and Lopez (1996). See also World Health Organization (2003c) on p. 160.

$$p^J = a - (b / n^J) q^J, \quad J = A,B.$$ [718] (113)

Taking into account (87) and noting that marginal cost of production are assumed to be zero in both countries, the optimal consumer surplus in country *J* is given by

$$s^{oJ} = \frac{1}{2} n^J \frac{a^2}{b} = n^J \tilde{s}.$$ [719] (114)

In (114), the optimal consumer surplus per capita is given by $\tilde{s}$. Similar to (95) and (100), Deardorff (1992, p. 43) orders inventions by decreasing values of the optimal per capita consumer surplus per dollar of research, $\tilde{s} / R$.
Furthermore, these values can – by assumption – be expressed as a linear function of the level of invention, *I*. Hence, the optimal consumer surplus, per capita and per dollar of research, *R*, given that *I* dollars have already been invested in the development of all goods that generate a per capita consumer surplus per dollar of research that is greater than or equal to $\tilde{s} / R$ is

$$\tilde{s}(I) = f - gI.$$ [720] (115)

Note that – analogous to the analysis of multiple inventions in a single country – $\tilde{s}(I)$ is of crucial importance for the analysis of multiple inventions in two countries as consumer surplus and monopoly profits can be expressed in terms of $\tilde{s}(I)$.
For instance, by multiplying (115) by population in country *J*, Deardorff (1992, p. 43) obtains the total optimal consumer surplus per dollar of research, *R*, in country *J* from the marginal invention, at the level of invention *I*,

$$s^{oJ} = n^J (f - gI), \quad J = A,B. \tag{116}$$

Recall from (98) that the monopoly profit, per unit of research cost, from the marginal invention, can be derived from the optimal consumer surplus, per unit of research, from the marginal invention. Consequently, keeping in mind that demand is linear, the monopoly profit in country *J* is

$$\pi^J (I) = \frac{1}{2} s^{oJ} (I) = \frac{1}{2} n^J (f - gI), \quad J = A,B.$$ [721] (117)

More specifically, (117) denotes the monopoly profit, per dollar of research, that is generated in country *J* when the product of the marginal invention is sold at the monopoly price. Furthermore, the consumer surplus per dollar of research from the marginal invention if consumers in country *J* pay the monopoly price is given by

---

718 See Deardorff (1992) on p. 42.
719 See Deardorff (1992) on p. 42.
720 See Deardorff (1992) on p. 43.
721 See Deardorff (1992) on p. 43.

$$s^{mJ}(I)=\frac{1}{4}s^{oJ}(I)=\frac{1}{4}n^{J}(f-gI),\quad J=A,B.\text{[722]} \tag{118}$$

Note that (118) follows from (92) and (99), respectively.
However, Deardorff (1992, p. 43ff) now calculates monopoly profit and total consumer surplus in two different cases of patent protection.
In the first case of restricted patent protection, patent protection is only provided in country A. In the second case, patent protection is provided in country A and extended to country B.
In order to calculate monopoly profit and total consumer surplus in both cases, the mathematical procedure is the following. First, (117) is used to calculate the level of invention, I, that will take place. Second, the level of total consumer surplus is found by integrating the relevant consumer surplus function up to the level of invention calculated in the first step. Third, monopoly profits are found by integrating the relevant profit functions up to the level of invention calculated in the first step.

4.2.1.2.1. Case 1: Restricted Patent Protection in an Open Economy with two Countries

As already mentioned before, patent protection is only provided in country A in this case. For instance, suppose that country A is an industrialized country that affords strong patent protection, i.e. the U.S. or Japan. One may also think of country A as a group of industrialized countries in the Northern Hemisphere and of country B as a group of developing countries in the Southern Hemisphere.
Nevertheless, monopoly profits can only be generated in country A but not in country B. Therefore, the level of invention under restricted patent protection, I^r, is the level for which monopoly profit per dollar of research, R, from the marginal invention is equal to one. This is, of course, the same rationale as in the case of monopolized inventions in a single country that we already know from (106). Formally, invention will take place up to the level I^r for which

$$\pi^{A}(I^{r})=1.\text{[723]} \tag{119}$$

Using (117) and knowing from (112) that $n^{A}=n\xi$, it follows from (119) that

$$\pi^{A}(I^{r})=\frac{1}{2}\xi n(f-gI^{r})=1$$
$$\Leftrightarrow \xi n(f-gI^{r})=2$$
$$\Leftrightarrow I^{r}=\frac{\xi nf-2}{\xi ng}.\text{[724]} \tag{120}$$

722 See Deardorff (1992) on p. 43.
723 See Deardorff (1992) on p. 43.
724 See Deardorff (1992) on p. 43.

As already mentioned before, total consumer surplus in country A is now calculated by integrating (118) up to the level given by (120) and taking into consideration from (112) that $n^A = \xi n$

$$S^{rA} = \int_0^{I^r} \frac{1}{4} n^A (f - gI) \mathrm{d} I = \left[\frac{1}{4} \xi n f I - \frac{1}{8} \xi n g I^2 \right]_0^{(\xi nf - 2)/\xi ng}$$

$$\Leftrightarrow S^{rA} = \frac{1}{4} \xi n f \frac{\xi n f - 2}{\xi n g} - \frac{1}{8} \xi n g \frac{(\xi n f - 2)^2}{\xi^2 n^2 g^2}$$

$$\Leftrightarrow S^{rA} = \frac{\xi^2 n^2 f^2 - 4}{8 \xi n g}. \quad (121)$$

[725]

Furthermore, recall from (117) and (118) that the monopoly profit per dollar of research is just twice the consumer surplus per dollar of research when consumers in country A pay the monopoly price.[726]

Moreover, as already mentioned before, monopoly profits are only generated in country A in the case of restricted patent protection. Consequently, total monopoly profit Π^r – defined as the sum of monopoly profits generated in country A and country B – is just equal to Π^{rA}. By taking into consideration (121), it is now straightforward to see that

$$\Pi^r = \Pi^{rA} = 2 S^{rA} = \frac{\xi^2 n^2 f^2 - 4}{4 \xi n g}. \quad (122)$$

[727]

As already mentioned, one may also interpret ξ as a measure for country A's share of the global burden of a specific disease.

Under this interpretation, we can see from (122) that there is a lower threshold for ξ, $\xi < 2/nf$, for which the total monopoly profit Π^r would be negative.[728]

In other words, if $\xi < 2/nf$, there would be no incentives for the innovating firms to invest in R&D for new medicinal products in the case of restricted patent protection.

However, in order to calculate the level of total consumer surplus in country B under restricted patent protection, S^{rB}, recall that – as patent protection is absent in country B – all invented goods are competitively supplied in country B.[729] More specifically, total consumer surplus in country B under restricted patent protection is obtained by integrating (116) up to the level given by (120) and by taking into consideration from (112) that $n^B = (1 - \xi) n$

725 See Deardorff (1992) on p. 43.

726 See Deardorff (1992) on p. 43.

727 See Deardorff (1992) on p. 43.

728 Note that the total monopoly profit given by (122) is negative if $\xi^2 n^2 f^2 < 4 \Leftrightarrow \xi < 2/nf$.

729 See Deardorff (1992) on p. 44.

$$S^{rB} = \int_0^{I^r} n^B(f - gI)\,\mathrm{d}I = \left[(1-\xi)nfI - \frac{1}{2}(1-\xi)ngI^2\right]_0^{(\xi nf-2)/\xi ng}$$

$$\Leftrightarrow S^{rB} = (1-\xi)nf\left(\frac{\xi nf - 2}{\xi ng}\right) - \frac{1}{2}(1-\xi)ng\frac{(\xi nf-2)^2}{\xi^2 n^2 g^2}$$

$$\Leftrightarrow S^{rB} = \frac{(1-\xi)(\xi^2 n^2 f^2 - 4)}{2\xi^2 ng}.^{730} \qquad (123)$$

It is now possible to calculate the net gain to all residents in country *A* and country *B*, respectively. In particular, the net gain to all residents in country *A* under restricted patent protection, N^{rA}, is defined as the sum of total consumer surplus in country *A* given by (121) plus the monopoly profits generated by the monopoly inventors from country *A* given by (122) minus the cost of invention given by (120).[731] Hence,

$$N^{rA} = S^{rA} + \Pi^r - I^r = \frac{\xi^2 n^2 f^2 - 4}{8\xi ng} + \frac{\xi^2 n^2 f^2 - 4}{4\xi ng} - \frac{\xi nf - 2}{\xi ng}$$

$$\Leftrightarrow N^{rA} = \frac{\xi^2 n^2 f^2 - 4 + 2\xi^2 n^2 f^2 - 8 - 8\xi nf + 16}{8\xi ng}$$

$$\Leftrightarrow N^{rA} = \frac{(\xi nf - 2)(3\xi nf - 2)}{8\xi ng}. \qquad (124)$$

As already mentioned before, new products are only invented by innovating firms in country *A*. Hence, the net gain to residents in country *B* under restricted patent protection is equal to the consumer surplus generated in country *B* given by (123). Put differently, $N^{rB} = S^{rB}$. Finally, we can now calculate the global net gain under restricted patent protection, N^{rW}, which is defined as the sum of the net gain to all residents in country *A* and the net gain to all residents in country *B*.[732] Hence,

$$N^{rW} = N^{rA} + N^{rB} = \frac{(\xi nf - 2)(3\xi nf - 2)}{8\xi ng} + \frac{(1-\xi)(\xi^2 n^2 f^2 - 4)}{2\xi^2 ng}$$

$$\Leftrightarrow N^{rW} = \frac{\xi(\xi nf - 2)(3\xi nf - 2) + 4(1-\xi)(\xi^2 n^2 f^2 - 4)}{8\xi^2 ng}$$

$$\Leftrightarrow N^{rW} = \frac{(\xi nf - 2)\left[\xi(3\xi nf - 2) + 4(1-\xi)(\xi nf + 2)\right]}{8\xi^2 ng}. \qquad (125)$$

Arguably, the case of restricted patent protection in an open economy with two countries *A* and *B* – with country *A* being an industrialized country where patent protection is afforded and all innovations take place and country *B* being a developing country where patent protection is not afforded – may describe the situation prior to the ratification and implementation of the TRIPS Agreement.

730 See Deardorff (1992) on p. 44.
731 See Deardorff (1992) on p. 44.
732 See Deardorff (1992) on p. 44.

Before we proceed to the analysis of extended patent protection in an open economy with two countries let us first summarize the findings of the previous sections.

Single invention in a single country
First, under the assumption that the single invention has already been developed, the monopoly output associated with patent protection is just 50 percent of the competitive output without patent protection.
Second, monopolistic production (patent protection) is detrimental to consumers as the consumer surplus under monopolistic production is just 25 percent of the consumer surplus under competitive production.
Third, monopolistic production (patent protection) is detrimental to national welfare as the total benefit to society under monopolistic production is just 75 percent of the total benefit to society under competitive production.

Multiple inventions in a single country
In contrast to the case of a single invention, a continuum of inventions is now considered in order to analyze explicitly the impact of patent protection on R&D incentives. The analysis leads to the following results.
First, patent protection fails to stimulate all worthwhile inventions as the level of invention under monopolistic conditions is lower than the optimal level of invention. The optimal level of invention includes all (worthwhile) inventions that generate a consumer surplus that exceeds their cost of research.
Second, patents lead to a deadweight loss to society associated with monopoly pricing.
Third, the trade-off between higher R&D incentives associated with monopoly rents and the deadweight loss due to monopoly pricing justifies the use of patent protection as along as the net gain to society under patent protection is positive.

Multiple inventions under restricted patent protection in an open economy with two countries
First, in this two-country case, monopoly profits can only be generated in the industrialized country A in the Northern Hemisphere but not in the developing country B in the Southern Hemisphere as patent protection is restricted to country A.
Second, the countries can be characterized by their share of the global burden of a specific disease.
Third, there is a certain threshold for country A's share of the global burden for which the total monopoly profit would be negative. In other words, if country A's share of the global burden of a specific disease is lower than this threshold pharmaceutical firms will not have any incentive to invest in R&D for medicines for this disease in the case of restricted patent protection.
However, the results regarding monopoly profits, consumer surplus, national net gains as well as global net gains under restricted patent protection provide us with a benchmark for the analysis of extended patent protection to be elaborated in the following section.
Following Deardorff (1992, p. 44ff), we first derive monopoly profits, consumer surplus and national as well as international net gains when patent protection is extended to country B. Then, we will explore the question as to which patent regime is beneficial from a national as well as a global welfare perspective.

4.2.1.2.2. Case 2: Extended Patent Protection in an Open Economy with two Countries

As already mentioned above, in this case patent protection is afforded in country A and extended to country B.[733] One may argue that the case of extended patent protection in an open economy with two countries describes the situation subsequent to the ratification and implementation of the TRIPS Agreement.
Nevertheless, as soon as a new product is patented in country A the inventor will be able to generate monopoly profits in country A as well as in country B. Of course, potential inventors will anticipate this and will make inventions up to the level of invention, I^e, that equates total profits – from the marginal invention and generated in country A and country B – to its cost of research.[734] In other words, I^e is the level of invention for which the total monopoly profit per dollar of research from the marginal invention is equal to one. In particular,

$$\pi^A(I^e)+\pi^B(I^e)=1.^{735} \tag{126}$$

We know from (117) that $\pi^A(I)=\left(n^A(f-gI)\right)/2$ and $\pi^B(I)=\left(n^B(f-gI)\right)/2$. More specifically, Deardorff (1992, p. 44) obtains from (126)

$$\frac{1}{2}n^A(f-gI^e)+\frac{1}{2}n^B(f-gI^e)=1$$
$$\Leftrightarrow \frac{1}{2}n(f-gI^e)=1$$
$$\Leftrightarrow I^e=\frac{nf-2}{ng}. \tag{127}$$

By looking at (120) and (127) it becomes apparent that $I^e \geq I^r$ as $\xi \leq 1$.[736] Analogous to the analysis of restricted patent protection in the previous section, total consumer surplus in country A under extended patent protection, S^{eA}, is now calculated by integrating (118) up to the level I^e given by (127) and taking into consideration from (112) that $n^A=\xi n$. Thus,

$$S^{eA}=\int_0^{I^e}\frac{1}{4}n^A(f-gI)\,\mathrm{d}I=\left[\frac{1}{4}\xi nfI-\frac{1}{8}\xi ngI^2\right]_0^{(nf-2)/ng}$$
$$\Leftrightarrow S^{eA}=\frac{1}{4}\xi nf\frac{(nf-2)}{ng}-\frac{1}{8}\xi ng\frac{(nf-2)^2}{n^2g^2}$$

733 For instance, see Grinols and Lin (2006) on p. 207. See also Deardorff (1992) on p. 44ff.
734 See Deardorff (1992) on p. 44.
735 See Deardorff (1992) on p. 44.
736 More specifically, $(nf-2)/ng \geq (\xi nf-2)/\xi ng \Leftrightarrow \xi nf-2\xi \geq \xi nf-2$ as $\xi \leq 1$.

$$\Leftrightarrow S^{eA} = \frac{\xi(n^2 f^2 - 4)}{8ng}.^{737} \tag{128}$$

Furthermore, the monopoly profit under extended patent protection generated in country *A*, Π^{eA}, can be found by integrating (117) up to the level I^e given by (127) and taking into consideration that $n^A = \xi n$. Therefore,

$$\Pi^{eA} = \int_0^{I^e} \frac{1}{2} n^A (f - gI)\,\mathrm{d}I = \left[\frac{1}{2}\xi nfI - \frac{1}{4}\xi ngI^2\right]_0^{(nf-2)/ng}$$

$$\Leftrightarrow \Pi^{eA} = \frac{1}{2}\xi nf \frac{(nf-2)}{ng} - \frac{1}{4}\xi ng \frac{(nf-2)^2}{n^2 g^2}$$

$$\Leftrightarrow \Pi^{eA} = \frac{\xi(n^2 f^2 - 4)}{4ng}.^{738} \tag{129}$$

However, as already mentioned before, inventors also generate monopoly profits in country *B* under extended patent protection.[739] Thus, the monopoly profit under extended patent protection generated in country *A*, Π^{eA}, is only a fraction of total profits.

In particular, the monopoly profit under extended patent protection generated in country *B*, Π^{eB}, can be found by integrating (117) up to the level I^e given by (127) and taking into consideration that $n^B = (1-\xi)n$. Therefore,

$$\Pi^{eB} = \int_0^{I^e} \frac{1}{2} n^B (f - gI)\,\mathrm{d}I = \left[\frac{1}{2}(1-\xi)nfI - \frac{1}{4}(1-\xi)ngI^2\right]_0^{(nf-2)/ng}$$

$$\Leftrightarrow \Pi^{eB} = \frac{1}{2}(1-\xi)nf \frac{(nf-2)}{ng} - \frac{1}{4}(1-\xi)ng \frac{(nf-2)^2}{n^2 g^2}$$

$$\Leftrightarrow \Pi^{eB} = \frac{(1-\xi)(n^2 f^2 - 4)}{4ng}.^{740} \tag{130}$$

Furthermore, Deardorff (1992, p. 45) calculates the total consumer surplus in country *B* under extended patent protection, S^{eB}, by integrating (118) up to the level I^e. Alternatively, it is straightforward to see from (117) and (118) that the consumer surplus in country *B* in this case is just 50 percent of the monopoly profit generated in country *B*. More specifically, taking into account (130), Deardorff (1992, p. 45) finds that

$$S^{eB} = \int_0^{I^e} \frac{1}{4} n^B (f - gI)\,\mathrm{d}I = \frac{1}{2}\Pi^{eB}$$

737 See Deardorff (1992) on p. 44.
738 See Deardorff (1992) on p. 44.
739 See Deardorff (1992) on p. 45.
740 See Deardorff (1992) on p. 45.

$$\Leftrightarrow S^{eB} = \frac{(1-\xi)(n^2 f^2 - 4)}{8ng}. \tag{131}$$

Furthermore, total monopoly profit under extended patent protection, Π^e, is the sum of the monopoly profit generated in country A given by (129) and the monopoly profit generated in country B given by (130):

$$\Pi^e = \Pi^{eA} + \Pi^{eB} = \frac{\xi(n^2 f^2 - 4)}{4ng} + \frac{(1-\xi)(n^2 f^2 - 4)}{4ng}$$

$$\Leftrightarrow \Pi^e = \frac{n^2 f^2 - 4}{4ng}.^{741} \tag{132}$$

The net gain to residents in country A under extended patent protection, N^{eA}, is the sum of total consumer surplus given by (128) and total monopoly profit given (132) minus the total cost of invention given by (127). Therefore, Deardorff (1992, p. 46) finds

$$N^{eA} = S^{eA} + \Pi^e - I^e = \frac{\xi(n^2 f^2 - 4)}{8ng} + \frac{2(n^2 f^2 - 4)}{8ng} - \frac{8(nf - 2)}{8ng}$$

$$N^{eA} = \frac{nf - 2}{8ng}\left(\xi(nf + 2) + 2(nf + 2) - 8\right)$$

$$\Leftrightarrow N^{eA} = \frac{nf - 2}{8ng}\left((2 + \xi)(nf + 2) - 8\right). \tag{133}$$

We can see from (133) that the net gain to residents in country A under extended patent protection increases if ξ increases.
Nevertheless, the net gain to residents in country B under extended patent protection, N^{eB}, is equal to the total consumer surplus given by (131):

$$N^{eB} = S^{eB}.^{742} \tag{134}$$

Finally, we can now obtain the net benefit to the world under extended patent protection, N^{eW}, from (133) and (134), respectively:

$$N^{eW} = N^{eA} + N^{eB} = \frac{nf - 2}{8ng}\left((2 + \xi)(nf + 2) - 8\right) + \frac{(1-\xi)(n^2 f^2 - 4)}{8ng}$$

$$\Leftrightarrow N^{eW} = \frac{nf - 2}{8ng}\left((2 + \xi)(nf + 2) - 8 + (1-\xi)(nf + 2)\right)$$

$$\Leftrightarrow N^{eW} = \frac{(nf - 2)(3nf - 2)}{8ng}.^{743} \tag{135}$$

---

741 See Deardorff (1992) on p. 45.
742 See Deardorff (1992) on p. 46.
743 See Deardorff (1992) on p. 46.

As already mentioned above, we can now explore the question as to which regime of patent protection is beneficial from a national as well as a global point of view.

4.2.1.2.3. Comparison of Restricted and Extended Patent Protection in an Open Economy with two Countries

4.2.1.2.3.1. Extended Patent Protection and Welfare in Country A

Intuitively, extending patent protection to country B makes firms in country A better off for the following reason: Firms located in country A generate monopoly profits not only in their domestic market but also in country B. In other words, total monopoly profits under extended patent protection are higher than total monopoly profits under restricted patent protection.

In particular, Deardorff (1992, p. 46) shows graphically that this intuition is correct. However, we will also mathematically show in the following that $\Pi^e \geq \Pi^r$ as – by assumption – $\xi \leq 1$. Taking into account (132) and (122), we will show that

$$\Pi^e = \frac{n^2 f^2 - 4}{4ng} \geq \Pi^r = \frac{\xi^2 n^2 f^2 - 4}{4\xi ng}$$
$$\Leftrightarrow \xi n^2 f^2 - 4\xi \geq \xi^2 n^2 f^2 - 4$$
$$\Leftrightarrow \xi n^2 f^2 + 4 \geq \xi^2 n^2 f^2 + 4\xi, \tag{136}$$

which is true as – by assumption – $\xi \leq 1$. More specifically, the first (second) term on the left-hand side of (136) is greater than or equal to the first (second) term on the right-hand side of (136). However, consumers in country A also benefit from extending patent protection to country B for the following reason. In both cases, consumers in country A only get the reduced consumer surplus of the monopoly case. However, they benefit from the additional goods that are invented when patent protection is extended to country B. Deardorff (1992, p. 46) only shows graphically that extending patent protection to country B makes consumers in country A better off.

Nevertheless, we will also formally show in the following that $S^{eA} \geq S^{rA}$ as $\xi \leq 1$. Taking into consideration (128) and (121) we have

$$S^{eA} = \frac{\xi(n^2 f^2 - 4)}{8ng} \geq S^{rA} = \frac{\xi^2 n^2 f^2 - 4}{8\xi ng}$$
$$\Leftrightarrow \xi^2 n^2 f^2 - 4\xi^2 \geq \xi^2 n^2 f^2 - 4$$
$$\Leftrightarrow \xi \leq 1. \tag{137}$$

It is now straightforward to see from (137) and (136) that residents in country A unambiguously benefit from extending patent protection to county B as it increases both consumer surplus and monopoly profits generated in country A.[744]
However, Deardorff (1992, p. 46ff) formally derives the net gains to residents in country A and country B from extending patent protection to country B. In particular, the net gain to residents in country A, Δ^A, is the difference between the net gain to residents in country A under extended patent protection, N^{eA}, given by (133), and the net gain to all residents in country A under restricted patent protection, N^{rA}, given by (124):

$$\Delta^A = N^{eA} - N^{rA} = \frac{nf-2}{8ng}\big((2+\xi)(nf+2)-8\big) - \frac{(\xi nf-2)(3\xi nf-2)}{8\xi ng}$$

$$\Leftrightarrow \Delta^A = \frac{1}{8\xi ng}\Big[(\xi nf-2\xi)\big((2+\xi)(nf+2)-8\big)-(\xi nf-2)(3\xi nf-2)\Big]$$

$$\Leftrightarrow \Delta^A = \frac{1}{8\xi ng}\Big[(\xi nf-2\xi)(\xi nf+2nf+2\xi-4)-\big(3\xi^2n^2f^2-8\xi nf+4\big)\Big]$$

$$\Leftrightarrow \Delta^A = \frac{1}{8\xi ng}\left[\begin{array}{l}\xi^2n^2f^2+2\xi n^2f^2+2\xi^2nf-4\xi nf \\ \qquad -2\xi^2nf-4\xi nf-4\xi^2+8\xi-3\xi^2n^2f^2+8\xi nf-4\end{array}\right]$$

$$\Leftrightarrow \Delta^A = \frac{1}{8\xi ng}\Big[-2\xi^2n^2f^2+2\xi n^2f^2-4\xi^2+8\xi-4\Big]$$

$$\Leftrightarrow \Delta^A = \frac{2(1-\xi)}{8\xi ng}\big(\xi n^2f^2-2(1-\xi)\big).^{745} \qquad (138)$$

It is straightforward to see that the first factor on the right-hand side of (138) is positive as long as $\xi < 1$. It is not quite clear, however, whether the second factor – in parentheses – on the right-hand side of (138) is positive or not. What we can say is that the second factor on the right-hand side of (138) is also positive if $\xi n^2 f^2 > 2(1-\xi)$. Therefore, in order to show that $\Delta^A > 0$, we have to show that $\xi n^2 f^2 > 2(1-\xi)$.
More specifically, Deardorff (1992, p. 46) suggests that for the net gain to residents in country A, Δ^A, to be positive it is a sufficient condition that the level of invention under restricted patent protection, I^r, given by (120) is positive. By looking at (120), it becomes apparent that $I^r > 0$ if $\xi nf > 2$. Taking this condition into account, we will see in the following that $\xi n^2 f^2 > 2(1-\xi)$ and thus $\Delta^A > 0$ if $\xi nf > 2$.
In order to see that this is true note first that $nf > 2$ if $\xi nf > 2$ as long as $\xi < 1$. Second, if $nf > 2$ and $\xi nf > 2$ it follows that $\xi n^2 f^2 > 2$ and finally that

$$\xi n^2 f^2 + 2\xi > 2 \qquad (139)$$

744 See also McCalman (2001) who estimates the value of transfers between countries resulting from the implementation of the TRIPS Agreement in order to quantify the impact of international patent harmonization. More specifically, McCalman (2001) finds that the U.S. is the major beneficiary of international patent harmonization. See also McCalman (2005).
745 See Deardorff (1992) on p. 46.

verifying that the net gain to residents in country A, Δ^A, given by (138) is positive.

4.2.1.2.3.2. Extended Patent Protection and Welfare in Country B

However, Deardorff (1992, p. 46ff) also shows that consumers in country *B* are likely to be worse off under extended patent protection as we will see in the following.[746] Intuitively, consumers in country *B* are worse off under extended patent protection if the loss of consumer surplus associated with monopoly pricing is higher then the extra consumer surplus that stems from the development of additional products stimulated by the extension of patent protection to country *B*.[747] As already mentioned above, the net gain to residents in country *B* under extended patent protection is equal to the total consumer surplus. Therefore, the change of welfare in country *B* from extending patent protection, Δ^B, is the difference between the net gain obtained under extended patent protection given by (131) and the net gain obtained under restricted patent protection given by (123). More specifically,

$$\Delta^B = N^{eB} - N^{rB} = \frac{(1-\xi)(n^2 f^2 - 4)}{8ng} - \frac{(1-\xi)(\xi^2 n^2 f^2 - 4)}{2\xi^2 ng}$$

$$\Leftrightarrow \Delta^B = \frac{1-\xi}{8\xi^2 ng}\left(\xi^2 n^2 f^2 - 4\xi^2 - 4\xi^2 n^2 f^2 + 16\right)$$

$$\Leftrightarrow \Delta^B = -\frac{1-\xi}{8\xi^2 ng}\left(3\xi^2 n^2 f^2 + 4(\xi^2 - 4)\right).^{748} \tag{140}$$

Deardorff (1992, p. 46ff) suggests that for the net effect on welfare in country *B* from extending patent protection, Δ^B, to be negative it is sufficient that ξnf only slightly exceeds the level required so that the net effect on welfare in country *A* from extending patent protection Δ^A is positive. Put differently, Deardorff (1992, p. 47) shows that, if ξnf only slightly exceeds 2, Δ^B will be negative. In particular, if

$$\xi nf > \sqrt{\frac{16}{3}} = 2.31 \tag{141}$$

then Δ^B given by (140) will be negative regardless of the value of the parameter ξ alone.[749] In order to see that this is true note that Δ^B is negative if the second factor on the right-hand side of (140) is positive, hence if $\left(3\xi^2 n^2 f^2 + 4\xi^2 - 16\right) > 0$ and thus $\xi nf > \sqrt{(16/3) - (4\xi^2/3)}$.[750]

---

746 See also McCalman (2001) and McCalman (2005).
747 See Deardorff (1992) on p. 46.
748 See Deardorff (1992) on p. 46.
749 See Deardorff (1992) on p. 47.
750 Note that if $\xi nf > \sqrt{16/3} = 2.31$ given by (141) it follows that $\xi nf > \sqrt{(16/3) - (4\xi^2/3)}$ as $\xi > 0$.

However, let us now take a closer look at the value of the parameter ξ and its impact on Δ^B. If ξ – being the portion of the world's population located in the innovating country A – exceeds a particular threshold, then Δ^B will be negative. In particular, if the second factor (in parentheses) on the right-hand side of (140) is positive, Δ^B will be negative. That is, Δ^B is negative if

$$3\xi^2 n^2 f^2 + 4(\xi^2 - 4) > 0$$
$$\Leftrightarrow \xi^2\left(3n^2 f^2 + 4\right) > 16$$
$$\Leftrightarrow \xi > \sqrt{\frac{16}{4+3n^2 f^2}}. \qquad (142)$$
[751]

In other words, if the fraction of the world's population living in the innovating country is sufficiently large, residents in the rest of the world will lose from an extension of patent protection.[752] In particular, Deardorff (1992, p. 47ff) shows that, under plausible circumstances, the extension of patent protection to country B decreases welfare in country B in spite of the fact that consumers in country B will benefit from increased inventive activities stimulated through the introduction of patent protection.[753]

To give an example, suppose that the optimal consumer surplus, per dollar of research, from the highest-priority invention for the world is twenty times its cost ($nf = 20$).[754] In order to understand the meaning of the term nf, recall from (115) that $\tilde{s}(I) = f - gI$ is the optimal consumer surplus, per capita and per dollar of research, given that I dollars have already been invested in the development of all goods that generate a per capita consumer surplus per dollar of research that is greater than or equal to $\tilde{s}/R$.[755] Hence, for the highest-priority invention it follows that $I = 0$ and thus that $\tilde{s}(0) = f$. In other words, f is the optimal consumer surplus, per capita and per dollar of research, from the highest-priority invention.[756] Furthermore, recall that n denotes the world's population. Consequently, nf is the optimal consumer surplus per dollar of research from the highest-priority invention for the world. In terms of pharmaceuticals, one could think of the highest-priority invention for the world as a medicine for a global disease that is widespread in both the developing world as well as the developed world such as cancer, diabetes or cardiovascular diseases.[757]

However, assuming that $nf = 20$, (142) implies that Δ^B is negative if the share of the world living in country A, ξ, is greater than only $\sqrt{16/1204} = 11.5$ percent. In other words, if the share of the world initially covered with patent protection is greater than

751 Note that this result differs from the result originally obtained by Deardorff (1992) on p. 47. However, Professor Deardorff agrees with us that our new result is correct.
752 See McCalman (2002) on p. 2. See also Deardorff (1992) on p. 47.
753 See Scherer (2000) on p. 1319 and Scherer (1993) on p. 112. See also Diwan and Rodrik (1991).
754 See Deardorff (1992) on p. 47.
755 See Deardorff (1992) on p. 43.
756 See Deardorff (1992) on p. 47.
757 See Lanjouw (2002b) on p. 3 and Table 2 on p. 29.

only 11.5 percent and $nf = 20$, the rest of the world (country *B*) is worse off if patent protection is extended.
Hence, under plausible circumstances, welfare in country *B* is likely to decrease if patent protection is extended to country *B*.
Moreover, we can see from (138) and (140) that – by taking into account (139) and (141) – the innovating country *A* benefits from extending patent protection at the expense of the non-innovating country *B* under plausible circumstances. However, the question of whether extending patent protection has a positive or negative impact on global welfare has not been answered yet. Therefore, we will elaborate on this question in the following section.

4.2.1.2.3.3. Extended Patent Protection and Global Welfare

Finally, we can now analyze the question as to whether extending patent protection to country *B* increases or decreases global welfare. In particular, the net gain to the world due to the extension of patent protection to country *B*, Δ^W, is the difference between the net benefit to the world under extended patent protection given by (135) and the global net gain under restricted patent protection given by (125):

$$\Delta^W = N^{eW} - N^{rW} = \frac{(nf-2)(3nf-2)}{8ng} - \frac{(\xi nf-2)\left[\xi(3\xi nf-2)+4(1-\xi)(\xi nf+2)\right]}{8\xi^2 ng}$$

$$\Leftrightarrow \Delta^W = \frac{(nf-2)(3\xi^2 nf-2\xi^2)}{8\xi^2 ng} - \frac{(\xi nf-2)(3\xi^2 nf-2\xi+4\xi nf-4\xi^2 nf+8-8\xi)}{8\xi^2 ng}$$

$$\Leftrightarrow \Delta^W = \frac{3\xi^2 n^2 f^2-6\xi^2 nf-2\xi^2 nf+4\xi^2}{8\xi^2 ng} - \frac{(\xi nf-2)(-\xi^2 nf+4\xi nf-10\xi+8)}{8\xi^2 ng}$$

$$\Leftrightarrow \Delta^W = \frac{3\xi^2 n^2 f^2-8\xi^2 nf+4\xi^2}{8\xi^2 ng} - \frac{-\xi^3 n^2 f^2+2\xi^2 nf+4\xi^2 n^2 f^2-10\xi^2 nf+20\xi-16}{8\xi^2 ng}$$

$$\Leftrightarrow \Delta^W = \frac{1-\xi}{8\xi^2 ng}\left(16-4\xi-\xi^2 n^2 f^2\right).\text{[758]} \qquad (143)$$

Let us now address the question of whether the extension of patent protection to the entire world is beneficial or detrimental to global welfare in the following.
Assume that $\xi \to 1$. In this case, the first factor on the right-hand side of (143) will be positive. Consequently, the question of whether (143) is positive or negative depends on the sign of the expression in parentheses. By setting $\xi = 1$, for mathematical convenience, it follows that if

$$16-4-n^2 f^2 < 0$$

$$\Leftrightarrow n^2 f^2 > 12$$

$$\Leftrightarrow nf > \sqrt{12} = 3.46, \qquad (144)$$

758 See Deardorff (1992) on p. 47.

then (143) will be negative for ξ sufficiently close to 1.[759] Recall that nf is the optimal consumer surplus per dollar of research from the highest-priority invention for the world's population. Most importantly, note that the following proposition holds.

Proposition 4:

Under the assumption that the highest-priority invention generates a consumer surplus for the world's population that is at least 3.5 times its cost, extending patent protection reduces global welfare once the fraction of the world in which patent protection is already provided given by ξ is sufficiently large. In other words, under the plausible condition expressed in (144), the extension of patent protection to the entire world is not optimal from a global welfare perspective.[760]

The intuition behind this result is the following. If all innovations are made in a specific part of the world, then the extension of patent protection to more and more countries has the positive effect that the inventors earn monopoly profits in a larger group of countries. Thus, they will have greater incentive to invest in R&D.[761]
There are, however, diminishing returns to this effect for the following reason.[762] As more and more countries afford patent protection, the extra market that can be covered becomes smaller as well as the extra invention that can be stimulated by the extension of patent protection.[763] Therefore, at some point the costs resulting from extending patent protection and thus monopoly pricing to existing innovations come to outweigh the benefits of making new innovations resulting from extending patent protection.[764]
Nevertheless, the analytical framework set up by Deardorff (1992, p. 49) is based on the assumption that per capita demands for newly invented products are the same in the industrialized world and in the developing world. This, however, may not be the case for medicines for neglected infectious and tropical diseases such as malaria, Dengue fever or the hookworm disease that are virtually non-existent in the Northern Hemisphere but rampant in the developing world. For instance, assume that the demand for medicines for these diseases in country A tends toward zero. Consequently, almost no R&D incentives for manufacturers would originate from demand in country A. In this case, the Deardorff (1992) model may not adequately incorporate the following potential benefit to residents in country B of extending patent protection to country B. More specifically, patent protection in country B would be likely to increase the incentives of the original manufacturers located in country A to invest in R&D for medicines that are particularly important for residents in country B.[765]

---

759 For instance, see Lai and Qiu (2003) on p. 185, footnote 3. See also Deardorff (1992) on p. 48.
760 See Grossman and Helpman (1995) on p. 1331 and Deardorff (1992) on p. 48.
761 See also Deardorff (1992) on p. 49.
762 See Deardorff (1992) on p. 49.
763 See Deardorff (1992) on p. 49.
764 See Deardorff (1992) on p. 49.
765 Note that one may also have to take into account the different levels of per capita income in the industrialized world and the developing world. We will come back to this issue in sections 6.1 and 6.2 in Chapter 6. See also McCalman (2002) on p. 2.

Diwan and Rodrik (1991) originally formulated a model in order to address this issue in their pioneering North-South trade model.

4.2.2. Patent Protection and North-South Trade

Diwan and Rodrik (1991) analyze the incentives of IPR developing and exporting Northern countries and IPR importing Southern countries to afford patent protection to innovating firms. The crucial assumption in their path-breaking North-South trade model is that the North and the South have different technological needs and thus have to compete with each other to promote R&D for their preferred technologies due to scarce resources for R&D. With respect to R&D for pharmaceutical products this assumption can be justified on the grounds that consumers in the North may prefer the development of new medicines for diseases that are prevalent in the North, i.e. cancer and heart diseases, whereas consumers in the South may benefit more from medicines for TB, malaria and other neglected infectious and tropical diseases. Diwan and Rodrik (1991) argue that the incentive effects to afford patent protection in the South to promote R&D for the preferred technology compete with the incentives in the South not to afford patent protection due to free-riding motives.

4.2.3. International Patent Agreements and International Harmonization of Patent Protection

In a complex game-theoretic model of a world economy with ongoing innovation in two heterogeneous countries in terms of market size and capacity for innovation, Grossman and Lai (2004) show that the international harmonization of patents is likely to benefit rich countries in the Northern Hemisphere at the expense of poor developing countries in the Southern Hemisphere.

In particular, Grossman and Lai (2004) analyze the trade-off between the static costs of strengthening patent protection in terms of increased deadweight losses and the dynamic benefits of stronger patent protection associated with increased innovation – i.e. having more products with higher quality – in both a closed economy and an open economy.[766]

More specifically, Grossman and Lai (2004, p. 1638) express the strength of patent protection in terms of the length of the patent granted by the national government and the vigor of the enforcement policy chosen by the national government.

Furthermore, patent duration and patent enforcement are assumed to be perfect substitutes as instruments of IPR protection.[767] Only if the duration of a patent is fully enforced by the government can the patent holder act as a monopolist, charging a monopoly price. If, however, the duration of the patent is not enforced, competitors

766 See Grossman and Lai (2004) on p. 1635ff.
767 See Grossman and Lai (2004) on p. 1639.

would imitate the product of the original designer without incurring R&D costs or licensing costs. In this case, the product would sell at the competitive price.[768]

4.2.3.1. Optimal Patent Policy in a Closed Economy

For a closed economy, Grossman and Lai (2004, p. 1639ff) derive an implicit formula for the optimal strength of patent protection that relates the marginal cost of strengthening patent protection in terms of deadweight loss to the marginal benefit of strengthening patent protection in terms of additional innovative activity.

Addressing the question of optimal patent policy originally formulated by Nordhaus (1969), Grossman and Lai (2004) find that the optimal patent protection is stronger the higher the responsiveness of innovation to strengthened patent protection, and the greater the finite economic life of a new product.[769]

Furthermore, Grossman and Lai (2004, p. 1640) find that optimal patent protection is stronger the greater the size of the market in terms of the number of consumers which are assumed to have identical preferences with respect to the product of the original innovator.[770] Whereas the first two findings accord well with intuition, the latter relationship between market size and the optimal strength of patent protection may call for further clarification.[771] Typically, when the economy is closed the optimal level of R&D is higher the greater the market size for the following reason:[772] Innovation is a public good and the Samuelson rule for the optimal provision of a public good calls for greater output of a public good – in the present case, through strengthened patent protection – when the benefits can be spread across more consumers.[773]

4.2.3.2. Optimal Patent Policies in a World Economy

The closed economy case aside, Grossman and Lai (2004, p. 1641ff) also consider a world economy with endogenous innovation in two countries that are heterogeneous in terms of their capability to innovate and their market size. In game-theoretic parlance, they analyze a non-cooperative game in which two heterogeneous countries simultaneously choose their patent policies.[774] The crucial difference between the closed economy model and the world economy model is that the benefits of innovation can spread beyond national boundaries in the latter model. In particular, Grossman and Lai

---

768 For instance, see Becker and Stigler (1974) for a general treatment of law enforcement. See also Landes and Posner (1975) and Friedman (1984) as to the private enforcement of law. See also Scotchmer (2006) on p. 69ff.

769 See Grossman and Lai (2004) on p. 1640.

770 See also Schmookler (1966) who elaborates on the idea that market size has a significant impact on innovative activities. See also Mansfield (1964), Grabowski and Vernon (2000b), and Acemoglu and Linn (2004).

771 See also Kremer and Glennerster (2004) on p. 55ff on the impact of market size on R&D incentives.

772 See Grossman and Lai (2004) on p. 1640.

773 See Samuelson (1954) and Samuelson (1955). See also Lévêque and Ménière (2004) on p. 7ff. We will come back to the analysis of the impact of market size on R&D incentives in the pharmaceutical industry in section 6.2 in Chapter 6.

774 See Grossman and Lai (2004) on p. 1641.

(2004, p. 1635) suggest that the trade-off between the static costs of strengthening patent protection in terms of increased deadweight losses and the dynamic benefits of stronger patent protection in terms of increased innovation in a world economy model is not as straightforward as in a model with a closed economy for the following reasons.

First, the heterogeneity of the countries in terms of market size and capacity to innovate leads to national differences in optimal patent protection.[775]

Second, a country's optimal patent protection also depends on the patent protection afforded by its trading partner for the following reason. In an open economy with two countries, the strength of patent rights afforded in one country affects the responsiveness of global innovation to a change in the other country's patent policies.[776] In particular, Grossman and Lai (2004, p. 1643ff) derive the best response functions for the two governments. For instance, the best response of the government in country *A* is defined as the strength of patent protection that maximizes aggregate welfare in country *A* as a function of the given patent policy of the government in country *B*. The main findings of the analysis are the following:

First, the formula for a country's optimal strength of patent protection equates the benefits and costs of strengthening patent protection. On the one hand, the benefits result from providing greater incentives for innovation to firms in both countries. On the other hand, the losses are given by the sum of the extra deadweight loss that stems from strengthening patent protection afforded to domestic firms and the extra loss in consumer surplus that stems from expanding the fraction of imported goods that are subject to monopoly pricing.[777]

Second, Grossman and Lai (2004, p. 1644ff) find that patent protection is weaker in each country in any Nash equilibrium in an open economy than it would be in the absence of trade. Put differently, the incentives that a government has for strengthening patent protection in a world in which countries are open to international trade are weaker than they would be in a closed economy.[778] This can be explained on the grounds that the ability of an open economy to promote innovation through strengthened patent protection is only a fraction of the ability of a closed economy as the innovating firms only earn part of their discounted profits within the country's borders.[779] The rationale behind this result is the following. Suppose that country *A* were to strengthen its patent protection. This would reduce the fraction of total discounted profits that the innovating firms earn in country *B* and thus, ceteris paribus, would reduce the responsiveness of global innovation to the patent policy in country *B*.[780] Hence, the marginal benefit to country *B* of strengthening its patent protection would decrease. Consequently, the government in country *B* would respond to the increase of patent protection in country *A* with a reduction of patent protection.[781] Of

775 See Grossman and Lai (2004) on p. 1645ff.
776 See Grossman and Lai (2004) on p. 1644ff.
777 See Grossman and Lai (2004) on p. 1644ff and on p. 1651ff.
778 See Grossman and Lai (2004) on p. 1644, Proposition 1.
779 See also Sykes (2002) on p. 65.
780 See Grossman and Lai (2004) on p. 1645.
781 See Grossman and Lai (2004) on p. 1645.

course, the same logic applies to the opposite case in which country *B* strengthens its patent protection.

The third result of the analysis of the optimal patent policy in an open economy is that the policy-setting game has a unique and stable Nash equilibrium.[782]

Fourth, Grossman and Lai (2004, p. 1645ff) suggest that a country that has a larger market for innovative products and a greater capacity to innovate, i.e. an industrialized country in the Northern Hemisphere, has a higher incentive to grant stronger patent protection than its counterpart in the Southern Hemisphere for the following reasons: Since patent protection results in a deadweight loss in the country where the patent is granted, the country that can more effectively spur innovation with a given strengthening of its patent protection will, ceteris paribus, have an incentive to provide stronger patent protection.[783] More specifically, as both the capacity to conduct R&D as well as the market is larger in the North than in the South, the bulk of the world's R&D is carried out in the North.[784] Therefore, the bulk of the world's profits from innovative products are generated in the North.[785] Furthermore, the marginal cost of strengthening patent protection in one country reflects the loss in consumer surplus on all protected products less the profits that are realized by domestic producers.[786] As the innovating firms in the North generate the bulk of the profits, the offset to marginal cost is larger in the North than in the South.[787] Consequently, the government in the North is less tempted to ease patent protection than the government in the South.

Fifth, Grossman and Lai (2004, p. 1647ff) analyze international patent agreements with respect to the question as to which combinations of patent policies maximize aggregate global welfare. In particular, the authors find that – compared to the unique Nash equilibrium in the non-cooperative game – the two countries can benefit from negotiating an international patent agreement so that at least one country is better off without making the other country worse off.[788] More specifically, the pareto-improving patent agreement ensures that the governments take into consideration the positive externalities that flow to foreign consumers when domestic patent protection is strengthened and that aggregate world patent protection is strengthened relative to the non-cooperative equilibrium.[789]

Lastly, Grossman and Lai (2004, p. 1649ff) find that the international harmonization of national patent protection – as stipulated in the TRIPS Agreement – is neither necessary nor sufficient for the efficiency of the global regime of intellectual property rights.[790] More specifically, if patent protection is stronger in the North than in the South in the initial non-cooperative equilibrium, harmonization can be achieved either by strengthening patent protection unilaterally in the South or by a combination of changes in the South and the North.[791] More specifically, Grossman and Lai (2004, p.

782 See Grossman and Lai (2004) on p. 1645, Proposition 2.
783 For instance, see Grossman and Lai (2004) on p. 1646, Proposition 3.
784 See **Table 3** on p. 86.
785 See Kremer and Glennerster (2004) on p. 30ff.
786 See Grossman and Lai (2004) on p. 1646.
787 See Grossman and Lai (2004) on p. 1646.
788 For instance, see Schäfer and Ott (2005) on p. 24ff on pareto improvements.
789 See Grossman and Lai (2004) on p. 1649.
790 See also McCalman (2001) and McCalman (2002).
791 See Grossman and Lai (2004) on p. 1649ff.

1650) find that, under the assumption that side payments are absent, the unilateral increase of patent protection in the South will harm the South, as the South would deviate from its best response to the North's choice of patent protection which is – by definition – harmful.

Furthermore, Grossman and Lai (2004) find that harmonization through a combination of policy changes in both countries that would achieve global efficiency requires a strengthening of patent protection in both the South and the North. More specifically, the North will necessarily benefit from a strengthening of patent protection in both countries whereas the South will possibly lose.[792] In particular, the probability that the South will lose in the course of bilateral policy changes is higher the larger the market in the North relative to the market in the South and the larger the capability to innovate in the North relative to the capability to innovate in the South.[793]

4.3. Empirical Evidence regarding Patent Protection in the Developing World

4.3.1. Empirical Evidence regarding the Underinvestment in R&D for Medicines for Neglected Infectious and Tropical Diseases

From an empirical point of view, the reforms associated with the TRIPS Agreement provide a unique opportunity to analyze the question as to what extent patents provide incentives for pharmaceutical companies to invest in R&D for new medicines for diseases that are rampant in the developing world.[794]

First, Lanjouw and MacLeod (2005, p. 4232) suggest that the TRIPS-related reforms represent a significantly large change in the protection of IPRs in the developing world. Second, the reforms affected both the vast majority of the world's population as all WTO members were required to implement a set of minimum standards for intellectual property protection as well as the growing pharmaceutical market in the developing world.[795]

Furthermore, one of the main arguments brought forward during the TRIPS negotiations in support of extending patent protection to the developing world was that raising the intellectual property standards in those countries would give pharmaceutical companies an incentive to invest in R&D for medicines of specific importance to consumers in the developing world.[796] Moreover, prior empirical evidence suggests that patent protection plays a crucial role in providing R&D incentives for pharmaceutical companies.[797] Therefore, one could expect the TRIPS-related reforms in the

792 See Grossman and Lai (2004) on p. 1650, Proposition 5.

793 See Grossman and Lai (2004) on p. 1649ff.

794 See Lanjouw and MacLeod (2005) on p. 4232.

795 For instance, see McCalman (2001) on p. 162. See also Lanjouw and MacLeod (2005) on p. 4232.

796 For instance, see Diwan and Rodrik (1991) on p. 28ff and Lanjouw and Cockburn (2001) on p. 266. See also Chen and Puttitanun (2005) on p. 475 and Helpman (1993) who argue that the South not necessarily benefits from extended patent protection.

797 See Mansfield (1986). See also Maskus (2000a) on p. 52ff. See also DiMasi et al. (1991) and DiMasi et al. (2003).

developing world to have an impact on the amount of R&D targeted at poor country markets.[798]

In particular, Lanjouw and Cockburn (2001) and the follow-up paper by Lanjouw and MacLeod (2005) explore the question of whether the change in IPRs in the developing world has led to more R&D on medicines for neglected infectious and tropical diseases that are rampant in the developing world.

4.3.1.1. Empirical Evidence regarding R&D for Medicines for Neglected Infectious and Tropical Diseases from 1975 to 1996

Lanjouw and Cockburn (2001) employ three indicators of R&D activity for medicines to treat tropical diseases in order to develop a "baseline" picture of R&D investment in medicines targeted to poor country markets.[799]

First, they examine trends – over the period from 1975 to 1996 – in worldwide patenting of medicines to treat tropical diseases as percentages of total pharmaceutical patenting as an indicator of early stage research in pharmaceuticals.[800] In particular, Lanjouw and Cockburn (2001, p. 271ff) find that patenting related to tropical diseases never exceeded 0.5 percent of overall pharmaceutical patenting. The authors find, however, interesting differences in the trends in worldwide patenting for specific tropical diseases. On the one hand, worldwide patenting related to malaria as percentages of total pharmaceutical patenting slightly increased from the early 80s until the early 90s and than decreased again.[801] On the other hand, worldwide patenting related to leprosy as percentages of total pharmaceutical patenting was significantly low over the entire period.[802]

The second, early indicator of pharmaceutical R&D activity in tropical diseases – extracted from approximately 3,900 biomedical journals published in more than 70 countries – is the frequency of references to tropical diseases in the biomedical literature as a percentage of all references.[803] In particular, Lanjouw and Cockburn (2001, p. 275ff) find that, taken together, references in the biomedical literature to tropical diseases were found in roughly 1.5 percent of all citation. Furthermore, they conclude that there is almost no change in these percentages over time. However, references to malaria became more frequent between the early 80s until the mid-90s whereas references to leprosy decreased significantly from the early 80s.[804]

Third, Lanjouw and Cockburn (2001, p. 279ff) consider trends in grants dispersed by the National Institutes of Health (NIH) as an indirect measure of the direction of pharmaceutical research. The corresponding data sets are extracted from the NIH Computer Retrieval of Information on Scientific Projects database – hereinafter CRIPS

798 See Lanjouw and MacLeod (2005) on p. 4232. See also Cohen et al. (2000).

799 See also Kremer (2002) on p. 70ff on the disease environment in the developing world. See also Lanjouw (2003) on p. 98ff.

800 See Lanjouw and Cockburn (2001) on p. 272, Table 2.

801 For instance, see Trouiller et al. (2002) on p. 2190 and Lanjouw and Cockburn (2001) on p. 272ff.

802 See Lanjouw and Cockburn (2001) on p. 273. See also Trouiller et al. (2002) on p. 2189ff.

803 See Lanjouw and Cockburn (2001) on p. 275ff.

804 For instance, see Lanjouw and Cockburn (2001) on p. 276ff, Figure 2.

database – of federally funded research grants by the U.S. Public Health Service.[805] In particular, the NIH administers and awards the majority of those grants that basically support research conducted by research institutes, hospitals and universities.[806] Other sources of grants are the Centers of Disease Control, the U.S. Food and Drug Administration (FDA) and other government agencies. Lanjouw and Cockburn (2001) suggest that there are three ways in which a change in the diseases of interest to the pharmaceutical industry may affect the trend in grants awarded by the NIH.

First, some grants are the direct result of Cooperative Research and Development Agreements (CRADAs) or Small Business Innovation Research (SBIR) submissions by private pharmaceutical companies.[807]

Second, Lanjouw and Cockburn (2001, p. 279) suggest that an arguably more limited way is that representatives of the pharmaceutical industry sit on NIH advisory councils and working group panels and thus may press for specific interests in these settings.

Third, as Cockburn and Henderson (1988) have shown, the for-profit research conducted by pharmaceutical company scientists is closely connected to the publicly funded research conducted by academic researchers through collaborative research. Therefore, Lanjouw and Cockburn (2001, p. 279) argue that this linkage is likely to have an impact on the direction of academic research and thus an impact on the characteristics of extramural grant proposals submitted to the NIH by academic researcher.

Other than in their analysis of worldwide patenting and biomedical citation trends where Lanjouw and Cockburn (2001) explore the trends for several tropical diseases, the authors only analyze the trends in NIH research grants directed at malaria research. In particular, they analyze – over the period from 1972 to 1996 – grant dollars related to malaria projects as percentages of the overall budget of the National Institute of Allergy & Infectious Diseases (NIAID) which is the originator of the bulk of federally funded grants for research related to tropical diseases. Lanjouw and Cockburn (2001, p. 280) find that malaria grants accounted for less than 2 percent of total NIAID grant dollars in 1972, remained more or less on this level until the mid-80s and then rose to a level of 3.7 percent in 1996. Note that the trends in NIH research grants directed at malaria research may only serve as an indicator of R&D activity for malaria medicines. However, this trend cannot be explained by patent law.[808]

To summarize the results of Lanjouw and Cockburn (2001), the analysis of three data sources – worldwide patenting, biomedical citations and NIH research grants – suggests a moderate increase in inventive activities relating to medicines for malaria beginning in the mid-1980s. However, the upward trend – in particular with respect to worldwide patenting and biomedical citations – seems to have disappeared in the late 90s.[809] Furthermore, there appears to be significantly less research activity directed

805 See http://crisp.cit.nih.gov/ (last visited February 13, 2008). See Lanjouw and Cockburn (2001) on p. 279.
806 See Lanjouw and Cockburn (2001) on p. 279ff.
807 See Lanjouw and Cockburn (2001) on p. 279.
808 We thank Hans-Bernd Schäfer for his comments in this respect.
809 See Lanjouw and Cockburn (2001) on p. 287ff. See also Lanjouw (2003) on p. 98ff.

toward other diseases specific to least-developed countries such as Chagas' disease or leprosy.[810]

Furthermore, Lanjouw and Cockburn (2001, p. 287) do not come to a definite conclusion with respect to the question of whether the strengthening of IPRs in the developing world associated with the TRIPS Agreement may contribute to an increase in R&D activities regarding medicines for diseases specific to the developing world.[811]

First, developing new medicines takes a significant amount of time and resources.[812] Hence, although strengthening IPRs in poor country markets may make those markets more attractive for pharmaceutical companies, the effect of the TRIPS Agreement on pharmaceutical research may take many years to become fully visible.[813]

Second, pharmaceutical firms remain sceptical about the prospects for effective enforcement of IPRs in the developing world due to the apparent reluctance of some governments to enforce IPRs for other products than pharmaceuticals, i.e. continual pirating of CDs in China, as well as due to bad experiences dealing with patent infringement in the developing world.[814]

Another reason that makes it difficult to address the question mentioned above, is that the TRIPS Agreement allowed some developing countries a grace period for adjustment to the new standard.[815] For instance, India only implemented full patent protection for pharmaceutical products in January 2005.

4.3.1.2. Empirical Evidence regarding R&D for Medicines for Tropical Diseases from 1975 to 2002

Nevertheless, the study initiated by Lanjouw and Cockburn (2001) serves as a baseline against which changes in R&D trends for tropical diseases in the following years can be analyzed. For instance, in a recent follow-up paper Lanjouw and MacLeod (2005) revisit and update the statistical series mentioned in the previous section. In particular, Lanjouw and Cockburn (2005, p. 4242) suggest that the level of pharmaceutical inventtive activities – more than a decade after the TRIPS Agreement was signed – related to neglected diseases specific to low-income countries still remains extremely low relative to overall pharmaceutical R&D.

For instance, just 1.25 percent of all citations in the biomedical literature were related to tropical diseases in 2004.[816] However, the authors find an upward trend in malaria related research between 1975 and 2002.

Nevertheless, Trouiller et al. (2002) – adopting a somewhat different approach compiling data by searches of the U.S. Food and Drug Administration (FDA) and the European Agency for the Evaluation of Medical Products (EMEA) – come to almost

810 See also 't Hoen (2005) on p. 2ff, Trouiller et al. (2002), and Kremer and Glennerster (2004) on p. 11ff.

811 See Abbott (2001) on p. 6ff. See also United Nations Development Programme (2001)on p. 109ff.

812 See Lanjouw and Cockburn (2001) on p. 287ff.

813 See Lanjouw and Cockburn (2001) on p. 281ff.

814 See Lanjouw and Cockburn (2001) on p. 286ff.

815 For instance, see Maskus (2000a) on p. 25. See also Lanjouw and Cockburn (2001) on p. 268ff and Thorpe (2002).

816 See Lanjouw and MacLeod (2005) on p. 4238.

the same conclusion as Lanjouw and Cockburn (2001) and Lanjouw and MacLeod (2005) that diseases that occur predominantly in the developing world remain largely unaddressed.

In their analysis of the outcomes of pharmaceutical R&D over the period from 1975 to 1999, Trouiller et al. (2002, p. 2188) find that only one percent of the 1,393 new pharmaceutical products marketed in this period were registered for tropical diseases although these diseases account for roughly one third of the worldwide disease burden. However, consistent with the results of Lanjouw and Cockburn (2001) and Lanjouw and MacLeod (2005), Trouiller et al. (2002, p. 2190) find that the biggest advance in drug R&D for tropical diseases has been made in malaria research.

4.3.2. Short-Term Welfare Effects of Global Patent Protection in Pharmaceuticals

Chaudhuri et al. (2006) empirically investigate the effects of the enforcement of patents for pharmaceutical products – as stipulated in the TRIPS Agreement – on prices and welfare in India with the objective to contribute to the ongoing controversy and debate regarding the potential adverse welfare effects of the TRIPS Agreement in developing countries.[817]

For this matter, India appears to be a leading example for four reasons.[818]

First, India is a major developing country that did not afford patents for pharmaceutical products prior to the ratification and implementation of the TRIPS Agreement.[819]

Second, health insurance coverage is virtually nonexistent so that Indian households have to cover all medical expenses.[820]

Third, the disease profile in India is both similar to that of many other low-income countries as well as significantly different from that of the majority of the industrialized countries.[821]

Finally, the Indian pharmaceutical industry is – in terms of volume – the largest producer of generic drugs in the world and has considerable imitative capabilities to domestically produce pharmaceutical products that are patented elsewhere.[822]

Given this natural setting for the analysis of the welfare effects of patent protection in the developing world, Chaudhuri et al. (2006, p. 1481ff) use detailed data on monthly pharmaceutical prices and sales from January 1999 to December 2000 in order to derive price and expenditure elasticities as well as supply-side parameters such as upper and lower bounds for marginal cost and markup for the fluoroquinolone sub-segment of the systematic antibacterials segment – a family of broad-spectrum antibiotics – in the Indian pharmaceuticals market.

---

817 See also Cooter and Schäfer (2008) on p. 56, footnote 61.
818 See Chaudhuri et al. (2006) on p. 1479.
819 For instance, see Lanjouw (1998) and Watal (2000). See Chaudhuri et al. (2006) on p. 1479.
820 See Chaudhuri et al. (2006) on p. 1479.
821 See Kremer and Glennerster (2004) on p. 7ff. See Chaudhuri et al. (2006) on p. 1479.
822 See Chaudhuri et al. (2006) on p. 1479. See also Lanjouw (1998), Lanjouw and MacLeod (2005), and Watal (2000).

After deriving the above stated estimates, Chaudhuri et al. (2006) analyze counterfactual scenarios that involve the withdrawal of one or more of the domestic pharmaceutical product groups of the fluoroquinolone subsegment.
The intuition behind this approach is that had U.S. patents for a certain broad-spectrum antibiotic been recognized in India, all domestic products containing that antibiotic would not be present in the Indian market.[823] Instead, only the foreign patented product(s) containing the specific antibiotic would be present in the market.[824] However, using the estimates for the price and expenditure elasticities as well as upper and lower bounds for marginal cost and markup, Chaudhuri et al. (2006) can – for several counterfactual scenarios – simulate prices and market shares.
Furthermore, Chaudhuri et al. (2006, p. 1495ff) calculate the welfare loss resulting from the additional expenditures that Indian consumers would need to incur to maintain their pre-TRIPS utility level in the face of the withdrawal of domestic products and upward price adjustments for the patented foreign product. For instance, Chaudhuri et al. (2006) estimate that the prices of foreign patented products would increase between 100 percent and 400 percent under the assumption that price regulation is absent.[825]
More specifically, Chaudhuri et al. (2006, p. 1506) find that the enforcement of patent protection in the fluoroquinolone subsegment alone would result in a large welfare loss for the Indian economy with a lower bound of US$144 million and an upper bound of US$450 million annually. The range of the estimated welfare loss, however, depends on several factors such as the way patent policies are implemented, the degree to which foreign pharmaceuticals producers respond to patent protection, and the extent of price regulation.[826]
Moreover, Chaudhuri et al. (2006, p. 1507) conclude that the overwhelming portion of this amount accounts for welfare losses to Indian consumers whereas only a small fraction of this amount accounts for forgone profits of Indian pharmaceutical firms.[827]
For instance, if prices were kept at their pre-TRIPS level the withdrawal of the domestic products in the fluoroquinolone subsegment would result in a total welfare loss of US$305 million annually.[828] Of this amount, forgone profits of Indian producers constitute approximately US$50 million which is roughly 16 percent of the total welfare loss.[829] More specifically, Chaudhuri et al. (2006, p. 1506) find that the major part of the total welfare loss – approximately 84 percent – derives from the loss of consumer welfare.
To sum up, Chaudhuri et al. (2006) focus on estimating the *static* costs of strengthening patent protection in India. They do not, however, address the question of whether a strengthening of international patent protection may spur global R&D resulting in potential dynamic benefits of innovation.[830] From our point of view, the stimulating

823 See Chaudhuri et al. (2006) on p. 1479.
824 See Chaudhuri et al. (2006) on p. 1479.
825 See also Lanjouw (1998) on p. 8ff for an analysis of the price-increasing effect associated with the introduction of pharmaceutical patents in India.
826 See Chaudhuri et al. (2006) on p. 1506.
827 See also Lanjouw (1998) on p. 12ff.
828 See Chaudhuri et al. (2006) on p. 1506.
829 See Chaudhuri et al. (2006) on p. 1506.
830 See Chaudhuri et al. (2006) on p. 1481.

effect of patent protection on R&D must also be taken into consideration in order to shed light on the ongoing debate regarding the welfare effects associated with the implementation of the TRIPS Agreement in developing countries.[831]

However, the major contribution of Chaudhuri et al. (2006) is that they are the first to derive estimates of the key price and expenditure elasticities and supply-side parameters in a developing economy in order to be able to analyze the impact of pharmaceutical patents on prices and welfare. Put differently, Chaudhuri et al. (2006) base their findings on actual estimates of the relevant parameters of demand and the structure of pharmaceuticals markets in developing countries whereas the findings in the prior literature were simply based on assumptions about market structure and demand characteristics.[832] Furthermore, whereas there is considerable theoretical literature on the welfare effects of patent protection in developing countries, the empirical work on this topic is still in its infancy.[833]

Finally, the ongoing debate regarding the welfare effects associated with the implementation of the TRIPS Agreement in developing countries mainly focuses on the issue of affordability of pharmaceutical products in developing countries.[834] Chaudhuri et al. (2006), however, provide further empirical evidence suggesting that the availability of pharmaceutical products is also important from a consumer welfare perspective. Consequently, their findings suggest that policymakers should assess policies that are related to the TRIPS Agreement not only in terms of their effects on the prices of pharmaceutical products, but also in terms of their effect on the availability of pharmaceutical products.[835]

4.3.3. International Redistribution of Income Associated with the Implementation of the TRIPS Agreement

A main concern that was raised by most developing countries was related to the potentially negative redistributive consequences that the international patent harmonization – as stipulated in the TRIPS Agreement – might have for them.[836] Put differently, the technology-importing developing countries raised concerns that they are likely to be exploited by the technology-exporting industrialized countries after the adoption of the TRIPS Agreement.[837]

Most notably, McCalman (2001) comprehensively estimates the value of transfers between countries resulting from the implementation of the TRIPS Agreement in order to quantify the impact of international patent harmonization.[838] In particular,

831 For instance, see the formal papers by Valletti and Szymanski (2006), Szymanski and Valletti (2005), Valetti (2006), Rey (2003), and Li and Maskus (2006) that look at the dynamic aspects of potentially patent-eroding parallel trade in the context of R&D for new medicines. We will elaborate on this issue in section 5.2.3.2 in Chapter 5.

832 See Chaudhuri et al. (2006) on p. 1478.

833 We thank Pranab Bardhan for his comment in this respect. See also Lanjouw (1998).

834 See Chaudhuri et al. (2006) on p. 1508.

835 See Chaudhuri et al. (2006) on p. 1507ff.

836 See Maskus (2000a) on p. 171ff.

837 For instance, see Chen and Puttitanun (2005) on p. 475 and Helpman (1993) on p. 1274. See also McCalman (2001) on p. 162 and Cooter and Schäfer (2008) on p. 44ff.

838 See also Maskus (2000a) on p. 182ff and McCalman (2005).

McCalman (2001, p. 162ff) adopts a structural model of innovation in an international setting in order to infer the value of patent rights in 29 countries, being a mix of both developing countries such as Brazil, India and South Africa as well as industrialized countries such as the U.S., Germany and Switzerland.[839]
More specifically, McCalman (2001) infers the value of patent rights in each country by relating local parameters to the decision to patent. For instance, these parameters include the strength of patent protection as well as the availability of enforcement institutions that permit the appropriation of the rents to an innovation.[840]
Put differently, the basic analytical framework set up by McCalman (2001, p. 162ff) relates the value of patent rights to both the sectoral coverage of patent protection – by providing information regarding the question as to whether sectors such as pharmaceuticals, foods, or chemicals are excluded from patent protection – and the availability of enforcement institutions in a country such as the availability of injunctions and burden of proof procedures.[841]
Moreover, by incorporating this relationship in his model, McCalman (2001, p. 162) analyzes the relationship between, on the one hand, patent institutions in a particular country and the rents associated with patent protection in that country on the other hand.
In particular, the estimation of this relationship enables McCalman (2001) to conduct the counterfactual experiment in which all countries adopt patent protection consistent with the TRIPS Agreement and thus provides a basis to analyze the question of how the value of patent protection is affected by the harmonization of patents. Put differently, the institutional parameters are set in line with those in compliance with the TRIPS Agreement, i.e. the coverage of patent protection is extended to all fields of technology such as pharmaceuticals and chemicals, "provided that they are new, involve an inventive step and are capable of industrial application".[842]
Furthermore, the counterfactual experiment approach allows McCalman (2001) to draw several conclusions with respect to the redistributive consequences of the TRIPS Agreement and the importance of patent protection.
First, patent protection is an important – although not the only – means for appropriating the rents of an innovation.[843] More specifically, McCalman (2001) calculates the ratio of the present value of patent protection and the R&D expenditures by business enterprises as given by OECD (1994) in order to provide a measure for the importance of patent protection. For instance, under the assumption that the entry into the R&D market is free one would expect this ratio to tend towards one if patent protection was the only means for appropriating the rents of an innovation.[844] McCalman (2001, p. 177), however, finds that Switzerland recoups roughly 25 percent of its R&D expenditures through patent protection. This is mainly due to the fact that almost 50

839 See also Maskus (2000a) on p. 184, Table 6.1.
840 See McCalman (2001) on p. 164.
841 See McCalman (2001) on p. 164ff. See also Scotchmer (2006) on p. 72 and Menell and Scotchmer (2007) on p. 1479ff. For a general treatment of the *ex post* efficiency of injunctions see Calabresi and Melamed (1972), Polinsky (1980), and Kaplow and Shavell (1996). For an analysis of the *ex ante* effects of injunctions in the IP context, see Schankerman and Scotchmer (2001).
842 See Art. 27(1) of the TRIPS Agreement. See also McCalman (2001) on p. 177ff.
843 See Levin et al. (1987). See also McCalman (2001) on p. 182.
844 See McCalman (2001) on p. 175ff.

percent of Swiss R&D expenditures are devoted to pharmaceuticals and chemicals and that the chemical and the pharmaceutical industries' reliance on patents to appropriate rents is significantly above average.[845] However, all other countries recoup less than one quarter of R&D expenditures from patent protection – with a ratio of 0.15 for the U.S. and Germany and 0.07 for Japan.[846]
Second, patent harmonization is likely to generate large transfers of income between countries, the U.S. being the major beneficiary, gaining almost six times more than Germany, the second largest beneficiary.[847] More specifically, McCalman (2001, p. 179) defines the net transfers associated with the TRIPS Agreement as the "difference between the increase in the value of patent rights held by residents of a country and the increased value of rights granted by that country".[848]
However, McCalman (2001) estimates that the U.S. would benefit from a net transfer associated with the TRIPS Agreement of more than $4.55 billion (1988 Dollars) on the patents applied for in 1988. Moreover, McCalman (2001, p. 180) puts these net transfers into perspective by comparing them to GDP and finds that the U.S. is also the largest beneficiary in terms of net transfer as percentage of GDP.
Furthermore, McCalman (2001) estimates that virtually all developing countries in the sample group generate a net transfer loss from patent harmonization. For instance, developing countries such as Brazil (with a value of –$0.93 billion net transfers associated with patent harmonization) and India (–$0.53 billion) are significant contributors to the transfer of income between countries.[849]
However, also industrialized countries such as Canada (–$1.02 billion) and the U.K. (–$0.54 billion) make significant contributions.[850] Canada's unexpectedly high estimated net loss resulting from harmonization needs further clarification. The potential for this net transfer loss appears to stem from the fact that Canada is the largest trading partner of the U.S. due to its proximity, significant market size, and the shared language.[851] In particular, prior to the TRIPS Agreement U.S. investors had only little incentive to seek patents in Canada because of weak enforcement of patent protection and the requirement that patents granted in Canada must be worked in Canada.[852] In contrast, Canadian investors sought more patents in the U.S. than investors from any other country prior to the implementation of the TRIPS Agreement.[853] Therefore, the harmonization of patent protection provides significant incentives and opportunities for U.S. innovators to seek patents in Canada because of stronger enforcement of patent protection and the removal of the working requirement under the TRIPS Agreement.[854]

845 See McCalman (2001) on p. 177.
846 See McCalman (2001) on p. 176, Table 3.
847 See Maskus (2000a) on p. 183ff. See also McCalman (2001) on p. 178ff.
848 See McCalman (2001) on p. 179, Table 4.
849 See Maskus (2000a) on p. 183ff and McCalman (2001) on p. 179, Table 4.
850 See McCalman (2001) on p. 178ff. See also Maskus (2000a) on p. 184, Table 6.1.
851 See McCalman (2001) on p. 178ff.
852 See also Pecorino (2002) with respect to the question as to whether reimports of drugs from Canada to the U.S. should be allowed. See also Ganslandt and Maskus (2004) on p. 1036ff. Note, however, that a comprehensive discussion of the NAFTA that is certainly important to the pharmaceutical trade between the U.S. and Canada is beyond the scope of this thesis. For instance, see Maskus (2000a) on p. 194ff for a discussion of the broad overlap between NAFTA and TRIPS.
853 See McCalman (2001) on p. 179ff.
854 For instance, see Maskus (2000a) on p. 185 and McCalman (2001) on p. 179ff.

However, Canadian innovators did not have corresponding opportunities in the U.S. as patent protection in the U.S. has already been relatively strong and properly enforced prior to the implementation of the TRIPS Agreement.[855] Finally, the high estimated net loss for Canada resulting from international patent harmonization may also serve as an explanation for Canada's willingness to align with developing countries regarding their main concern that the harmonization of patents – as stipulated in the TRIPS Agreement – has negative redistributive consequences for them.[856]
To summarize, McCalman (2001) suggests that the international patent harmonization associated with the TRIPS Agreement clearly shifts the international legal framework to favour U.S. innovating firms at the expense of the technology-importing developing countries.

4.3.3.1. Comment on McCalman (2001)

Indeed, McCalman (2001) provides interesting insights with respect to the transfer of income between countries associated with the implementation of the TRIPS Agreement by providing a thorough means to quantify the impact of international patent harmonization. Nevertheless, it should be noted that McCalman (2001) conducts the counterfactual experiment for a *given* set of innovations.[857] Therefore, the basic framework does not elaborate on the link between patent protection and its impact on R&D.[858] Put differently, the benefits of any increase in R&D and thus innovation in response to the implementation of the TRIPS Agreement have not been included. From our point of view, the potential long-term benefits through increased innovation associated with the TRIPS Agreement must also be taken into consideration in order to fully characterize the welfare impact of the TRIPS Agreement.[859]
However, as already mentioned above, the international harmonization of patent protection is fiercely debated in the global trading system. Another closely related and also highly debated issue is the question as to whether parallel imports (or re-imports) undermine patent rights and whether they should be permitted or prohibited. We will elaborate on this issue in the following chapter.

855 See McCalman (2001) on p. 180.
856 For instance, see Maskus (2000a) on p. 185. See also McCalman (2001) on p. 180.
857 For instance, see McCalman (2001) on p. 162.
858 For instance, see Valletti and Szymanski (2006), Szymanski and Valletti (2005), Valetti (2006), and Li and Maskus (2006) as to the dynamic effects of potentially patent-eroding parallel trade in the context of R&D for new medicines.
859 For instance, see Maskus (2000a) on p. 186ff.

5. Legal and Economic Analysis of Parallel Imports

5.1. Introduction

In this chapter, we develop a simple double marginalization model with complete information, in which an original manufacturer of a pharmaceutical product faces potential competition from parallel imports by a foreign exclusive distributor. The model suggests that parallel imports will never occur in the sub-game perfect Nash equilibrium, as it will always be beneficial for the manufacturer to monopolize the home country by undercutting the price of the re-imported pharmaceutical product. However, the question as to whether it is optimal for the manufacturer to charge the monopoly price in the home country depends on the level of trade costs and the level of heterogeneity of the two countries, in terms of market size and price elasticity of demand.

Moreover, we shall analyze the impact of parallel trade on the manufacturer's profit and on global welfare for low, intermediate, and high trade costs and different levels of heterogeneity of the two countries.

More specifically, our model suggests that parallel trade – provided that it is a credible threat – reduces the profit of the manufacturer and thus reduces his incentives to invest in R&D. If, however, trade costs are high, parallel trade is a non-credible threat as it is not a worthwhile business activity for the foreign distributor and thus does not have any impact on the profit of the manufacturer.

Furthermore, we will show that parallel trade has positive welfare properties if the two countries are sufficiently heterogeneous in terms of market size and if trade costs are intermediate and low, respectively. If, however, the countries are virtually homogenous in terms of market size, parallel trade may be detrimental to global welfare for specific levels of trade costs.

The second part of this chapter elaborates on the idea that differences in national price regulation in the pharmaceutical sector are a major cause for the occurrence of parallel trade.

In the third part of this chapter, we shall draw some conclusion as to parallel imports and the problem of underinvestment of R&D into neglected infectious and tropical diseases. In particular, we shall address the question as to whether parallel imports should be permitted or prohibited from a developing country's perspective.

5.2. Parallel Trade and the Pricing of Pharmaceutical Products in a Double Marginalization Game

5.2.1. Introduction

Parallel imports are also known as gray-market imports.[860] More specifically, a parallel-imported product is a legitimately manufactured product under IP protection that is first placed into circulation in one country.[861] Then, the product is imported to a second country without the consent of the owner of the IPRs that are attached to the product in the second country.[862] For instance, parallel imports occur when a trading firm buys quantities of a particular drug in a low-price country such as Portugal and then imports them into a high-price country such as Germany without the approval of the exclusive distributor that owns the licensed patent rights in Germany.[863]

Parallel imported products are not counterfeited or pirated but are legitimate products.[864] However, they may not carry the original producer's warranty and may be packaged differently.[865] Moreover, parallel importing firms ordinarily purchase a product in one country at a price that is lower than the price at which the product is sold in the second country (arbitrage between markets).[866]

The ability of an owner of intellectual property rights to exclude parallel trade stems from the importing country's treatment of exhaustion of intellectual property rights.[867]

On the one hand, under a regime of national exhaustion intellectual property rights end upon first sale within a country, and right-holders are awarded the right to prevent parallel imports from other countries.[868] Hence, right owners retain full rights for distributing their goods either themselves or through authorized dealers; this also includes the right to exclude imports.[869]

On the other hand, a regime of international exhaustion of intellectual property rights makes parallel imports from other countries legal, as "rights are exhausted upon first sale anywhere".[870] Countries permitting parallel imports do not provide rightful owners with full rights for distributing their goods themselves, effectively invalidating any right to control the import of goods in circulation abroad.[871]

---

860 See Maskus (2000a) on p. 208. See also Maskus (2001) on p. 2.
861 See Maskus (2000a) on p. 208.
862 See Maskus (2000a) on p. 208.
863 For instance, see Chard and Mellor (1989) and Danzon (1998). See also Maskus (2001) on p. 1.
864 See Maskus (2000a) on p. 208ff.
865 See Maskus (2001) on p. 2ff. See also Maskus (2000a) on p. 208.
866 See Ganslandt and Maskus (2004) on p. 1035ff.
867 See Maskus (2000a) on p. 208.
868 See Maskus (2001) on p. 3. See also Hilty (2000) and Maskus (2000a) on p. 208ff.
869 See Maskus (2000a) on p. 208ff.
870 See Maskus (2001) on p. 3.
871 See Maskus (2000a) on p. 208.

A third option is regional or community exhaustion.[872] Under a regime of regional or community exhaustion of intellectual property rights, rights are exhausted upon first sale within any member country of the community and parallel trade is allowed within the community.[873] However, parallel imports from a non-member country are prohibited.

In particular, the regulation of parallel imports in the field of pharmaceuticals has become a critical issue in the global trading system, as the welfare effects of parallel imports of pharmaceuticals are generally ambiguous.[874] In particular, there is tension between two major objectives of public policy.

On the one hand, a major long-run public policy objective is to stimulate the innovation and development of new medicines by awarding pharmaceutical producers with a patent on new medicines.[875] In particular, pharmaceutical producers shall benefit from the higher prices of medicines protected by a patent, in order to be able to cover high R&D costs.

On the other hand, public policy should also ensure broad access to affordable existing medicines in the short-run.[876] Hence there is a trade-off between access to affordable medicines in the short-run and higher (monopoly) drug prices to stimulate R&D in the long-run.[877]

The research-intensive pharmaceutical sector relies heavily on patents, as Mansfield (1986) has shown.[878] In particular, the value of a patent depends on the monopoly power afforded in terms of "scope for price differentiation",[879] which depends on the existence of barriers to parallel trade.[880] Put differently, the value of patent rights depends, to a certain extent, on "the scope for price discrimination within the area of exhaustion."[881] Furthermore, the narrower the area of exhaustion the greater is the scope for price differentiation, and thus the higher is *ceteris paribus* the value of a patent.[882] Consequently, advocates of strong patent rights for new pharmaceutical products support a global policy of banning parallel imports.[883] For instance, representatives of the pharmaceutical industry argue that if parallel importation of pharmaceuticals were permitted it would cut profits in the pharmaceutical industry, and thus

872 See Desogus (2008) for an excellent legal analysis with respect to the regime of regional exhaustion of intellectual property rights in the EU and antitrust issues in the European pharmaceutical market.

873 See Maskus (2001) on p. 3.

874 See Maskus and Chen (2004) and Danzon and Towes (2003). See also Maskus (2001) and Ganslandt and Maskus (2004) on p. 1036ff.

875 See Ganslandt and Maskus (2004) on p. 1036.

876 See Ganslandt and Maskus (2004) on p. 1036.

877 See Maskus (2001) on p. 23.

878 For instance, Mansfield (1986) in a ranking of industries' reliance on patent protection for innovation showed that the pharmaceutical sector is more than twice as dependent on patent protection as the next sector (chemicals). See also Harhoff and Reitzig (2004) on p. 457, Harhoff et al. (2003), Bale (1998), Zweifel and Breyer (1997), and OECD (2000).

879 See Ganslandt and Maskus (2004) on p. 1036.

880 See Ganslandt and Maskus (2004) on p. 1036.

881 See Ganslandt and Maskus (2004) on p. 1037.

882 See Ganslandt and Maskus (2004) on p. 1037.

883 For instance, see Barfield and Groombridge (1998). See also Bale (1998).

would reduce the incentives to invest in R&D for new drugs.[884] Furthermore, they argue that this would slow down innovation of new pharmaceuticals.
Nevertheless, policy makers in many developing countries not endowed with the technical and non-technical input factors required for innovation support an open regime of parallel imports.[885] In particular, they place a larger emphasis on the affordability of pharmaceuticals than on promoting R&D abroad, arguing that it is important to be able to purchase pharmaceuticals from the cheapest sources possible.[886] Of course, the vast majority of new inventions in the world have been and are generated by the pharmaceutical companies in the developed nations.[887] For instance, the big multinational pharmaceutical companies, in terms of world market sales, are all based either in Europe or in the U.S..[888]
The opposition to restricting parallel trade in most developing countries reflects concerns that domestic prices for pharmaceuticals would actually be higher under price discrimination.[889] However, as we will see in the following it is questionable whether this is a valid argument from an economic point of view. In economic parlance, parallel trade of pharmaceutical products limits the scope for third-degree price discrimination of a monopolistic pharmaceuticals producer.[890] In third-degree price discrimination, a monopolistic pharmaceuticals producer sells output to different people or to segmented markets at different prices, but individuals in the same segmented market or group pay the same price per unit of output.[891] Basic economic theory tells us that, if the segmented markets are heterogeneous in terms of average income and price elasticities of demand, profit-maximizing prices for a monopolist are likely to differ between those markets.[892] In general, the monopolist will charge relatively high prices in markets with low price elasticity of demand, typically in highly developed countries, and relatively low prices in markets with high price elasticity of demand, typically in developing countries.[893] Parallel imports limit the scope for third-degree price discrimination.[894] More specifically, on the one hand, the price in a low-income country with a high price elasticity of demand is likely to increase if parallel trade is permitted.[895] On the other hand, the price that is charged in

884 For instance, see Danzon (1998).
885 See Maskus (2000a) on p. 211.
886 See Maskus (2001) on p. 2.
887 See Sykes (2002) on p. 47.
888 For instance, see **Table 3** on p. 86.
889 See Maskus (2001) on p. 4. See also Maskus (2000a) on p. 212ff and Abbott (1998).
890 Throughout the analysis we assume that a patent on a new pharmaceutical product gives the manufacturing firm that holds the patent a temporary monopoly.
891 See Robinson (1933), Schmalensee (1981b), Varian (1985), and Hausman and MacKie-Mason (1988) for an analysis of the effect on social welfare of third-degree price discrimination. See also Varian (1996) on p. 431ff.
892 See the model of third-degree price discrimination on p. 95 of this thesis.
893 See Maskus (2001) on p. 13ff.
894 See Ganslandt et al. (2005) on p. 216ff. See also Sykes (2002) on p. 63ff and Scherer (1980) on p. 316.
895 For instance, see Ganslandt and Maskus (2004) on p. 1042 on price convergence in the parallel trade context.

a high-income country with a low price elasticity of demand is likely to fall if parallel imports are permitted.[896]

The following section outlines the legal framework regarding parallel trade. In particular, we focus on Article 6 of the TRIPS Agreement and on the regime of regional exhaustion in the EU.

Then, we will give an overview of the two main strands of the existing formal literature on parallel trade. The first strand of formal papers analyzes the determinants of parallel trade. However, the second strand involves the dynamic effects of parallel trade on the decision to invest in R&D for new products.

Finally, we contribute to the first strand of literature mentioned above and develop a new double marginalization model as a three-stage game of complete information, played between a monopolistic producer of pharmaceuticals in one country and an exclusive distributor in another country. In particular, we analyze the question as to why parallel imports in a game with complete information may actually occur in equilibrium.

5.2.2. Legal Framework regarding Parallel Trade

Under a regime of national exhaustion of IPRs, an IPR owner can prevent competition resulting from the parallel import of his product from another country where it is sold either by himself or by an exclusive distributor. For instance, the IPR owner can take action against a parallel importing firm for infringing a patent, copyright, or trademark. Furthermore, the owner can include a restriction notice in licensing and purchasing agreements in order to prevent parallel trade, i.e. by attaching a label to the product which indicates that the product is not for re-sale in its home country or by implementing a supply quota.[897] However, the extent to which contractual restrictions such as labels or quotas can be lawfully adopted depends on whether they are anticompetitive under prevailing competition laws or not.[898]

In contrast, under a regime of international exhaustion (regional exhaustion), the IPR owner looses his exclusive right once the product is launched on a market for the first time, with the result that parallel imports from abroad (from countries inside the region) are not prohibited.[899] As we shall see in more detail in the following sections, the European Court of Justice (ECJ) held in various cases that the free circulation of goods within the common market takes precedence over the protection of intellectual property rights and that parallel trade within the common market is legal, at least

896 See Ganslandt and Maskus (2004) on p. 1042. See also Ganslandt et al. (2005) on p. 216ff. See also Sykes (2002) on p. 63ff and Scherer (1980) on 316.

897 See Holmberg et al. (2003) who report that quantity limits for parallel import products are highly significant for the Swedish market. See also Simon (2004). For an overview of reactive and proactive strategies of multinational companies to combat parallel trade activities see Cavusgil and Sikora (1988). For instance, the authors identified price cutting, supply interference, and acquisition of the re-importing firm as reactive strategies. Furthermore, the authors identified product differentiation, strategic uniform pricing, establishing legal precedence, and lobbying as proactive strategies. See also Palia and Keown (1991).

898 See Fink (2005) on p. 172ff. See also Gallini and Hollis (1999) and Desogus (2008).

899 See Maskus (2000a) on p. 208ff.

within very broad limits.[900] Furthermore, private contractual provisions in licensing and purchasing agreements explicitly prohibiting parallel trade within the common market would automatically be void because these are incompatible with the common market.[901]

In the remainder of the section, we shall first describe the treatment of the principle of the exhaustion of intellectual property rights within the WTO framework focusing on Article 6 of the TRIPS Agreement. The second part gives a description of the treatment of parallel trade in the EU. Finally, the third part elaborates on the different national legal frameworks regarding parallel trade, i.e. in the U.S., Japan, Australia, and New Zealand.

5.2.2.1. Parallel Trade and the WTO

In general, countries are free to determine their preferred exhaustion regime for each form of intellectual property rights.[902] Put differently, countries can freely decide on whether to permit or ban parallel trade, as long as they are not bound by an international agreement.[903] However, no international convention or multilateral agreement on intellectual property rights has so far mandated a particular regime of exhaustion of intellectual property rights.[904]

The only provision in the various multilateral WTO agreements that explicitly deals with the treatment of parallel trade is Article 6 of the TRIPS Agreement.[905] In particular, American negotiators in the Uruguay Round tried to include a global standard of national exhaustion of IPRs in the TRIPS Agreement, in order to ban parallel imports aimed at protecting innovative industries, such as the pharmaceutical industry, as well as other industries, such as the music and film industries.[906] Nevertheless, it was not possible to reach such an agreement with regard to a global standard of national exhaustion of IPRs, because the views on the net benefits of parallel imports were too divergent.[907] For instance, some WTO members such as Switzerland and the U.S. tried to include a global standard of national exhaustion of IPRs in the TRIPS Agreement, while other countries such as Australia, India, and New Zealand defended the principle of international exhaustion.[908] Therefore, Article 6 of the TRIPS Agreement simply prescribes that:

900 Hereinafter the following references to cases are to those of the ECJ if not stated otherwise. See Case C-187/80 *Merck & Co. Inc. vs. Stephar B.V. and Petrus Stephanus Exler*. See also Case C-56/64 *Etablissements Consten S.A. and Grundigverkaufs-GmbH. vs. E.E.C. Commission*. See also Darbà and Rovira (1998).

901 See Article 81 of the EC Treaty.

902 See Maskus (2000a) on p. 208ff.

903 See Fink (2005) on p. 173ff.

904 See Fink (2005) on p. 173ff.

905 See Fink (2005) on p. 173ff. See also Maskus (2000a) on p. 208ff.

906 See Maskus (2000a) on p. 208ff. See also Fink (2005) on p. 173ff.

907 See Fink (2005) on p. 173ff.

908 See Gervais (2003) on p. 11ff. See also Chard and Mellor (1989), and Gallus (2005) on p. 78ff.

"For the purposes of dispute settlement under this Agreement, subject to the provisions of Articles 3 and 4, nothing in this Agreement shall be used to address the issue of the exhaustion of intellectual property rights."

Hence, it seems that the compromise reached in Article 6 is simply to exclude the treatment of parallel imports from dispute settlement and to preserve the territorial privilege for regulating parallel trade.[909] Furthermore, Paragraph 5(d) of the Declaration on the TRIPS Agreement and Public Health (hereafter "Doha Declaration") affirmed this interpretation. In particular, it prescribes that:

"The effect of the provisions in the TRIPS Agreement that are relevant to the exhaustion of intellectual property rights is to leave each Member free to establish its own regime for such exhaustion without challenge, subject to the MFN and national treatment provisions of Articles 3 and 4."[910]

Indeed, the flexibility to allow parallel trade was crucially important for many developping countries, as they perceived parallel imports to be an "effective antidote"[911] to concerns about potential price increases for pharmaceuticals, due to strengthened patent protection in the course of the ratification and implementation of the TRIPS Agreement.[912] Furthermore, many developing countries were in favor of permitting parallel trade, arguing that it would allow licensees in developing countries to obtain export markets for high-technology products, such as pharmaceuticals.[913]

5.2.2.2. Parallel Trade in the EU

The European Union (EU) applies a regime of regional exhaustion to all fields of intellectual property within the Community.[914] Put differently, "exhaustion applies

---

909 See Gervais (2003) on p. 11ff. See also Maskus (2001) on p. 4 and Yusuf and Moncayo von Hase (1992). However, after failing to include the principle of national exhaustion in the TRIPS Agreement, the U.S. then exchanged commitments on limiting parallel trade with Singapore in the U.S.-Singapore Free Trade Agreement, which came into force in 2004, and with Australia in the U.S.-Australia Free-Trade Agreement, which came into force in 2005. For instance, the International Intellectual Property Alliance provides a detailed list regarding the current status of U.S. negotiations on Free Trade Agreements with several other countries on http://www.iipa.com./fta_issues.html (last visited March 24, 2009). See also Gallus (2005) on p. 77ff, Hestermeyer (2007) on p. 233, Correa (2000b), Slotboom (2003), and Fink (2005) on p. 173ff.

910 The full text is available on http://www.wto.org/English/tratop_e/dda_e/dohaexplained_e.htm (last visited March 24, 2009). See also Garrison (2006) on p. 53.

911 See Maskus (2001) on p. 4.

912 See Maskus (2001) on p. 11ff and Maskus (2000a) on p. 209. See also Watal (2001).

913 See Szymanski and Valletti (2005) on p. 714ff. See also Abbott (1998) who supported the developing countries' point of view, arguing that a restriction on parallel trade was an unjustified inhibition of free trade.

914 See Case C-15/74 *Centrafarm BV and Others vs. Sterling Drug Inc.*, and Case C-355/96 *Silhouette International Schmiedt GmbH & Co. KG vs. Hartlauer Handelsgesellschaft mbH.* See also Müller-Langer (2008b) on p.17ff, Crampes et al. (2005) on p. 8ff. and Barnard (2004) on p. 162ff. See also Maskus (2000b) on p. 1272ff, Darbà and Rovira (1998) and Desogus (2008).

upon first sale anywhere in the EU".[915] In particular, the ECJ has held that free circulation of goods within the common market takes precedence over protection of IPRs.[916] For instance, in the initial case for patents, *Merck vs. Stephar*, the ECJ concluded that a holder of a patent who decides to market his product in two EU countries cannot prevent parallel trade between the two countries. For example, the patent holder is not awarded the right to prevent parallel trade by bringing summary proceedings against the parallel-importing firm for patent infringement, despite differences in patent protection in those countries.[917] Furthermore, the primacy of free circulation of goods within the common market over patent protection has been upheld by the ECJ's ruling in *Merck vs. Primecrown*.[918] In particular, the ECJ held that the existence of differential national price regulations in pharmaceuticals in the EU does not justify the prevention of parallel imports – i.e. by taking action against infringement of a patent – from EU countries with lower (highly regulated) prices to EU countries with higher (less regulated) prices.[919] Indeed, varying national regulatory practices that result in differences in prices for the same pharmaceutical product across EU countries are a major cause for arbitrage, as parallel-importing firms are able to buy pharmaceutical products from wholesalers in low-price countries such as Portugal, Spain, or Greece and re-sell them in high-priced countries such as Germany, Sweden, or the UK.[920]

Recent evidence regarding parallel trade of pharmaceutical products within the EU shows that parallel trade is a considerable business activity. For instance, the York Health Economics Consortium (2003) estimated that the UK market for parallel-traded pharmaceutical products represented around £1,300 million (€2,000 million) in 2002. Furthermore, the consortium estimated that parallel-traded pharmaceuticals accounted for around 10 percent of the total drug bill in Denmark in 2002.[921]

Nevertheless, exhaustion in the EU has important limitations. For instance, the ECJ concluded in *EMI vs. CBS* and *Silhouette vs. Hartlauer* that exhaustion "does not extend to countries outside the common market."[922] Hence, the ECJ established a regime of regional exhaustion or "Community exhaustion" but rejected the principle of

915 See Ganslandt and Maskus (2004) on p. 1039ff.

916 See Ganslandt and Maskus (2004) on p. 1038ff.

917 See Case C-187/80 *Merck & Co. Inc. vs. Stephar B.V. and Petrus Stephanus Exler*. See also the initial cases for trademarks, Case C-56/64 *Etablissements Consten S.A. and Grundigverkaufs-GmbH. vs. E.E.C. Commission*, and for copyrights, Case C-78/70 *Deutsche Grammophon Gesellschaft mbH. vs. Metro-SB-Grossmärkte GmbH & Co. K.G.*. See also Ganslandt and Maskus (2004) on p. 1038ff.

918 See Ganslandt and Maskus (2004) on p. 1039.

919 See Joined Cases C-267-268/95 *Merck & Co. Inc. and Others vs. Primecrown Limited and Others*. See also Case C-15/74 *Centrafarm BV and others vs. Sterling Drug Inc.* See also Wagener et al. (2006) on p. 230, Danzon (1998) on p. 295ff, and Maskus (2000b) on p. 1272ff.

920 See Kanavos and Costa-i-Font (2005) on p. 755ff. See also Maskus (2000a) on p. 214ff and Maskus and Ganslandt (2002) on p. 63ff, Table 3.1. In particular, Maskus and Ganslandt (2002) show that there was a significant variability of drug prices within the EU in 1998. For instance, Maskus and Ganslandt (2002) find that the British price of a particular drug was 45 percent higher than the price of the same drug in Spain in 1998. See also Maskus and Ganslandt (2002), on p. 71, Table 3.3.

921 See also Valletti and Szymanski (2006) on p. 501.

922 See Ganslandt and Maskus (2004) on p. 1039. See also Case C-51/75 *EMI Records Limited vs. CBS United Kingdom Limited*. See Case C-355/96 *Silhouette International Schmiedt GmbH & Co. KG vs. Hartlauer Handelsgesellschaft mbH.*

international exhaustion.[923] Furthermore, the ECJ established in *Pharmon vs. Hoechst* that regional exhaustion does not extend to products that are marketed in a member state under a compulsory license.[924]
Another important issue with regard to potential restrictions for parallel trade within the common market is the question as to whether supply quotas for foreign wholesalers imposed by original manufacturers are illegal under Article 81 of the EC Treaty.[925] Most importantly, the ECJ concluded in *Bundesverband der Arzneimittel-Importeure and Commission of the European Communities vs. Bayer* that unilateral supply quota systems are not necessarily prohibited under Article 81 of the EC Treaty, as long as they do not constitute a contractual agreement prohibiting parallel trade.[926] Put differently, unilateral restraints on sales from an original manufacturer to foreign wholesalers are not necessarily illegal under Article 81 of the EC Treaty.[927] However, any contractual agreement explicitly prohibiting parallel trade within the common market would be void under Article 81 of the EC Treaty.
To sum up, on the one hand, the EU system basically allows parallel imports within its territory, despite the fact that national IP regimes and national price regulations may differ between member states, as long as the product has not been marketed under a compulsory license within the EU.[928] On the other hand, parallel imports from outside the EU are not allowed under the EU system, so that IPR owners can invoke their rights and prevent competition from parallel imports.

5.2.2.3. National Legal Frameworks regarding Parallel Trade

Exhaustion policies vary widely between developed and developing countries and even among developed countries themselves, as the following summary will show.[929]
Let us first consider national policies with regard to parallel trade in some high-income countries such as the U.S., Japan, Australia, and New Zealand.
The U.S. has a mixed policy on parallel imports.[930] Within its territory, the country employs what is known as the "first-sale doctrine", under which rights of the seller or manufacturer are exhausted when a good has been first placed on the national market outside the vertical distribution chain.[931] Hence, price discrimination against American

923 See also Szymanski and Valletti (2005) on p. 712ff.
924 See Case C-19/84 *Pharmon B.V. vs. Hoechst AG*. See Maskus (2000b) on p. 1272ff. See also Ganslandt and Maskus (2004) on p. 1039ff.
925 See Ganslandt and Maskus (2004) on p. 1039.
926 See Joined cases C-2/01 P and C-3/01 P *Bundesverband der Arzneimittel-Importeure e.V. and Commission of the European Communities vs. Bayer AG*. See also Smits (2006) on p. 65ff. See also Rey and Venit (2004) for an excellent analysis of the economic implications of parallel trade in medicines in Europe.
927 See also Smits (2006) on p. 65ff.
928 See Maskus (2000a) on p. 209ff.
929 See Maskus (2000a) on p. 209ff. See also Fink (2005) on p. 173ff, Maskus and Chen (2005) on p. 193 (Table 8.1), and Maskus (2001) on p. 3ff.
930 See Maskus (2000a) on p. 209ff.
931 See U.S. Supreme Court case *Bobbs-Merrill Co. vs. Straus*, 210 U.S. 339 (1908). The "first-sale doctrine" was later codified in section 109(a) of the Copyright Act of 1976. See also Szymanski and Valletti (2005) on p. 712ff, and Maskus and Chen (2004) on p. 553.

consumers is ruled out, as U.S. firms cannot prevent consumers from re-selling goods anywhere within the U.S..

With regard to parallel imports in trademarked goods, the U.S. applies a "common-control exception".[932] Under this rule, U.S. trademark owners can block parallel imports, i.e. by using statutory provisions relating to the exclusion of imports, except when they are in a parent-subsidiary relationship with the foreign trademark owner or when both trademark owners are owned by the same entity.[933] Furthermore, the trademark owner's ability to block parallel imports rests on his ability to demonstrate that the imported product does not have the same quality as the original product and that this difference in quality is likely to cause consumer confusion.[934] One may argue that these principles suggest that parallel imports of pharmaceutical products are permitted, as they are identical to the original product; however, U.S. law explicitly prohibits the re-importation of pharmaceutical products unless the drug is imported by the original manufacturer of the drug (21 U.S.C. 381 (d)).[935]

However, because of the large differences in prices for prescription drugs between the U.S. and Canada, parallel trade in pharmaceuticals became an important issue in the 2004 U.S. presidential elections, as many states encouraged American consumers to buy from parallel-trading internet pharmacies, despite the dubious legality of parallel trade in pharmaceuticals under federal law.[936] For instance, Graham and Robson (2000) estimated that brand-name drugs are significantly cheaper in Canada than in the U.S. at both the wholesale and retail level.[937] Indeed, parallel trade has become a considerable business activity, as recent IMS estimates suggest. For instance, compared to 2002, the value of U.S. re-importation of prescription drugs from Canada increased by 134 percent to US$1.100 million in 2003.[938]

However, other high-income countries such as Japan, Australia, and New Zealand are substantially more open to parallel trade than the U.S..[939] In Japan, parallel imports in trademarked and patented goods are allowed with two exceptions.[940] First, parallel imports are not allowed in case the original sale of the product was subject to foreign price regulation.[941] Second, parallel imports can be explicitly barred by contractual provisions.[942] Another high-income country that has a far more liberal view on parallel

---

932 See U.S. Supreme Court case *K Mart Corporation vs. Cartier*, 486 U.S. 281 (1987). See also Maskus (2001) on p. 5, Gallini and Hollis (1999) on p. 7ff, Palia and Keown (1991) on p. 49ff, Maskus and Chen (2004) on p. 553ff, and Kanavos et al. (2004) on p. 36ff.

933 See Maskus (2000a) on p. 209.

934 See Maskus (2001) on p. 5.

935 See the Prescription Drug Marketing Act of 1987. See Valletti and Szymanski (2006) on p. 500.

936 See Szymanski and Valletti (2005) on p. 713ff. See also Valletti and Szymanski (2006) on p. 500 and Ganslandt and Maskus (2004) on p. 1036ff.

937 See also U.S. House of Representatives (1998) that compared the international prices of prescription drugs. In particular, the report concluded that prices for pharmaceutical products in Maine were 70 percent higher than in Canada and 102 percent higher than in Mexico.

938 See http://open.imshealth.com/IMSinclude/i_article_20040726.asp (last visited, January 10, 2009).

939 See Maskus (2000a) on p. 211 and Abbott (1998).

940 For instance, see *BBS Kraftfahrzeugtechnik AG. vs. K.K. Racimex Japan, K.K. Jap Auto Products* (Japanese Supreme Court decision from July 1st, 1997).

941 See Maskus (2001) on p. 5 and Fink (2005) on p. 174.

942 See Maskus (2001) on p. 5.

trade is Australia.[943] Furthermore, New Zealand applies a system of international exhaustion with respect to copyright.[944]

Furthermore, as the summary of exhaustion regimes of various developing and least-developed countries in **Appendix 6** shows, the exhaustion regimes and thus the restraints on parallel trade vary widely in the developing world.[945] A large number of countries, such as Argentina, India and South Africa, apply a regime of international exhaustion.[946] More specifically, Argentina and South Africa have enacted laws allowing parallel imports of pharmaceuticals.[947] However, just to name a few, countries such as Brazil, Mexico, and Nigeria adopt a regime of national exhaustion of IPRs and thus allow the right holder to prevent parallel trade.[948]

To summarize, exhaustion regimes and thus the restraints on parallel trade vary widely between developed and developing countries and even amongst developed countries.[949] Furthermore, these differences in exhaustion regimes and the corresponding divergent views on the net benefits of parallel imports have created a fierce debate in recent years.[950] However, as we shall see in the following sections, the law and economics approach to parallel trade appears to be a highly attractive and promising field of research, given the complex legal and economic issues involved, which can significantly contribute to this debate.

5.2.3. Literature on Parallel Trade and R&D for Pharmaceuticals

Before proceeding with the model, we will give an overview of the two main strands of the existing formal literature on parallel imports.[951]

First, the vast majority of formal papers applying game-theoretic tools analyzes the determinants of parallel imports, i.e. price discrimination by monopolistic manufacturers, vertical price control by multinational enterprises or national price regulations.

However, the second and limited strand of literature involves the dynamic effects of parallel trade on the decision to invest in R&D for new products, which is certainly a crucially important issue for the research-intensive pharmaceutical industry.

943 For instance, see the Australian Copyright Amendment (Parallel Importation) Bill 2002 to the Copyright Act 1968, available on http://www.aph.gov.au/LIBRARY/Pubs/bd/2001-02/02bd133.htm (last visited March 24, 2009). See also Maskus (2000a) on p. 211.

944 See Copyright (Removal of the Prohibition on Parallel Importing) Amendment Act 1998. See also Copyright (Parallel Importation of Films and Onus of Proof) Amendment Act 2003, available on the New Zealand Ministry of Economic Development homepage, http://www.med.govt.nz/ (last visited March 24, 2009). See also Fink (2005) on p. 174.

945 See also Maskus (2000a) on p. 210, Table 7.1.

946 See Kanavos et al. (2004) on p. 39.

947 See Section 15C of the South African Medicines and Related Substances Control Amendment Act, 1997. See also Maskus (2001) on p. 5ff.

948 See the analysis of the intellectual property laws of over 70 developing and least-developed countries undertaken by Thorpe (2002).

949 See Maskus (2000a) on p. 209ff.

950 See Fink (2005) on p. 174ff and Maskus (2000a) on p. 210ff.

951 For an overview of less formal policy-oriented reviews on parallel trade see Szymanski and Valletti (2005) on p. 715ff. See Tarr (1985), Danzon (1998), Darbà and Rovira (1998), NERA et al. (1999), and OECD (2002).

5.2.3.1. Determinants of Parallel Trade

Maskus (2000a) and Maskus (2000b) provide an excellent overview of the economic theories on the causes of parallel trade and the main arguments in favour of banning parallel imports.

First, in many circumstances efficient international distribution of goods and services requires multinational enterprises that typically build markets through exclusive territorial dealership rights, in order to vertically control the operations of their official licensees.[952] Nevertheless, in foreign markets it is likely to be difficult to enforce private contractual provisions that prohibit sales outside the authorized distribution chain, so that parallel trade may occur.[953]

In particular, Maskus and Chen (2004) elaborate on this idea and offer a sophisticated theory of parallel imports in the context of vertical price controls.[954] Maskus and Chen (2004) analyze the nature of contractual relationships between a domestic manufacturer and a foreign independent and exclusive distributor through which the manufacturer sells his product abroad, in order to determine the optimal level of parallel trade. In particular, the manufacturer offers the exclusive foreign distributor a two-part wholesale tariff consisting of a wholesale price and a franchise fee.[955]

The analysis suggests that the possibility of parallel trade affects the manufacturer's pricing decision when fixing the wholesale price it charges the foreign distributor. Furthermore, the threat of parallel trade may reduce vertical pricing efficiency and thus reduce social welfare.[956]

However, Maskus and Chen (2004) conclude that the effect of parallel trade on global welfare is not unambiguous. In fact, they show that global welfare is U-shaped with respect to the cost of engaging in parallel trade, i.e. transportation costs.[957]

First, suppose that parallel trade costs are very low, i.e. transportation costs tend toward zero. In this case, Maskus and Chen (2004) conclude that the manufacturer cannot deter parallel trade in equilibrium by raising the wholesale price and thus that a welfare-reducing distortion in the vertical pricing scheme is not created. Put differently, parallel trade has good welfare properties if trade costs are sufficiently low, as it reallocates goods between the two countries without creating welfare-reducing distortions in the vertical pricing scheme.[958]

However, consider now the other extreme case, that parallel trade costs are so high that parallel trade is not feasible. In this case, Maskus and Chen (2004) conclude that parallel trade is not a real threat and that the manufacturer sets an efficient wholesale price.

---

952 See Maskus (2000a) on p. 213 and Maskus (2000b) on p. 1277ff. See also Maskus and Chen (2002) and Maskus and Chen (2004).

953 See Maskus (2000b) on p. 1277. See also Maskus and Chen (2002) and Maskus (2000a) on p. 213.

954 See also Gallini and Hollis (1999) who explore the nature of the contractual relationships between trademark or copyright owners and authorized distributors that may employ trademark and copyright law to prevent parallel trade.

955 See Maskus and Chen (2004) on p. 554ff.

956 See Maskus and Chen (2004) on p. 567.

957 See Maskus and Chen (2004) on p. 560.

958 See Maskus and Chen (2004) on p. 552.

If, however, trade costs are neither too low nor too high the manufacturer can deter parallel trade by raising the wholesale price and thus reducing vertical pricing efficiency. Finally, Maskus and Chen (2004, p. 561) suggest that the optimal policy regarding parallel trade shall either reduce any existing trade barriers and thus trade costs as much as possible or raise trade costs as much as possible. However, the optimal policy should not leave trade costs at some intermediate value.[959]

A second determinant for parallel trade is that parallel importing firms have the incentive to free ride on investments in marketing as well as on the before- and after-sales services of official licensees and authorized distributors.[960] For instance, assume that an authorized distributor in the territorial market *A* invests in marketing and sales activities that are associated with the sale of a certain product in market *A*. Consequently, the distributor in market *A* will charge a markup on top of the procurement cost so that he can earn a return on those investments.[961] Furthermore, suppose that the marketing and sales activities mentioned above are substantially cheaper in the territorial market *B*, or that they are not even provided by the authorized distributor in territorial market *B*.[962] In this case, parallel importing firms that purchase the product in market *B* and re-sell the product in market *A* free ride on the investments in marketing and sales services made by the official distributor in market *A*.[963]

Third, in some industries such as the pharmaceutical industry national governments intervene in private markets by regulating prices in order to achieve particular social objectives, i.e. to make medicines affordable for low-income consumers and to limit public health budgets.[964] As these government interventions result in significant international price differences there is a potential for arbitrage between markets, as parallel importing firms may purchase a certain product in more regulated (lower-price) markets and re-sell the product in less regulated (higher-price) markets.[965]

In a recent paper, Jelovac and Bordoy (2005) identify international differences between the regulatory regimes in the pharmaceuticals area as a main determinant of international price discrimination.[966] In particular, Jelovac and Bordoy (2005) explore the welfare implications of permitting parallel trade of pharmaceutical products in a model in which countries may differ along two dimensions.

First, countries may be different in terms of governmental health insurance reimbursement policies, as is reflected in the patient's level of co-payment for buying a pharmaceutical product.[967]

---

959 See Maskus and Chen (2004) on p. 561.

960 See Maskus (2000a) on p. 213. See also Chard and Mellor (1989) and Barfield and Groombridge (1999) on p. 228.

961 See Maskus (2000b) on p. 1278.

962 See Maskus (2000b) on p. 1278ff.

963 See Maskus (2000b) on p. 1275ff, Maskus (2000a) on p. 212ff, and Fink (2005) on p. 176ff.

964 See Maskus (2000a) on p. 214ff. See also Maskus (2000b) on p. 1279ff.

965 See Danzon (1997). See also Ganslandt and Maskus (2004) on p. 1035ff. See also Maskus and Ganslandt (2002) on p. 63ff, Table 3.1, for information on per dosage prices for 20 major drugs in 14 countries in 1998.

966 See also Szymanski and Valletti (2005) on p. 715ff.

967 See Jelovac and Bordoy (2005) on p. 6.

Second, countries may differ in terms of drug needs, as is reflected in the distribution of the valuations for the pharmaceutical product among their population.[968] In particular, Jelovac and Bordoy (2005, p. 18) show that parallel trade increases total welfare when countries share the same health system and only differ in the distribution of the valuations for the pharmaceutical product among their population. In this case, parallel trade leads to an efficient re-allocation of consumption from consumers with a relatively low valuation of the pharmaceutical product in the exporting country towards consumers with a relatively high valuation of that product in the importing country.[969]

If, however, the countries only differ in terms of their health insurance reimbursement policies, parallel trade decreases total welfare, as it re-allocates drug consumption from consumers with relatively high valuation of the pharmaceutical product towards consumers with relatively low valuation of that drug.[970] However, Jelovac and Bordoy (2005) do not consider the dynamic effects of parallel trade on R&D for new pharmaceutical products.

In a recent paper, Ganslandt and Maskus (2004) also take into account international differences between the regulatory regimes in the pharmaceuticals area. However, Ganslandt and Maskus (2004) particularly focus on the econometric analysis of the price impact of parallel trade in pharmaceutical products within the EU. Interestingly, despite the importance of parallel trade from a welfare perspective, their analysis is the first systematic economic investigation into the price impacts of parallel trade in pharmaceuticals.[971]

In particular, Ganslandt and Maskus (2004) explore the effect of the entry of parallel traders on the prices of pharmaceutical producers in Sweden from 1994 to 1999. Prior to Sweden's entry into the European Union on January 1, 1995 parallel imports of pharmaceuticals were prohibited. However, after its entry Sweden had to adopt the EU-wide principle of exhaustion of patent distribution rights and thus permitted parallel trade. Therefore, the Swedish market provides a natural example for testing and estimating the effect of the exogenous shock to the patented pharmaceutical market, due to the introduction of parallel trade.[972] Ganslandt and Maskus (2004) find that the prices of pharmaceutical products that faced competition from parallel trade fell relative to the prices of other pharmaceutical products from 1994 to 1999. In particular, Ganslandt and Maskus (2004) come to the conclusion that parallel trade significantly reduced prices, by 12-19 percent, relative to other pharmaceutical products not subject to competition from parallel trade. Arguably, parallel trade represents a significant form of competition in Sweden.

Finally, Richardson (2002) analyzes a two-stage game in which welfare-maximizing national governments simultaneously choose whether to permit or prohibit parallel trade in the first stage. In the second stage, a monopolistic manufacturer of a homogenous good sets a price for that good in each country. By assumption, welfare in the country in which the monopolist is located is given by the sum of the domestic

968 See Jelovac and Bordoy (2005) on p. 6.
969 See Jelovac and Bordoy (2005) on p. 18, proposition 1.
970 See Jelovac and Bordoy (2005) on p. 18, proposition 2.
971 See Ganslandt and Maskus (2004) on p. 1037.
972 See Ganslandt and Maskus (2004) on p. 1038.

consumer surplus and the global profits of the monopolist.[973] However, welfare in all other countries is simply domestic consumer surplus. Richardson (2002, p. 243ff) shows that it is a global Nash equilibrium for all countries to permit parallel trade, resulting in a globally uniform price for the product. The idea behind this result is the following.

On the one hand, the countries that prefer to permit parallel trade are those countries that would be discriminated against if parallel trade were prohibited, i.e. high-price countries with a relatively low price elasticity of demand.[974] Those countries can prevent price discrimination by permitting parallel trade.

On the other hand, those countries that might favour discrimination, i.e. low-price countries with a relatively high price elasticity of demand, cannot enforce price discrimination on a global scale when high-price countries permit parallel trade.[975]

Finally, Richardson (2002) examines more realistic settings, taking tariffs and lobbying by producers into account in order to analyze the question as to why barriers to parallel trade can actually be observed in practice. However, Richardson (2002) does not take into consideration the dynamic effects of parallel trade on the monopolist's decision to invest in R&D for new products.

5.2.3.2. Dynamic Effects of Parallel Trade on the Investment in R&D

As we have already mentioned earlier, the question as to how much a monopolistic manufacturer is willing to invest in R&D for new products is clearly of crucial importance to the research-intensive pharmaceutical industry. However, the literature on this issue is rather limited. To the best of our knowledge, Valletti and Szymanski (2006), Szymanski and Valletti (2005), Valeti (2006), Rey (2003), and Li and Maskus (2006) are the few exceptions of formal papers that look at the dynamic aspects of parallel trade in the context of R&D for new medicines.

In particular, this issue has been addressed in a recent paper by Valletti and Szymanski (2006) who have extended the well-known analysis of Malueg and Schwartz (1994) by endogenizing the quality of the good sold. More specifically, Valletti and Szymanski (2006) consider a model of product innovation in which a higher investment in R&D enables the manufacturer to discover products with higher quality. In particular, Valletti and Szymanski (2006) analyze a two-stage game in which a manufacturer chooses the quality of the product sold in the first stage and then chooses prices in the second stage. Furthermore, Valletti and Szymanski (2006) discuss the following basic trade-off between the positive *ex post* welfare properties of parallel trade, and the negative *ex ante* impact of parallel trade on aggregate welfare, respectively. In the second stage of the game, taking the level of product quality as fixed, a uniform pricing regime induced by parallel trade *ex post* results in higher aggregate welfare as long as demand dispersion across markets is sufficiently low.[976] However, in the first

973 See Richardson (2002) on p. 235ff. See also Deardorff (1992).

974 See Richardson (2002) on p. 237.

975 See Richardson (2002) on p. 237ff.

976 See Valletti and Szymanski (2006) on p. 507, proposition 3.

stage of the game, the threat of parallel trade reduces *ex ante* the incentive to invest and thus results in lower product quality.[977]

In a recent paper, Szymanski and Valletti (2005) analyze the policy implications of parallel trade in a model of vertical product differentiation with endogenous product quality. However, Szymanski and Valletti (2005, p. 730ff) also take into account the possibility that national governments may impose price caps as well as compulsory licences on patented products. Szymanski and Valletti (2005, p. 734) come to the conclusion that parallel trade entirely destroys the incentives to invest in R&D for new products if the national government of a foreign country issues a compulsory license on the patented product and unilaterally sets a fixed price equal to marginal cost to be paid to the patent holder.

If, however, the manufacturer has the option to either supply a high-quality product or a low-quality product to the foreign country and the foreign government offers the manufacturer a binding contract to issue a compulsory license at a capped price only for the low-quality product, then parallel trade has no effect on investment incentives.[978]

In another recent game-theoretic article, Valetti (2006) analyzes the question as to how a uniform pricing regime induced by parallel trade *ex ante* affects the incentives of a monopolistic manufacturer of pharmaceuticals to invest in R&D for new pharmaceutical products where the level of investment affects the quality of the new pharmaceutical product. Valletti (2006, p. 316) assumes that the markets in which the manufacturer sells his products differ in terms of marginal cost of manufacturing and delivering the product as well as in consumer demand in terms of the maximum willingness-to-pay of consumers.

However, in his analysis of the incentives to invest in R&D, Valetti (2006) reaches the conclusion that two trade-offs arise.

On the one hand, when differential pricing is demand-based, uniform pricing induced by parallel trade has good *ex post* welfare properties[979] but bad *ex ante* properties in terms of lower incentives to invest in R&D in order to obtain a better-quality product.[980]

On the other hand, when differential pricing is cost-based, uniform pricing induced by parallel trade has bad *ex post* welfare properties[981] but good *ex ante* properties in terms of higher incentives to invest in R&D in order to obtain a better-quality product.[982]

Rey (2003) provides another formal analysis that looks at the dynamic aspects of parallel trade. As in most countries pharmaceutical products are not directly purchased by consumers but by national governments at a regulated price, Rey (2003) analyzes the relationship between pharmaceutical companies and national governments in a game in which two national governments *H* and *L* contribute towards spurring investment through regulated prices.

977 See Valletti and Szymanski (2006) on p. 505, proposition 2.
978 See Szymanski and Valletti (2005) on p. 735.
979 See Valetti (2006) on p. 318, corollary 1.
980 See Valetti (2006) on p. 319.
981 See Valetti (2006) on p. 318, corollary 1.
982 See Valetti (2006) on p. 319.

On the one hand, government *H* has a high willingness to pay and places strong emphasis on high R&D for new medicines.[983]
On the other hand, government *L* has a low willingness to pay and places less emphasis on high R&D for new medicines.[984]
In particular, Rey (2003) shows that – once parallel trade is permitted – there is an equilibrium where government *H* reduces its contribution to R&D and sets a lower price, while government *L* maintains the same policy as in the absence of parallel trade.[985] Put differently, in this equilibrium parallel trade leads to a uniform alignment on the lowest level of R&D, which adversely affects both countries due to reduced incentives to invest in R&D for new medicines.[986]
Finally, in a recent article, Li and Maskus (2006) extend the model set out by Maskus and Chen (2002) to a framework with endogenous investment in process innovation. Li and Maskus (2006) analyze the impact of parallel trade on cost-reducing R&D in a vertical-pricing model in which a manufacturer invests in cost-reducing R&D and sells its product in another market through a distributor. In particular, they show that the distortions associated with parallel trade reduce the monopolist's incentive to invest in cost-reducing R&D.
However, we shall contribute to the first strand of formal literature on the determinants of parallel trade, with our double marginalization model to be elaborated in the following sections.

5.2.4. Double Marginalization Game with Complete Information

5.2.4.1. The Model

In this section, we develop a three-stage double marginalization game with complete information.[987] Player One is a monopolistic manufacturing pharmaceutical firm located in country *A*, henceforth *m*. Player Two is a single authorized independent firm located in country *B*, henceforth *r*, and is responsible for the distribution and retail of the manufacturer's product. We assume that efficient international distribution of the pharmaceutical product requires the manufacturer to build a market in country *B* through exclusive territorial dealership rights.[988] For instance, suppose that the exclusive distributor in country *B* has already established costly distribution channels.[989] Furthermore, we assume that the two countries differ in per capita income

983 See Rey (2003) on p. 17.
984 See Rey (2003) on p. 17, footnote 17.
985 See Rey (2003) on p. 21, proposition 1.
986 See Rey (2003) on p. 22ff.
987 See Feess (2000) on p. 319ff for an excellent introduction on monopoly theory. See also Weise et al. (2005) on p. 305ff. See also Fudenberg and Tirole (1996) on p. 65ff.
988 See Maskus and Chen (2002) and Maskus and Chen (2004) who originally formulated the theory of parallel imports in the context of vertical price controls.
989 Furthermore, as noted by Maskus (2000a) on p. 213, exclusive territorial dealership rights facilitate the manufacturer's monitoring of marketing efforts as well as the enforcement of product quality in foreign markets. One may also argue that the exclusive distributor can collect information on local

and in price elasticity of demand for a new medicine. The main purpose of this model is to analyze the pricing strategies of a producer of pharmaceuticals and an exclusive distributor. In particular, we analyze the question as to whether parallel imports may occur in equilibrium or not.

The strategies available to the manufacturer and the distributor are the different prices they might charge. We will assume that negative prices are not feasible, but that any non-negative price can be charged.[990] Moreover, we assume that the payoff functions for the manufacturer and the distributor are simply their profit. The timing of the game is as follows:

In the first stage, the manufacturing firm chooses the wholesale price p_B^w, $p_B^w \in [0,\infty)$, at which he sells the pharmaceutical product to the distributor in country *B*.

In the second stage, the distributor chooses the retail price p_B, $p_B \in [0,\infty)$, in country *B*.

In the third stage, the manufacturer *m* and the exclusive distributor *r* simultaneously choose the price at which they sell the product in country *A* in a Bertrand model of duopoly, e.g. p_A^m, $p_A^m \in [0,\infty)$, and p_A^r, $p_A^r \in [0,\infty)$, respectively. We assume that the product re-imported by the distributor from country *B* to country *A* is a perfect substitute for the pharmaceutical product sold by the manufacturer in country *A*.[991]

Consider a model with two countries *A* and *B*. Demand for a specific pharmaceutical product in country *A* is

$$D_A(p_A) = \gamma a - bp_A \tag{145}$$

with $\gamma > 1$. p_A denotes the price in country *A*. The pharmaceutical product is produced by a monopolistic manufacturing firm that holds a patent on the medicine in both countries. For simplicity, we assume that marginal costs of production *c* are equal to zero in both countries. This is a common assumption in models that deal with the strategic decisions of pharmaceutical companies, as the marginal cost of production are negligibly small compared to the cost of research and development.[992] Demand for the pharmaceutical product in Country *B* is

$$D_B(p_B) = a - bp_B. \tag{146}$$

γ is a measure for the homogeneity of the two countries. If γ tends towards 1 the two countries are virtually homogenous. Put differently, the higher is γ the more heterogeneous are the two countries.

---

tastes at lower costs than the manufacturer and that the distribution process exhibits economies of scale (Gallini and Hollis (1999) on p. 2). Hence, in the presence of large set-up costs of distribution channels, large costs of collecting information on local tastes and economies of scale in distribution, it can be an efficient means for the manufacturer to leave the responsibility for distribution and retail of the product with the single independent distributor. Indeed, many multinational firms build international marketing and production networks, maintain head offices in various countries, and are organized around subsidiaries which have significant decision-making power for the local market.

990 For instance, assume that disposal costs are equal to zero.

991 See Ganslandt and Maskus (2004) on p. 1041.

992 For instance, see Ganslandt and Maskus (2001) on p. 6.

As $\gamma > 1$ we can see from (145) and (146) that the price elasticity of demand[993] in country A, $E^A(p)$, is lower than the price elasticity of demand in country B, $E^B(p)$, for any given price p as

$$E^A(p) = \left|\frac{bp}{\gamma a - bp}\right| < \left|\frac{bp}{a - bp}\right| = E^B(p). \tag{147}$$

Thus, standard economic theory tells us that, in the absence of parallel imports, the single manufacturer engages in third-degree price discrimination and sets a price in country A that exceeds the price in country B.[994] Put differently, the larger is the size of the market in country A and the more inelastic is the demand in country A, the higher is the price in country A. However, consumers in the smaller country B where demand is elastic receive the pharmaceutical product at a lower price.[995]

We assume that there is an exclusive distributor in country B that is officially approved by the authorities in country A for re-importing the quantities of the pharmaceutical product he can buy from the monopolistic manufacturing firm in country A. Hence the distributor sells to consumers in country B at first, but may also engage in parallel trade from country B to country A. We also assume that arbitrage by individual consumers between B and A is legally prohibited.[996] We moreover suppose that the marginal costs of engaging in parallel trade are t. The costs of parallel trade include distribution cost as well as advertising cost. For instance, the costs of re-packaging and re-labelling are incurred by the parallel-importing distributor as well as other parallel trade-specific transaction costs such as import duties on parallel trade.[997] Furthermore, we assume that the parallel import product is a perfect substitute for the product sold by the original pharmaceutical producer in country A.[998]

5.2.4.2. *Analysis*

Before we proceed to the analysis of the three-stage double marginalization game with complete information as outlined in the previous section – this game being played between a monopolistic manufacturer in country A and an exclusive distributor in country B in order to endogenously derive the prices charged in country A and country B – consider the following two benchmark cases:

---

993 See Schäfer and Ott (2004) on p. 71ff for a definition of the price elasticity of demand. See also Varian (1996) on p. 266ff and Pindyck and Rubinfeld (2005) on p. 32ff.

994 In third-degree price discrimination, the monopolist sells output to different people or segmented markets at different prices, but individuals in the same segmented market or group pay the same price per unit of output. For instance, different admission prices for students or senior citizens in cinemas, theaters, amusement parks etc. are typical examples for third-degree price discrimination. See Varian (1999) on p. 440ff for a general model of third-degree price discrimination. See also Tirole (1988) on p. 137.

995 See Tirole (1988) on p. 137.

996 See Ganslandt and Maskus (2004) on p. 1041.

997 See NERA et al. (1999) on p. 15. See also Maskus and Chen (2004) on p. 566, Li and Maskus (2006) on p. 447, and Arfwedson (2004) on p. 8.

998 See also Ganslandt and Maskus (2004) on p. 1041.

In the first case, the question as to how the manufacturer would choose prices for maximizing profits if he directly served customers in both countries and parallel imports were prohibited is analyzed. Hence, we first analyze the manufacturer's optimal decision in the absence of an exclusive distributor in country *B* and thus without potential competition from parallel imports as a first benchmark.
In the second case, a two-stage double marginalization game with complete information played between the manufacturer in country *A* and the distributor in country *B* is analyzed. The manufacturing firm can engage in the retail of the pharmaceutical product in country *A*, but can only sell the product in country *B* through a distributor. Furthermore, the distributor in country *B* has a monopoly on the retailing business in country *B*. However, we assume that the manufacturer of the patented product can prevent parallel imports of his product from country *B*, i.e. under a regime of national exhaustion of intellectual property rights.
Finally, we will relax the latter assumption in the analysis of the three-stage double marginalization game with complete information, in which potential competition may arise from parallel imports in order to answer the question as to whether parallel imports may occur in equilibrium or not.

5.2.4.2.1. Third-Degree Price Discrimination under a Regime of National Exhaustion of IPRs

We assume that the manufacturer of the patented product is awarded the right to prevent parallel imports of his product from country *B*.[999] Put another way, the manufacturer retains full rights for distributing the patented product which also includes the right to exclude parallel imports from country *B*.[1000] To given an example, in the U.S., a pharmaceutical company that holds a patent on a specific prescription drug is protected from parallel imports of this drug by an explicit right of importation.[1001] Furthermore, we assume that there is no exclusive distributor in country *B* and that the manufacturing firm can engage in third-degree price discrimination. The manufacturing firm maximizes profits generated in country *A* according to

$$\max_{p_A}(\gamma a - bp_A)p_A.^{1002} \tag{148}$$

Furthermore, from (148) we obtain the following first order condition

$$\gamma a - 2bp_A = 0. \tag{149}$$

Consequently, the profit maximizing (monopoly) price is given by

$$p_A^* = \frac{\gamma a}{2b}. \tag{150}$$

999 See Maskus (2001) on p. 3. See also Maskus (2000a) on p. 208ff.
1000 See Maskus (2000a) on p. 208ff. See also Gallini and Hollis (1999) on p. 7ff on the use of trademark and copyright law as instruments for preventing parallel imports.
1001 For instance, see Arfwedson (2004) on p. 4.
1002 See also Ganslandt and Maskus (2004) on p. 1042.

The manufacturing firm maximizes profits generated in country *B* according to

$$\max_{p_B}(a-bp_B)p_B. \quad (151)$$

The first order condition is given by

$$a-2bp_B=0 \quad (152)$$

and the profit-maximizing price is consequently

$$p_B^*=\frac{a}{2b}. \quad (153)$$

By looking at (150) and (153) it becomes apparent that in the case of national exhaustion of intellectual property rights and price discrimination the manufacturing firm will set a price p_A^* in country *A* that exceeds the price p_B^* in country *B*, as the price elasticity of demand in country *A* is lower than that in country *B*, seeing as $\gamma>1$.[1003] By inserting (150) into (145) we have

$$D_A(p_A^*)=\gamma a-b\left(\frac{\gamma a}{2b}\right)=\frac{\gamma a}{2}. \quad (154)$$

Moreover, by inserting (153) into (146) we obtain

$$D_B(p_B^*)=a-b\left(\frac{a}{2b}\right)=\frac{a}{2}. \quad (155)$$

Correspondingly, total profit $\Pi(p_A^*,p_B^*)$, defined as the sum of the profit generated in country *A*, $\Pi_A(p_A^*)$, and the profit generated in country *B*, $\Pi_B(p_B^*)$, is given by

$$\Pi(p_A^*,p_B^*)=\Pi_A(p_A^*)+\Pi_B(p_B^*)=p_A^*D_A(p_A^*)+p_B^*D_B(p_B^*)$$
$$\Leftrightarrow \Pi(p_A^*,p_B^*)=\frac{\gamma a}{2b}\frac{\gamma a}{2}+\frac{a}{2b}\frac{a}{2}$$
$$\Leftrightarrow \Pi(p_A^*,p_B^*)=\frac{(\gamma a)^2+a^2}{4b}. \quad (156)$$

Interestingly, we can see from (156) that the total profit of the monopolist increases if γ increases. Put differently, the higher the market size in country *A* for a given *a* the higher is the monopolist's total profit provided that he is awarded the right to prevent parallel imports from country *B*. Comparing (150) to (153) we find that the difference

1003 For instance, see Tirole (1988) on p. 137.

between the profit-maximizing price in country A and the profit-maximizing price in country B increases if countries are increasingly heterogeneous.

5.2.4.2.2. Double Marginalization Game without Parallel Imports

As already noted before, a major determinant of parallel trade elaborated in the formal literature on parallel trade is that multinational firms that build markets through exclusive territorial dealership and distribution rights may find it difficult to enforce private contracts that prohibit parallel trade "outside the authorized distribution chain".[1004] For instance, recent EU case law suggests that a private contractual provision prohibiting parallel trade, at least within the common market, would be void.[1005] To give an example, a German pharmaceutical company that sells a patented pharmaceutical product at low prices to Portugal while charging a high price in Germany cannot prevent parallel trade simply by declaring that the export product is "not for re-sale in Germany".[1006]

In game-theoretic parlance, suppose that the manufacturing firm can itself become involved in the retail of the pharmaceutical product in country A, but sells the product in country B through an exclusive distributor. Furthermore, we assume that the distributor in country B has a monopoly on the retailing business in country B.[1007] We make the simplifying assumption that retailing in country B does not involve any cost, except for the cost incurred by the distributor in buying the units of the pharmaceutical product from the manufacturing firm. Demand for the pharmaceutical product at the retail level is given by the demand curve $D_B(p_B) = a - bp_B$, where p_B is the retail price in country B.

In the first stage, the manufacturing firm sets a wholesale price p_B^w for the distributor, and the distributor sets a price p_B for the retail trade in country B in the second stage.[1008] To keep matters simple, we will first assume that the manufacturer is awarded the right to prevent parallel imports of the pharmaceutical product from country B, i.e. he is awarded an explicit right of importation of the pharmaceutical product.[1009] Arbitrage by individual consumers between the two countries is legally prohibited.[1010] The distributor is quoted a wholesale price p_B^w, which the distributor must pay per unit at wholesale.

Using backward induction we start with the second stage. In the second stage, the distributor chooses which retail price p_B he will charge his customers in country B.

1004 See Maskus (2000a) on p. 213.

1005 The following references to cases are to those of the ECJ. See Case C-187/80 *Merck & Co. Inc. vs. Stephar B.V. and Petrus Stephanus Exler*. See also Case C-56/64 *Etablissements Consten S.A. and Grundigverkaufs-GmbH. vs. E.E.C. Commission*, and Case C-78/70 *Deutsche Grammophon Gesellschaft mbH. vs. Metro-SB-Grossmärkte GmbH & Co. K.G.*. See also Joined Cases C-267-268/95 *Merck & Co. Inc. and Others vs. Primecrown Limited and Others.*

1006 For instance, see Maskus (2000b) on p. 1270ff.

1007 For an example of a monopoly selling to another monopoly see Kreps (1990) on p. 309ff.

1008 See Spengler (1950). See also Kreps (1994) on p. 273ff and Tirole (1995) on p. 379ff.

1009 For instance, see Arfwedson (2004) on p. 4.

1010 See Ganslandt and Maskus (2004) on p. 1044.

The distributor, facing wholesale price p_B^w, will treat p_B^w as his marginal cost and will set p_B in order to maximize his profit $\pi(p_B)$.[1011] Thus

$$\max_{p_B}\left(p_B - p_B^w\right)D_B(p_B). \tag{157}$$

By inserting (146) into (157) and reformulating (157) we obtain the following first order condition

$$\frac{\partial\pi\left(p_B, p_B^w\right)}{\partial p_B} = a - 2bp_B + bp_B^w = 0$$
$$\Leftrightarrow p_B = \frac{a + bp_B^w}{2b}. \tag{158}$$

Furthermore, this gives

$$\pi\left(p_B^w\right) = \left(\frac{a + bp_B^w}{2b} - p_B^w\right)\left(a - b\left(\frac{a + bp_B^w}{2b}\right)\right)$$
$$\Leftrightarrow \pi\left(p_B^w\right) = \frac{\left(a - bp_B^w\right)^2}{4b}. \tag{159}$$

In the first stage, the manufacturing firm sets the wholesale price at p_B^w, anticipating that the distributor will purchase $\left(a - bp_B^w\right)/2$. Hence the manufacturer's profit generated in country *B*, $\Pi_B(p_B^w)$, will be

$$\Pi_B(p_B^w) = p_B^w\left(\frac{a - bp_B^w}{2}\right)$$
$$\Leftrightarrow \Pi_B(p_B^w) = \frac{a}{2}p_B^w - \frac{b}{2}p_B^{w2} \tag{160}$$

which gives the following first order condition

$$bp_B^w = \frac{a}{2}$$
$$\Leftrightarrow p_B^{w*} = \frac{a}{2b}. \tag{161}$$

Inserting (161) into (158) and reformulating (158) we obtain

1011 Note that the manufacturer's profit is denoted by Π and the distributor's profit by π, respectively.

$$p_B = \frac{3}{2}\frac{a}{2b}$$
$$\Leftrightarrow p_B = \frac{3}{2} p_B^{w*} . \quad (162)$$

We can see from (162) that the distributor marks up the price of the pharmaceutical product by 50 percent, compared to the wholesale price p_B^{w*}. However, if the manufacturer were directly engaged in the retail business in country *B*, he would set a price $p_B^* = a/(2b)$ as given by (153) in the previous section. By comparing (153) with (162) it becomes apparent that, if the manufacturer were to sell the pharmaceutical product directly, more would be sold at a lower price than when the manufacturer must go through a distributor that has a monopoly on the retailing business in country *B*.
Inserting (161) into (160) we obtain the equilibrium profit of the manufacturer generated in country *B*

$$\Pi_B = \frac{a^2}{8b} . \quad (163)$$

The profit generated in country *A* is $\Pi_A = (\gamma a)^2 / 4b$ which we can directly obtain from the maximization problem given in (156). Moreover, by inserting (161) into (159) we obtain the equilibrium profit of the distributor

$$\pi = \frac{a^2}{16b} . \quad (164)$$

So far, we have assumed that the distributor is not allowed to re-import quantities of the pharmaceutical product into country *A*, i.e. under a global regime of national exhaustion of intellectual property rights. In the following section, we relax this assumption and allow for parallel imports, in order to explore the important strategic decision faced by the manufacturer as to at which wholesale price the pharmaceutical product is sold to the distributor in country *B*, anticipating that part of the quantities sold can be re-imported.

5.2.4.2.3. Double Marginalization Game with Parallel Imports

The main purpose of the double marginalization game with complete information elaborated in this section is to analyze the pricing strategies of the manufacturing firm *m* and the exclusive distributor *r*. In particular, we wish to analyze the question as to whether parallel imports may or may not occur in equilibrium. Furthermore, we assume that the manufacturer cannot contractually limit or even prohibit parallel trade by imposing supply quotas on the distributor in country *B*.[1012] The timing of the game

1012 See Joined cases C-2/01 P and C-3/01 P *Bundesverband der Arzneimittel-Importeure e.V. and Commission of the European Communities vs. Bayer AG*. See also case C-277/87 *Sandoz prodotti farmaceutici SpA vs. Commission of the European Communities.*

played between the manufacturer in country A and the distributor in country B is as follows.

In the first stage, the manufacturing firm chooses the wholesale price p_B^w at which it sells the pharmaceutical product to the distributor in country B.

In the second stage, the distributor chooses the retail price p_B in country B.

In the third stage, the monopolist and the distributor simultaneously choose the price at which they sell the product in country A in a Bertrand duopoly model.

We solve the game starting with the last stage and working backwards to the first stage, in order to look for the sub-game perfect Nash equilibrium.

5.2.4.2.3.1. Backward Induction

We start with the last stage where the manufacturer and the distributor play a Bertrand game[1013] and simultaneously choose prices for the pharmaceutical product in country A.[1014] We assume that the pharmaceutical product re-imported by the distributor from country B to country A is a perfect substitute for the pharmaceutical product sold by the manufacturer in country A.[1015] In looking for the Bertrand equilibrium this section will demonstrate different scenarios in terms of the prices the manufacturer and the distributor are charging, as well as in terms of the demand they are serving in country A. Prices and demand served must be consistent with the following rules:[1016] if the manufacturer and the distributor charge unequal prices, the low-price firm serves the entire market at the low price. Furthermore, the high-price firm gets no sales. However, if the manufacturer and the distributor charge the same price, total market demand is equally divided between them. Let us suppose that the quantity consumers demand from the manufacturer is

---

1013 One may argue that the application of a Cournot quantity competition framework instead of a Bertrand price competition would be more suitable to model the strategic interaction at the third stage. However, from the author's point of view, Bertrand's approach has a certain modeling advantage over the Cournot setup and seems to be a better approximation to reality in the pharmaceutical industry for various reasons. First, as already noted earlier, parallel trade is an important issue in the context of third-degree price discrimination, as parallel trade erodes the monopolist's ability to discriminate prices across markets. Hence, one may argue that prices and not quantities should be the decision variables in a model that elaborates on these issues in the first place. Second, since prices are the decision variables in our model and not just an endogenous consequence of the firms' output decisions, we do not need to resort to any additional mechanism such as an (artificial) auctioneer to determine the market-clearing price (Vega-Redondo (2003) on p. 153ff). Put differently, the main modeling advantage of the Bertrand setup is that it includes an explicit description of all components required for understanding how the market actually operates, whereas the Cournot framework resorts to an additional theoretical mechanism to determine the market-clearing price. Finally, since the marginal cost of production in the pharmaceutical industry is negligibly small, one may also argue that capacities and output can be changed relatively easily compared to other industries. Hence, it may not be possible to vindicate the Cournot setup on the grounds of the well-known argument originally formulated by Kreps and Scheinkman (1983) that - by introducing capacity constraints - a two-stage game in which firms simultaneously choose capacities in the first stage and (Bertrand) prices in the second stage is equivalent to a one-stage Cournot game.

1014 See Bertrand (1883). See also Feess (2000) on p. 411ff.

1015 See Ganslandt and Maskus (2004) on p. 1041.

1016 See Kreps (1990) on p. 331.

$$q_A^m = \begin{cases} \gamma a - bp_A^m & if\, p_A^m < p_A^r \\ \dfrac{\gamma a - bp_A^m}{2} & if\, p_A^m = p_A^r \\ 0 & if\ p_A^m > p_A^r. \end{cases} \tag{165}$$

Similarly, the quantity that consumers demand from the distributor is given by

$$q_A^r = \begin{cases} \gamma a - bp_A^r & if\, p_A^r < p_A^m \\ \dfrac{\gamma a - bp_A^r}{2} & if\, p_A^r = p_A^m \\ 0 & if\ p_A^r > p_A^m. \end{cases} \tag{166}$$

By assumption the manufacturer has fixed cost of zero and marginal cost of zero. Furthermore, we assume that the distributor also has fixed cost of zero. However, by assumption, the distributor treats the sum of the wholesale price p_B^w and the per unit cost of engaging in parallel trade t as his marginal cost of selling the pharmaceutical product in country A in the third stage.

First, note that a firm would never charge a price that is lower than its marginal cost. In this case, the firm could increase its profits by simply reducing the quantities produced. On the one hand, the manufacturer could supply a positive quantity of the product as long as the price is non-negative, as his marginal costs are zero. On the other hand, the distributor would not charge a price smaller than his marginal cost $p_B^w + t$. Hence, the manufacturer can monopolize the market in country A and steal all of the customers from the parallel importing distributor by setting a price that is infinitesimally smaller than the marginal cost of the distributor. Put differently, the manufacturer will always set the price $p_A^m < p_B^w + t$. Consequently, the distributor will not stay in the market in country A and will not engage in parallel trade. At this point we can already formulate one of the main results of the analysis of the double marginalization game with complete information.

Proposition 5:

Parallel imports will never occur in any sub-game perfect Nash equilibrium in a double marginalization game with complete information and Bertrand price competition in the last stage.

Note that this result holds for any non-negative p_B^w and any positive t.

In the second stage, the distributor anticipates that he will be driven out of the market in country A in the third stage. Hence the maximization problem of the distributor is identical to the maximization problem we have already discussed before [see (157)–(159)]. For instance, the distributor will choose a price $p_B = (a + bp_B^w)/2b$.

Working backwards to the first stage, the maximization problem of the manufacturer is to maximize the total profit generated in country A and country B, subject to the constraint stated in $p_A^m \leq p_B^w + t$[1017] and subject to the non-negativity restrictions stated in $p_A^m \geq 0$ and $p_B^w \geq 0$. Mathematically, what the constraint and the non-negativity restrictions do is to narrow the range of the profit function. After the constraints are added we can admit only those values of p_A^m and p_B^w which satisfy the constraints. Note that we have to adopt the Kuhn-Tucker Method to find a maximum, as we are dealing with an optimization problem with inequality constraints. In fact, the Kuhn-Tucker Method is just a generalization of the Lagrange-Multiplier Method for optimization problems with inequality constraints.[1018] Adopting the Kuhn-Tucker Method, we first have to identify the maximization problem. Secondly, we will define the Lagrange function by multiplying each constraint with the corresponding Lagrange multiplier and by adding it to the original profit function. And thirdly, we will derive the first-order conditions that a solution for the maximization problem must satisfy. First, the maximization problem has the following format:

$$max\, \Pi(p_A^m, p_B^w) = \left(\gamma a - bp_A^m\right) p_A^m + p_B^w \left(\frac{a\text{-}bp_B^w}{2}\right)$$

$$\begin{aligned} &\text{subject to} \quad p_A^m \geq 0 \\ &\text{and} \quad p_B^w \geq 0 \\ &\text{and} \quad p_A^m - p_B^w \leq t. \end{aligned} \tag{167}$$

Second, let us write the classical type of the Lagrangian function, L, as follows

$$L(p_A^m, p_B^w; \lambda_1, \lambda_2, \lambda_3) = \left(\gamma a - bp_A^m\right) p_A^m + p_B^w \left(\frac{a\text{-}bp_B^w}{2}\right) + \lambda_1 p_A^m + \lambda_2 p_B^w + \lambda_3 \left(t + p_B^w - p_A^m\right). \tag{168}$$

Third, we obtain the following first-order conditions:

$$\frac{\partial L}{\partial p_A^m} = \gamma a - 2bp_A^m + \lambda_1 - \lambda_3 = 0, \tag{169}$$

$$\frac{\partial L}{\partial p_B^w} = \frac{a}{2} - bp_B^w + \lambda_2 + \lambda_3 = 0, \tag{170}$$

$$\lambda_1 p_A^m = 0, \tag{171}$$

$$\lambda_2 p_B^w = 0, \tag{172}$$

$$\lambda_3 \left(t + p_B^w - p_A^m\right) = 0. \tag{173}$$

$$p_A^m \geq 0, p_B^w \geq 0, \tag{174}$$

1017 Note that the manufacturer always sets a price in country A that undercuts the distributor's marginal costs. The manufacturer undercuts the distributor's marginal cost at least by an infinitely small ε.

1018 See Kuhn and Tucker (1951). See also Chiang (1984) on p. 722ff and Eichberger (2004) on p. 402ff.

$$t + p_B^w - p_A^m \geq 0. \tag{175}$$

$$\lambda_1 \geq 0, \lambda_2 \geq 0, \lambda_3 \geq 0. \tag{176}$$

We must now find solutions $\left(p_A^m, p_B^w, \lambda_1, \lambda_2, \lambda_3\right)$ that can satisfy all conditions given by (169)–(176). Therefore it is appropriate to discuss various cases that differ as to the extent to which the constraints are binding. For instance, if $\lambda_1 > 0$, it follows from (171) that $p_A^m = 0$. To give another example, if $p_A^m > 0$, it follows from (171) that $\lambda_1 = 0$.[1019] As we have three Lagrange multipliers λ_1, λ_2 and λ_3 that are either positive or equal to zero, we have to distinguish between nine different cases.

After checking each of the nine cases with regard to the question as to whether it satisfies all conditions given by (169)–(176) we obtain two solutions: $\left(p_A^{m*}, p_B^{w*}, \lambda_1^*, \lambda_2^*, \lambda_3^*\right)$ and $\left(p_A^{m**}, p_B^{w**}, \lambda_1^{**}, \lambda_2^{**}, \lambda_3^{**}\right)$. The first solution is given by:

$$\begin{pmatrix} p_A^{m*} = \frac{a}{6b}(2\gamma+1) + \frac{1}{3}t, \\ p_B^{w*} = \frac{a}{6b}(2\gamma+1) - \frac{2}{3}t, \\ \lambda_1^* = 0, \\ \lambda_2^* = 0, \\ \lambda_3^* = \frac{a}{3}(\gamma-1) - \frac{2b}{3}t. \end{pmatrix} \tag{177}$$

We can see from (177) that the optimal price the manufacturer sets in country *A* always exceeds the optimal wholesale price the manufacturer charges the distributor in country *B* as $t > 0$. More specifically, the difference between p_A^{m*} and p_B^{w*} is equal to *t*. Furthermore, we can see from (177) that the optimal wholesale price decreases if *t* increases, and that the optimal price the manufacturer sets in country *A* increases if *t* increases, respectively. Put differently, the higher the parallel trade cost *t* for a given γ and thus the less profitable parallel trade the higher is p_A^{m*} and the lower p_B^{w*}.

However, we can also see from (177) that the non-negativity restriction for λ_3^* is only satisfied for specific values for the parameter *t*. Therefore, let us now determine this threshold for *t*.

$$\lambda_3^* = \frac{a}{3}(\gamma-1) - \frac{2b}{3}t \geq 0$$

$$\Leftrightarrow t \leq \frac{a}{2b}(\gamma-1). \tag{178}$$

1019 The conditions which imply that either the Lagrange multiplier is zero or a constraint binding are called complementary slackness conditions. See also Chiang (1984) on p. 722ff.

Henceforth, we will refer to this threshold given by (178) as the *upper* bound for the trade cost, that is $\bar{t} = a(\gamma - 1)/2b$.
To conclude the discussion with respect to the first solution, the outcome $(p_A^{m*}, p_B^{w*}, \lambda_1^*, \lambda_2^*, \lambda_3^*)$ given by (177) only satisfies each of the eight conditions given by (169)-(176) if $t \le \bar{t}$.[1020] If, however, $t > \bar{t}$, i.e. for high parallel trade cost and a relatively low γ, $(p_A^{m*}, p_B^{w*}, \lambda_1^*, \lambda_2^*, \lambda_3^*)$ is not a solution for the maximization problem given by (167), due to the fact that the non-negativity restriction for λ_3^* would not be satisfied. Thus we have to consider the second solution $(p_A^{m**}, p_B^{w**}, \lambda_1^{**}, \lambda_2^{**}, \lambda_3^{**})$ given by

$$\begin{pmatrix} p_A^{m**} = \frac{\gamma a}{2b}, \\ p_B^{w**} = \frac{a}{2b}, \\ \lambda_1^{**} = 0, \\ \lambda_2^{**} = 0, \\ \lambda_3^{**} = 0. \end{pmatrix} \tag{179}$$

When we compare (179) with (150) and (161), we find that p_A^{m**} is equal to the monopoly price in a double marginalization game in which parallel imports are prohibited,[1021] and p_B^{w**} is equal to the profit-maximizing wholesale price in a double marginalization game in which parallel imports are prohibited, respectively. Intuitively, if the two countries are virtually homogeneous ($\gamma \to 1$) and the parallel trade costs are so high that $t > \bar{t}$, the distributor will not be willing to engage in parallel trade. Put differently, if $t > \bar{t}$, the outcome of the double marginalization game in which parallel imports are permitted is equal to the outcome of the double marginalization game in which the manufacturer is awarded the right to prevent parallel imports.

1020 See **Appendix 7** for the proof that for the non-negativity restriction for p_B^{w*} to be satisfied it is sufficient that the non-negativity restriction for λ_3^* is satisfied.

1021 Note that the monopoly price in country *A* in a double marginalization game without parallel imports is equal to the monopoly price under third-degree price discrimination given by (150).

5.2.4.3. Effects of Parallel Trade Freedom on Profits, Consumer Surplus, National and Global Welfare

5.2.4.3.1. Equilibrium Prices and Quantities

Table 4 provides a summary of the equilibrium prices and quantities in country *A* and country *B* when the manufacturer is awarded the right to prevent parallel trade and when parallel trade is permitted for low trade cost (denoted by subscript *l*), intermediate trade cost (denoted by subscript *i*) and high trade cost (denoted by subscript *h*).

For instance, we obtain the equilibrium retail price under a regime of international exhaustion when parallel trade is allowed and intermediate trade cost denoted by $p^{*}_{(B,i)}$ by plugging the equilibrium wholesale price $p^{w*}_{(B,i)}$ into the reaction function of the distributor given by (158).

Furthermore, we obtain the equilibrium quantities by plugging the relevant equilibrium prices into the relevant demand functions. For instance, we obtain the equilibrium quantity in country *B* under a regime of international exhaustion and intermediate trade cost denoted by $q^{*}_{(B,i)}$ by plugging $p^{*}_{(B,i)}$ into the demand function given by (146).

Table 4 *Equilibrium Prices and Quantities*

	Manufacturer can prevent parallel imports		
	Scenario 1-3 (high, intermediate and low *t*)		
	Parallel imports permitted	**Parallel imports permitted**	
	Scenario 1 high *t*: $t > \bar{t}$	**Scenario 2 intermediate *t*:** $\underline{t} \le t \le \bar{t}$	**Scenario 3 low *t*:** $t < \underline{t}$
Equilibrium price in country *A*	$p_A^{m**} = p_{(A,h)}^{m*} = \frac{a\gamma}{2b}$	$p_{(A,i)}^{m*} = \frac{a\gamma}{3b} + \frac{a}{6b} + \frac{t}{3}$	$p_{(A,l)}^{m*} = \frac{a\gamma}{3b} + \frac{a}{6b} + \frac{t}{3}$
Equilibrium quantity in country *A*	$q_A^{**} = q_{(A,h)}^{*} = \frac{a\gamma}{2}$	$q_{(A,i)}^{*} = \frac{2a\gamma}{3} - \frac{a}{6} - \frac{bt}{3}$	$q_{(A,l)}^{*} = \frac{2a\gamma}{3} - \frac{a}{6} - \frac{bt}{3}$
Equilibrium wholesale price in country *B*	$p_B^{w**} = p_{(B,h)}^{w*} = \frac{a}{2b}$	$p_{(B,i)}^{w*} = \frac{a\gamma}{3b} + \frac{a}{6b} - \frac{2t}{3}$	Country *B* will not be served
Equilibrium retail price in country *B*	$p_B^{**} = p_{(B,h)}^{*} = \frac{3a}{4b}$	$p_{(B,i)}^{*} = \frac{7a}{12b} + \frac{a\gamma}{6b} - \frac{t}{3}$	Country *B* will not be served
Equilibrium quantity in country *B*	$q_B^{**} = q_{(B,h)}^{*} = \frac{a}{4}$	$q_{(B,i)}^{*} = \frac{5a}{12} - \frac{a\gamma}{6} + \frac{bt}{3}$	Country *B* will not be served

In order to double-check that the results in **Table 4** are correct, note that the equilibrium prices and quantities in country *A* and country *B* in both situations with and without parallel imports are identical if we set $t = \bar{t} = a(\gamma - 1)/2b$ which we will call the upper bound for *t*. If trade costs exceed the upper bound, we will refer to them as high trade costs. Furthermore, we know from the analysis in the previous sections that the equilibrium prices and quantities for high trade costs are the same in both cases when the manufacturer is awarded the right to prevent parallel imports and when parallel imports are permitted, i.e. $p_B^{w**} = p_{(B,h)}^{w*}$.

There is, however, also a lower bound for *t* under a regime of international exhaustion of intellectual property rights with parallel trade as we will see in the following.

The distributor will only be willing to sell the product in country *B* as long as he can sell a quantity of the product in country *B* that is equal to or greater than zero and as long as the retail price he can charge is equal to or greater than the wholesale price set by the manufacturer. Put differently,

$$
\begin{aligned}
& q^*_{(B,i)} \geq 0 \\
& \Leftrightarrow \frac{5a}{12} - \frac{a\gamma}{6} + \frac{bt}{3} \geq 0 \\
& \Leftrightarrow t \geq \frac{a}{2b}\left(\gamma - \frac{5}{2}\right).
\end{aligned} \tag{180}
$$

Alternatively, we can derive the participation constraint for the distributor as follows.

$$
\begin{aligned}
& p^*_{(B,i)} \geq p^{w*}_{(B,i)} \\
& \Leftrightarrow \frac{7a}{12b} + \frac{a\gamma}{6b} - \frac{t}{3} \geq \frac{a\gamma}{3b} + \frac{a}{6b} - \frac{2t}{3} \\
& \Leftrightarrow t \geq \frac{a}{2b}\left(\gamma - \frac{5}{2}\right).
\end{aligned} \tag{181}
$$

Henceforth, we will refer to this threshold given by (181) as the *lower* bound for the trade cost, that is $\underline{t} = a(\gamma - (5/2))/2b$. Intuitively, if trade costs are very low, i.e. $t < \underline{t}$, potential competition from parallel trade is so fierce that the manufacturer has to charge such a high wholesale price in country *B* in order to deter parallel trade that the distribution of the good in country *B* becomes unprofitable. In this case, the market in country *B* will not be served. We will come back to this issue at the end of this chapter where we analyze the welfare effects of parallel trade for different combinations of the parameters *t* and γ.

However, we can see from the previous analysis that we have to deal with three different scenarios.

First, parallel trade costs are so high – more specifically $t > \bar{t}$ – that parallel trade is not a worthwhile activity for the distributor and thus a non-credible threat. In other words, for very high trade costs, the equilibrium outcome will be the same no matter whether or not the manufacturer is awarded the right to prevent parallel trade. More specifically, parallel trade does not have any impact on profits, consumer surplus, and welfare in both countries. Consequently, parallel trade does not have any impact on global welfare if trade costs are very high.

However, the analysis of the second scenario with trade costs at an intermediate level is not trivial. As we will see in the following, for intermediate trade costs, the manufacturer will strategically set prices in order to deter parallel trade under a regime of international exhaustion of IPRs. However, the wholesale price will be sufficiently low so that the distribution of the product in country *B* is still a worthwhile activity.

In the third scenario with very low trade costs – more specifically $t < \underline{t}$ – the manufacturer will charge such a high wholesale price in country *B*, in order to deter parallel trade under a regime of international exhaustion of IPRs that the market in country *B* ends up not being served.

In the following sections, we will analyze the impact of parallel trade on the profit of the manufacturer and on global welfare for the second and the third scenario mentioned above.

5.2.4.3.2. Effect of Parallel Trade Freedom on the Profit of the Manufacturer

In the following sections, we will show that the following proposition holds.

Proposition 6:
The threat of parallel trade – under a regime of international exhaustion of IPRs – leads to lower profits of the manufacturer (i) if trade costs are intermediate and (ii) if trade costs are low, respectively.

5.2.4.3.2.1. Effect of Parallel Trade Freedom on the Manufacturer's Profit for Intermediate Trade Costs

At an intermediate level of *t*, $\underline{t} \leq t \leq \bar{t}$, the equilibrium profit of the manufacturer if parallel trade is permitted is given by[1022]

$$\Pi_i^* = \Pi_{(A,i)}^* + \Pi_{(B,i)}^* = p_{(A,i)}^{m*} q_{(A,i)}^* + p_{(B,i)}^{w*} q_{(B,i)}^*$$

$$\Leftrightarrow \Pi_i^* = \left(\frac{a\gamma}{3b} + \frac{a}{6b} + \frac{t}{3}\right)\left(\frac{2a\gamma}{3} - \frac{a}{6} - \frac{bt}{3}\right) + \left(\frac{a\gamma}{3b} + \frac{a}{6b} - \frac{2t}{3}\right)\left(\frac{5a}{12} - \frac{a\gamma}{6} + \frac{bt}{3}\right)$$

$$\Leftrightarrow \Pi_i^* = \frac{a^2}{24b} - \frac{at}{3} - \frac{bt^2}{3} + \frac{a^2\gamma}{6b} + \frac{at\gamma}{3} + \frac{a^2\gamma^2}{6b}. \tag{182}$$

However, at an intermediate level of *t*, the equilibrium profit of the manufacturer if he is awarded the right to prevent parallel trade is given by

$$\Pi_i^{**} = \Pi^{**} = \Pi_A^{**} + \Pi_B^{**} = p_A^{m**} q_A^{**} + p_B^{w**} q_B^{**}$$

$$\Leftrightarrow \Pi_i^{**} = \frac{a\gamma}{2b}\frac{a\gamma}{2} + \frac{a}{2b}\frac{a}{4}$$

$$\Leftrightarrow \Pi_i^{**} = \Pi^{**} = \frac{a^2}{8b} + \frac{a^2\gamma^2}{4b}. \tag{183}$$

Note that $\Pi_i^{**} = \Pi_l^{**} = \Pi_h^{**} = \Pi^{**}$ as the profit of the manufacturer is always the same if he is awarded the right to prevent parallel trade. The question arises as to whether parallel trade – at an intermediate level of *t* – has a positive or negative impact on the profit of the manufacturer. In particular, let $\Delta\Pi_i$ denote the difference between the equilibrium profit of the manufacturer if parallel trade is permitted given by (182) and the equilibrium profit of the manufacturer if he has the right to prevent parallel trade given by (183). Hence,

1022 Recall that the manufacturer's profit is denoted by Π and the distributor's profit by π, respectively.

$$\Delta\Pi_i = \Pi_i^* - \Pi_i^{**}$$
$$\Leftrightarrow \Delta\Pi_i = \frac{a^2}{24b} - \frac{at}{3} - \frac{bt^2}{3} + \frac{a^2\gamma}{6b} + \frac{at\gamma}{3} + \frac{a^2\gamma^2}{6b} - \frac{a^2}{8b} - \frac{a^2\gamma^2}{4b}$$
$$\Leftrightarrow \Delta\Pi_i = -\frac{a^2}{12b} - \frac{at}{3} - \frac{bt^2}{3} + \frac{a^2\gamma}{6b} + \frac{at\gamma}{3} - \frac{a^2\gamma^2}{12b}. \qquad (184)$$

Note that $\Delta\Pi_i$ is a quadratic function of t which is an important feature we will elaborate upon in the following. It is straightforward to see that a negative $\Delta\Pi_i$ would indicate that the manufacturer can generate a higher profit if he were awarded the right to prevent parallel trade. In other words, in order to show that, for intermediate trade costs, parallel trade harms the manufacturer it is sufficient to show that $\Delta\Pi_i$ is negative. Intuitively, $\Delta\Pi_i = 0$ if $t = \bar{t}$ as the equilibrium quantities and prices are identical in both situations with and without parallel trade. In order to see that this intuition is correct, set $t = \bar{t} = a(\gamma-1)/2b$ in (184):

$$\Delta\Pi_i = -\frac{a^2}{12b} - \frac{a\left(\frac{a}{2b}(\gamma-1)\right)}{3} - \frac{b\left(\frac{a}{2b}(\gamma-1)\right)^2}{3} + \frac{a^2\gamma}{6b} + \frac{a\gamma\left(\frac{a}{2b}(\gamma-1)\right)}{3} - \frac{a^2\gamma^2}{12b}$$
$$\Leftrightarrow \Delta\Pi_i = -\frac{a^2}{12b} - \frac{a^2\gamma}{6b} + \frac{a^2}{6b} - \frac{a^2\gamma^2}{12b} + \frac{2a^2\gamma}{12b} - \frac{a^2}{12b} + \frac{a^2\gamma}{6b} + \frac{a^2\gamma^2}{6b} - \frac{a^2\gamma}{6b} - \frac{a^2\gamma^2}{12b}$$
$$\Leftrightarrow \Delta\Pi_i = 0. \qquad (185)$$

Furthermore, note that $\Delta\Pi_i$ has its maximum at $t = \bar{t}$ as

$$\frac{\partial\Delta\Pi_i}{\partial t} = -\frac{a}{3} - \frac{2bt}{3} + \frac{a\gamma}{3} = 0$$
$$\Leftrightarrow t = \frac{a}{2b}(\gamma-1) \qquad (186)$$

and

$$\frac{\partial^2\Delta\Pi_i}{\partial^2 t} = -\frac{2b}{3} < 0 \qquad (187)$$

as $b > 0$. To summarize, $\Delta\Pi_i$ is a quadratic function of t and has its maximum at $\bar{t}$. Furthermore, $\Delta\Pi_i = 0$ at $\bar{t}$. Hence, $\Delta\Pi_i$ is negative for any other value of the parameter t. Therefore, for intermediate trade costs, parallel trade harms the manufacturer as it leads to a lower profit [*Proposition 6(i)*].

However, an important point in favor of banning parallel trade is the following. By the time the manufacturer chooses to invest in R&D for a new product, he will be more willing to do so, anticipating that he will be able to raise more money from the new

product. In other words, under the assumption that the R&D investment leads with certainty to the development of a new product, the maximum amount that the manufacturer is willing to invest in R&D for the product is just the profit that he can generate.[1023] As the profit of the manufacturer if he is awarded the right to prevent parallel trade is higher than his profit under parallel trade freedom, the incentive of the manufacturer to invest in R&D – for intermediate trade costs – is higher if he can prevent parallel trade.[1024]
However, let us now turn to the question whether the same reasoning applies to the case with low trade costs in the following.

5.2.4.3.2.2. Effect of Parallel Trade Freedom on the Manufacturer's Profit for Low Trade Costs

In this section, we consider the case of very low trade costs, $t<\underline{t}$. Recall that trade costs are assumed to be positive. Hence, we can see from $t<\underline{t}=a(\gamma-(5/2))/2b$ that γ must be greater than 5/2 in this case. For smaller values of the parameter γ we would automatically end up in one of the other two scenarios mentioned above. Intuitively, if γ is very low, i.e. $\gamma \to 1$, parallel trade may not be a highly attractive business activity for the distributor even if trade costs are very low.
However, if trade costs are very low and $\gamma > 5/2$, the market in country *B* will end up not being served. Hence, the manufacturer will only generate a profit in country *A* if parallel trade is permitted. The profit is given by

$$\Pi_l^* = p_{(A,l)}^{m*} q_{(A,l)}^*$$
$$\Leftrightarrow \Pi_l^* = \left(\frac{a\gamma}{3b}+\frac{a}{6b}+\frac{t}{3}\right)\left(\frac{2\gamma a}{3}-\frac{a}{6}-\frac{bt}{3}\right)$$
$$\Leftrightarrow \Pi_l^* = -\frac{a^2}{36b}-\frac{at}{9}-\frac{bt^2}{9}+\frac{a^2\gamma}{18b}+\frac{at\gamma}{9}+\frac{2a^2\gamma^2}{9b}. \tag{188}$$

However, for low trade cost, the equilibrium profit of the manufacturer if he is awarded the right to prevent parallel trade is given by

$$\Pi_l^{**} = \Pi_i^{**} = \frac{a^2}{8b}+\frac{a^2\gamma^2}{4b}. \tag{189}$$

The question arises as to whether the threat of parallel trade – for low trade cost – has a positive or negative impact on the profit of the manufacturer. In particular, let $\Delta\Pi_l$ denote the difference between the equilibrium profit of the manufacturer if parallel trade is permitted and the equilibrium profit of the manufacturer if he has the right to prevent parallel trade. Hence,

---

1023 See also Deardorff (1992) on p. 40.
1024 See also Valletti and Szymanski (2006) on p. 504.

$$\Delta\Pi_l = \Pi_l^* - \Pi_l^{**}$$

$$\Leftrightarrow \Delta\Pi_l = -\frac{a^2}{36b} - \frac{at}{9} - \frac{bt^2}{9} + \frac{a^2\gamma}{18b} + \frac{at\gamma}{9} + \frac{2a^2\gamma^2}{9b} - \frac{a^2}{8b} - \frac{a^2\gamma^2}{4b}$$

$$\Leftrightarrow \Delta\Pi_l = -\frac{11a^2}{72b} - \frac{at}{9} - \frac{bt^2}{9} + \frac{a^2\gamma}{18b} + \frac{at\gamma}{9} - \frac{a^2\gamma^2}{36b}. \tag{190}$$

We can see from (190) that $\Delta\Pi_l$ is a quadratic function of *t*. Let us now find the maximum of $\Delta\Pi_l$. We obtain the maximum as follows

$$\frac{\partial\Delta\Pi_l}{\partial t} = -\frac{a}{9} - \frac{2bt}{9} + \frac{a\gamma}{9} = 0$$

$$\Leftrightarrow t = \frac{a}{2b}(\gamma - 1) \tag{191}$$

and

$$\frac{\partial^2\Delta\Pi_l}{\partial^2 t} = -\frac{2b}{9} < 0 \tag{192}$$

as $b > 0$. $\Delta\Pi_l$ has its maximum at $\bar{t} = a(\gamma-1)/2b$. Hence, in order to show that $\Delta\Pi_l$ is negative for $t < \underline{t}$ it is sufficient to show that $\Delta\Pi_l$ is negative at $\bar{t}$. Therefore, by plugging $\bar{t} = a(\gamma-1)/2b$ into $\Delta\Pi_l$ given by (190) we obtain

$$\Delta\Pi_l = -\frac{11a^2}{72b} - \frac{a\left(\frac{a}{2b}(\gamma-1)\right)}{9} - \frac{b\left(\frac{a}{2b}(\gamma-1)\right)^2}{9} + \frac{a^2\gamma}{18b} + \frac{a\gamma\left(\frac{a}{2b}(\gamma-1)\right)}{9} - \frac{a^2\gamma^2}{36b}$$

$$\Leftrightarrow \Delta\Pi_l = -\frac{11a^2}{72b} - \frac{a^2}{18b}(\gamma-1) - \frac{a^2}{36b}(\gamma-1)^2 + \frac{a^2\gamma}{18b} + \frac{a^2\gamma}{18b}(\gamma-1) - \frac{a^2\gamma^2}{36b}$$

$$\Leftrightarrow \Delta\Pi_l = -\frac{a^2}{8b} < 0 \tag{193}$$

as $a > 0$ and $b > 0$. From (193), it follows that, for low trade costs, the profit of the manufacturer – if he is awarded the right to prevent parallel trade – is higher than the profit of the manufacturer if parallel trade is permitted. Therefore, for low trade cost, (the threat of) parallel trade harms the manufacturer as it leads to a lower profit [see *Proposition 6* (ii)].[1025]

Let us now summarize the results of the analysis of the impact of parallel trade freedom on the manufacturer's profit for intermediate costs (scenario 2) and low trade

1025 See also Crampes et al. (2006) for an analysis of the threat of parallel trade and its impact on prices in the context of bundling, i.e. a firm bundles its main product which is a tradable good with a non-traded service.

costs (scenario 3). Our model shows that parallel trade freedom harms the manufacturer in both scenarios as it reduces his profit [see *Proposition 6*].[1026] Hence, if the unique social objective were to spur R&D for new pharmaceutical products by protecting the manufacturer who holds a patent on the pharmaceutical product in country *A* and country *B*, our model suggested that the manufacturer should be awarded the right to prevent parallel trade.

However, the protection of the manufacturer is clearly not the only social objective. Indeed, we have to take a closer look at the welfare effects of parallel trade. Therefore, a central purpose of the following sections is to explore the question as to whether parallel trade should be permitted or prohibited from a global welfare perspective if trade costs are at an intermediate level (scenario 2) and if trade costs are low (scenario 3). Note that permitting parallel trade does not have any impact on global welfare if trade costs are very high (scenario 1).

However, in order to be able to calculate global welfare, we first have to derive the profit of the distributor, consumer surplus, as well as welfare in country *A* and country *B* under scenario 2 and 3.

5.2.4.3.3. Profit of the Distributor

5.2.4.3.3.1. Profit of the Distributor if Parallel Trade is Prohibited

If the manufacturer is awarded the right to prevent parallel trade, the profit of the distributor for high, intermediate and low trade costs is the same for all scenarios and given by

$$\pi^{**} = \pi_h^* = \left(p_B^{**} - p_B^{w**}\right) q_B^{**}$$

$$\Leftrightarrow \pi^{**} = \pi_h^* = \left(\frac{3a}{4b} - \frac{a}{2b}\right)\frac{a}{4}$$

$$\Leftrightarrow \pi^{**} = \pi_h^* = \frac{a^2}{16b}. \qquad (194)$$

Note that the profit of the distributor if parallel trade is permitted but trade costs are high, π_h^*, is also given by (194).

5.2.4.3.3.2. Profit of the Distributor for Intermediate Trade Costs if Parallel Trade is Permitted

As already mentioned above, for intermediate trade costs the market in country *B* will be served so that the distributor will make a profit according to

1026 See also Scherer and Watal (2002a) on p. 38ff.

$$\pi_i^* = \left(p_{(B,i)}^* - p_{(B,i)}^{w*}\right) q_{(B,i)}^*$$

$$\Leftrightarrow \pi_i^* = \left(\frac{7a}{12b} + \frac{a\gamma}{6b} - \frac{t}{3} - \frac{a\gamma}{3b} - \frac{a}{6b} + \frac{2t}{3}\right)\left(\frac{5a}{12} - \frac{a\gamma}{6} + \frac{bt}{3}\right)$$

$$\Leftrightarrow \pi_i^* = \frac{25a^2}{144b} + \frac{5at}{18} + \frac{bt^2}{9} - \frac{5a^2\gamma}{36b} - \frac{at\gamma}{9} + \frac{a^2\gamma^2}{36b}. \tag{195}$$

5.2.4.3.3.3. Profit of the Distributor if Parallel Trade is Permitted and Trade Costs are Low

Recall that neither the distribution of the good in country *B* nor parallel trade is a worthwhile business activity if trade costs are low as the manufacturer strategically charges a prohibitively high wholesale price in country *B* in order to deter parallel trade. Hence, we set the profit of the distributor for low trade costs equal to zero if parallel trade is permitted.

5.2.4.3.4. Consumer Surplus in Country A

5.2.4.3.4.1. Consumer Surplus in Country A if the Manufacturer has the Right to Prevent Parallel Trade

In general, we obtain the consumer surplus by calculating the area between the demand function and the market price. Taking into account that demand in country *A* is given by the linear function (145) and taking into account that $a\gamma / b$ is the intercept of the demand function with the vertical (price) axis, we obtain the consumer surplus in country *A* if the manufacturer has the right to prevent parallel trade as follows.

$$CS_A^{**} = CS_{(A,h)}^* = \frac{1}{2} q_A^{**} \left(\frac{a\gamma}{b} - p_A^{m**}\right)$$

$$\Leftrightarrow CS_A^{**} = CS_{(A,h)}^* = \frac{1}{2} \frac{a\gamma}{2} \left(\frac{a\gamma}{b} - \frac{a\gamma}{2b}\right)$$

$$\Leftrightarrow CS_A^{**} = CS_{(A,h)}^* = \frac{a^2\gamma^2}{8b}. \tag{196}$$

Note that the consumer surplus in country *A*, if parallel trade is permitted but trade costs are high, $CS_{(A,h)}^*$, is also given by (196).

5.2.4.3.4.2. Consumer Surplus in Country A for Intermediate Trade Costs if Parallel Trade is Permitted

Analogous to the calculation in the previous section, the consumer surplus in country *A* for intermediate trade costs is given by

$$CS^*_{(A,i)} = \frac{1}{2}\left(\frac{a\gamma}{b} - p^{m*}_{(A,i)}\right)q^*_{(A,i)}$$
$$\Leftrightarrow CS^*_{(A,i)} = \frac{1}{2}\left(\frac{2a\gamma}{3b} - \frac{a}{6b} - \frac{t}{3}\right)\left(\frac{2a\gamma}{3} - \frac{a}{6} - \frac{bt}{3}\right)$$
$$\Leftrightarrow CS^*_{(A,i)} = \frac{a^2}{72b} + \frac{at}{18} + \frac{bt^2}{18} - \frac{a^2\gamma}{9b} - \frac{2at\gamma}{9} + \frac{2a^2\gamma^2}{9b}. \tag{197}$$

5.2.4.3.4.3. Consumer Surplus in Country A for Low Trade Costs if Parallel Trade is Permitted

The consumer surplus in country A for low trade costs is given by

$$CS^*_{(A,l)} = \frac{a^2}{72b} + \frac{at}{18} + \frac{bt^2}{18} - \frac{a^2\gamma}{9b} - \frac{2at\gamma}{9} + \frac{2a^2\gamma^2}{9b}. \tag{198}$$

5.2.4.3.5. Consumer Surplus in Country B

5.2.4.3.5.1. Consumer Surplus in Country B if the Manufacturer has the Right to Prevent Parallel Trade

Taking into account that demand in country B is given by the linear function (146) and taking into account that a/b is the intercept of the demand function with the vertical (price) axis, we obtain the consumer surplus in country B if the manufacturer is awarded the right to prevent parallel trade as follows.

$$CS^{**}_B = CS^*_{(B,h)} = \frac{1}{2}\left(\frac{a}{b} - p^{**}_B\right)q^{**}_B$$
$$\Leftrightarrow CS^{**}_B = CS^*_{(B,h)} = \frac{1}{2}\left(\frac{a}{b} - \frac{3a}{4b}\right)\frac{a}{4}$$
$$\Leftrightarrow CS^{**}_B = CS^*_{(B,h)} = \frac{a^2}{32b}. \tag{199}$$

Note that the consumer surplus in country B if parallel trade is permitted but trade costs are high, $CS^*_{(B,h)}$, is also given by (199).

5.2.4.3.5.1.1. Consumer Surplus in Country B with Intermediate Trade Costs if Parallel Trade is Permitted

Analogous to the calculation in the previous section, the consumer surplus in country B for intermediate trade costs is given by

$$CS^*_{(B,i)} = \frac{1}{2}\left(\frac{a}{b} - p^*_{(B,i)}\right)q^*_{(B,i)}$$
$$\Leftrightarrow CS^*_{(B,i)} = \left(\frac{5a}{24b} - \frac{a\gamma}{12b} + \frac{t}{6}\right)\left(\frac{5a}{12} - \frac{a\gamma}{6} + \frac{bt}{3}\right)$$
$$\Leftrightarrow CS^*_{(B,i)} = \frac{25a^2}{288b} + \frac{5at}{36} + \frac{bt^2}{18} - \frac{5a^2\gamma}{72b} - \frac{at\gamma}{18} + \frac{a^2\gamma^2}{72b}. \quad (200)$$

5.2.4.3.5.1.2. Consumer Surplus in Country B with Low Trade Costs if Parallel Trade is Permitted

Recall that the distribution of the good in country B is not a worthwhile business activity if trade costs are low as the manufacturer charges a prohibitively high wholesale price in country B in order to deter parallel trade. Hence, we set consumer surplus in country B equal to zero if parallel trade is permitted and trade costs are low.

5.2.4.3.6. Welfare in Country A

5.2.4.3.6.1. Welfare in Country A if Parallel Trade is Prohibited

Welfare in country A if the manufacturer has the right to prevent parallel trade is given by the sum of the total profit generated by the manufacturer given by (183) and the consumer surplus in country A given by (196).[1027] Hence,

$$W^{**}_A = W^*_{(A,h)} = \Pi^{**} + CS^{**}_A = \frac{a^2}{8b} + \frac{a^2\gamma^2}{4b} + \frac{a^2\gamma^2}{8b}$$
$$\Leftrightarrow W^{**}_A = W^*_{(A,h)} = \frac{a^2}{8b} + \frac{3a^2\gamma^2}{8b}. \quad (201)$$

Note that welfare in country A if parallel trade is permitted but trade costs are high, $W^*_{(A,h)}$, is also given by (201).

5.2.4.3.6.2. Welfare in Country A with Intermediate Trade Costs if Parallel Trade is Permitted

Welfare in country A if parallel trade is permitted and trade costs are at an intermediate level is given by the sum of the profit of the manufacturer given by (182) and the consumer surplus in country A given by (197). Hence,

1027 See also Müller-Langer (2008a) on p. 23ff.

$$W^*_{(A,i)} = \Pi^*_i + CS^*_{(A,i)} = \frac{a^2}{24b} - \frac{at}{3} - \frac{bt^2}{3} + \frac{a^2\gamma}{6b} + \frac{at\gamma}{3} + \frac{a^2\gamma^2}{6b} + \frac{a^2}{72b} + \frac{at}{18} + \frac{bt^2}{18} - \frac{a^2\gamma}{9b} - \frac{2at\gamma}{9} + \frac{2a^2\gamma^2}{9b}$$

$$\Leftrightarrow W^*_{(A,i)} = \frac{a^2}{18b} - \frac{5at}{18} - \frac{5bt^2}{18} + \frac{a^2\gamma}{18b} + \frac{at\gamma}{9} + \frac{7a^2\gamma^2}{18b}. \tag{202}$$

5.2.4.3.6.3. Welfare in Country A with Low Trade Costs if Parallel Trade is Permitted

Welfare in country A if parallel trade is permitted and trade costs are low is given by the sum of the profit of the manufacturer given by (188) and the consumer surplus given by (198)

$$W^*_{(A,l)} = \Pi^*_l + CS^*_{(A,l)} = -\frac{a^2}{36b} - \frac{at}{9} - \frac{bt^2}{9} + \frac{a^2\gamma}{18b} + \frac{at\gamma}{9}$$
$$+ \frac{2a^2\gamma^2}{9b} + \frac{a^2}{72b} + \frac{at}{18} + \frac{bt^2}{18} - \frac{a^2\gamma}{9b} - \frac{2at\gamma}{9} + \frac{2a^2\gamma^2}{9b}$$

$$\Leftrightarrow W^*_{(A,l)} = -\frac{a^2}{72b} - \frac{at}{18} - \frac{bt^2}{18} - \frac{a^2\gamma}{18b} - \frac{at\gamma}{9} + \frac{4a^2\gamma^2}{9b}. \tag{203}$$

5.2.4.3.7. Welfare in Country B

5.2.4.3.7.1. Welfare in Country B if Parallel Trade is Prohibited

Welfare in country B if the manufacturer has the right to prevent parallel trade is given by the sum of the profit generated by the distributor given by (194) and the consumer surplus in country B given by (199)

$$W^{**}_B = W^*_{(B,h)} = \pi^{**} + CS^{**}_B = \frac{a^2}{16b} + \frac{a^2}{32b}$$

$$\Leftrightarrow W^{**}_B = W^*_{(B,h)} = \frac{3a^2}{32b}. \tag{204}$$

Note that welfare in country B if parallel trade is permitted but trade costs are high, $W^*_{(B,h)}$, is also given by (204).

5.2.4.3.7.2. Welfare in Country B with Intermediate Trade Costs if Parallel Trade is Permitted

Welfare in country B – if parallel trade is permitted and trade costs are at an intermediate level – is the sum of the profit generated by the distributor given by (195) and the consumer surplus in country B given by (200)

$$W^*_{(B,i)} = \pi^*_i + CS^*_{(B,i)} = \frac{25a^2}{144b} + \frac{5at}{18} + \frac{bt^2}{9} - \frac{5a^2\gamma}{36b} - \frac{at\gamma}{9} + \frac{a^2\gamma^2}{36b} + \frac{25a^2}{288b} + \frac{5at}{36} + \frac{bt^2}{18} - \frac{5a^2\gamma}{72b} - \frac{at\gamma}{18} + \frac{a^2\gamma^2}{72b}$$

$$\Leftrightarrow W^*_{(B,i)} = \frac{75a^2}{288b} + \frac{15at}{36} + \frac{3bt^2}{18} - \frac{15a^2\gamma}{72b} - \frac{3at\gamma}{18} + \frac{3a^2\gamma^2}{72b}$$

$$\Leftrightarrow W^*_{(B,i)} = \frac{25a^2}{96b} + \frac{5at}{12} + \frac{bt^2}{6} - \frac{5a^2\gamma}{24b} - \frac{at\gamma}{6} + \frac{a^2\gamma^2}{24b}. \tag{205}$$

5.2.4.3.7.3. Welfare in Country B with Low Trade Costs if Parallel Trade is Permitted

Welfare in country B is equal to zero if trade costs are low, $\underline{t} = a(\gamma - (5/2))/2b > t$. Note that we end up in this situation only for relatively high values of the parameter γ, more specifically if $\gamma > 5/2$ as t is assumed to be positive.

5.2.4.3.8. Effect of Parallel Trade Freedom on Global Welfare

5.2.4.3.8.1. Global Welfare if Parallel Trade is Prohibited

If the manufacturer is awarded the right to prevent parallel trade, global welfare is given by the sum of welfare in country A given by (201) and welfare in country B given by (204). More specifically,

$$W^{**} = W^{**}_A + W^{**}_B = \frac{a^2}{8b} + \frac{3a^2\gamma^2}{8b} + \frac{3a^2}{32b}$$

$$\Leftrightarrow W^{**} = W^*_h = \frac{7a^2}{32b} + \frac{3a^2\gamma^2}{8b}. \tag{206}$$

Note that global welfare, if parallel trade is permitted but trade costs are high, W^*_h, is also given by (206).

5.2.4.3.8.2. Global Welfare if Parallel Trade is Permitted and Trade Costs are Intermediate

By adding welfare in country A given by (202) and welfare in country B given by (205) we obtain global welfare if trade costs are at an intermediate level and parallel trade is permitted:

$$W^*_i = W^*_{(A,i)} + W^*_{(B,i)} = \frac{a^2}{18b} - \frac{5at}{18} - \frac{5bt^2}{18} + \frac{a^2\gamma}{18b} + \frac{at\gamma}{9} + \frac{7a^2\gamma^2}{18b} + \frac{25a^2}{96b} + \frac{5at}{12} + \frac{bt^2}{6} - \frac{5a^2\gamma}{24b} - \frac{at\gamma}{6} + \frac{a^2\gamma^2}{24b}$$

$$\Leftrightarrow W^*_i = \frac{91a^2}{288b} + \frac{5at}{36} - \frac{bt^2}{9} - \frac{11a^2\gamma}{72b} - \frac{at\gamma}{18} + \frac{31a^2\gamma^2}{72b}. \tag{207}$$

5.2.4.3.8.3. Global Welfare if Parallel Trade is Permitted and Trade Costs are Low

We already know from the previous analysis that in this case the distribution of the pharmaceutical product in country *B* is not a worthwhile business activity. Put differently, the profit of the distributor, consumer surplus as well as welfare in country *B* are equal to zero if parallel trade is permitted and trade costs are low. Consequently, global welfare is equal to welfare in country *A*. More specifically, welfare in country *A* and thus global welfare in this case is given by (203):

$$W_l^* = W_{(A,l)}^* = -\frac{a^2}{72b} - \frac{at}{18} - \frac{bt^2}{18} - \frac{a^2\gamma}{18b} - \frac{at\gamma}{9} + \frac{4a^2\gamma^2}{9b}. \quad (208)$$

[1028]

5.2.4.3.9. Net Effect of Parallel Trade Freedom on Global Welfare

In the following sections, we will analyze the impact of parallel trade freedom on global welfare for three different scenarios. More specifically, for the cases of high, intermediate, and low trade costs, we derive the net effect of parallel trade freedom on global welfare by subtracting global welfare if the manufacturer has the right to prevent parallel trade from global welfare if parallel trade is permitted.

The intuition behind this is the following. If this difference is negative, parallel trade is detrimental to global welfare and thus the manufacturer should be awarded the right to prevent parallel trade. If, however, this difference is positive, it would indicate that global welfare is higher if parallel trade is permitted.

5.2.4.3.9.1. Net Effect of Parallel Trade Freedom on Global Welfare if Trade Costs are High

We already know from the analysis in the previous sections that the outcome of the double marginalization game if parallel trade is permitted is equal to the outcome of the double marginalization game without parallel trade if trade costs are high, $t > \bar{t}$. Consequently, the profits of the manufacturer and the distributor, consumer surplus as well as welfare in country *A* and country *B* are equal, regardless of whether parallel trade is prohibited or permitted. Therefore, even if parallel trade were permitted, the (non-credible) threat of parallel trade would not have any impact on global welfare because parallel trade is not a worthwhile business activity for the distributor due to prohibitively high trade costs.

However, let us now analyze the other two cases with intermediate and low trade costs in which potential competition from parallel trade may arise as parallel trade is a worthwhile business activity for the exclusive distributor.

1028 See also **Appendix 8** for a summary of the results of our analysis.

5.2.4.3.9.2. Net Effect of Parallel Trade Freedom on Global Welfare if Trade Costs are at an Intermediate Level

5.2.4.3.9.2.1. Net Effect of Parallel Trade Freedom on Global Welfare for Intermediate Trade Costs and $\gamma \geq 5/2$

In this section, we will show that the following proposition holds.

Proposition 7: Parallel trade freedom increases global welfare if trade costs are intermediate and $\gamma \geq 5/2$.

Let the net effect of parallel trade on global welfare be denoted by ΔW_i if trade costs are at an intermediate level, $\underline{t} \leq t \leq \bar{t}$. In particular, we obtain ΔW_i by subtracting global welfare if parallel trade is prohibited given by (206) from global welfare if parallel trade is permitted and trade costs are at an intermediate level given by (207)

$$\Delta W_i = W_i^* - W^{**} = \frac{91a^2}{288b} + \frac{5at}{36} - \frac{bt^2}{9} - \frac{11a^2\gamma}{72b} - \frac{at\gamma}{18} + \frac{31a^2\gamma^2}{72b} - \left(\frac{7a^2}{32b} + \frac{3a^2\gamma^2}{8b}\right)$$

$$\Leftrightarrow \Delta W_i = \frac{7a^2}{72b} + \frac{5at}{36} - \frac{bt^2}{9} - \frac{11a^2\gamma}{72b} - \frac{at\gamma}{18} + \frac{a^2\gamma^2}{18b}. \tag{209}$$

Note that ΔW_i is a quadratic function of *t*. The question arises as to whether (209) is positive or negative. If (209) is positive, parallel trade freedom has a positive effect on global welfare. If, however, (209) is negative, parallel trade freedom is detrimental to global welfare. First, note that $\Delta W_i = 0$ at $t = a(\gamma - 1)/2b$:

$$\Leftrightarrow \Delta W_i = \frac{7a^2}{72b} + \frac{5a\left(a(\gamma-1)/2b\right)}{36} - \frac{b\left(a(\gamma-1)/2b\right)^2}{9} - \frac{11a^2\gamma}{72b} - \frac{a\gamma\left(a(\gamma-1)/2b\right)}{18} + \frac{a^2\gamma^2}{18b}$$

$$\Leftrightarrow \Delta W_i = \frac{7a^2}{72b} + \frac{5a^2\gamma}{72b} - \frac{5a^2}{72b} - \frac{a^2}{36b}\left(\gamma^2 - 2\gamma + 1\right) - \frac{11a^2\gamma}{72b} - \frac{a^2\gamma}{36b}(\gamma - 1) + \frac{a^2\gamma^2}{18b}$$

$$\Leftrightarrow \Delta W_i = 0. \tag{210}$$

In other words, ΔW_i is equal to zero at the upper bound for *t*. Hence, in order to show that ΔW_i and thus the effect of parallel trade freedom on global welfare is positive it is sufficient to show that ΔW_i is a monotonically decreasing function of *t* for $\underline{t} \leq t \leq \bar{t}$. Let us first find out whether ΔW_i has a unique maximum by differentiating (209) with respect to *t*.

$$\frac{\partial \Delta W_i}{\partial t} = \frac{5a}{36} - \frac{2bt}{9} - \frac{a\gamma}{18} = 0$$

$$\Leftrightarrow t_i^{max} = \frac{a}{2b}\left(\frac{5}{4} - \frac{\gamma}{2}\right). \tag{211}$$

Note that t_i^{max} is the unique maximum as $\partial^2 \Delta W_i / \partial^2 t = -2b/9 < 0$ as $b > 0$. As t_i^{max} is the unique maximum, ΔW_i decreases in t for any $t > t_i^{max}$. In other words, if $t > a((5/4)-(\gamma/2))/2b$, ΔW_i decreases in *t*. Furthermore, taking into account that $\Delta W_i = 0$ at $t = a(\gamma - 1)/2b$, it follows that $\Delta W_i > 0$ for $t > a((5/4)-(\gamma/2))/2b$. In the following, we show for which values of the parameter γ t_i^{max} is smaller than or equal to the lower bound $\underline{t}$:

$$t_i^{max} = \frac{a}{2b}\left(\frac{5}{4} - \frac{\gamma}{2}\right) \leq \frac{a}{2b}\left(\gamma - \frac{5}{2}\right)$$
$$\Leftrightarrow \gamma \geq \frac{5}{2}. \tag{212}$$

In other words, for $\gamma \geq 5/2$ the unique maximum of ΔW_i is located on the left-hand side of the lower bound for *t*. Furthermore, ΔW_i monotonically decreases in *t* on the interval between the lower bound and the upper bound for *t*. Hence, taking into account that $\Delta W_i = 0$ at the upper bound for *t*, ΔW_i and thus the impact of parallel trade on global welfare is positive if $\gamma \geq 5/2$ as stated in *Proposition 7* on p. 183 of this thesis.

5.2.4.3.9.2.2. Net Effect of Parallel Trade Freedom if Trade Costs are at an Intermediate Level and $\gamma < 5/2$

If $\gamma < 5/2$, we cannot apply the same logic as in the previous section in order to answer the question as to whether ΔW_i is positive or negative. Note that – for $\gamma < 5/2$ – the lower bound $\underline{t} = a(\gamma - (5/2))/2b$ would be negative. However, as *t* is assumed to be positive we set the lower bound for *t* equal to zero in this case. Furthermore, note that also for $\gamma < 5/2$, ΔW_i has its unique maximum at $t_i^{max} = a((5/4)-(\gamma/2))/2b$ [(211)] which is positive as $\gamma < 5/2$. Hence, the question arises as to whether ΔW_i is positive or negative at the lower bound for *t*. For instance, if we can show that ΔW_i is positive at $t = 0$ this would imply that ΔW_i is also positive between the lower bound and the upper bound taking into account that $\Delta W_i = 0$ at the upper bound for *t*. In the following we will show that ΔW_i is positive at $t = 0$ if $7/4 \leq \gamma < 5/2$.

5.2.4.3.9.2.2.1. Net Effect of Parallel Trade Freedom on Global Welfare for Intermediate Trade Costs and $7/4 \leq \gamma < 5/2$

In this section, we will show that the following proposition holds.

Proposition 8: Freedom of parallel trade increases global welfare if trade costs are at an intermediate level and $7/4 \le \gamma < 5/2$.

By setting $t = 0$ in (209) we obtain

$$\Delta W_i = \frac{7a^2}{72b} - \frac{11a^2\gamma}{72b} + \frac{a^2\gamma^2}{18b}. \tag{213}$$

Note that ΔW_i given by (213) is greater than or equal to zero if $\gamma \ge 7/4$.[1029] Consequently, if $\gamma \ge 7/4$, ΔW_i is positive between zero and the upper bound for *t*. Thus, parallel trade freedom has a positive impact on global welfare if $7/4 \le \gamma < 5/2$ [see *Proposition 8*].
However, let us now consider the case if $1 < \gamma < 7/4$.

5.2.4.3.9.2.2.2. Net Effect of Parallel Trade Freedom on Global Welfare for Intermediate Trade Costs and $1 < \gamma < 7/4$

In this section, we will give an example in order to illustrate that the following proposition holds.

Proposition 9: Freedom of parallel trade can have negative welfare properties if trade costs are at an intermediate level and γ *is sufficiently low* $[1 < \gamma < 7/4]$.

We already know from the previous section that $\Delta W_i = 0$ at the upper bound $\bar{t} = a(\gamma - 1)/2b$. However, by looking at (209), it becomes apparent that ΔW_i has another null at

$$t = \frac{a}{2b}\left(\frac{7}{2} - 2\gamma\right) \tag{214}$$

as

$$\Delta W_i = \frac{7a^2}{72b} + \frac{5a}{36}\frac{a}{2b}\left(\frac{7}{2} - 2\gamma\right) - \frac{b}{9}\frac{a^2}{4b^2}\left(\frac{7}{2} - 2\gamma\right)^2 - \frac{11a^2\gamma}{72b} - \frac{a\gamma}{18}\frac{a}{2b}\left(\frac{7}{2} - 2\gamma\right) + \frac{a^2\gamma^2}{18b}$$
$$\Leftrightarrow \Delta W_i = \frac{7a^2}{72b} + \frac{35a^2}{144b} - \frac{5a^2\gamma}{36b} - \frac{a^2}{36b}\left(\frac{49}{4} - 14\gamma + 4\gamma^2\right) - \frac{11a^2\gamma}{72b} - \frac{7a^2\gamma}{72b} + \frac{a^2\gamma^2}{18b} + \frac{a^2\gamma^2}{18b}$$
$$\Leftrightarrow \Delta W_i = 0. \tag{215}$$

1029 For instance, we can see from (213) that $7 - 11\gamma + 4\gamma^2 = 0$ if $\gamma = 7/4$ and that $7 + 4\gamma^2 > 11\gamma$ if $\gamma > 7/4$.

Note that – in contrast to the previous sections – (214) is positive in this case as $\gamma < 7/4$. However, the following example illustrates that *Proposition 9* holds.

Example 1
We set $a = 100, b = 1/2$ and $\gamma = 13/8$. **Figure 8** shows that ΔW_i has one null at $t = 25$ [see (214)] and the other null at $t = 62.5$ which is also the upper bound. Furthermore, ΔW_i has its unique maximum at $t_i^{max} = 43.75$ [see (211)] and the lower bound at $t = 0$.

Figure 8 *Net Welfare Effect of Parallel Trade Freedom ($a = 100, b = 1/2$ and $\gamma = 13/8$)*

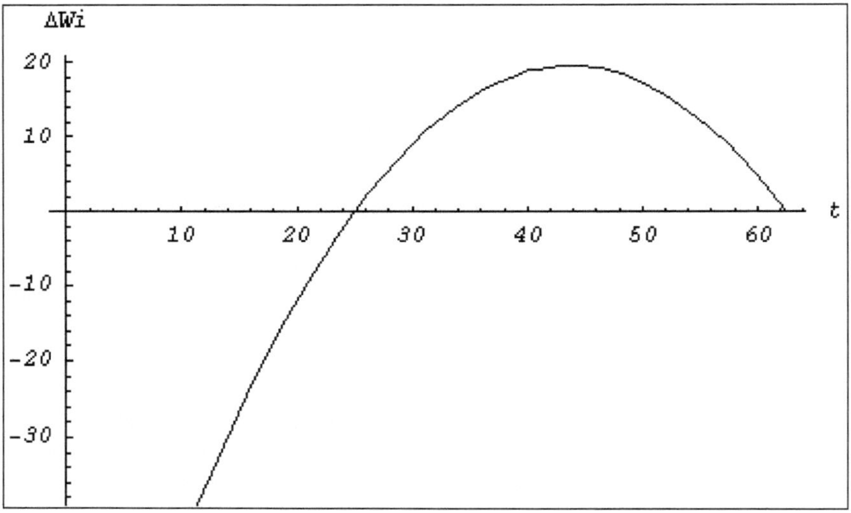

We can see from **Figure 8** that $\Delta W_i < 0 \ \forall t \in (0, 25)$ which suggests that *Proposition 9* holds.

5.2.4.3.9.3. Net Effect of Parallel Trade on Global Welfare if Trade Costs are Low

In this section, we shall show that the following proposition holds.

Proposition 10: Freedom of parallel trade increases global welfare if trade costs are low and γ is sufficiently high ($\gamma > 5/2$).

If trade costs are low, $t > \underline{t}$, the effect of parallel trade freedom on global welfare, ΔW_l, is given by the difference between global welfare if parallel trade is permitted given by (208) and global welfare if the manufacturer is awarded the right to prevent parallel trade given by (206). Hence,

$$\Delta W_l = W_l^* - W^{**} = -\frac{a^2}{72b} - \frac{at}{18} - \frac{bt^2}{18} - \frac{a^2\gamma}{18b} - \frac{at\gamma}{9} + \frac{4a^2\gamma^2}{9b} - \frac{7a^2}{32b} - \frac{3a^2\gamma^2}{8b}$$

$$\Leftrightarrow \Delta W_l = -\frac{67a^2}{288b} - \frac{at}{18} - \frac{bt^2}{18} - \frac{a^2\gamma}{18b} - \frac{at\gamma}{9} + \frac{5a^2\gamma^2}{72b}. \quad (216)$$

Note that ΔW_l is a quadratic function of *t*. Moreover, recall that – as *t* is assumed to be positive – γ must be greater than 5/2. For smaller values of the parameter γ we would automatically end up in one of the other scenarios mentioned above.
However, by differentiating (216) we obtain

$$\frac{\partial \Delta W_l}{\partial t} = -\frac{a}{18} - \frac{bt}{9} - \frac{a\gamma}{9} = 0$$

$$\Leftrightarrow t_l^{max} = -\frac{a}{b}\left(\frac{1}{2} + \gamma\right). \quad (217)$$

Note that t_l^{max} is the unique maximum as $\partial^2 \Delta W_l / \partial^2 t = -b/9 < 0$ as $b > 0$. Furthermore, note that $t_l^{max} < 0$ as $a > 0$, $b > 0$ and $\gamma > 0$.
However, by setting $t = 0$ in (216) we obtain

$$\Delta W_l = -\frac{67a^2}{288b} - \frac{16a^2\gamma}{288b} + \frac{20a^2\gamma^2}{288b}. \quad (218)$$

We can see from (218) that – at $t = 0$ – $\Delta W_l > 0$ if $\gamma > 5/2$.[1030] Furthermore, by setting $t = \underline{t} = a(\gamma - (5/2))/2b$ in (216) it becomes apparent that

$$\Delta W_l = -\frac{67a^2}{288b} - \frac{a\left(\frac{a}{2b}\left(\gamma - \frac{5}{2}\right)\right)}{18} - \frac{b\left(\frac{a}{2b}\left(\gamma - \frac{5}{2}\right)\right)^2}{18} - \frac{a^2\gamma}{18b} - \frac{a\gamma\left(\frac{a}{2b}\left(\gamma - \frac{5}{2}\right)\right)}{9} + \frac{5a^2\gamma^2}{72b}$$

$$\Leftrightarrow \Delta W_l = -\frac{67a^2}{288b} - \frac{a^2\gamma}{36b} + \frac{5a^2}{72b} - \frac{a^2\gamma^2}{72b} + \frac{5a^2\gamma}{72b} - \frac{25a^2}{288b} - \frac{a^2\gamma}{18b} - \frac{a^2\gamma^2}{18b} + \frac{5a^2\gamma}{36b} + \frac{5a^2\gamma^2}{72b}$$

$$\Leftrightarrow \Delta W_l = -\frac{a^2}{4b} + \frac{a^2\gamma}{8b}. \quad (219)$$

Note that (219) is positive as $\gamma > 5/2$.[1031] Consequently, taking into account that ΔW_l is a quadratic function of *t*, $t_l^{max} < 0$, $\Delta W_l > 0$ at $t = 0$, and $\Delta W_l > 0$ at $\underline{t}$, it is straightforward to see that ΔW_l is positive if trade costs are low and γ sufficiently high ($\gamma > 5/2$) [see *Proposition 10*].

1030 For instance, note that $20\gamma^2 - 16\gamma - 67 > 0$ if $\gamma > 5/2$.

1031 For instance, note that $\gamma - 2 > 0$ if $\gamma > 5/2$.

5.2.4.4. Conclusion as to the Model of Parallel Trade and the Pricing of Pharmaceutical Products

Our model suggests that parallel imports in a double marginalization game with complete information will never occur in the sub-game perfect equilibrium, as it is always beneficial for the manufacturer to monopolize the market in country *A* at the third stage. However, the question arises as to how the manufacturer strategically chooses prices in order to prevent the occurrence of parallel trade.

As we have shown, this depends on the level of the parameters γ and t for given values for a and b. If $t > \bar{t}$, potential competition from parallel trade does not arise and thus the manufacturer will always charge the monopoly price in country *A* and the optimal wholesale price in country *B*. One tentative interpretation of this outcome is that parallel trade is a non-credible threat if parallel trade cost are high and the two countries are virtually homogeneous, i.e. if $\gamma \to 1$. If, however, $t \le \bar{t}$, potential competition from parallel trade arises and the manufacturer strategically sets the wholesale price in country *B* and the price in country *A*, in order to prevent that parallel trade occurs.

Moreover, we have shown that – provided that parallel trade is permitted – country *B* ends up not being served at all if trade costs are very low, $t < \underline{t}$, and γ sufficiently high, i.e. $\gamma > 5/2$.

As to the impact of parallel trade on the profit of the manufacturer, we come to the following conclusion. If parallel trade is permitted, the credible threat of parallel trade leads to lower profits of the manufacturer and thus reduces his incentives to invest in R&D [see *Proposition 6*].

As to the welfare properties of parallel trade, parallel trade freedom increases global welfare if γ is sufficiently high, $\gamma > 5/2$ [see *Proposition 7* and *Proposition 10*]. If, however, trade costs are intermediate and γ is sufficiently low, $1 < \gamma < 7/4$, parallel trade freedom can have negative welfare properties [see *Proposition 9*].

Finally, as a first idea for further research, we suggest a more elaborate theoretical and empirical analysis of the parameter t which is of significant importance for the results of our model. For instance, suppose that t is very low. In this case, country *B* is likely to end up not being served at all under parallel trade freedom.

As already mentioned, costs of re-packaging and re-labelling are incurred by the parallel-importing distributor as well as other parallel trade-specific transaction costs such as import duties on parallel trade. One may argue that the parameter t can to some extent be influenced by the manufacturer, i.e. through special labelling, language, warnings etc. that make re-packaging and re-labelling more expensive for the parallel-importing distributor.[1032]

Intuitively, on the one hand, the manufacturer may prefer to make parallel trade as costly as possible, in order to prevent parallel trade. Consider again the case of very low parallel trade costs where country *B* ends up not being served. In this case, it may

1032 For instance, see Maskus and Ganslandt (2002) on p. 69ff. See also REMIT Consultants (1991) and Gallini and Hollis (1999) on p. 2ff.

be beneficial for the manufacturer to increase t so that he can sell his product in country B even under parallel trade freedom.

On the other hand, to increase t through special labelling, language and warnings may also be costly for the manufacturer so that a trade-off arises between the costs of increasing t and the benefit from preventing parallel trade.

As a second idea for further research, we suggest analyzing the strategic behaviour of foreign governments to protect consumers in their country from excessive pricing, i.e. through price caps or compulsory licensing.

5.3. Parallel Trade of Pharmaceutical Products in the Context of National Price Regulation

In the following section, we shall elaborate on the analytical framework originally formulated by Ganslandt and Maskus (2004) in order to analyze the question as to whether parallel trade occurs when national governments set a price cap on pharmaceutical products and when the quantities available for parallel trade are limited.

Let us first take a look at the main differences between the Ganslandt and Maskus (2004) model and our own double marginalization model in the following.

First, Ganslandt and Maskus (2004) suppose that the original manufacturer of a pharmaceutical product takes the price in country B as given. More specifically, Ganslandt and Maskus (2004, p. 1040) assume that the market in country B is regulated in the sense that the autonomous government in country B sets a cap on the price charged to retail outlets in country B. As a consequence, demand in country B is not explicitly modeled in the Ganslandt and Maskus (2004) model. In contrast, we assume in our double marginalization model that the market both in country A and in country B is unregulated. Put differently, in our model, the manufacturer of pharmaceuticals does not take the price in country B as given, and demand in country B is explicitly taken into consideration.

Second, Ganslandt and Maskus (2004) assume that the volumes available for parallel trade are limited. In contrast, we do not explicitly assume in our model that volumes available for parallel trade are limited. Nevertheless, the manufacturer sets prices strategically in order to deter the occurrence of parallel trade.

Third, Ganslandt and Maskus (2004) take into consideration fixed cost of parallel trade as well as per unit cost of parallel trade whereas we only consider per unit cost of parallel trade.

Fourth, Ganslandt and Maskus (2004, p. 1044ff) provide an empirical analysis of the price effects of parallel trade. In particular, Ganslandt and Maskus (2004) estimate that drug prices fell by 12-19% after Sweden's entry into the EU that required the country to permit parallel trade. However, Ganslandt and Maskus (2004) do not mathematically derive the net effects of parallel trade on global welfare.

We will now take a closer look at the Ganslandt and Maskus (2004) model in the following section.

5.3.1. Model of Parallel Trade with a Price Cap and a Quantity Limit

Ganslandt and Maskus (2004, p. 1039ff) develop a model of price arbitrage between two countries A and B based on the assumption that the quantities of pharmaceutical products available for parallel trade are limited. Ganslandt and Maskus (2004) justify this assumption on various grounds. First, original pharmaceutical producers tend to cap production levels permitted to licensees abroad aiming at restricting the quantities of pharmaceutical products available for parallel trade.[1033] For instance, Holmberg et al. (2003) analyze the organization of pharmaceutical goods distribution in the Nordic Countries and find that quantity limits of parallel import products are highly significant for the Swedish market. According to pharmacy managers, there is often a shortage of parallel import products, and wholesalers often cannot meet the demand for parallel import products.[1034]

However, Ganslandt and Maskus (2004, p. 1040) suggest that, from a theoretical point of view, the assumed quantity limit is a means to take into consideration the increasing marginal cost of parallel imports. For instance, recent evidence with respect to parallel imports from Canada to the U.S. suggests that it is increasingly costly for parallel import firms to find large quantities available for re-importation.[1035] That is, supply control systems used by major pharmaceutical producers impose significant restrictions on sales to Canadian drug wholesalers and induce parallel import firms to circumvent the supply control systems at high costs.[1036] According to Ganslandt and Maskus (2004, p. 1040), parallel importing firms buy products from the cheapest distributor of the product first, from the second-cheapest distributor second and so on. Nevertheless, demand for a specific pharmaceutical product in country A is denoted by

$$D_A(p) = \gamma a - \frac{1}{2}p. \quad (220)$$ [1037]

Note that, for mathematical convenience, the slope parameter in (220) is set equal to 1/2. A substitute medicine does not exist, so that only the own-price appears in the demand function in (220).[1038] By assumption, marginal costs of production c are equal to zero in both countries. This is a common assumption in models that deal with the

1033 See Ganslandt and Maskus (2004) on p. 1039ff. In particular, Ganslandt and Maskus (2004) refer to recent evidence from the U.S. that major pharmaceutical manufacturers use supply control systems to limit re-imports of prescription drugs from Canadian online pharmacies to consumers in the U.S.. Note, however, that – as to parallel trade within the EU – any contractual agreement explicitly prohibiting parallel trade would be void under Article 81 of the EC Treaty. See also Smits (2006) on p. 65ff and Rey and Venit (2004).

1034 See Ganslandt and Maskus (2004) on p. 1040, footnote 7.

1035 See Ganslandt and Maskus (2004) on p. 1040, Simon (2004), and Pugh (2003). See also Graham (2000) and Graham and Robson (2000) for an analysis of prescription drug prices in Canada and the U.S..

1036 See Arfwedson (2004) on p. 58ff. See also Ganslandt and Maskus (2004) on p. 1040, footnote 8 and footnote 9.

1037 See Ganslandt and Maskus (2004) on p. 1040. We added the γ in the demand function in order to facilitate comparisons between the Ganslandt and Maskus (2004) model and our own model.

1038 See Ganslandt and Maskus (2004) on p. 1040.

output decisions of pharmaceutical companies, as the marginal cost of production is negligibly small compared to the fixed cost of research and development.[1039]
The manufacturer of the pharmaceutical product holds a patent on the product in both countries.[1040] The government in country *B* is able to set a cap on the price, $\overline{p}_B$, that is charged to retail outlets, such as pharmacies and hospitals, in country *B*.[1041]
Moreover, Ganslandt and Maskus (2004, p. 1041) assume that $\overline{p}_B$ is always strictly binding in country *B*, whereas the price in country *A* is unregulated. Hence, the manufacturer of pharmaceuticals sells the patented pharmaceutical product in country *A* at price *p*. Moreover, he sells the product in country *B* at price $\overline{p}_B$. As already mentioned above, the assumption of an exogenously given price ceiling in country *B* constitutes a central difference between the Ganslandt and Maskus model and our double-marginalization model elaborated in the previous sections in which the retail price in country *B* is endogenous.
However, Ganslandt and Maskus (2004, p. 1041) assume that there is a small number of symmetric firms that engage in parallel trade (henceforth, parallel-importing firms). Furthermore, Ganslandt and Maskus (2004) assume that commercial arbitrage undertaken by those parallel-importing firms is permitted, whereas arbitrage between country *B* and country *A* undertaken by individual consumers is prohibited.[1042] According to Ganslandt and Maskus (2004, p. 1041), parallel trade generates a fixed cost, *T*. For instance, in the EU, parallel traders are required to meet the standards for manufacturers of pharmaceuticals and to acquire a costly Parallel Import Product License, i.e. issued by the EMEA.[1043] Furthermore, the variable trade costs are *t* per unit shipped from country *B* to country *A*.[1044] More specifically, costs of repackaging the product, i.e. newly added package inserts, are incurred by the parallel importing firms.[1045] Furthermore, Ganslandt and Maskus (2004, p. 1041) assume that the parallel-imported pharmaceutical product is a perfect substitute for the pharmaceutical product sold by the original manufacturer in country *A*. In order to ensure that the entire quantity of the pharmaceutical product shipped to country *A* is sold, the parallel import price is assumed to be lower than the price set by the pharmaceutical producer.[1046] More specifically, the parallel-import quantity is denoted by *X* and the manufacturer's residual demand in country *A* is therefore given by

$$D_A^m(p) = D_A(p) - X.^{1047} \tag{221}$$

1039 See also Ganslandt and Maskus (2001) on p. 6.
1040 See Ganslandt and Maskus (2004) on p. 1040.
1041 See Rey and Venit (2004) on p. 176ff and Ganslandt and Maskus (2004) on p. 1041. See also Danzon (1997) and Szymanski and Valletti (2005) on p. 750ff.
1042 See also Outterson (2004) for an analysis of pharmaceutical arbitrage. See also Matteucci and Reverberi (2005). See Ganslandt and Maskus (2004) on p. 1041.
1043 See Arfwedson (2004) on p. 8ff.
1044 See Ganslandt and Maskus (2004) on p. 1041.
1045 See Arfwedson (2004) on p. 20. See also Maskus and Ganslandt (2002) on p. 57.
1046 See Ganslandt and Maskus (2004) on p. 1041.
1047 See Ganslandt and Maskus (2004) on p. 1041.

Ganslandt and Maskus (2004, p. 1041ff) model the strategic interaction between the original manufacturer and the parallel importers as a multi-stage game and use backward induction to find the unique sub-game perfect Nash equilibrium.

More specifically, $N=\{1,...,n\}$ denotes the finite number of symmetric parallel importers.

In the first stage, n parallel importers apply for an approval permit from competent authorities in country A in order to be permitted to import the product from country B, i.e. to get a Parallel Import Product License.[1048] Parallel import firms will enter the market if two conditions are fulfilled. First, the application for approval is successful, and second, the expected profit is non-negative.[1049]

In the second stage, according to Ganslandt and Maskus (2004, p. 1041), each parallel import firm i simultaneously ships a quantity x_i from country B to country A, incurring the per-unit trade cost t. The quantity x_i shipped by each of the symmetric parallel-import firms is known to all firms.[1050]

In the third stage, the pharmaceuticals producer sets the market-clearing price p in country A, whereas he takes the price in country B, $\overline{p}_B$, as given.[1051]

The analysis which applies backward induction to find the unique sub-game perfect Nash equilibrium is outlined in the following section.

5.3.2. Analysis of the Model of Parallel Trade with a Price Cap and a Quantity Limit

Starting with the final stage, the manufacturer of the pharmaceutical product maximizes profits generated in country A and country B according to

$$\Pi(p)=D_A^m(p)p+X\overline{p}_B=(\gamma a-\frac{1}{2}p-X)p+X\overline{p}_B \tag{222}$$

where Π denotes the profit of the manufacturer.[1052] By differentiating (222), we obtain

$$\frac{\partial\Pi(p)}{\partial p}=\gamma a-p-X=0. \tag{223}$$

By rearranging (223), the profit-maximizing price can be written as follows

$$p(X)=\gamma a-X.^{1053} \tag{224}$$

1048 See Arfwedson (2004) on p. 8ff.

1049 See Ganslandt and Maskus (2004) on p. 1041.

1050 See Ganslandt and Maskus (2004) on p. 1041.

1051 See Maskus and Ganslandt (2002) on p. 57 as to the regulation of prices of pharmaceutical products. See also Ganslandt and Maskus (2004) on p. 1041.

1052 See Ganslandt and Maskus (2004) on p. 1042.

1053 See also Ganslandt and Maskus (2004) on p. 1042.

Note that the profit-maximizing price given by (224) is a function of the total quantity that is shipped from country *B* to country *A*. Furthermore, we can see from (224) that $p'(X)=-1<0$. Put differently, the price *p* falls if the quantity of parallel imports *X* increases.[1054] Intuitively, stronger competition from parallel trade in terms of increasing sales volumes decreases the market power of the manufacturer who holds a patent on the pharmaceutical product in both countries.[1055] Recall that we come to a similar result in our double marginalization model. More specifically, the credible threat of parallel trade reduces the market power of the manufacturer and reduces his profit. Note, however, that our model suggests that the mere threat of parallel trade is sufficient to reduce the market power of the manufacturer.

However, we can also see from (224) that the price in country *A* increases if γ increases.

Working backwards to the second stage, Ganslandt and Maskus (2004, p. 1043ff) now find the non-cooperative quantities chosen by the symmetric parallel import firms. Each parallel import firm *i* maximizes

$$\pi_i(x_i)=p(X)x_i-(\overline{p}_B+t)x_i-T \tag{225}$$

where *p(X)* is given by (224) and π_i denotes the parallel import firm *i*'s profit.[1056] Fixed costs of parallel trade are denoted by *T*.[1057] Note that the maximization problem is the same for each of the symmetric parallel import firms. Hence, by differentiating (225), the *n* interior first order conditions follow:

$$\frac{\partial\pi_i(x_i)}{\partial x_i}=\frac{\partial\left((\gamma a-X)x_i-(\overline{p}_B+t)x_i-T\right)}{\partial x_i}=0$$
$$\Leftrightarrow \gamma a-2x_i-\sum\nolimits_{-i}x_{-i}-(\overline{p}_B+t)=0\,. \tag{226}$$

Note that, in (226), all parallel import firms other than firm *i* are denoted by subscript $-i$.[1058] Note that $\sum_{-i}x_{-i}=(n-1)x_i$, as the *n* parallel import firms are symmetrical. Therefore, by rearranging (226), the unique sub-game equilibrium quantity can be written as follows

$$\gamma a-2x_i-(n-1)x_i=\overline{p}_B+t$$
$$\Leftrightarrow x_i(n)=\frac{\gamma a-(\overline{p}_B+t)}{n+1}.\text{[1059]} \tag{227}$$

1054 See Ganslandt and Maskus (2004) on p. 1042.
1055 See also Malueg and Schwartz (1994) on p. 117ff as to the profit-eroding impact of uniform pricing induced by parallel trade. See also Arfwedson (2004) on p. 1ff with respect to the R&D incentive-reducing impact of parallel trade.
1056 See also Ganslandt and Maskus (2004) on p. 1042.
1057 See Ganslandt and Maskus (2004) on p. 1041.
1058 See Ganslandt and Maskus (2004) on p. 1043.
1059 See also Ganslandt and Maskus (2004) on p. 1043.

Note that $x_i(n)$ increases if the parameter γ increases, and that it decreases if the marginal costs of parallel trade $(\overline{p}_B + t)$ increase.[1060] Intuitively, the higher the demand for the pharmaceutical product in country *A* and the lower the marginal costs of parallel trade, the more attractive will be parallel trade as a business activity for the parallel-importing firms.

In the sub-game perfect Nash equilibrium with *n* symmetric parallel import firms, the total parallel import quantity is given by

$$X(n) = nx_i(n) = \frac{n}{n+1}\left(\gamma a - (\overline{p}_B + t)\right) \tag{228}$$

which increases if the number of parallel import firms, *n*, increases.[1061] Substituting *X* in (224) for *X* given by (228), we obtain the equilibrium price as a function of *n*

$$p(n) = \gamma a - \frac{n}{n+1}\left(\gamma a - (\overline{p}_B + t)\right).^{1062} \tag{229}$$

Note that – as *X(n)* increases if the number of parallel import firms *n* increases [see (228)] – the equilibrium price in country *A* falls if *n* increases. In other words, the higher the number of parallel-importing firms and thus the higher the quantities traded, the stronger is the competition for the manufacturer in country *A* stemming from parallel trade. Hence, parallel trade limits the market power of the manufacturer who holds a patent on the pharmaceutical product in country *A* and country *B*.

Moreover, Ganslandt and Maskus (2004, p. 1043) suggest that the equilibrium price in country *A* converges to the predetermined price in country *B* plus per unit trade costs if the number of parallel-importing firms increases [see (229) if $n \to \infty$].

Most notably, we come to a similar result in our double marginalization model if parallel trade costs are not prohibitively high so that parallel trade is a credible threat. More specifically, we find that $p_A^{m*} = p_B^{w*} + t$ [see (177)]. Nevertheless, the equilibrium wholesale price in country *B*, p_B^{w*}, is an endogenous variable in our model and not exogenously given as in the Ganslandt and Maskus (2004) model.

Working backwards to the first stage, Ganslandt and Maskus (2004, p. 1043) determine the equilibrium number of parallel import firms. More specifically, under the assumption that parallel import firms will only enter the market if expected profits are non-negative, Ganslandt and Maskus (2004, p. 1043) suggest that the free-entry equilibrium condition for any parallel import firm *i* is given by

$$\left(p(n) - (\overline{p}_B + t)\right)x_i(n) - T \geq 0. \tag{230}$$

Note that *p(n)* is given by (229). $x_i(n)$ is the corresponding sub-game perfect Nash equilibrium quantity given by (227). Under the assumption that – for mathematical

1060 See also Scherer and Watal (2002a) on p. 49ff as to the regulation of prices of pharmaceutical products in developed and developing countries. See also Maskus and Ganslandt (2002) on p. 57.

1061 See Ganslandt and Maskus (2004) on p. 1043.

1062 See Ganslandt and Maskus (2004) on p. 1043.

convenience – n is a continuous variable, by rearranging (230) the equilibrium number of parallel import firms is given by

$$\left(\left(\frac{\gamma a+n(\overline{p}_B+t)}{n+1}\right)-(\overline{p}_B+t)\right)\left(\frac{\gamma a-(\overline{p}_B+t)}{n+1}\right)-T=0$$
$$\Leftrightarrow(\gamma a+n(\overline{p}_B+t)-(n+1)(\overline{p}_B+t))(\gamma a-(\overline{p}_B+t))=(n+1)^2T$$
$$\Leftrightarrow n^*=\frac{\gamma a-(\overline{p}_B+t)}{\sqrt{T}}-1.^{1063} \qquad (231)$$

Note that (231) is positive if T is sufficiently small. For instance, if $\sqrt{T}<\gamma a-(\overline{p}_B+t)$ and thus $T<(\gamma a-(\overline{p}_B+t))^2$ it follows that the first term on the right-hand side of (231) is greater than 1 and n^* is a positive number.
Moreover, we can see from (231) that $\frac{\partial n^*}{\partial \overline{p}_B}<0$, $\frac{\partial n^*}{\partial t}<0$, $\frac{\partial n^*}{\partial T}<0$, and $\frac{\partial n^*}{\partial \gamma}>0$. Put differently, the equilibrium number of parallel import firms n^* decreases if the predetermined price in country B, $\overline{p}_B$, the variable trade cost t and the fixed cost T increase, and it increases if the size of the market in country A increases.[1064]
By inserting n^* given by (231) into (229) we obtain the equilibrium price in country A

$$p^*=\gamma a-\left(\frac{\gamma a-(\overline{p}_B+t)}{\sqrt{T}}-1\right)\left(\frac{\sqrt{T}}{\gamma a-(\overline{p}_B+t)}\right)(\gamma a-(\overline{p}_B+t))$$
$$\Leftrightarrow p^*=\gamma a-\left(\gamma a-(\overline{p}_B+t)-\sqrt{T}\right)$$
$$\Leftrightarrow p^*=\overline{p}_B+t+\sqrt{T}.^{1065} \qquad (232)$$

We can see from (232) that the equilibrium price in country A increases if the predetermined price in country B, the per unit costs of parallel trade, t, and the fixed costs of parallel trade increase. In other words, the less attractive parallel trade is due to unfavorable cost structures the smaller is the market power reducing impact of parallel trade in country A and thus the higher is the price in country A.
However, by inserting n^* given by (231) into (228) we obtain the equilibrium parallel import quantity

$$X^*=\left(\frac{\gamma a-(\overline{p}_B+t)}{\sqrt{T}}-1\right)\frac{\sqrt{T}(\gamma a-(\overline{p}_B+t))}{\gamma a-(\overline{p}_B+t)}$$
$$\Leftrightarrow X^*=\gamma a-\overline{p}_B-t-\sqrt{T}. \qquad (233)$$

1063 See also Ganslandt and Maskus (2004) on p. 1043.
1064 See Ganslandt and Maskus (2004) on p. 1043.
1065 Note that Ganslandt and Maskus (2004) algebraically neither derive $p(n^*)$ nor $X(n^*)$. However, from the author's point of view, it is crucially important to derive $p(n^*)$ as well as $X(n^*)$ in order to analyze the impact of a change in the predetermined price in country B, T and t on the equilibrium price in country A and on the equilibrium quantity of parallel imports.

We can see from (233) that the equilibrium volume of parallel trade decreases if the predetermined price in country *B*, the per unit trade costs, *t*, and the fixed cost, *T*, increase and that it increases if the parameter γ increases.

To sum up, in contrast to our model, Ganslandt and Maskus (2004) show that the monopolistic manufacturer of pharmaceuticals located in country *A* is willing to accommodate parallel trade if the volumes available for parallel trade are limited. Put differently, quantity limits may serve as an explanation why parallel trade may actually occur in equilibrium. Our model, however, suggests that parallel trade does not occur in equilibrium (and thus wasteful transportation costs and repacking costs are not incurred) but that the mere threat of parallel trade – provided that it constitutes a credible threat – is sufficient to reduce the market power of the manufacturer.

Moreover, a crucial assumption in the Ganslandt and Maskus (2004) model is that the price in the foreign market, $\overline{p}_B$, is exogenously given. Of course, this assumption simplifies the algebra in a very convenient way.

However, from our point of view, the price that a monopolistic producer charges abroad is an important strategic variable and may not necessarily be seen as exogenously given. In fact, the wholesale price that the manufacturer of pharmaceuticals charges exclusive distributors in foreign markets is of particular importance as to the distributor's incentives to engage in parallel trade, as we have shown in our double marginalization model.

Nevertheless, pharmaceutical markets are highly regulated and small countries without real pharmaceutical manufacturing capacity often impose price caps to circumvent patent law.[1066] Hence, it appears to be important to take caps for pharmaceutical prices into consideration in a formal model of parallel trade. Consequently, as an idea for further research, we suggest extending our double marginalization model in this respect and formally addressing the issue of national regulation of pharmaceutical prices in a follow-up paper.

5.4. Parallel Trade and the Availability of Patented Pharmaceutical Products in the Developing World

Countries can freely decide whether to permit or ban parallel trade.[1067] As already mentioned in section 5.2.2.1, Article 6 of the TRIPS Agreement – being the only provision in the various international agreements on IPRs that deals with the treatment of parallel trade – preserves the territorial privilege for regulating parallel trade.[1068]

At the negotiations that led to the TRIPS Agreement, and later on to the Doha Declaration, it became apparent that the freedom to allow parallel trade was crucially

1066 For instance, see Danzon (1997), Matteucci and Reverberi (2005) and OECD (2000). See also Szymanski and Valletti (2005) on p. 734ff. We thank Hans-Bernd Schäfer for his comment in this respect.

1067 See Fink (2005) on p. 173ff.

1068 See Fink (2005) on p. 173ff. See also Maskus (2000a) on p. 208ff, Maskus (2000b) on p. 1271, Gervais (2003) on p. 11ff, Gallus (2005) on p. 77ff, Hestermeyer (2007) on p. 233, Correa (2000b), and Slotboom (2003).

important for many developing countries.[1069] They argued that parallel trade would be an effective means of mitigating potential price increases for pharmaceuticals resulting from the strengthened patent protection set out in the TRIPS Agreement.[1070] Furthermore, they argued that parallel trade would allow domestic licensees to obtain export markets for pharmaceuticals.[1071]

Nevertheless, many authors have argued that third-degree price discrimination by pharmaceutical manufacturers is desirable to ensure the availability of affordable medicines in low-income countries, and therefore that parallel trade flowing from low-income countries to high-income countries should be prohibited.[1072]

More specifically, consumers in low-income countries with a high price elasticity of demand are more likely to have access to cheaper patented pharmaceutical products when the manufacturer of the pharmaceutical products can successfully engage in third-degree price discrimination than when parallel trade forces prices towards uniformity.[1073]

We agree with the thesis that cross-national price discrimination without parallel trade is desirable from a developing countries' perspective.

First, our parallel trade model suggests that the (credible) threat of parallel trade leads to the convergence of prices in country A and country B up to the trade costs t.

Second, our model suggests that the equilibrium retail price in country B under parallel trade freedom – with country B being the country with a higher price elasticity of demand – typically exceeds the equilibrium retail price in country B under a regime of national exhaustion of IPRs without parallel trade.[1074] Furthermore, the equilibrium quantity in country B under parallel trade freedom is typically lower than the equilibrium quantity in country B under a regime of national exhaustion of IPRs without parallel trade.[1075] Put differently, a lower quantity of the pharmaceutical product is sold in country B at a higher price under parallel trade freedom as compared to a situation without parallel trade. Consequently, parallel trade is *ceteris paribus*

1069 For instance, see Abbott (1998) on p. 620 and Bale (1998) on p. 645. See also Valletti and Szymanski (2006) on p. 501, Maskus and Chen (2004) on p. 553ff, Maskus (2001) on p. 4, and Watal (1998).

1070 See Maskus (2001) on p. 11ff and Maskus (2000a) on p. 209. See also Watal (2001).

1071 See Szymanski and Valletti (2005) on p. 714ff. See also Abbott (1998) who supported the developing countries' point of view, arguing that a restriction on parallel trade was an unjustified inhibition of free trade.

1072 See Ganslandt et al. (2005) on p. 209ff, Scherer and Watal (2002a) on p. 41, Scherer and Watal (2002b) on p. 925ff, Maskus (2001) on p. 41ff, Maskus (2000b) on p. 1276ff, and Maskus and Ganslandt (2002) on p. 77ff. See also Word Health Organization and World Trade Organization (2002) on p. 210ff and on p. 218ff, Kremer (2002) on p. 76ff and Commission on Intellectual Property Rights (2002) on p. 41ff. See also Hausman and MacKie-Mason (1988), Batson (1998) on p. 489ff, Danzon and Towes (2003) on p. 184ff, Malueg and Schwartz (1994), and Fink (2005) on p. 177.

1073 For instance, see Scherer and Watal (2002a) on p. 43. See also World Health Organization and World Trade Organization (2002) on p. 220ff, Ganslandt et al. (2005) on p. 215ff, and Garrison (2006) on p. 16.

1074 See **Appendix 9**. See also Scherer and Watal (2002a) on p. 43ff for an example of niche-pricing of pharmaceutical products in South Africa. More specifically, Scherer and Watal (2002a) suggest that multinational pharmaceutical companies charge a small but very rich minority of the South African population with high drug prices although the unambiguous fact that South Africa is a low-income country would suggest that drug prices are low.

1075 See **Appendix 10**.

detrimental to country *B* as welfare in country *B* – with domestic welfare being equal to domestic consumer surplus – is lower under parallel trade freedom.

Maskus and Ganslandt (2002, p. 78) suggest in a non-technical article on parallel trade in pharmaceuticals and its implications for low-income countries that, under plausible circumstances, parallel trade may increase prices in low-income countries and that smaller markets might end up not being served.

Indeed, the analysis of our parallel trade model shows that this assertion is correct if trade costs are low and γ is relatively high. More specifically, we find that – for low trade costs – potential competition from parallel trade is so fierce that the manufacturer has to charge such a high wholesale price in country *B* in order to deter parallel trade that the distribution of the pharmaceutical product in country *B* becomes unprofitable. In this case, the market in county *B* will not be served.[1076] Consequently, it would be desirable for country *B* to discourage parallel trade and to encourage price discrimination in order to open the otherwise unserved domestic market.[1077]

Moreover, several authors have argued that parallel trade reduces the profit of the manufacturer and therefore – if profits are accurately foreseen – reduces his incentives to invest in R&D for new pharmaceutical products.[1078]

We agree with this argument because our parallel trade model suggests that the credible threat of parallel trade always leads to a lower profit of the manufacturer of a patented pharmaceutical product. Thus, parallel trade freedom is likely to reduce the incentives of the manufacturer to invest in R&D for new pharmaceutical products in the first place even though the product could be patented in both countries.[1079] Put another way, under the reasonable assumption that pharmaceutical R&D programmes are sensitive to profit reductions, parallel trade freedom undermines the innovation-stimulating effect of patent protection by reducing the capability of the original manufacturer of a patented pharmaceutical product to engage in third-degree price discrimination.[1080] This issue is of particular importance for pharmaceutical R&D into diseases of particular interest to developing countries such as neglected infectious and tropical diseases.[1081] If developing countries were to make widespread use of parallel trade in medicines for these diseases, the threat of parallel trade could offset incentives to more R&D into those diseases emerging from stronger patent protection in the developing world as stipulated in the TRIPS Agreement and the Doha Declaration.[1082]

1076 For instance, see **Table 4** on p. 170. See also Scherer and Watal (2002a) on p. 41ff and Ganslandt et al. (2005) on p. 216.

1077 For instance, see Fink (2005) on p. 178. See also Varian (1985) and Maskus (2001) on p. 41.

1078 For instance, see Szymanski and Valletti (2005) on p. 722ff, Scherer and Watal (2002a) on p. 49, and Valletti and Szymanski (2006) on p. 502ff.

1079 See also Maskus (2001) on p. 23ff.

1080 For instance, see Ganslandt et al. (2005) on p. 209 and on p. 217, Maskus and Ganslandt (2002) on p. 78, Scherer and Watal (2002a) on p. 38ff, Bale (1998) on p. 643, and Malueg and Schwartz (1994). See also Szymanski and Valletti (2005) on p. 707ff, Lanjouw (1998), Atik and Lidgard (2006) on p. 1044ff, and Fink (2005) on p. 178ff. See also Lanjouw (2003) on p. 107ff and Kremer (2002) on p. 74ff as to the likely political backlash in high-income countries if – under third-degree price discrimination – pharmaceutical prices in low-income countries are significantly lower.

1081 See Maskus and Ganslandt (2002) on p. 78.

1082 For instance, see Maskus and Ganslandt (2002) on p. 78. See also Maskus (2001) on p. 42ff.

Consequently, in order to encourage affordable provision of medicines and to stimulate pharmaceutical R&D, developing countries should rather aid market segmentation and thus facilitate price discrimination by prohibiting parallel trade flowing from low-income to high-income countries.[1083]

However, several authors suggest that even if strong patent protection in the developing world were successfully enforced and parallel trade were prohibited, the problem of underinvestment in R&D for neglected infectious and tropical diseases would still not be mitigated.[1084] We will address this issue in the following chapter.

1083 See also World Health Organization and World Trade Organization (2002) on p. 213, Kremer (2002) on p. 76ff, Commission on Intellectual Property Rights (2002) on p. 41ff, Subramanian (1999) on p. 11ff, Malueg and Schwartz (1994), and Fink (2005) on p. 184.

1084 For instance, see Lanjouw (2003) on p. 100ff, Lanjouw and Cockburn (2001), Glennerster and Kremer (2001) on p. 35ff, Webber and Kremer (2001) on p. 738, and Kremer (2001a).

6. Solutions for the Problem of Underinvestment in R&D for Medicines for Neglected Infectious and Tropical Diseases

6.1. Introduction

The introduction of patent protection in the developing world alone is not sufficient for solving the problem of underinvestment in R&D for neglected infectious and tropical diseases.[1085] Furthermore, even if patent protection provided an adequate incentive mechanism to successfully stimulate R&D, there would still remain the problem that patented medicines may not be affordable for large groups of consumers in poor countries.[1086]

Therefore, in this chapter we consider:[1087]

- which incentive mechanisms may be adequate to promote research into neglected infectious and tropical diseases; and
- which mechanisms may help to improve low-cost access to medicine in low-income countries?

The first part of this chapter provides an overview of the empirical literature on the impact of expected market size on innovation. This includes an analysis of the impact of stronger patent protection in developing countries on local R&D.

The second part deals with push programs such as publicly-funded research institutions and targeted R&D tax credits to stimulate research. It shows that push programs are particularly suitable to promote basic research, but that moral hazard and adverse selection problems reduce their effectiveness.

The third part of this chapter provides an analysis of pull programs such as prizes, patent buyouts, and advanced purchase commitments. Such programs link payment to successful innovation. Pull programs reduce shirking incentives of researchers and increase their incentives to concentrate their research efforts on marketable innovations. In particular, pull programs are suitable to improve access to affordable medicines in low-income countries.

1085 See World Health Organization (2002) on p. 20. See also Maurer (2005) on p. 10, Kettler (2002) on p. 667ff, Lanjouw (2003) on p. 100ff, Lanjouw and Cockburn (2001), Glennerster and Kremer (2001) on p. 35ff, and Webber and Kremer (2001) on p. 738. See also Kremer (2001a), Kremer (2001b), Kremer (2002), Attaran and Gillespie-White (2001), Attaran (2004), World Health Organization and World Trade Organization (2002) on p. 213, and Outterson (2004) on p. 244ff. See also Penrose (1973) for an early analysis of the benefits and costs of patent protection in the developing world.

1086 For instance, see World Health Organization (2001a) on p. 86. See also Scherer and Watal (2002b) on p. 938ff and Watal (2000) on p. 747ff. See also Kremer and Glennerster (2004) on p. 34ff.

1087 See also Kremer and Glennerster (2004) on p. 37.

Finally, we show that a combination of push and pull programs – as supplements rather than substitutes for patent protection – is an appropriate strategy to stimulate research into neglected infectious and tropical diseases.

6.2. Insufficient Market Size and Low Expected Market Returns to Research

6.2.1. Impact of Market Size on Innovation

Market size causes innovation. In his empirical work, Schmookler (1966) elaborates on the idea that market size has a significant impact on innovative activities.[1088] In particular, Schmookler (1966) finds a significant statistical relationship between sales of goods in a certain field such as petroleum refining and the amount of R&D investment and patent applications in that field.[1089] Griliches (1957) finds that the development of hybrid corn strains appropriate for a particular region is largely determined by the expected market size of that region.[1090] Similarly, Mansfield (1964) shows that – in industries such as petroleum, drugs and steel – there is a significant relationship between expected profits and R&D expenditures of large firms.

As to the market entry of manufacturers of generics, Scott Morton (1999) estimates a significant positive impact of the market size of pharmaceutical products in terms of sales revenue on the amount of generic drug entry.[1091]

Grabowski and Vernon (2000b) analyze the impact of a pharmaceutical firm's expected returns on the firm's R&D expenditure, and find a significant positive relationship.[1092]

Acemoglu and Linn (2004) analyze the empirical relationship between current and future market size of pharmaceutical products and the entry of new pharmaceutical products and innovation.[1093] They find a significant and robust impact of future market size on the entry of new pharmaceutical products. They show that the entry of new pharmaceutical products in a specific category grows by 4 percent if the potential market size for that category increases by 1 percent. Acemoglu and Linn (2004) conclude that this significant and robust impact of market size on market entry of pharmaceutical products has important implications for the direction of pharmaceutical R&D. They suggest that pharmaceutical R&D is directed toward more profitable markets and categories. Moreover, the empirical evidence provided by Acemoglu and Linn (2004) suggests that pharmaceutical R&D directed at medicines for neglected infectious diseases is likely to be very low as potential consumers' ability to pay for

1088 See Schmookler (1966) on p. 104ff. See also Schmookler (1962).

1089 See Schmookler (1966) on p. 104ff and on p. 137ff. See also Kremer and Glennerster (2004) on p. 55ff.

1090 See also Hayami and Ruttan (1971).

1091 See also Scott Morton (2000).

1092 See also Grabowski and Vernon (1994) for an analysis of the returns to R&D for pharmaceutical products marketed in the U.S. between 1980 and 1984. See also Grabowski et al. (2002) and Grabowski and Vernon (2000a).

1093 See also Acemoglu and Linn (2003).

new products is low and potential markets for new products are small. This is discussed further below.

6.2.2. Pharmaceutical R&D and Low Expected Market Returns in the Developing World

Several works by Harvard Professor Michael Kremer are based on the premise that pharmaceutical markets in the poorest countries are too small to trigger significant R&D for medicines for neglected infectious diseases that are prevalent in these countries.[1094]

He shows that low incomes are only one among several explanations why potential markets for vaccines for neglected infectious diseases are too small and research incentives for private pharmaceutical companies are suboptimal.[1095] In particular, there are several failures in the market for vaccines.[1096]

First, the consumption of a vaccine by one person has a positive external effect on other people as every additional vaccinated person reduces the spread of disease.[1097] However, individuals do not take the positive external effect on others into consideration when they decide whether to be vaccinated or not.[1098]

Second, many consumers in the developing world appear to be more willing to pay for drugs to treat a disease than for prevention through vaccination as the benefits from vaccination are less evident.[1099] This problem may be exacerbated by a lack of appropriate information about the benefits of vaccination due to a high level of illiteracy in poor countries and unsuccessful public health communications.[1100]

Third, children would benefit most from vaccination as they are most susceptible to diseases such as malaria because of their weak immune systems.[1101] However, even though the extra future earnings that they would generate if they were vaccinated and stayed healthy may exceed the costs of vaccination, they cannot contract with the vaccine supplier to pay for the vaccine out of those future earnings.[1102]

Furthermore, Kremer and Glennerster (2004) argue that the social returns to malaria vaccine innovation are likely to be at least ten times higher than the private returns to R&D for malaria vaccines.[1103] This gap between social and private returns results in suboptimal incentives for the pharmaceutical industry to pursue R&D for socially valuable malaria vaccines.

1094 See Kremer (2002) on p. 70ff and Kremer and Glennerster (2004) on p. 25ff. See also Kremer (2001a) on p. 44ff and Kremer (2001b). See also Maurer (2005) on p. 10 and World Health Organization and World Trade Organization (2002) on p. 210ff.

1095 See Kremer (2001a) on p. 44ff and Kremer and Glennerster (2004) on p. 37ff. See also Kremer and Snyder (2003).

1096 See Kremer (2001a) on p. 44ff.

1097 See Kremer and Glennerster (2004) on p. 29.

1098 See Kremer (2001a) on p. 45.

1099 See Kremer (2001a) on p. 45.

1100 See Rozek and Tully (1999) on p. 815ff. See also Kremer (2001a) on p. 45.

1101 See World Health Organization (2005) and World Health Organization (2003a).

1102 See Kremer (2001a) on p. 45.

1103 See also Nadiri (1993), Mansfield et al. (1977), and Kremer (2001a) on p. 50ff.

Nevertheless, Kettler (2002) suggests that a main factor for the underinvestment in pharmaceutical R&D into neglected infectious diseases is the low estimated market size for medicines for these diseases.[1104] Although a large number of consumers in the developing world lack effective medicines for such diseases, their purchasing power is too low to generate a sufficiently large market to stimulate R&D.[1105] In these circumstances pharmaceutical companies judge that the return on R&D investment in neglected infectious diseases will be less than the return on an equivalent investment in medicines for the developed world.[1106]

Recent estimates of the Pharmaceutical Research and Manufacturers of America (PhRMA) for the year 2007 suggest that only 0.5 percent of their market is in Africa, 1.3 percent in Latin America and 5.7 percent in the Asia-Pacific region.[1107] Interestingly, the share of the African market dropped from 1.0 percent in 1998 to 0.5 in 2007.[1108] By far largest market in 2007 was the U.S. market at 67.7 percent, followed by the European market at 18.3 percent.[1109]

It has also been argued that emerging pharmaceutical industries in developing countries such as India, Brazil or Argentina will invest in R&D for medicines for neglected infectious diseases if stronger patent protection is afforded in these countries.[1110] This idea suggests that local R&D for medicines for neglected infectious diseases in endemic regions may help to eradicate them. We will address this issue in the following section.

6.2.3. Impact of Patent Protection on the Domestic Pharmaceutical Industry in the Developing World

Kettler and Modi (2001) analyze patterns of patenting and R&D activities in India in order to address the question of whether the introduction of patent protection for pharmaceutical products in India will help to stimulate local R&D for medicines for neglected infectious diseases. They find that Indian pharmaceutical companies capable of conducting R&D for new pharmaceutical products are more likely to target diseases that are prevalent in industrialized countries with large and profitable global markets, i.e. diabetes and cancer, instead of neglected infectious and tropical diseases.

The survey data from India provided by Lanjouw and Cockburn (2001) seems to confirm the results by Kettler and Modi (2001). Lanjouw and Cockburn (2001) consider whether the introduction of patent protection for new pharmaceutical products in India lead to more R&D for medicines for neglected infectious diseases. They

1104 See Kettler (2002) on p. 657ff. See also World Health Organization and World Trade Organization (2002) on p. 210ff.

1105 See also Lanjouw (2002a) on p. 88ff, Maurer (2005) on p. 38, and Ganslandt et al. (2005) on p. 207ff.

1106 See Webber and Kremer (2001) on p. 736.

1107 See PhRMA (2009), Table 9 on p. 57. See also PhRMA (2008), Table 6 on p. 56 with respect to R&D by geographic area. See also Maurer (2005) on p. 38 for a summary of PhRMA member sales in 2002.

1108 See also Kremer (2002) on p. 70.

1109 See PhRMA (2005), Table 9 on p. 40.

1110 For instance, see Kettler (2002) on p. 667ff.

use measures of R&D constructed from the biomedical literature, i.e. frequency of citations of specific diseases, NIH grant allocations for malaria projects and survey evidence from Indian pharmaceutical companies. The results of the survey data obtained from India's leading pharmaceutical companies suggest that Indian pharmaceutical companies follow a global strategy and focus on global diseases prevalent in industrialized countries.[1111] In a follow-up paper Lanjouw and MacLeod (2005) come to the conclusion that, while there was a significant increase in overall pharmaceutical R&D in India from 1998 to 2003, R&D investment in neglected infectious and tropical diseases fell.

To sum up, insufficient expected market returns from R&D for medicines for neglectted infectious and tropical diseases are the major cause of underinvestment in R&D into these diseases. There is also significant evidence that, even where stronger patent protection is available, this is not sufficient to shift the research priorities of developing country's pharmaceutical industries to R&D for medicines for neglected diseases.[1112] Instead, stronger patent protection in the developing world is more likely to stimulate local R&D for medicines for global diseases that produce higher market returns.

So stronger protection of intellectual property rights in developing countries alone does not provide sufficient incentives for R&D into medicines for neglected infectious diseases.[1113] Therefore, additional mechanisms alongside the stronger patent protection stipulated in the TRIPS Agreement are required to promote R&D for medicines for neglected infectious diseases. We will elaborate on this issue in the following sections. In particular, we will focus on the question as to whether so-called push or pull programs are suitable for promoting such R&D.

6.3. Push Programs and R&D for Neglected Infectious Diseases

A program that subsidizes research inputs through direct funding such as research grants[1114] or tax credits for R&D investment is called a push program.[1115] Current push programs aimed at promoting R&D into malaria research are the Medicines for Malaria Venture[1116] and the Malaria Vaccine Initiative.[1117]

1111 See also Scherer and Watal (2001) on p. 11.
1112 See Kettler (2002) on p. 667ff. See also Kettler and Modi (2001), Lanjouw and MacLeod (2005), and Scherer and Watal (2002b).
1113 See Kettler (2002) on p. 667ff.
1114 See Maurer (2005) on p. 22ff.
1115 See United Nations Development Programme (2001) on p. 99. See also Kremer and Glennerster (2004) on p. 45ff and Webber and Kremer (2001) on p. 737. See also Trouiller et al. (2002) on p. 2191.
1116 See http://www.mmv.org (last visited March 24, 2009).
1117 See Kremer and Glennerster (2004) on p. 45.

Grants to a university or a government laboratory are also push programs.[1118] In this section, we examine the question as to whether a push incentive mechanism is an adequate device to stimulate R&D for medicines for neglected infectious diseases.
First, we analyze the efficacy of publicly-funded research such as research grants. In particular, we will examine the question as to whether public funding provides adequate incentives to promote research into vaccines for neglected infectious diseases.
Second, we elaborate on the question as to whether R&D tax credits are an appropriate means to encourage R&D into neglected infectious diseases.

6.3.1. Publicly-Funded Research Institutions

Large publicly-funded research institutions such as universities or the U.S. National Institutes of Health certainly play a significant role in promoting basic research.[1119] They help to create non-patentable fundamental scientific knowledge that provides a platform for downstream discoveries of the profit-seeking pharmaceutical industry.[1120] This publicly available fundamental scientific knowledge generated by publicly-funded research institutions reduces research costs incurred by the pharmaceutical industry. Thus, it potentially increases private incentives to invest in applied research.[1121]
However, experiences with publicly-funded programs to finance commercial R&D of marketable pharmaceutical products suggest that push programs are subject to moral hazard and adverse selection problems due to asymmetric information between researchers and governmental research administrators.[1122] For instance, the USAID's malaria vaccine push program in the 1980s was characterized by external evaluators as unrealistic and mediocre.[1123] The evaluators concluded that two of three research teams should not get additional funding.[1124] However, the project director ignored the recommendations of the external evaluators.[1125] Instead, he provided the USAID Office of Procurement with information that resulted in full funding for all three research teams.[1126] Later on, two of three teams were indicted for theft and criminal conspiracy in diverting grant funds into their private accounts.[1127] Additional examples for publicly-funded research programs to finance commercial R&D that failed

1118 See Webber and Kremer (2001) on p. 737ff.
1119 See Glennerster and Kremer (2001) on p. 35. See also Webber and Kremer (2001) on p. 737, Scotchmer (2006) on p. 17ff, Lévêque and Ménière (2004) on p. 8, and Kremer and Glennerster (2004) on p. 49ff.
1120 See Scherer (2000) on p. 1298. See also Webber and Kremer (2001) on p. 737.
1121 See also Scotchmer (2006) on p. 127ff.
1122 See Kremer (2002) on p. 82ff. See also Glennerster and Kremer (2001) on p. 39ff and Kremer (1998) on p. 1143.
1123 See Kremer and Glennerster (2004) on p. 48.
1124 See Kremer and Leino (2004) on p. 231.
1125 See Kremer and Leino (2004) on p. 231.
1126 See Glennerster and Kremer (2001) on p. 48.
1127 See Kremer and Leino (2004) on p. 231.

spectacularly are the supersonic transport plane,[1128] the nuclear breeder reactor[1129] and the Carter administration's synthetic fuel program.[1130]
Nevertheless, moral hazard problems may arise because governmental research administrators cannot perfectly monitor the research activities of the funded researchers. Furthermore, researchers, once they are funded, may have incentives to redirect resources to non-core research activities,[1131] to put effort in unrelated more rewarding research projects, or to prepare the next grant application instead of focussing on the funded research project.[1132]
Effective performance management of researchers together with reputation effects and contingency of future funding on previous performance may help to mitigate the moral hazard problems.[1133] For instance, suppose that a researcher applies for public funding for several subsequent research projects. If the researcher fails to perform in one of the early research projects because he strays from the funded research project, he may not get funds for a subsequent research project. Thus, he is likely to have higher incentives to perform under repeated interaction than in a one-shot situation.[1134]
From a theoretical point of view, adverse selection problems with publicly-funded push programs may arise because they pay for research inputs on the grounds of the *ex ante* evaluation of potential product delivery and not on the grounds of successful product development.[1135] More specifically, researchers have better information than governmental research administrators about the probability of success of a research program designated to be funded.[1136] Researchers may also have incentives to overestimate the probability of success of the research program, i.e. in order to get the funding in the first place or to increase the amount awarded.[1137]
However, due to the lack of appropriate information governmental research administrators may neither be able to determine which research projects should be funded nor which diseases should be targeted.[1138] Hence, asymmetric information with respect to the probability of success of research projects may result in the funding of research projects that only have a small probability of success.[1139] Or even worse, governmental research administrators may decide not to fund a worthwhile research project with a high probability of success when they doubt that the information on the probability of success they are provided with is credible.[1140]
These problems may be mitigated when a private pharmaceutical firm or research institution is only paid by a governmental agency after it has successfully developed a specific marketable pharmaceutical product. In this case, researchers will have strong

1128 See Glennerster and Kremer (2001) on p. 40.
1129 See Kremer and Glennerster (2004) on p. 51.
1130 See Glennerster and Kremer (2001) on p. 40.
1131 See Webber and Kremer (2001) on p. 737.
1132 See Kremer and Glennerster (2004) on p. 49. See also Kremer (2002) on p. 82ff.
1133 See Gallini and Scotchmer (2002) on p. 53ff. See also Maurer (2005) on p. 23.
1134 See Gallini and Scotchmer (2002) on p. 54. See also Kremer (2002) on p. 75ff.
1135 See Maurer (2005)on p. 22ff. See also Kremer and Glennerster (2004) on p. 49ff.
1136 See Kremer and Glennerster (2004) on p. 49ff.
1137 See Kremer and Glennerster (2004) on p. 49ff.
1138 See Kremer (2002) on p. 82ff.
1139 See Kremer and Glennerster (2004) on p. 50.
1140 See Kremer (2002) on p. 82ff.

incentives to evaluate the likelihood of success of its research projects more realistically and to focus on the development of the desired product. Consequently, moral hazard and adverse selection problems would be mitigated.[1141] We will come back to this issue in our discussion of alternatives to publicly-funded push programs below where we elaborate on pull mechanisms to spur pharmaceutical R&D such as prizes, patent buyouts, and advanced purchase commitments.

To sum up, public funding may serve as a mechanism to promote basic research that is not patentable and that is therefore likely to be a financially unattractive business activity for the private sector. Nevertheless, several negative examples suggest that publicly-funded research programs are subject to moral hazard and adverse selection problems that reduce the efficacy of such programs. However, fundamental scientific knowledge has positive spillover effects on the private sector. Therefore, publicly-funded research programs to encourage fundamental research would be recommendable if the moral hazard and adverse selection problems mentioned above were successfully mitigated through the use of effective performance management, i.e. in the case of repeated interaction.

6.3.2. Targeted R&D Tax Credits

In contrast to publicly-funded research institutions, targeted R&D tax credits[1142] – being a specific type of tax relief[1143] – are a direct contribution to pharmaceutical companies in order to promote R&D into specific neglected diseases.[1144] However, publicly-funded research institutions as well as R&D tax credits are push mechanisms that finance research inputs rather than research outputs.[1145] For instance, in the U.S., pharmaceutical companies are eligible for a 20 percent R&D tax credit. Nevertheless, a bill introduced in the U.S. Congress that proposed to increase the R&D tax credit for R&D into vaccines for HIV, tuberculosis, and malaria to 30 percent was never passed into law.[1146]

As already mentioned above, the private returns to R&D into neglected infectious and tropical diseases are much lower than the social returns to R&D into these diseases.[1147] This results in private firms investing less than is socially optimal.[1148] R&D tax credits

---

1141 See Kremer and Glennerster (2004) on p. 50.

1142 See Hall (1993) and Dixon and Greenhalgh (2002) on p. 41ff. See also Hall and Van Reenen (2000) for a survey of the econometric evidence on the efficacy of R&D tax credits. See Kremer (2002) on p. 83. See also Trouiller et al. (2001) on p. 949 and Kremer and Glennerster (2004) on p. 51. See also World Trade Organization (2004) on p. 174 for several arguments in favour of publicly financing basic research through R&D tax credits. See also World Trade Organization (2006), Table 3 on p. 84 for an overview of government-financed R&D expenditures through tools such as R&D tax concessions in various developed and developing countries from 1999 to 2003.

1143 See World Trade Organization (2006) on p. 84, footnote 117.

1144 See Kremer and Glennerster (2004) on p. 51ff.

1145 See Kremer and Glennerster (2004) on p. 52.

1146 See U.S. Vaccines for the New Millenium Act of 2001 (S. 895, 107th Congress, introduced May 16, 2001). See also Kremer and Glennerster (2004) and Kremer (2001a) on p. 55ff.

1147 See Dixon and Greenhalgh (2002) on p. 41ff.

1148 See World Trade Organization (2004) on p. 174ff.

address this problem. They are a means to provide private pharmaceutical companies with higher incentives to invest in R&D for new pharmaceutical products.

However, targeted R&D tax credits subsidize research inputs for a specific pharmaceutical product rather than rewarding successful product development. Therefore, R&D tax credits are subject to similar monitoring problems as other push mechanisms.[1149]

First, pharmaceutical companies have better information about the characteristics of their R&D than the governmental agency that determines the qualification of R&D expenditures to a targeted tax credit program.[1150] Consequently, pharmaceutical companies may have incentives to use their superior knowledge to maximize their claims through creative accounting.[1151] To give an example, vaccines typically include both antigens specific to certain organisms as well as adjuvants. Adjuvants are substances that typically have no direct effects by themselves but that increase the efficacy of a vaccine by sensitizing the immune response.[1152] Now suppose that an adjuvant was originally developed for a vaccine that does not qualify for a targeted R&D tax credit. Nevertheless, the adjuvant can also be used in a vaccine that qualifies for a targeted R&D tax credit. In this case, the pharmaceutical company will have incentives to claim that the adjuvant was actually designed for the latter vaccine in order to maximize their claims.[1153]

A second general problem with targeted R&D tax credits may arise because tax credits can only serve as an incentive mechanism to promote R&D into specific diseases if firms have tax liabilities.[1154] However, most biotechnology firms neither generate current profits nor have tax liabilities so that targeted R&D tax credits may not be effective in this case.[1155]

Nevertheless, as to R&D for medicines for neglected infectious diseases, i.e. a malaria vaccine appropriate for residents in low-income countries, the following problems with targeted R&D tax credits may arise.

For instance, a targeted R&D tax credit could be claimed by a pharmaceutical company pursuing R&D for types of the pharmaceutical product that are not appropriate for low-income countries.[1156] Suppose that a pharmaceutical company claims a targeted tax credit for R&D into a malaria vaccine. Nevertheless, health needs of residents in low-income countries with respect to a malaria vaccine significantly differ from health needs of residents in high-income countries.[1157] For instance, a malaria vaccine appropriate for travellers or military personnel that only spend a limited period of time in poor regions where malaria is prevalent may have different

1149 See Kremer (2001a) on p. 55ff.

1150 See Kremer and Glennerster (2004) on p. 51ff.

1151 See Kremer (2002) on p. 82ff. See also Gallini and Scotchmer (2002) on p. 53ff and Kremer and Glennerster (2004) on p. 53.

1152 See Kremer and Glennerster (2004), footnote 1 on p. 53.

1153 See Kremer and Glennerster (2004) on p. 52ff.

1154 See Kremer and Glennerster (2004) on p. 53.

1155 See Kremer and Glennerster (2004) on p. 53.

1156 See United Nations Development Programme (2001) on p. 100.

1157 See Diwan and Rodrik (1991). See also Kremer and Glennerster (2004) on p. 52ff.

characteristics than a malaria vaccine appropriate for residents that permanently live in those regions.[1158]

On the one hand, a malaria vaccine for consumers in high-income countries is more likely to focus on the early life-cycle stage of the malaria parasite when it is transmitted from an Anopheles mosquito to its human host.[1159] This stage is called the sporozoite-stage of malaria. However, a malaria vaccine that focuses on the sporozoite-stage of malaria may only provide temporary protection and thus may not be adequate for consumers in low-income countries.[1160] On the other hand, a malaria vaccine appropriate for residents of poor regions where malaria is prevalent would have to target the malaria parasite on the later merozoite-stage of malaria when merozoite spores infect and destroy red blood cells in order to provide durable instead of temporary protection.[1161]

The problem that pharmaceutical products may not be appropriate for use in low-income countries may also arise with tax credits for R&D into an HIV vaccine. Most commercial R&D into an HIV vaccine focuses on the clade B HIV subtype that dominates in the U.S. and in Europe.[1162] In Africa, however, the clade C HIV subtype dominates, and it is not known yet whether a vaccine against the clade B HIV subtype would also be effective against the clade C HIV subtype.[1163] Hence, a targeted tax credit for R&D into an HIV vaccine could be claimed by a pharmaceutical company pursuing R&D for an HIV vaccine type that may not be appropriate for consumer in low-income countries.[1164]

One may argue that the problems mentioned above could be mitigated by restricting the targeted R&D tax credit into malaria vaccine research focussing on the merozoite-stage of malaria or HIV vaccine research focussing on clade C. However, it might be counterproductive to restrict research in that manner for the following reasons. An HIV vaccine designed for a specific HIV subtype might turn out to be effective against other HIV subtypes or a malaria vaccine focussing on the early sporozoite-stage might turn out to provide both temporary and long-term protection.[1165]

To sum up, a targeted R&D tax credit for malaria or HIV research may result in vaccines that are appropriate for consumers in high-income countries but inappropriate for consumers in poor regions where the diseases are prevalent. In other words, if the main objective was to promote research into vaccines that are appropriate for consumers in low-income countries where neglected infectious diseases are widespread, targeted R&D tax credits may not fully achieve this objective. The two examples mentioned above suggest that it may be difficult to promote research inputs into specific types of vaccines due to the scientific complexity of pharmaceutical R&D. They also suggest that alternative incentive mechanisms that reward the

---

1158 See Kremer (2002) on p. 82ff. See also Kremer and Glennerster (2004) on p. 52.
1159 See Kremer and Glennerster (2004) on p. 52ff.
1160 See United Nations Development Programme (2001) on p. 100 and Kremer (2002) on p. 82ff. See also Kremer and Glennerster (2004) on p. 52ff.
1161 For instance, see Anderson et al. (1996) on p. 58ff and Breman et al. (2004) on p. 12. See also Kremer and Glennerster (2004) on p. 52ff.
1162 For instance, see OECD (2007). See also Kremer and Glennerster (2004) on p. 52.
1163 See Kremer and Glennerster (2004) on p. 52.
1164 See Kremer and Glennerster (2004) on p. 52ff.
1165 See Kremer and Glennerster (2004) on p. 52ff.

development of a specific vaccine on the grounds of the assessment of its efficacy once it is developed may be more appropriate than a targeted R&D tax credit that rewards research inputs. We will come back to this issue below where we analyze the efficacy of pull mechanisms to spur research into neglected infectious diseases.

There is another drawback associated with targeted R&D tax credits with respect to the access of affordable new medicines for neglected infectious diseases in low-income countries.[1166] They cannot mitigate the core problem that residents in poor regions do not have access to affordable medicines once they are developed.[1167] For instance, assuming that patent rights are afforded in low-income countries as prescribed in the TRIPS Agreement, prices of new pharmaceutical products may still be too high for the vast majority of consumers in low-income countries during the life of the patent. In other words, even if targeted R&D tax credits successfully stimulated the development of new and effective pharmaceutical products, poor people in those regions where neglected infectious diseases are widespread may still not benefit from these products because of unaffordable (monopoly) prices. Consequently, additional mechanisms are required to secure affordable access to new pharmaceutical products in low-income countries.

To conclude, targeted R&D tax credits subsidize R&D inputs instead of rewarding the successful development of a desired pharmaceutical product. Furthermore, they are subject to monitoring problems due to asymmetric information with respect to the qualification of private R&D expenditures to a targeted tax credit program. They may also provide pharmaceutical companies with incentives to make use of creative accounting and may promote R&D into medicines inappropriate for consumers in low-income countries. Therefore, additional mechanisms next to targeted R&D tax credits are necessary to improve affordable access to medicines for neglected infectious diseases for residents in low-income countries.

6.3.3. Conclusion as to Push Programs

Given the dearth of R&D for medicines for neglected infectious diseases, direct public funding of basic research into these diseases may be an appropriate option to provide a platform for downstream discoveries of the pharmaceutical sector.[1168]

However, moral hazard and adverse selection problems as well negative experiences in the past suggest that publicly-funded research institutions may not be the optimal solution to finance the development of marketable pharmaceutical products. More specifically, incentive problems arise because public funds pay for research inputs on the grounds of an *ex ante* assessment of the probability of success of research programs instead of rewarding successful product development.[1169]

Similar incentive problems arise when research is financed through targeted R&D tax credits.

1166 See Kremer and Glennerster (2004) on p. 52.

1167 See Kremer and Glennerster (2004) on p. 52.

1168 See Scherer (2000) on p. 1298. See also Webber and Kremer (2001) on p. 737 and Glennerster and Kremer (2001) on p. 37ff.

1169 See Kremer and Glennerster (2004) on p. 49.

Therefore, additional mechanisms alongside publicly funded push programs are necessary in order to encourage private pharmaceutical companies to develop medicines for neglected infectious diseases and to improve affordable access to those medicines for residents of low-income countries. We will, therefore, address the question as to whether pull programs such as prizes or advanced purchase commitments are effective mechanisms to mitigate the problems mentioned above.

6.4. Pull Programs and R&D for Neglected Infectious Diseases

In contrast to push programs, pull programs such as prizes, advanced purchase commitments and patent buyouts reward research output rather than research input.[1170] For instance, a pull program rewards the actual creation of a desired medicine or a vaccine but not the R&D input itself.[1171] Nevertheless, we will see in the following that pull programs may not be adequate to encourage basic research.[1172]

In the first part of this section, we will analyze the advantages and disadvantages of prizes as an incentive mechanism to stimulate research.

The second part provides an analysis of the efficacy of patent buyouts as an incentive mechanism for R&D into medicines for neglected infectious diseases.

Third, we will elaborate on the efficacy of the U.S. Orphan Drug Act as an incentive mechanism to stimulate research into rare diseases such as Huntington's diseases or Lou Gehrig's Disease. The U.S. Orphan Drug Act provides an example of an incentive mechanism designed to encourage research into medicines with low expected market returns.

In the fourth part of this section, we analyze the proposal to use advanced purchase commitments to stimulate vaccine research into neglected infectious diseases brought forward by Michael Kremer and Rachel Glennerster.[1173]

Finally, we compare push and pull programs with respect to the question as to which mechanism spurs research into neglected infectious diseases more efficiently.

6.4.1. Prizes

In the following, we will focus on targeted prizes.[1174] A targeted prize is a payment that is made to a researcher conditional the achievement of a particular outcome, i.e. a technical specification of a desired drug or vaccine.[1175]

1170 For instance, see United Nations Development Programme (2001) on p. 99.

1171 See Kremer (2002) on p. 83ff. See also Webber and Kremer (2001) on p. 737ff. See also United Nations Development Programme (2001) on p. 100, box 5.3, and Callan and Gillespie (2007) on p. 164ff.

1172 For instance, see Kremer and Glennerster (2004) on p. 54.

1173 See Kremer (2001a) and Kremer (2001b). See also Kremer and Glennerster (2004) on p. 68ff.

1174 See Maurer (2005) on p. 20. See also Scotchmer (2006) on p. 40ff.

1175 See Gallini and Scotchmer (2002) on p. 53ff. See also Maurer (2006) on p. 377ff.

An early example of a targeted prize from ancient times is that offered by King Hiero II of Syracuse for anyone who could find out whether his new crown was made of pure gold by determining its volume.[1176] Hiero II suspected that the goldsmith who produced the crown abstracted some of the gold he provided him with and that the goldsmith used silver instead to keep the weight of the crown at the same level.[1177] However, at that time, nobody knew how to measure the volume of an object with such an irregular shape.[1178] Archimedes unintentionally solved the problem when he took a bath in an overly full bath tub and perceived that the volume of the water that ran out of the bath tub was equal to the volume of the immersed parts of his body.[1179]
Another example of prizes is the £10,000, £15,000 and £20,000 prize of the British government, in 1713, for anyone who could invent a method for measuring longitude within 60, 40, and 30 minutes, respectively.[1180]
Furthermore, when Napoleon was in need of more efficient ways to feed his troops on the battlefield he awarded a 12,000 francs prize that led to the development of food canning in 1809.[1181]
Further examples for prizes are the prize that Edward Jenner received from the British parliament for developing a smallpox vaccine in 1796,[1182] the Wolfskehl prize for solving Fermat's Last Theorem, established in 1908,[1183] and the Rockefeller prize for developing a diagnostic test for gonorrhea that is appropriate for use in developing countries.[1184]

6.4.1.1. Advantages of Prizes

First, suppose that a new drug or vaccine is successfully stimulated through a prize, i.e. the smallpox vaccine developed by Edward Jenner mentioned above, and donated to the public or made available to the public at manufacturing cost. In this case, the drug or vaccine is not subject to inefficient (monopoly) pricing associated with the market exclusivity provided by a patent.[1185] More specifically, prizes avoid deadweight losses associated with patent protection.[1186]

1176 See Vitruvius, De Architectura, Book IX, paragraphs 9-12, available on http://penelope.uchicago.edu/Thayer/E/Roman/Texts/Vitruvius/9*.html (last visited March 24, 2009). See also Kremer and Glennerster (2004) on p. 59ff.
1177 See Kremer and Glennerster (2004) on p. 59ff.
1178 See Kremer and Glennerster (2004) on p. 59ff.
1179 See Kremer and Glennerster (2004) on p. 59ff.
1180 See Encyclopaedia Britannica (1959) on p. 220. See also Kremer and Glennerster (2004) on p. 61ff and Sobel (1995).
1181 See Glennerster and Kremer (2001) on p. 35. See also Kremer and Glennerster (2004) on p. 60 and Falkman (1999) on p. 64. See also Wright (1983) on p. 704, footnote 5, and Burke (1978) on p. 234.
1182 See Lévêque and Ménière (2004) on p. 8. See also MacLeod (1988).
1183 See Kremer and Glennerster (2004) on p. 60. The theorem was proven by Andrew Wiles in 1997.
1184 See Kremer (1998) on p. 1164ff. See also Rockefeller Foundation (1997).
1185 See Gallini and Scotchmer (2002) on p. 53ff. See also Maurer (2005) on p. 20.
1186 See Wright (1983) on p. 693 and Scotchmer (2006) on p. 41. See also Shavell and Van Ypersele (2001) who compare reward systems to patents and copyrights. In particular, the authors argue that

Second, in contrast to push programs which finance research inputs,[1187] prizes are not likely to be subject to moral hazard problems.[1188] As a researcher will only receive the prize once the desired drug or vaccine is successfully developed, incentives to stray from the task or shift research priorities to other projects are lower under a prize mechanism.[1189]
Third, the technical specification of a prize could be designed to spur the development of a drug or vaccine appropriate for use in low-income countries.[1190] For instance, the prize for the development of a malaria vaccine may only be awarded if it fulfills specific requirements. For example, the requirement that the vaccine should prevent not less than 50 percent of Plasmodium falciparum malaria which is the most dangerous malaria type with the highest mortality rate and which is particularly widespread in Sub-Saharan Africa.[1191]
Fourth, in contrast to patents, the innovator to be awarded with a prize for successfully developing a specific drug does not have to fear profit-reducing infringement. That is, he does not incur high costs of litigation and identifying alleged patent infringers.[1192]

6.4.1.2. Disadvantages of Prizes

The first disadvantage of prizes is that, if the sponsor of a prize does not have accurate information of the prospective benefits and costs of the innovation to be awarded, the reward is likely to differ from the social value of the innovation resulting in either underpayment or overpayment for the innovation.[1193] In other words, the core difficulty with respect to prizes is to determine how large the prize should be.[1194]
Second, sponsors have incentives to renege on their promise once the invention is made, e.g. by creating reasons that the invention is useless and not eligible for the prize.[1195] For instance, John Harrison's prize for inventing a very exact chronometer to measure longitude in 1762 was delayed for more than a decade as the British Board of Longitude tried to prove that astronomical solutions were superior to the chronometer.[1196] It was not until 1773 that Harrison was paid in full.[1197] This example suggests that it is of crucial importance that the rules of a prize, i.e. the process for

---

reward systems stimulate R&D without creating monopoly power associated with patents. Moreover, they argue that an optional reward system is superior to IPRs.

1187 See Maurer (2005) on p. 20.

1188 For instance, see Maurer (2005) on p. 20.

1189 See Maurer (2005) on p. 20.

1190 See Gallini and Scotchmer (2002) on p. 55ff.

1191 See World Health Organization (2005) on p. 11ff. See also Maurer (2006) on p. 377ff.

1192 See Gallini and Scotchmer (2002) on p. 55. See also the analysis of patent breadth in section 3.2.2.2 in Chapter 3 of this thesis.

1193 See Gallini and Scotchmer (2002) on p. 55ff. See also Lévêque and Ménière (2004) on p. 8 and Maurer (2005) on p. 20.

1194 See Hollis (2005) on p. 3ff.

1195 See Maurer (2006) p. 377ff. See also Kremer and Glennerster (2004) on p. 61ff, Maurer (2005) on p. 20 and Gallini and Scotchmer (2002) on p. 55ff.

1196 See Gallini and Scotchmer (2002) on p. 55ff, footnote 2. See also Kremer and Glennerster (2004) on p. 61ff and Sobel (1995).

1197 See Encyclopaedia Britannica (1959) on p. 220.

assessing the value of an innovation, are clear and well specified in advance, and enforceable by a court.[1198] In other words, the sponsor has to adopt a credible commitment strategy *ex ante* to reduce his ability to renege *ex post* in order to prevent the erosion of incentives to innovate.[1199] Finally, the time-inconsistency problem mentioned above may also be solved through a bonding mechanism, i.e. a conflict resolution mechanism.[1200]

Third, Maurer (2005, p. 20) suggests that publicly-funded prizes are likely to be politically less favorable than patents because large lump-sum (governmental) prize payments are more visible to voters than patent revenues spread over a large number of doses.

Fourth, equivalent to patent race problems mentioned in section 3.2.1.2.3 in Chapter 3 of this thesis, prizes may result in a wasteful prize race in which R&D investments are duplicated when several firms compete for a prize.[1201] More specifically, if prizes offer the full social value of an innovation, competing firms may allocate excessive resources to their research under very specific conditions.[1202] For instance, competition may only arise if a firm that starts to invest in R&D at a later stage than its opponents can still get ahead of its rival. If, however, accelerated R&D programs and "leapfrogging" are not possible, patent races as well as prize races are not likely to happen.

Another disadvantage of prizes compared to patents stems from the fact that public or private sponsors are required to finance the prize.[1203] If a prize is publicly financed, it may eliminate deadweight loss associated with patents as mentioned above. However, public financing, i.e. through taxation of other goods, creates its own distortions.[1204]

To sum up, the usefulness of targeted prizes is indeed limited to cases where the desired innovation can be described ahead of time.[1205]

Nevertheless, by linking payment to successful development of an innovation prizes reduce shirking incentives of researchers.[1206] Prizes are less vulnerable to moral hazard and adverse selection problems than push mechanisms. Therefore, prizes appear to be an appropriate incentive mechanism to promote basic research where monitoring is typically difficult.[1207]

1198 See Kremer and Glennerster (2004) on p. 62.

1199 See Maurer (2005) on p. 20.

1200 We thank Hans-Bernd Schäfer for his comment in this respect.

1201 See Gallini and Scotchmer (2002) on p. 73, footnote 5. See also Loury (1979).

1202 See Wright (1983) on p. 693. In particular, Wright (1983) provides the first formal treatment regarding the advantages and disadvantages of several incentive mechanisms such as patents and prizes when the public research authority and researchers have asymmetric information with respect to research costs and rewards to innovation.

1203 See Maurer (2005) on p. 20.

1204 See Lévêque and Ménière (2004) on p. 8.

1205 See Maurer (2005) on p. 20.

1206 For instance, see Glennerster and Kremer (2001) on p.63ff. See also Maurer (2005) on p. 20.

1207 See Maurer (2006) on p. 379.

6.4.2. *Patent Buyouts*

Kremer (1998) examines the potential of patent buyouts to promote innovations and analyzes the use of auctions to determine patent buyout prices.[1208] Kremer (1998) argues that patent buyouts may eliminate the monopoly price distortions and increase incentives for original research.

We shall analyze the question as to whether the patent buyout mechanism proposed by Kremer is appropriate to spur research into medicines for neglected infectious diseases.

6.4.2.1. Description of the Patent Buyout Mechanism

Kremer (1998) suggests that the patent authority should offer to buy relevant patents at a price that is equal to its estimated private value plus a markup that reflects the ratio of the social to private value of the invention.

Under the assumption that the value of the invention is observable by competitors of the patent-holding firm,[1209] the market value of the patent would be estimated through a sealed-bid second-price auction.[1210]

In the following sections, we will briefly address the question how the market value of a patent could be estimated through a sealed-bid second-price auction and how large the markup mentioned above should be.

6.4.2.1.1. Sealed-bid Second-price Auction

Kremer (1998) suggests that the patent authority would place most of the bought patents in the public domain so that the innovation can be produced and marketed at a competitive price.[1211] However, only a small fraction of the bought patents would be sold to the firm with the highest bid at a price equal to the second highest bid in order to provide the auction participants with incentives to disclose their true expectations of the market value of the patent.[1212] The patent authority would randomly choose which patent will eventually be sold to the high bidder and thus will not be placed in the public domain.[1213] Note that – even though only a small fraction of the bought and

---

1208 For instance, see OECD (2007). See also Glennerster and Kremer (2001) on p. 38ff.

1209 See Scotchmer (2006) on p. 43. See also Hopenhayn et al. (2006) for a somewhat different buyout scheme to reward innovators – in the context of sequential innovation – that does not rely on information provided by rival firms competing with the innovator.

1210 A sealed-bid second-price auction is commonly also referred to as *Vickrey auction*. See Vickrey (1961). See also Kremer (1998) on p. 1146ff, Mas-Colell et al. (1995) on p. 866, and Tirole (1988) on p. 364. Furthermore, see McAfee and McMillan (1987) for an excellent overview of the formal literature on auctions.

1211 See also Maurer (2005) on p. 26. See also Scotchmer (2006) on p. 43.

1212 See Kremer (1998) on p. 1147.

1213 For instance, Scotchmer (2006) on p. 43.

auctioned patents will be sold – the auction participants will make the same bid as if the auction participant with the highest bid would receive the patent with certainty.[1214] However, even if the private value of a patent could be correctly estimated through the sealed-bid second-price auction, the patent holder may not be willing to participate voluntarily in the patent buyout mechanism as long as he does not realize a price for the patent that exceeds its market value.[1215] Therefore, Kremer (1998) proposes that the price at which the patent authority buys the patent from the patent-holder is equal to the market value of the patent, as determined through the sealed-bid second-price auction, times a specific markup in order the provide the patent holder with an incentive to sell the patent.

6.4.2.1.2. Determination of the Markup

Nadiri (1993) and Mansfield et al. (1977) estimate that the social returns to innovations are typically twice as large as the private returns to innovations.[1216] Based on this estimate, Kremer (1998) suggests that the patent authority should offer the patent-holder to purchase the patent at a price equal to the estimated market value of the patent times a markup equal to the ratio of social returns to innovation and private returns to innovation.[1217] Put differently, the patent authority should offer to buy the patent at a price that is at least twice as large as the estimated market value of the patent, as determined by the sealed-bid second-price auction.[1218]

6.4.2.2. Advantages of Patent Buyouts

First, as the price that the original developer of a patented innovation can realize from selling the patent to the patent authority typically exceeds the private value of the patent, patent buyouts are likely to increase private R&D incentives.[1219] Thus, they may help to mitigate the market failure that private returns on R&D are typically lower than social returns on R&D.[1220]

Second, as most of the patents bought will be put in the public domain so that the innovation can be produced and marketed at a competitive price,[1221] the deadweight losses due to inefficient monopoly pricing associated with patents will be eliminated in

---

1214 See Scotchmer (2006) on p. 43. See also Maurer (2005) on p. 26ff and Menell and Scotchmer (2007).

1215 See Kremer (1998) on p. 1146ff.

1216 See also Kremer and Glennerster (2004) on p. 40, Bernstein and Nadiri (1988), Bernstein and Nadiri (1989) and Lichtenberg (1992).

1217 See Kremer (1998) on p. 1147.

1218 Furthermore, Kremer (1998) shows on p. 1149ff that the markup is likely to mitigate the problem that bids might be low due to the winner's curse problem associated with informational asymmetries [Milgrom and Weber (1982) and Hendricks and Porter (1988)]. More specifically, the winner's curse problem may arise if the original innovator has private knowledge about the value of the patent that is superior to the knowledge of the bidders.

1219 For instance, see OECD (2007) as well as Kremer (1998) on p. 1148 and on p. 1152ff. See also Scotchmer (2006) on p. 42.

1220 See also Kremer and Glennerster (2004) on p. 40.

1221 See Maurer (2005) on p. 26.

those cases.[1222] Kremer (1998) suggests that the pharmaceutical sector would be a natural area to try the buyout scheme for the following reason.[1223] When bought patents are put in the public domain, pharmaceutical markets are likely to be relatively competitive compared to the patent-induced monopoly situation with large monopoly markups.[1224] Moreover, considerable information about medicinal products is gathered during the procedure of a new medicine's approval for patient use, i.e. through the EMEA in the EU or the FDA in the U.S.. Hence, auction participants could use this information to make informed bids.[1225]
Finally, monopoly profits would be eliminated in those cases in which the bought patent is put in the public domain.[1226] Hence, patent buyouts potentially mitigate the problem that competitors of the original innovator typically have incentives to invest in wasteful duplicative research in substitute products in order to steal profits from the innovator. These substitute products are often referred to as "me-too" drugs in the pharmaceutical sector.[1227] Producers of competing "me-too" drugs typically modify the original production process to such an extent that patent infringement is avoided.[1228]

6.4.2.3. Disadvantages of Patent Buyouts

First, the second-price auction which is of crucial importance for an effective operation of patent buyouts is potentially vulnerable to collusive behavior between the patent-holder and auction participants.[1229] Patent-holders have incentives to pay auction participants to make a bid that is higher than their true valuation of the patent in order to increase buyout prices.[1230] As already mentioned above, most of the bought patents are put in the public domain and only a small fraction of them would actually be sold to the highest bidders.[1231] Hence, on the one hand, the bribed bidders would only have a low probability of having to pay the patent authority. On the other hand, the patent-holders would have certainty of getting an inflated price.[1232] However, Kremer (1998) suggests several mechanisms for preventing collusive behavior, i.e. sealed bids, punishing colluding firms or rewards for whistle blowers among others.
Second, patent buyouts may aggravate the problem of patent races and wasteful duplication of R&D expenses as the price that the patent authority would pay for a patent is typically higher than its private (commercial) value.[1233]

1222 See Kremer (1998) on p. 1148.
1223 See also Scotchmer (2006) on p. 43.
1224 See Kremer (1998) on p. 1163ff.
1225 See Kremer (1998) on p. 1163.
1226 For instance, Scotchmer (2006) on p. 43.
1227 See Kremer (1998) on p. 1148. See also Kremer and Glennerster (2004) on p. 100ff.
1228 For instance, see Kremer and Glennerster (2004) on p. 37.
1229 See Kremer (1998) on p. 1157ff.
1230 See Kremer (2001a) on p. 60, footnote 21. See also Kremer (1998) on p. 1157ff.
1231 See Scotchmer (2006) on p. 43.
1232 See Kremer (1998) on p. 1157ff.
1233 See Gallini and Scotchmer (2002) on p. 60, footnote 5. See also Scotchmer (2006) on p. 43 and on p. 112ff.

Finally, patent buyouts are a visible lump-sum payment and thus are likely to be politically less attractive than less visible patent revenues spread over a large number of doses.[1234] Michael Kremer suggests in a subsequent paper, that buying a patent from a pharmaceutical manufacturer in a multi-billion-dollar patent buyout deal financed with tax money may generate some public resentment.[1235]

6.4.2.4. Conclusion as to Patent Buyouts

Patent buyouts may supplement the present system of encouraging innovative activeties through patents and publicly-financed push mechanisms such as research grants or publicly-financed research institutions.[1236] Moreover, patent buyouts would not be mandatory as patent holders are free to choose whether to sell their patent or not.[1237]

Note, however, that the patent buyout mechanism originally formulated by Kremer (1998) is actually a more sophisticated version of a prize. Patent buyouts provide the patent authority with a mechanism to turn a patent into a prize of the estimated market value of the patent times a mark-up that reflects the ratio of social returns to innovation and private returns to innovation.[1238]

Patent holders are likely to benefit from participating in the buyout mechanism as they would realize a price that is typically significantly higher than the private value of the patent.[1239] Furthermore, patent buyouts are likely to increase R&D incentives to a level that is closer to the socially optimal level.[1240] They also eliminate distortions associated with monopoly pricing.[1241]

Finally, patent buyouts are likely to mitigate the problem that competitors of the original manufacturer of a patented product typically have incentives to invest in wasteful "me-too" research.[1242]

To conclude, patent buyouts appear to be a particularly suitable incentive mechanism to promote research into medicinal products.[1243]

With respect to medicines for neglected infectious diseases, patent buyouts potentially mitigate the incentive problem as the buyout price is typically higher than the commercial value of the patent which would lead to higher R&D incentives.[1244]

Patent buyouts may also mitigate the problem that consumers in low-income countries do not have access to affordable medicines, as medicinal products would be produced and marketed at a competitive price that is significantly lower than the monopoly price.[1245]

1234 See Maurer (2005) on p. 26.
1235 See Kremer (2001a) on p. 61ff.
1236 For instance, see OECD (2007). See also Kremer (1998) on p. 1163ff.
1237 See Kremer (1998) on p. 1139.
1238 For instance, see Scotchmer (2006) on p. 43. See also Kremer (1998) on p. 1147.
1239 See Kremer (1998) on p. 1141.
1240 See Kremer (1998) on p. 1138.
1241 See Kremer (1998) on p. 1138.
1242 For instance, see Kremer and Glennerster (2004) on p. 37.
1243 See also Scotchmer (2006) on p. 43.
1244 For instance, see Kremer (1998) on p. 1146.
1245 See Kremer (1998).

However, let us now consider a successful example of an incentive mechanism designed to encourage research into diseases that used to be neglected simply due to the fact that too few people actually suffered from them.

6.4.3. *Orphan Drugs*

Huntington's disease, Lou Gehrig's Disease and Tourette syndrome are referred to as rare diseases or conditions as only a very small number of people suffer from them.[1246] Under normal market conditions, the prospective market for medicines for these rare diseases is too small to stimulate research by the private pharmaceutical sector.[1247] In other words, under normal market conditions, there would virtually be no research into these rare diseases. Therefore, drugs to cure these rare diseases are commonly referred to as "orphan drugs".[1248] Whereas the rare diseases mentioned above are not necessarily diseases of poverty such as neglected infectious diseases, they share the same core problem that – under normal market conditions – the pharmaceutical sector would be reluctant to develop new medicines to treat and cure those diseases.

The main difference, however, is that additional incentive programs to stimulate research into rare diseases have already been successfully established in industrialized countries.[1249] For instance, the U.S. Orphan Drug Act became effective in 1983[1250] and Japan and Australia established orphan drug systems based on the U.S. model in 1993 and 1998, respectively.[1251] Furthermore, the European Regulation on Orphan Medicinal Products was approved by the European Parliament in 1999.[1252]

The U.S. Orphan Drug Act provides R&D incentives in the form of regulatory assistance, i.e. fast-track regulatory approval, research grants and tax credits for clinical testing and R&D expenses incurred in connection with research into orphan drugs.[1253] More specifically, the Orphan Drug Act defines rare diseases as diseases which affect less than 200,000 persons in the U.S.[1254] However, from the pharmaceutical industry's perspective, the arguably most important feature of the Orphan Drug Act is the promise of seven years of market exclusivity from the date of

---

1246 See Morris et al. (2005) on p. 15. See also http://www.fda.gov/orphan/oda.htm (last visited March 24, 2009). See also Haffner (1999).

1247 See Regulation (EC) No. 141/2000 of the European Parliament and of the Council (December 16, 1999).

1248 For instance, see United Nations Development Programme (2001) on p. 100. See also Kremer and Glennerster (2004) on p. 56ff.

1249 For instance, see United Nations Development Programme (2001) on p. 100.

1250 See http://www.fda.gov/orphan/oda.htm (last visited March 24, 2009). See also Kremer and Glennerster (2004) on p. 56.

1251 See Henkel (1999); available on http://www.fda.gov/fdac/features/1999/399_orph.html (last visited March 24, 2009).

1252 See http://ec.europa.eu/health/ph_threats/non_com/rare_6_en.htm (last visited March 24, 2009). See also Regulation (EC) No. 141/2000 of the European Parliament and of the Council on orphan medicinal products (December 16, 1999).

1253 For instance, see http://www.fda.gov/orphan/oda.htm (last visited March 24, 2009).

1254 For the exact wording of the Orphan Drug Act see http://www.fda.gov/orphan/oda.htm (last visited March 24, 2009). See also Kremer and Glennerster (2004) on p. 56 and Grabowski and Vernon (2000b) on p. 25ff.

approval.[1255] In the pharmaceutical sector, developers of the initial product often face competition from subsequent "me-too" drugs that skirt IP protection.[1256] Put differently, initial developers face a risk that copycat products capture much of the market of the initial product, even if it is protected by a patent. This risk may discourage R&D into the initial product in the first place even though patent protection would be available. The Orphan Drug Act's provision to guarantee market exclusivity to the initial product particularly aims at discouraging the development of "me-too" drugs. It is widely seen as a crucially important element of the act to stimulate research into orphan drugs.[1257]

Recent evidence suggests that the combination of push mechanisms such as grants and tax benefits and pull mechanisms such as the promise of market exclusivity as provided by the Orphan Drug Act successfully stimulates the development of medicines for rare diseases.[1258] For instance, as of October 4, 2007, the total number of approved orphan drugs since 1983 is 315.[1259] In contrast, fewer than 10 such medicinal products for rare diseases were marketed in the decade prior to the Orphan Drug Act.

To sum up, as to the underinvestment of R&D into neglected infectious diseases, the Orphan Drug Act may serve as a successful and tested model of a combination of push incentives such as tax credits and grants and pull incentives such as the promise of market exclusivity over a certain period.[1260]

However, it is important to note that, on the one hand, a promise of market exclusivity for orphan drugs in high-income countries such as the U.S., Japan or Australia is likely to provide appropriate incentives to stimulate research into rare diseases because of the patient's high ability to pay in those countries.

One the other hand, market exclusivity that discourages the development of "me-too" drugs may not be sufficient to stimulate research into neglected infectious diseases because of the consumer's inability to pay for new medicines in low-income countries.[1261]

1255 See Section 527 of the Orphan Drug Act and the FDA homepage; http://www.fda.gov/orphan/progovw.htm (last visited March 24, 2009). However, Art. 8 of the Regulation (EC) No. 141/2000 of the European Parliament and of the Council on orphan medicinal products prescribes that, in Europe, the duration of market exclusivity for orphan drugs is ten years. See also Haffner (1999) on p. 565ff.

1256 See Kremer and Glennerster (2004) on p. 100ff.

1257 For instance, see Shulman and Manocchia (1997). See also Kremer and Glennerster (2004) on p. 101.

1258 See the FDA homepage; http://www.fda.gov/orphan/designat/list.htm (last visited March 24, 2009). See also Kremer and Glennerster (2004) on p. 56. See also Lichtenberg and Waldfogel (2003), Henkel (1999), and Shulman and Manocchia (1997). Furthermore, Bloom et al. (2002) – from a panel of nine countries over a 19-year period – find evidence that R&D tax credits have a positive impact on R&D activities.

1259 See the FDA homepage; http://www.fda.gov/orphan/designat/list.htm (last visited March 24, 2009).

1260 For instance, see United Nations Development Programme (2001) on p. 100. See also Kremer (2001b) on p. 92ff and Kettler (2002) on p. 670ff.

1261 See Kettler (2002) on p. 670ff.

6.4.4. Advanced Purchase Commitments

Advanced purchase commitments are *ex ante* commitments by national governments, international organizations or private foundations to purchase a certain quantity at a certain price of a drug or vaccine yet to be invented.[1262] For instance, a government could sign a contract to buy from a pharmaceutical company a malaria vaccine suitable for use in low-income countries yet to be invented. The vaccine could be required to meet certain technical criteria such as safety, efficacy and usability and that passes a market-test regarding its suitability for use in low-income recipient countries.[1263] If the vaccine is successfully invented the purchaser could then make the vaccine available to countries in need at a price that is lower than the monopoly price.[1264]
As already mentioned above, the core problem with respect to the underinvestment in R&D for neglected infectious diseases is that the expected returns to research into those diseases are too small to stimulate sufficient research investments by the pharmaceutical industry.[1265] The main purpose of an advanced purchase commitment is to mitigate this problem by creating a sufficiently large expected market of medicines for neglected infectious diseases.[1266]

6.4.4.1. Advantages of Advanced Purchase Commitments

First, the arguably most attractive feature of a suitably designed advanced purchase commitment is that it reduces market uncertainty and that it increases the expected market for a desired drug or vaccine as it specifies a guaranteed price and the quantity to be purchased in advance.[1267] More specifically, advanced purchase commitments may create markets in previously unprofitable areas such as neglected infectious diseases.[1268]
Second, in contrast to push mechanisms such as research grants, advanced purchase commitments reward successful research output rather than research input.[1269] Consequently, advanced purchase commitments are less vulnerable to moral hazard problems than push programs.[1270] In particular, the developer of a malaria vaccine will only sell a certain quantity of a vaccine at a certain price if the vaccine is successfully developed, fulfills all technical criteria and passes the market-test of suitability in low-

---

1262 For instance, see World Health Organization (2006) on p. 89ff, OECD (2007) and Maurer (2006) on p. 377ff. See also Kremer and Glennerster (2004) on p. 76ff, Kremer (2002) on p. 83ff, Sachs et al. (1999), Berndt and Hurvitz (2005), and Batson and Ainsworth (2001).
1263 For instance, see OECD (2007) and Kremer and Glennerster (2004) on p. 76ff. See also Kremer and Glennerster (2000), Kremer (2001a), and Kremer (2001b).
1264 See Kremer and Glennerster (2004) on p. 86ff.
1265 See Kremer and Glennerster (2004) on p. 86ff.
1266 For instance, see United Nations Development Programme (2001) on p. 100. See also Kettler (2002) on p. 672ff and Webber and Kremer (2001) on p. 738ff.
1267 See Webber and Kremer (2001) on p. 738ff. See also Kremer (2002) on p. 85ff and Global Alliance for Vaccines and Immunization (2005).
1268 See Morris et al. (2005) on p. 14. See also World Health Organization (2006) on p. 89ff.
1269 See Webber and Kremer (2001) on p. 738ff. See also Kremer and Glennerster (2004) on p. 63ff.
1270 For instance, see Kremer and Glennerster (2004) on p. 63ff.

income countries. Consequently, his incentives to stray from the task are lower under an advanced purchase mechanism than under a push mechanism.[1271]

Third, suppose that the sponsor is less than entirely confident about the scientific prospects for success of the development of a malaria vaccine due to huge scientific hurdles.[1272] On the one hand, a sponsor may not be inclined to provide direct push support to finance research into a malaria vaccine because he may not be willing to bear the risk of financing a project that eventually fails.[1273] One the other hand, he might be more willing to make an advanced purchase commitment even when scientific prospects for success of the development of a malaria vaccine are not entirely clear.[1274] However, pharmaceutical companies supposedly have better information than sponsors or buyers about the feasibility of scientific research. Hence, under an advanced purchase mechanism, those pharmaceutical companies that think that the development of a malaria vaccine is scientifically feasible and commercially attractive will pursue research into the vaccine.[1275] In other words, advanced purchase commitments – by setting incentives for pharmaceutical companies to follow those research strategies that they think will result in marketable pharmaceutical products – imitate the R&D incentives that a market typically provides.[1276]

Fourth, suppose that the buyer of a vaccine or drug promoted through an advanced purchase commitment makes the medicines available to consumers in low-income countries either for free or at a relatively low price.[1277] In this case, advanced purchase commitments would help to mitigate both central problems with respect to neglected infectious diseases: the underinvestment of R&D into those diseases on the one hand, and the lack of access to affordable drugs and vaccines in low-income countries, on the other hand.[1278]

Fifth, under an advanced purchase commitment, IPRs are protected because quantities of the desired drug or vaccine to be promoted through the purchase commitment are only bought from legitimate manufacturers.[1279]

However, advanced purchase commitments are also subject to several problems as we shall see in the following section.

6.4.4.2. Disadvantages of Advanced Purchase Commitments

First, advanced purchase commitments are like prizes subject to a "time inconsistency" problem.[1280] Prior to the development of a desired drug or vaccine buyers such as governments or private foundations have incentives to promise a guaranteed price that

1271 See also Glennerster and Kremer (2001) on p. 38.
1272 See Kremer and Glennerster (2004) on p. 63.
1273 For instance, see Kremer and Glennerster (2004) on p. 63ff.
1274 See Kremer and Glennerster (2004) on p. 63ff.
1275 See Kremer and Glennerster (2004) on p. 63.
1276 See Glennerster and Kremer (2001) on p. 38. See also Webber and Kremer (2001) on p. 738ff.
1277 For instance, see World Health Organization (2001a) on p. 84. See also Kremer and Glennerster (2004) on p. 63ff.
1278 See also Kremer (2002) on p. 83.
1279 See Webber and Kremer (2001) on p. 738ff.
1280 See Kremer and Glennerster (2004) on p. 65.

– at a given specified quantity – allows the innovating firm to cover its R&D costs.[1281] However, buyers have incentives to renege on their promise *ex post* when the R&D investment is sunk in order to obtain the drug or vaccine at the lowest possible price.[1282] Potential innovators, however, anticipate this hold-up problem and will be reluctant to invest in risky and expensive R&D in the first place or may charge a premium before they take part in such a pull program.[1283] Consequently, in order to mitigate the hold-up problem, an explicit-long-term commitment with clear, judicially enforceable rules is of crucial importance.[1284] One way to address the problem that the buyers or sponsors have incentives to renege on their promise is the establishment of an adjudication committee[1285] that is independent from the sponsor or buyer. The main purpose of this committee is to evaluate whether a vaccine or drug promoted through a purchase commitment satisfies the eligibility requirements or not.[1286] Furthermore, the committee could consist of decision-makers trusted by potential innovators in order to enhance the credibility of the advanced purchase commitment.[1287] In particular, due to its independence and its composition, the adjudication committee would provide the credibility needed to mitigate the hold-up problem.[1288] As already mentioned above, the establishment of a legally binding commitment is crucially important. Morantz and Sloane (2001) suggest that a suitably designed advanced vaccine purchase commitment constitutes a legally-binding and enforceable contract.[1289]

A second problem with advanced purchase commitments stems from the fact that sponsors must specify the desired innovation to be promoted through the purchase commitment beforehand.[1290] Advanced purchase commitments may therefore not be an appropriate mechanism to promote basic research as it is typically difficult to specify the output of basic research and appropriate eligibility requirements in advance.[1291] In contrast to basic research, however, it is easier to specify what is meant by an efficacious and safe drug or vaccine that fulfills certain criteria such as safety, efficacy and usability. Institutions such as the European Medicines Agency

1281 See Kremer and Glennerster (2000) on p. 2ff.

1282 See Webber and Kremer (2001) on p. 739. See also Kremer and Glennerster (2000) on p. 2ff, Morris et al. (2005) on p. 14ff, and Maurer (2005) on p. 17ff.

1283 See Maurer (2005) on p. 19. See also Kremer and Glennerster (2000) on p. 2ff.

1284 For instance, see United Nations Development Programme (2001) on p. 100. See also Kremer and Glennerster (2004) on p. 116ff.

1285 See Kremer (2002) on p. 85. See also Kremer and Glennerster (2004) on p. 78ff.

1286 For instance, see Kremer and Glennerster (2004) on p. 78ff.

1287 See Kremer and Glennerster (2004) on p. 78ff.

1288 See Kremer and Glennerster (2004) on p. 78ff.

1289 See also Sullivan (1988) suggesting that publicly advertised contests constitute legally binding contracts. See also Kremer and Glennerster (2004) on p. 117ff.

1290 See Kremer (2002) on p. 84.

1291 See Kremer and Glennerster (2004) on p. 65. However, as noted by Kremer (2002) on p. 84, some basic research outputs can be specified beforehand as the prize for proving Fermat's last theorem shows.

(EMEA)[1292] or the U.S. Food and Drug Administration (FDA) are already specialized and in charge of making such specifications.[1293]
Third, similar to the problem of setting an adequate prize in advance that neither overpays nor underpays, it may be difficult to set an adequate guaranteed price in advance in order to spur research because expected R&D expenses are variable and difficult to estimate.[1294] In other words, advanced purchase commitments may result in either underpayment or overpayment.[1295] On the one hand, given a certain quantity, if the buyer, i.e. a government or a private foundation, sets the guaranteed price too low, the advanced purchase mechanism fails to stimulate R&D.[1296] On the other hand, given a certain quantity, if the buyer sets the price too high, the additional benefit may cause wasteful duplication of research efforts by competing firms.[1297] However, from the sponsor's perspective, given a certain quantity, it would be optimal to find the lowest price that still successfully promotes the development of the desired vaccine or drug.[1298]
Finally, advanced purchase commitments might be politically less attractive than patents because (governmental) payments are more visible to the public than patent revenues spread over a large number of doses.[1299]

6.4.4.3. Conclusion as to Advanced Purchase Commitments

Advanced purchase commitments appear to be an appropriate incentive mechanism to stimulate research into drugs or vaccines for neglected infectious diseases for the following two reasons.
First, advanced purchase commitments help to mitigate the core problem of under-investment in R&D for neglected infectious diseases. They increase the incentives of the private pharmaceutical sector to invest in research into neglected diseases through a market-oriented approach.[1300]
Second, suppose that the buyers of the drug or vaccine such as national governments or international organizations provide consumers in low-income countries with medicines at zero cost or a modest co-payment. In this case, advanced purchase

---

1292 Established as the European Agency for the Evaluation of Medicinal Products by Council Regulation (EEC) No. 2309/93 (July 22, 1993) it was renamed as the European Medicines Agency by Regulation (EC) No. 726/2004 of the European Parliament and of the Council (March 31, 2004).
1293 See Kremer and Glennerster (2004) on p. 65.
1294 For instance, see DiMasi et al. (2003) on p. 169 for estimates of discovery costs in the pharmaceutical sector ranging between US$684 million and $US 936 million at 95 percent confidence. See also DiMasi et al. (1991).
1295 See Maurer (2005) on p. 17.
1296 For instance, see Maurer (2005) on p. 17ff.
1297 See Maurer (2005) on p. 17.
1298 See Maurer (2006) on p. 377ff.
1299 See Maurer (2005) on p. 17. See also Farlow et al. (2005) on p. 6ff. However, Kremer and Glennerster (2004), on p. 115ff, suggest that the U.S., several European countries and the WHO have recently endorsed vaccine purchase commitments.
1300 See Kremer (2002) on p. 83ff.

commitments may also help to mitigate the problem that consumers in low-income countries lack access to affordable medicines.[1301]

However, in order to mitigate the hold-up problem mentioned above, advanced purchase commitments must fulfill the following conditions. First, the purchase commitment must be legally-binding and enforceable.[1302] Second, an independent adjudication committee assesses whether a drug or vaccine candidate fulfills the eligibility conditions.[1303] Furthermore, a thorough estimation of expected R&D expenses is required in order to avoid underpayment or overpayment. Arguably, this is a challenging task due to the fact that pharmaceutical research is subject to high risks and unpredictability.[1304]

Nevertheless, advanced purchase commitments do not appear to be an appropriate incentive mechanism to stimulate basic research as basic research outputs typically cannot be determined beforehand.[1305] As already mentioned above, push mechanisms such as publicly-funded research institutions or research grants are more appropriate to stimulate basic research.

6.4.5. Conclusion as to Pull Programs

The core benefit of pull programs is that the sponsors of the program only have to pay when an innovation is successfully developed.[1306] By linking payment to successful development, pull programs decrease shirking incentives of researchers and increase their incentives to concentrate their research efforts on marketable innovations.[1307]

The U.S. Orphan Drug Act provides a tested benchmark of how research into diseases with a small expected market can be stimulated successfully through a combination of push and pull mechanisms.[1308]

As to neglected infectious diseases, pull programs such as the advanced vaccine purchase commitment brought forward by Michael Kremer and Rachel Glennerster have the potential to increase the incentives of pharmaceutical companies to develop medicines for neglected diseases through a market-oriented and transparent approach.[1309]

The main limitation of targeted prizes is that the desired innovation has to be specified in advance.[1310] Nonetheless, patent buyouts which are a special form of prize also work in cases where the desired innovation cannot be specified in advance. Nevertheless, the problem that desired innovations have to be specified in advance is

1301 See also Kremer and Glennerster (2004) on p. 68ff.
1302 See Kremer and Glennerster (2004) on p. 116ff.
1303 See Kremer and Glennerster (2004) on p. 78ff.
1304 For instance, see El Feki (2005).
1305 See World Health Organization (2006) on p. 89ff.
1306 See Kremer and Glennerster (2004)on p. 63ff.
1307 See Kremer (2002) on p. 83ff.
1308 For instance, see Kremer and Glennerster (2004)on p. 56ff.
1309 See Kremer (2001a), Kremer (2001b) and Kremer and Glennerster (2000). See also Kremer and Glennerster (2004)on p. 63ff.
1310 See Glennerster and Kremer (2001) on p. 36ff.

less severe in the case of advanced drug or vaccine purchase commitments as we will see below.

Advanced purchase commitments and patent buyouts are two closely related approaches to stimulate research.[1311] Both mechanisms are market-based and link payment to successful development of a desired product.[1312]

A crucially important feature of both advanced purchase commitments as well as patent buyouts is that they potentially mitigate the problem that consumers in low-income countries lack access to affordable medicines.[1313] On the one hand, in a patent buyout scheme, bought patents are typically placed in the public domain so that innovations can be produced and marketed at a competitive price which is typically lower than the monopoly price.[1314] On the other hand, buyers of a vaccine or drug for neglected infectious diseases promoted through an advanced purchase commitment would typically make the medicines available to the patients in low-income countries either for free or at a modest co-payment.[1315]

Nevertheless, it is of crucial importance that the advanced commitment is legally-binding and enforceable in order to mitigate the hold-up problem once the innovation is made.[1316] Furthermore, the auction mechanism to determine the buyout price in a buyout scheme must be safeguarded against collusive behavior between auction participants and the patent-holder.[1317]

However, there are also some practical differences between advanced purchase commitments and patent buyouts.

On the one hand, patent buyouts do no require that the desired innovation is specified in advance. On the other hand, advanced purchase commitments require that the sponsor determines specific details of the desired innovation beforehand.[1318] However, this may be a minor problem in case of advanced drug or vaccine purchase commitments because institutions such as the European Medicines Agency or the U.S. Food and Drug Administration are already specialized and in charge of making such specifications.[1319]

The second difference between patent buyouts and advanced purchase commitments in the context of pharmaceutical research is that advanced purchase commitments are less vulnerable to problems associated with the detection of harmful side effects after the development and regulatory approval of a medicinal product.[1320] For instance, suppose that unacceptable harmful side effects are detected subsequent to a patent buyout. In this case, the patent authority may have to engage in a potentially wasteful fight with the innovators to recover the buyout money from them.[1321] In contrast to patent

1311 See Kremer and Glennerster (2004) on p. 68ff.
1312 See Kremer and Glennerster (2004) on p. 68ff.
1313 For instance, see Kremer and Glennerster (2004) on p. 68ff.
1314 See Kremer (1998) on p. 1137ff.
1315 For instance, see Kremer and Glennerster (2004) on p. 68ff.
1316 See Kremer and Glennerster (2004) on p. 116ff.
1317 See Kremer (1998) on p. 1157ff.
1318 See Kremer (2002)on p. 83ff. See also Kremer and Glennerster (2004) on p. 69.
1319 See Glennerster and Kremer (2001) on p. 36. See also Kremer (2002) on p. 83ff and Kremer and Glennerster (2004) on p. 65.
1320 See Kremer and Glennerster (2004) on p. 70.
1321 See Kremer and Glennerster (2004) on p. 70.

buyouts, a sponsor participating in an advanced purchase program could relatively easy suspend the purchase of a drug or vaccine as soon as unacceptable harmful side effects are detected.[1322]

Finally, advanced purchase commitments may be politically more appealing than patent buyouts as they do not involve a substantial visible lump-sum payment.[1323] In other words, advanced purchase commitments are likely to generate less public resentment than patent buyouts because the purchase payments are successively spread over a large number of doses.

To sum up, for pharmaceutical products such as vaccines that could relatively easily be specified in advance by governmental agencies, a legally-binding and enforceable advanced purchase commitment is likely to be as effective as patent buyouts in terms of stimulating research into medicines for neglected infectious diseases and affordable access to medicines in low-income countries.[1324] However, advanced purchase commitments are likely to be politically more attractive than patent buyouts and less vulnerable to collusive behaviour.[1325]

6.5. Parallel Trade and Medicines for Neglected Infectious Diseases

One of the main results of our parallel trade model in Chapter 5 is that low-income countries with a high price elasticity of demand are likely to benefit from banning parallel trade of pharmaceutical products flowing from low-income countries to high-income countries.

To the extent that price discrimination opens otherwise unserved markets in low-income countries there is an important rationale for low-income countries to discourage parallel trade from low-income countries to high-income countries.[1326] Furthermore, even if low-income countries were served under parallel trade freedom, they are still likely to benefit from the price-reducing impact of cross-country price discrimination. Hence, there is also an important rationale for discouraging parallel trade to high-income countries in this case. We conclude that cross-country price discrimination may help to improve low-cost access to medicines in low-income countries.

1322 See Kremer and Glennerster (2004) on p. 70.

1323 See Maurer (2005) on p. 19 and on p. 27. See also Kremer and Glennerster (2004) on p. 70.

1324 See Kremer (2001a) on p. 60, footnote 21.

1325 See Kremer and Glennerster (2004) on p. 70.

1326 See also Ganslandt et al. (2005) on p. 217ff for the interesting proposal that parallel trade within a particular group of low-income countries (as classified by the United Nations) should be permitted. It is aimed at ensuring access to affordable essential medicines in the group of low-income countries where diseases such as malaria and tuberculosis are widespread but that parallel trade flowing from low-income countries to high-income countries should be prohibited. In other words, Ganslandt et al. (2005) suggest a regime of regional exhaustion within a particular low-income area but strict controls in order to prevent parallel trade of low-priced drugs flowing from this area to high-income countries. See also Maskus and Ganslandt (2002) on p. 79 with respect to the idea of regional exhaustion regimes among low-income countries.

However, it is noteworthy that price discrimination under a regime of national exhaustion of IPRs without parallel trade may only serve as a supplement rather than as a substitute for the push and pull incentive mechanisms mentioned above. Even if patent protection in the developing world were successfully enforced and parallel trade prohibited, the problem of underinvestment in R&D for neglected infectious diseases could not be fully solved. As already mentioned before, insufficient market size and low expected market returns to research into neglected infectious diseases are decisive in this respect.

6.6. Conclusions and Policy Recommendations

This chapter addressed the following two closely related questions:
Which incentive mechanisms may mitigate the problem of underinvestment in R&D for neglected infectious and tropical diseases?
Which mechanisms may secure access to affordable medicines for consumers in low-income countries?
In the first part of this chapter, we elaborated on the fact that expected market returns to research into neglected infectious diseases in low-income countries are too low to promote significant R&D into those diseases.[1327] There is a strong positive statistical association between expected market size and R&D investments.[1328] Furthermore, empirical evidence suggests that the prospects of patents in the developing world are not sufficient to promote research into neglected infectious disease that is adequate to the social and economics costs of those diseases.[1329]
In the second part of the chapter, we analyzed different push programs that finance research inputs, i.e. publicly-funded research institutions and targeted R&D tax credits. The third part of the chapter gave an overview of various pull programs to promote R&D for neglected infectious diseases such as prizes, patent buyouts and advanced purchase commitments. We also provided a description of the U.S. Orphan Drug Act which may serve as a useful example how to promote research into diseases with low expected market returns.
However, several of the push and pull incentive mechanisms mentioned above have been proposed to mitigate (a) the problem of underinvestment in R&D for neglected infectious diseases and (b) the lack of access to affordable medicines for consumers in low-income countries.[1330]

1327 See Kremer (2002) on p. 82ff, Lanjouw (2003) on p. 100ff, Attaran and Gillespie-White (2001), and Attaran (2004).
1328 See Schmookler (1966) on p. 104ff. See also Schmookler (1962), Griliches (1957), Scott Morton (1999), Grabowski and Vernon (2000b), Acemoglu and Linn (2004), and Kremer (2001b) on p. 95ff.
1329 See Trouiller et al. (2002). See also Lanjouw and Cockburn (2001), Lanjouw and MacLeod (2005) and Maurer (2005) on p. 10, Kremer (1998) on p. 36, and Kremer and Glennerster (2004) on p. 37.
1330 For instance, see Maurer (2005) for an overview of various push and pull mechanisms. As to advanced vaccine purchase commitments see Kremer and Glennerster (2004). Furthermore, see Kremer (1998) for a discussion of patent buyouts.

Nonetheless, push mechanisms such as research grants and publicly-financed research institutions appear to be more suitable than pull mechanisms such as advanced purchase commitments to promote basic research for the following reasons.
Absent any subsidization of research inputs, private incentives to invest in basic research are suboptimal because basic innovations such as basic scientific knowledge may not be patentable nor commercially exploitable.[1331] Furthermore, the results of basic research are typically not specifiable in advance so that basic research usually cannot be stimulated through an advanced purchase commitment.[1332] Nevertheless, basic research discoveries – although they may not be directly commercially exploitable – provide a basis for subsequent applied research that is patentable and commercially exploitable.[1333] As already mentioned, push mechanisms are vulnerable to moral hazard and adverse selection problems due to asymmetric information between researchers and research administrators.
Furthermore, push mechanisms do not help to mitigate the problem that expected private returns to research into neglected infectious diseases are too low to stimulate sufficient research.[1334]
Therefore, additional incentive mechanisms are necessary (a) to promote research into neglected infectious diseases and (b) to improve access to affordable medicines in low-income countries.
Both the pull mechanisms of patent buyouts and advanced purchase commitments potentially help mitigate these problems.
As to patent buyouts, the buyout price would typically be at least twice as large as the private value of the patent and thus potentially increases R&D incentives.[1335] Furthermore, bought patents would typically be placed in the public domain so that an innovation can be produced and marketed at a competitive price.[1336] This would mitigate the problem that consumers in low-income countries do not have access to affordable medicines when manufactures of pharmaceuticals charge monopoly prices.
Legally-binding and enforceable advanced purchase commitments are also likely to promote pharmaceutical research into neglected infectious diseases through a transparent market-oriented approach.[1337] Furthermore, sponsors involved in an advanced purchase commitment would typically provide consumers in low-income countries with medicines at zero cost or a modest co-payment and thus would help to mitigate the second problem mentioned above.
However, advanced purchase commitments appear to be more appropriate than patent buyouts as they are likely to be at least as effective as patent buyouts in terms of

1331 See Scotchmer (2006) on p. 135ff and on p. 156.
1332 See Kremer and Glennerster (2004) on p. 54 and on p. 65. See also World Health Organization (2006) on p. 89ff.
1333 For instance, see Scotchmer (2006), chapter 5, for an excellent treatment of cumulative innovations. See also Scherer (2000) on p. 1298, Webber and Kremer (2001) on p. 737, and Glennerster and Kremer (2001) on p. 37ff.
1334 See Kremer and Glennerster (2004) on p. 54.
1335 See Kremer (1998) on p. 1148 and on p. 1152ff. See also Scotchmer (2006) on p. 42 and Kremer and Glennerster (2004) on p. 40.
1336 See Maurer (2005) on p. 26. See also Kremer (1998) on p. 1148.
1337 See Kremer (2002) on p. 83ff.

stimulating research but politically more appealing and less vulnerable to collusive behaviour.[1338]

To conclude, a combination of push and pull programs – supplemented by a ban of parallel trade flowing from low-income countries to high-income countries – appears to be the appropriate strategy to stimulate research into neglected infectious diseases.[1339] On the one hand, early-stage (basic) research should be supported through push mechanisms such as research grants or publicly-financed research institutions.[1340] On the other hand, pull mechanisms such as legally-binding and enforceable purchase commitments potentially stimulate research into neglected infectious diseases and mitigate the problem that consumers in low-income countries lack affordable access to essential medicines.

1338 See Kremer and Glennerster (2004) on p. 70.

1339 For instance, see Council Regulation (EC) No. 953/2003 of 26 May 2003 to avoid trade diversion into the European Union of certain key medicines. According to Article 1 of this regulation, parallel trade of tiered priced medicines for neglected infectious diseases from low-income countries to high-income countries shall be prohibited. See also Fink (2005) on p. 172 and World Health Organization (2006) on p. 89.

1340 See also Maurer (2005) on p. 73ff.

7. Conclusion and Ideas for Further Research

Infectious diseases kill 14 million people around the world every year, with 90 percent of these deaths occurring in the developing world. Furthermore, in the last 25 years, almost 1,400 new medicines have been developed, but only 1 percent of these were for tropical diseases which particularly afflict people in developing countries.
We examined recent developments in international patent protection with respect to the observable underinvestment in R&D for neglected infectious diseases and with respect to the lack of access to affordable medicines in low-income countries.
In Chapter 2, we outlined the legal landscape regarding patent protection with respect to medicines for neglected infectious diseases. We focussed on the relevant provisions regarding patent protection stated in the TRIPS Agreement. IP protection in industrialized countries in the Northern Hemisphere where the bulk of new inventions are made is typically stronger than that in developing countries in the Southern Hemisphere. The TRIPS Agreement is aimed at strengthening the status of IP protection around the world by establishing minimum standards for IPRs. The most significant transition period in the area of pharmaceuticals expired on January 1, 2005. Virtually all WTO member countries with pharmaceutical manufacturing capacities are now obliged to grant patents for pharmaceuticals. In particular, developing countries with generic manufacturing capacities such as India or Brazil that did not grant patents for pharmaceuticals before the TRIPS Agreement came into effect are now obliged to do so.[1341] Consequently, manufacturers of pharmaceuticals are more likely to successfully prevent the manufacture of generic substitutes for patented pharmaceuticals. Hence, the international harmonization of patent protection may indirectly result in a lower availability of affordable medicines in low-income countries. To find a solution to this problem is of the utmost urgency.
Chapter 3 provided a survey of the economic analysis of patents – i.e. patent races, optimal patent design and the problem of fragmented patents in biomedical research – as well as the economics of drug development and pricing. We contributed to the formal literature on the tragedy of the anticommons by generalizing the model originally formulated by Schulz et al. (2002). We came to the conclusion that – in the context of malaria research – the infinite fragmentation of patents on research technologies would result in a complete waste of the potential value of the patented technologies.
Chapter 4 focussed on microeconomic theory with respect to patent protection in the developing world and on the empirical evidence regarding underinvestment in R&D for medicines for neglected diseases.
First, we described the model originally formulated by Deardorff (1992) that suggests that the extension of patent protection from an IP exporting country, i.e. a developed

1341 See also Hestermeyer (2007) on p. 75.

country in the Northern Hemisphere, to an IP importing county, i.e. a developing country in the Southern Hemisphere, is likely to increase welfare in the IP exporting country but may decrease welfare in the IP importing country. Nevertheless, the overall effect on global welfare of extending patent protection to the whole world is ambiguous. The analysis suggests that – under plausible conditions – the extension of patent protection to IP importing countries may reduce welfare once the fraction of the world in which patent protection is already provided is sufficiently large. At some point the costs associated with extended patent protection and monopoly pricing to existing innovations may come to outweigh the benefits of making new innovations resulting from extending patent protection. Furthermore, Grossman and Lai (2004) make a strong game-theoretic argument to support the proposition that the international harmonization of patent protection is neither necessary nor sufficient for the efficiency of the global regime of intellectual property rights. Also McCalman (2001) estimates that virtually all developing countries in his sample group generate a transfer loss from international patent harmonization. Hence, we conclude that – from a theoretical and empirical point of view – the international harmonization of patent protection stated in the TRIPS Agreement may be detrimental to consumers in the developing world even if we take into consideration the positive impact of patent protection on innovation.

In the second part of Chapter 4, we elaborated the empirical evidence regarding the investment in R&D for medicines for neglected diseases in order to analyze the question as to whether stronger patent protection in the developing world is likely to stimulate R&D for medicines for such diseases. More specifically, recent empirical evidence suggests that there is still not sufficient R&D into neglected infectious diseases whereas R&D efforts on malaria research have slightly increased in the last two decades.

As an idea for further research we suggest the empirical analysis of the impact of the availability of patents, the rule of law,[1342] and per capita income on the direction of pharmaceutical R&D. For instance, we propose to test the following hypothesis: if the per capita income increases in a certain country or region the number of patents for medicines for diseases prevalent in this country or region also increases.

Chapter 5 focuses on the economic rationale behind parallel imports and their impact on drug pricing in the pharmaceutical industry. We develop a double marginalization model with complete information, in which an original manufacturer of a pharmaceutical product faces potential competition from parallel imports by a foreign exclusive distributor. The model suggests that parallel imports will never occur in the sub-game perfect Nash equilibrium, as it will always be beneficial for the manufacturer to monopolize the home country by undercutting the price of the re-imported pharmaceutical product. However, the question as to whether it is optimal for the manufacturer to charge the monopoly price in the home country depends on the level of trade costs and the level of heterogeneity of the two countries, in terms of market size and price elasticity of demand. We come to the conclusion that the credible threat of parallel imports – for each possible combination of trade costs and heterogeneity of the two countries – reduces the profit of the original manufacturer of pharmaceuticals

1342 For instance, see Kaufmann et al. (2004), Kaufmann et al. (2002), and Kaufmann et al. (1999). See also Cooter and Schäfer (2007) on p. 11.

and thus diminishes his incentive to invest in R&D in the first place. In game-theoretic parlance, our model suggests that parallel trade undermines patent protection by reducing the capability of the original manufacturer of a patented pharmaceutical product to engage in third-degree price discrimination. Therefore, we conclude that if the unique social objective were to stimulate research, innovators should be awarded the right to prevent parallel imports. Furthermore, we argue that cross-country price discrimination is beneficial to low-income countries. Low-income countries typically have a high price elasticity of demand. Thus, they are likely to have access to cheaper medicines when the innovator can successfully engage in price discrimination. Put differently, parallel trade freedom that makes cross-country price discrimination unfeasible is likely to reduce welfare in low-income countries. Hence, we conclude that a global regime of banning parallel imports from low-income countries to high-income countries is desirable from a developing country's perspective.

However, the net effect of parallel imports on global welfare is not unambiguous and depends on the level of trade costs and the heterogeneity of the two countries. We show that parallel imports have positive welfare properties if the two countries are sufficiently heterogeneous in terms of market size and if trade costs are either at an intermediate or low level. If, however, countries are virtually homogenous in terms of market size, parallel imports may be detrimental to global welfare for specific levels of trade costs.

As an idea for further research, we propose to incorporate national price regulation of pharmaceutical products in our double marginalization model in order to analyze both the impact of price caps on the occurrence of parallel trade in equilibrium as well as the strategic behaviour of foreign governments to protect consumers in their country from excessive (monopoly) pricing.

Chapter 6 focussed on additional mechanisms to stimulate R&D for pharmaceutical products alongside patent protection. We analyzed push mechanisms that typically subsidize research inputs, i.e. publicly-funded research institutions and targeted R&D tax credits. Furthermore, we analyzed the efficacy of pull mechanisms such as advanced purchase commitments and patent buyouts that link payment to successful development of a desired innovation. We conclude that push mechanisms are more suitable than pull mechanisms to stimulate basic (non-patentable) research. However, pull mechanisms, such as legally-binding and enforceable advanced purchase commitments, potentially stimulate research into neglected infectious diseases and may help mitigate the problem that consumers in low-income countries lack access to affordable medicines.

Appendix

Appendix 1: Child and Adult Mortality in the Developing World

Developing countries with high child and high adult mortality (Africa)
Algeria, Angola, Benin, Burkina Faso, Cameroon, Cape Verde, Chad, Comoros, Equatorial Guinea, Gabon, Gambia, Ghana, Guinea, Guinea- Bissau, Liberia, Madagascar, Mali, Mauritania, Mauritius, Niger, Nigeria, Sao Tome and Principe, Senegal, Seychelles, Sierra Leone, Togo.

Developing countries with high child and very high adult mortality (Africa)
Botswana, Burundi, Central African Republic, Congo, Côte d'Ivoire, Democratic Republic of the Congo, Eritrea, Ethiopia, Kenya, Lesotho, Malawi, Mozambique, Namibia, Rwanda, South Africa, Swaziland, Uganda, United Republic of Tanzania, Zambia, Zimbabwe.

Developing countries with low child and low adult mortality (The Americas)
Antigua and Barbuda, Argentina, Bahamas, Barbados, Belize, Brazil, Chile, Colombia, Costa Rica, Dominica, Dominican Republic, El Salvador, Grenada, Guyana, Honduras, Jamaica, Mexico, Panama, Paraguay, Saint Kitts and Nevis, Saint Lucia, Saint Vincent and the Grenadines, Suriname, Trinidad and Tobago, Uruguay, Venezuela.

Developing countries with high child and high adult mortality (The Americas)
Bolivia, Ecuador, Guatemala, Haiti, Nicaragua, Peru.

Developing countries with low child and low adult mortality (Eastern Mediterranean)
Bahrain, Iran, Jordan, Kuwait, Lebanon, Libyan Arab, Jamahiriya, Oman, Qatar, Saudi Arabia, Syrian Arab Republic, Tunisia, United Arab Emirates.

Developing countries with high child and high adult mortality (Eastern Mediterranean)
Afghanistan, Djibouti, Egypt, Iraq, Morocco, Pakistan, Somalia, Sudan,Yemen.

Developing countries with low child and low adult mortality (South-East Asia)
Indonesia, Sri Lanka, Thailand.

Developing countries with high child and high adult mortality (South-East Asia)
Bangladesh, Bhutan, Democratic People's Republic of Korea, India, Maldives, Myanmar, Nepal, Timor-Leste.

Developing countries with low child and low adult mortality (Western Pacific)
Cambodia, China, Cook Islands, Fiji, Kiribati, Lao People's Democratic Republic, Malaysia, Marshall Islands, Micronesia, Mongolia, Nauru, Niue, Palau, Papua New Guinea, Philippines, Republic of Korea, Samoa, Solomon Islands, Tonga, Tuvalu, Vanuatu, Viet Nam.

Source: World Health Organization (2003c)

Appendix 2: Generalized Set-Up for the Tragedy of the Anticommons in a Game with two Patent Owners

Suppose that two pharmaceutical companies A and B hold a patent on particular technologies required to do research for a potential malaria vaccine. Furthermore, suppose that any third-party firm that wishes to use the two technologies needs to obtain access to both patents. There is a continuum of third-party firms. Each firm is characterized by its willingness to pay for the two licenses, w. w is uniformly distributed across $[0, a/b]$. Let p_i, $i \in \{A, B\}$, denote the price of Firm i that it charges for the use of its patented research tool. Thus, a third-party firm has to pay a total price P of p_A+p_B.[1343] It is straightforward to see that a third-party firm will be willing to pay total price P in order to use both patented technologies if it is smaller than his willingness to pay w.[1344] We assume that the demand for patents is $Q = a - b(p_A + p_B)$. Firm A generates a profit of

$$\pi^A(p_A, p_B) = p_A(a - b(p_A + p_B)).^{1345} \tag{19*}$$

Analogously, Firm B's profit function is given by

$$\pi^B(p_B, p_A) = p_B(a - b(p_A + p_B)). \tag{20*}$$

Assume that both firms choose the prices for the licenses simultaneously, each taking the price of the other firm as given.[1346] In this simultaneous-move game, we can therefore use the Nash equilibrium concept to determine the profit-maximizing prices.[1347]

$$\max_{p_A} \pi^A(p_A, p_B) = ap_A - bp_A^2 - bp_A p_B$$

$$\frac{\partial \pi^A}{\partial p_A} = a - 2b\,p_A - b\,p_B = 0$$

$$\Leftrightarrow p_A^*(p_B) = \frac{1}{2b}(a - bp_B).^{1348} \tag{21*}$$

Firm A's reaction curve given by (21*) expresses Firm A's profit-maximizing price as a function of Firm B's price. Furthermore, for Firm B we obtain:

$$p_B^*(p_A) = \frac{1}{2b}(a - b\,p_A). \tag{22*}$$

1343 See Schulz et al. (2002) on p. 600.
1344 See Schulz et al. (2002) on p. 601.
1345 See Buchanan and Yoon (2000) on p. 9. See also Schulz et al. (2002) on p. 601.
1346 See Buchanan and Yoon (2000) on p. 9ff.
1347 For instance, see Mas-Colell et al. (1995) on p. 384ff and Pindyck and Rubinfeld (2005) on p. 441ff.
1348 See Schulz et al. (2002) on p. 601.

The Nash equilibrium is the intersection of the two reaction curves. In order to determine the profit-maximizing price for Firm *A* substitute p_B in (21*) with p_B^* given by (22*). By rearranging (21*), we then obtain:

$$p_A = \frac{1}{2b}\left(a - b\left(\frac{1}{2b}(a - bp_A)\right)\right)$$

$$\Leftrightarrow p_A = \frac{1}{2b}\left(\frac{a}{2} + \frac{bp_A}{2}\right)$$

$$\Leftrightarrow 4bp_A = a + bp_A$$

$$\Leftrightarrow p_A^* = \frac{a}{3b}.\text{[1349]} \qquad (23^*)$$

And for Firm *B*:

$$p_B^* = \frac{a}{3b}.\text{[1350]} \qquad (24^*)$$

It follows that the total equilibrium price *P* for both licenses is $2a/3b$.
Moreover, we can determine the demand for patents by substituting $P=2a/3b$ into the general demand function. Thus, total demand is *a/3*. Moreover, the total revenue is given by:

$$TR = PQ = \left(\frac{2a}{3b}\right)\left(\frac{a}{3}\right) = \frac{2a^2}{9b}.\text{[1351]} \qquad (25^*)$$

As a benchmark, Schulz et al. (2002, p. 601) derive the profit-maximizing price *P* for a license for the use of both patented technologies if a single firm were the owner of both patents. The profit of the single firm is given by:

$$\pi(P) = P(a - bP). \qquad (26^*)$$

By differentiating (26*), it follows for the profit-maximizing price P^*:

$$\frac{\partial \pi(P)}{\partial P} = a - 2bP = 0$$

$$\Leftrightarrow P^* = \frac{a}{2b}.\text{[1352]} \qquad (27^*)$$

Consequently, the total revenue is given by:

1349 See Buchanan and Yoon (2000) on p. 10.
1350 See Buchanan and Yoon (2000) on p. 10. See also Schulz et al. (2002) on p. 601.
1351 See Buchanan and Yoon (2000) on p. 10.
1352 See Schulz et al. (2002) on p. 601. See also Buchanan and Yoon (2000) on p. 8ff.

$$TR = \left(a - b\left(\frac{a}{2b} \right) \right) \left(\frac{a}{2b} \right)$$

$$\Leftrightarrow TR = \frac{a}{2} \frac{a}{2b}$$

$$\Leftrightarrow TR = \frac{a^2}{4b}. \qquad (28^*)$$

It is straightforward to see from (23*), (24*), and (27*) that $P^* < p_A^* + p_B^*$ as $1/2 < 2/3$. Furthermore, we can see from (25*) and (28*) that the total revenue of a monopoly patent holder is higher than the total revenue if patents are fragmented as $1/4 > 2/9$.

Appendix 3: Derivation of a General Equation for p_j^*

We know that

$$p_j^* = \frac{1}{2}(1 - \sum_{k \in N/\{j\}} p_k) \ \forall i, j \in N. \tag{35}$$

In the following we will first reformulate p_j^*. Then, we plug in $p_i^* = \frac{1}{2}(1 - \sum_{k \in N/\{i\}} p_k)$. Finally, we get the general equation for p_j^* after some simple reformulations:

$$p_j = \frac{1}{2}\left(1 - \sum_{k \in N/\{i,j\}} p_k - p_i^*\right)$$

$$\Leftrightarrow p_j = \frac{1}{2}\left(1 - \sum_{k \in N/\{i,j\}} p_k - \frac{1}{2}\left(1 - \sum_{k \in N/\{i\}} p_k\right)\right)$$

$$\Leftrightarrow p_j = \frac{1}{2} - \frac{1}{2}\sum_{k \in N/\{i,j\}} p_k - \frac{1}{4} + \frac{1}{4}\sum_{k \in N/\{i,j\}} p_k + \frac{1}{4}p_j$$

$$\Leftrightarrow p_j = \frac{1}{4} - \frac{1}{4}\sum_{k \in N/\{i,j\}} p_k + \frac{1}{4}p_j$$

$$\Leftrightarrow \frac{3}{4}p_j = \frac{1}{4} - \frac{1}{4}\sum_{k \in N/\{i,j\}} p_k$$

$$\Leftrightarrow p_j^* = \frac{1}{3} - \frac{1}{3}\sum_{k \in N/\{i,j\}} p_k. \tag{36}$$

Appendix 4: Derivation of a General Equation for p_i^*

We know that

$$p_i^* = \frac{1}{2}(1 - \sum_{k \in N/\{i\}} p_k) \tag{34}$$

In the following we will first reformulate p_i^*. Then, we plug in $p_j^* = \frac{1}{2}(1 - \sum_{k \in N/\{j\}} p_k)$. Finally, we get the general equation for p_i^* after some simple reformulations:

$$p_i = \frac{1}{2}\left(1 - \sum_{k \in N/\{i,j\}} p_k - p_j^*\right)$$

$$\Leftrightarrow p_i = \frac{1}{2}\left(1 - \sum_{k \in N/\{i,j\}} p_k - \frac{1}{2}\left(1 - \sum_{k \in N/\{j\}} p_k\right)\right)$$

$$\Leftrightarrow p_i = \frac{1}{2} - \frac{1}{2}\sum_{k \in N/\{i,j\}} p_k - \frac{1}{4} + \frac{1}{4}\sum_{k \in N/\{j,i\}} p_k + \frac{1}{4} p_i$$

$$\Leftrightarrow p_i = \frac{1}{4} - \frac{1}{4}\sum_{k \in N/\{i,j\}} p_k + \frac{1}{4} p_i$$

$$\Leftrightarrow \frac{3}{4} p_i = \frac{1}{4} - \frac{1}{4}\sum_{k \in N/\{i,j\}} p_k$$

$$\Leftrightarrow p_i^* = \frac{1}{3} - \frac{1}{3}\sum_{k \in N/\{i,j\}} p_k . \tag{37}$$

Appendix 5: Proof that the Total Revenue of a Monopoly Patent Holder is Higher than the Total Revenue if Patents are Fragmented

In the following we will show that $TR(1) > TR(n)$. We know from (43) that $TR(1) = 1/4$ and that $TR(n) = n/(n+1)^2$. Consequently,

$$TR(1) > TR(n)$$
$$\Leftrightarrow \frac{1}{4} > \frac{n}{(n+1)^2}$$
$$\Leftrightarrow (n+1)^2 > 4n$$
$$\Leftrightarrow n^2 + 2n + 1 > 4n$$
$$\Leftrightarrow n^2 - 2n + 1 > 0$$
$$\Leftrightarrow (n-1)^2 > 0 \text{ q.e.d.}$$

Appendix 6: Summary of Exhaustion Regimes in 28 Developing and Least-Developed Countries

Country	Exhaustion Regime
Argentina	International exhaustion
Barbados	National exhaustion
Belize	National exhaustion
Bolivia	International exhaustion
Botswana	National exhaustion
Brazil	National exhaustion
Colombia	International exhaustion
Costa Rica	International exhaustion
Dominican Republic	International exhaustion
Guatemala	International exhaustion
Honduras	International exhaustion
India	International exhaustion
Madagascar	National exhaustion
Malaysia	International exhaustion
Mexico	National exhaustion
Morocco	National exhaustion
Namibia	National exhaustion
Nicaragua	International exhaustion
Nigeria	National exhaustion
Peru	International exhaustion
Phillipines	National exhaustion
Republic of Korea	International exhaustion
South Africa	International exhaustion
Sri Lanka	International exhaustion
Suriname	National exhaustion
Tunisia	International exhaustion
Uruguay	International exhaustion
Venezuela	International exhaustion

Sources: WIPO (based on notifications made by Members to the WTO), Kanavos et al. (2004) on p. 39, Maskus and Chen (2002) on p. 322, Thorpe (2002) on p. 29ff, and Garrison (2006) on p. 53ff.

Appendix 7: Proof with respect to the Non-Negativity Restriction for the Equilibrium Wholesale Price in Country B

In the following we show that for the non-negativity restriction for p_B^{w*} to be satisfied it is sufficient that the non-negativity restriction for λ_3^*, $t \leq \frac{a}{2b}(\gamma-1)$, is satisfied. Recall that $p_B^{w*} = \frac{a}{6b}(2\gamma+1) - \frac{2}{3}t \geq 0$

$\Leftrightarrow \frac{2}{3}t \leq \frac{a}{6b}(2\gamma+1)$

$\Leftrightarrow t \leq \frac{a}{4b}(2\gamma+1)$.

Hence, the non-negativity restriction for p_B^{w*} is satisfied if the non-negativity restriction for λ_3^* is satisfied as $\frac{a}{4b}(2\gamma+1) > \frac{a}{2b}(\gamma-1)$ and $1 > -2$.

Appendix 8: Equilibrium Profits, Consumers Surplus and Global Welfare

	Parallel imports prohibited		
	Scenario 1-3 (high, intermediate and low *t*)		
	Parallel imports permitted	**Parallel imports permitted**	
	Scenario 1 (high *t*)	**Scenario 2 (intermediate *t*)**	**Scenario 3 (low *t*)**
Equilibrium profit of the manufacturer	$\Pi^{**} = \Pi_h^* = \Pi_A^{**} + \Pi_B^{**} = \frac{a^2}{8b} + \frac{a^2\gamma^2}{4b}$	$\Pi_i^* = \Pi_{(A,i)}^* + \Pi_{(B,i)}^* = \frac{a^2}{24b} - \frac{at}{3} - \frac{bt^2}{3} + \frac{a^2\gamma}{6b} + \frac{at\gamma}{3} + \frac{a^2\gamma^2}{6b}$	$\Pi_l^* = -\frac{a^2}{36b} - \frac{at}{9} - \frac{bt^2}{9} + \frac{a^2\gamma}{18b} + \frac{at\gamma}{9} + \frac{2a^2\gamma^2}{9b}$
Equilibrium profit of the distributor	$\pi^{**} = \pi_h^* = \frac{a^2}{16b}$	$\pi_i^* = \frac{25a^2}{144b} + \frac{5at}{18} + \frac{bt^2}{9} - \frac{5a^2\gamma}{36b} - \frac{at\gamma}{9} + \frac{a^2\gamma^2}{36b}$	Country *B* will not be served
Consumer surplus in country *A*	$CS_A^{**} = CS_{(A,h)}^* = \frac{a^2\gamma^2}{8b}$	$CS_{(A,i)}^* = \frac{a^2}{72b} + \frac{at}{18} + \frac{bt^2}{18} - \frac{a^2\gamma}{9b} - \frac{2at\gamma}{9} + \frac{2a^2\gamma^2}{9b}$	$CS_{(A,l)}^* = \frac{a^2}{72b} + \frac{at}{18} + \frac{bt^2}{18} - \frac{a^2\gamma}{9b} - \frac{2at\gamma}{9} + \frac{2a^2\gamma^2}{9b}$
Consumer surplus in country *B*	$CS_B^{**} = CS_{(B,h)}^* = \frac{a^2}{32b}$	$CS_{(B,i)}^* = \frac{25a^2}{288b} + \frac{5at}{36} + \frac{bt^2}{18} - \frac{5a^2\gamma}{72b} - \frac{at\gamma}{18} + \frac{a^2\gamma^2}{72b}$	Country *B* will not be served
Welfare in country *A*	$W_A^{**} = W_{(A,h)}^* = \Pi^{**} + CS_A^{**} = \frac{a^2}{8b} + \frac{3a^2\gamma^2}{8b}$	$W_{(A,i)}^* = \Pi_i^* + CS_{(A,i)}^* = \frac{a^2}{18b} - \frac{5at}{18} - \frac{5bt^2}{18} + \frac{a^2\gamma}{18b} + \frac{at\gamma}{9} + \frac{7a^2\gamma^2}{18b}$	$W_{(A,l)}^* = -\frac{a^2}{72b} - \frac{at}{18} - \frac{bt^2}{18} - \frac{a^2\gamma}{18b} - \frac{at\gamma}{9} + \frac{4a^2\gamma^2}{9b}$
Welfare in country *B*	$W_B^{**} = W_{(B,h)}^* = \pi^{**} + CS_B^{**} = \frac{3a^2}{32b}$	$W_{(B,i)}^* = \pi_i^* + CS_{(B,i)}^* = \frac{25a^2}{96b} + \frac{5at}{12} + \frac{bt^2}{6} - \frac{5a^2\gamma}{24b} - \frac{at\gamma}{6} + \frac{a^2\gamma^2}{24b}$	Country *B* will not be served

Global welfare	$W^{**}=W_h^*=W_A^{**}+W_B^{**}$ $=\frac{7a^2}{32b}+\frac{3a^2\gamma^2}{8b}$	$W_i^*=W_{(A,i)}^*+W_{(B,i)}^*$ $=\frac{91a^2}{288b}+\frac{5at}{36}-\frac{bt^2}{9}$ $-\frac{11a^2\gamma}{72b}-\frac{at\gamma}{18}+\frac{31a^2\gamma^2}{72b}$	$W_l^*=-\frac{a^2}{72b}-\frac{at}{18}-\frac{bt^2}{18}$ $-\frac{a^2\gamma}{18b}-\frac{at\gamma}{9}+\frac{4a^2\gamma^2}{9b}$

In order to double-check that the results in the second and third column of the table are correct, note that the equilibrium profits and the levels of consumer surplus and welfare in country A and country B as well as global welfare in both situations with and without parallel imports are identical for the case that $t=a(\gamma-1)/2b$ which is the upper bound for t.

Appendix 9: Impact of Parallel Trade Freedom on the Equilibrium Retail Price in Country *B*

Note that parallel trade is a non-credible threat if trade costs are high. In this case, parallel trade freedom does not have any impact on the equilibrium retail price in country *B*, i.e. $p_B^{**} = p_{(B,h)}^{*} = 3a/4b$ [**Table 4** on p. 170]. Furthermore, if trade costs are low, country *B* will not be served. Let us now consider the case that trade costs are at an intermediate level.

In the following we will show that the equilibrium retail price in country *B* under parallel trade freedom, $p_{(B,i)}^{*}$, is greater than or equal to the equilibrium retail price under price discrimination without parallel trade, p_B^{**}, if trade costs are at an intermediate level, i.e. $\frac{a}{2b}\left(\gamma-\frac{5}{2}\right)\le t\le\frac{a}{2b}(\gamma-1)$:

$$p_B^{**}=\frac{3a}{4b}\le p_{(B,i)}^{*}=\frac{7a}{12b}+\frac{a\gamma}{6b}-\frac{t}{3}$$

$$\Leftrightarrow\frac{9a}{12b}\le\frac{7a}{12b}+\frac{a\gamma}{6b}-\frac{t}{3}$$

$$\Leftrightarrow\frac{a}{6b}\le\frac{a\gamma}{6b}-\frac{t}{3}$$

$$\Leftrightarrow\frac{t}{3}\le\frac{a\gamma}{6b}-\frac{a}{6b}$$

$$\Leftrightarrow\frac{t}{3}\le\frac{a}{6b}(\gamma-1)$$

$$\Leftrightarrow t\le\frac{a}{2b}(\gamma-1)\text{ q.e.d.}$$

Appendix 10: Impact of Parallel Trade Freedom on the Equilibrium Quantity in Country *B*

Note that parallel trade is a non-credible threat if trade costs are high. In this case, parallel trade freedom does not have any impact on the equilibrium quantity in country *B*, i.e. $q_B^{**} = q^*_{(B,h)} = a/4$ [**Table 4** on p. 170]. Furthermore, if trade costs are low, country *B* will not be served. Let us now consider the case that trade costs are at an intermediate level.

In the following we will show that the equilibrium quantity in country *B* under parallel trade freedom, $q^*_{(B,i)}$, is lower than or equal to the equilibrium quantity under price discrimination without parallel trade, q_B^{**}, if trade costs are at an intermediate level, i.e. $\frac{a}{2b}\left(\gamma-\frac{5}{2}\right) \leq t \leq \frac{a}{2b}(\gamma-1)$:

$$q_B^{**} = \frac{a}{4} \geq q^*_{(B,i)} = \frac{5a}{12} - \frac{a\gamma}{6} + \frac{bt}{3}$$

$$\Leftrightarrow -\frac{2a}{12} \geq -\frac{a\gamma}{6} + \frac{bt}{3}$$

$$\Leftrightarrow \frac{a\gamma}{6} - \frac{a}{6} \geq \frac{bt}{3}$$

$$\Leftrightarrow \frac{a}{6b}(\gamma-1) \geq \frac{t}{3}$$

$$\Leftrightarrow \frac{a}{2b}(\gamma-1) \geq t \quad \text{q.e.d.}$$

Bibliography

Abbott, F. M. (1998), "First Report (Final) to the Committee on International Trade Law of the International Law Association on the Subject of Parallel Importation", *Journal of International Economic Law*, 1(4), 607-636.

Abbott, F. M. (2001), "The TRIPS Agreement, Access to Medicines and the WTO Doha Ministerial Conference", *Quaker United Nations Office Occasional Paper No. 7*,

Abbott, F. M. (2002), "The Doha Declaration on the TRIPS Agreement and Public Health: Lighting a Dark Corner at the WTO", *Journal of International Economic Law*, 5(2), 469-505.

Abbott, F. M. (2005), "The WTO Medicines Decision: World Pharmaceutical Trade and the Protection of Public Health", *American Journal of International Law*, 99(2), 317-358.

Acemoglu, D. and J. Linn (2003), *Market Size in Innovation: Theory and Evidence from the Pharmaceutical Industry*, NBER Working Paper No. 10038, Washington, D. C.: National Bureau of Economic Research.

Acemoglu, D. and J. Linn (2004), "Market Size in Innovation: Theory and Evidence from the Pharmaceutical Industry", *Quarterly Journal of Economics*, 119(3), 1049-1090.

Adelman, D. E. (2005), "The Irrationality of Speculative Gene Patents", *Advances in the Study of Entrepreneurship, Innovation, & Economic Growth*, 16, 123-154.

Anderson, J., M. MacLean, and C. Davies (1996), *Malaria Research: An Audit of International Activity*, Unit for Policy Research in Science and Medicine (PRISM) Report No. 7, London: Wellcome Trust.

Anton, J. J. and D. A. Yao (2007), "Finding "Lost" Profits: An Equilibrium Analysis of Patent Infringement Damages", *Journal of Law, Economics & Organization*, 23(1), 186-207.

Aoki, R. (1991), "R&D Competition for Product Innovation: An Endless Race", *American Economic Review, Papers and Proceedings*, 81(2), 252-256.

Arfwedson, J. (2004), *Parallel Trade in Pharmaceuticals*, IPI Policy Report No. 182, Lewisville: Institute for Policy Innovation.

Arndt, C. and J. D. Lewis (2000), "The Macro Implications of HIV/AIDS in South Africa: A Preliminary Assessment", *South African Journal of Economics*, 68(5), 856-887.

Arrow, K. J. (1959), *Economic Welfare and the Allocation of Resources for Invention*, RAND Corporation, Economics Division P-1856-RC, RAND Corporation.

Arrow, K. J. (1962), "Economic Welfare and the Allocation of Resources for Invention" in Nelson, R. R. (ed.), *The Rate and Direction of Inventive Activity: Economic and Social Factors*, 609-625, Princeton, New Jersey: Princeton University Press.

Atik, J. and H. H. Lidgard (2006), "Embracing Price Discrimination: TRIPS and the Suppression of Parallel Trade in Pharmaceuticals", *University of Pennsylvania Journal of International Economic Law*, 27, 1043-1076.

Attaran, A. (2004), "How Do Patents and Economic Policies Affect Access to Essential Medicines in Developing Countries?" *Health Affairs*, 23(3), 155-166.

Attaran, A. and L. Gillespie-White (2001), "Do Patents for Antiretroviral Drugs Constrain Access to AIDS Treatment in Africa?" *Journal of the American Medical Association*, 286(15), 1886-1892.

Bale, H. E. (1998), "The Conflicts between Parallel Trade and Product Access and Innovation: The Case for Pharmaceuticals", *Journal of International Economic Law*, 1(4), 637-653.

Ballance, R., J. Pogány, and H. Forstner (1992), *The World's Pharmaceutical Industry. An International Perspective on Innovation, Competition and Policy*, Vienna: United Nations Industrial Development Organization.

Barfield, C. E. and M. A. Groombridge (1998), "The Economic Case for Copyright Owner Control over Parallel Imports", *Journal of World Intellectual Property*, 1(6), 903-939.

Barfield, C. E. and M. A. Groombridge (1999), "Parallel Trade in the Pharmaceutical Industry: Implications for Innovation, Consumer Welfare, and Health Policy", *Fordham Intellectual Property, Media and Entertainment Law Journal*, 10(1), 185-266.

Barnard, C. (2004), *The Substantive Law of the EU - The Four Freedoms*, New York: Oxford University Press.

Batson, A. (1998), "Win-Win Interactions between the Public and Private Sectors", *Nature Medicine: Vaccine Supplement*, 4(5), 487-491.

Batson, A. and M. Ainsworth (2001), "Private Investment in AIDS Vaccine Development: Obstacles and Solutions", *Bulletin of the World Health Organization*, 79(8), 721–727.

Becker, G. S. (1968), "Crime and Punishment: An Economic Approach", *Journal of Political Economy*, 76(2), 169-217.

Becker, G. S. and G. J. Stigler (1974), "Law Enforcement, Malfeasance, and Compensation of Enforcers", *Journal of Legal Studies*, 3(1), 1-18.

Bell, C., S. Devarajan, and H. Gersbach (2003), *The Long-Run Economic Costs of AIDS: Theory and Application to South Africa*, Washington, D.C.: World Bank.

Bell, F. W. (1986), "Mitigating the Tragedy of the Commons", *Southern Economic Journal*, 52(3), 653-664.

Benson, T. (2005), *Brazil and U.S. Maker Reach Deal on AIDS Drug*, New York Times, July 9, 2005.

Bently, L. and B. Sherman (2004), *Intellectual Property Law*, Oxford: Oxford University Press.

Bergquist, R. (2004), *Prospects for Schistosomiasis Vaccine Development*, UNICEF-UNDP-World Health Organization Programme for Research and Training in Tropical Diseases, http://www.who.int/tdr/publications/tdrnews/news71/schisto.htm.

Berndt, E. R. and J. A. Hurvitz (2005), "Vaccine Advance-Purchase Agreements for Low-Income Countries: Practical Issues", *Health Affairs*, 24(3), 653-665.

Bernstein, J. I. and M. I. Nadiri (1988), "Interindustry R&D Spillovers, Rates of Return, and Production in High-Tech Industries", *American Economic Review*, 78(2), 429-434.

Bernstein, J. I. and M. I. Nadiri (1989), "Research and Development and Intra-Industry Spillovers: An Empirical Applications of Dynamic Duality", *Review of Economic Studies*, 56(186), 249-269.

Bertrand, J. (1883), "Théorie mathématique de la richesse sociale", *Journal des Savants*, 499-508.

Bessen, J. and R. M. Hunt (2003), *An Empirical Look at Software Patents*, Working Paper: No. 03-17/R, Federal Reserve Bank of Philadelphia.

Bessen, J. and E. Maskin (2006), *Sequential Innovation, Patents, and Imitation*, Economics Working Papers 0025, Institute for Advanced Study, School of Social Science.

Bettcher, D. W., D. Yach, and G. E. Guindon (2000), "Global Trade and Health: Key Linkages and Future Challenges", *Bulletin of the World Health Organization*, 78(4), 521-534.

Blair, R. D. and T. F. Cotter (1998), "An Economic Analysis of Damages Rules in Intellectual Property Law", *William and Mary Law Review*, 39, 1585-1694.

Blair, R. D. and T. F. Cotter (2005), *Intellectual Property - Economic and Legal Dimensions of Rights and Remedies*, New York: Cambrigde University Press.

Bloland, P. B. (2001), *Drug Resistance in Malaria*, Geneva: World Health Organization.

Bloom, N., R. Griffith, and J. Van Reenen (2002), "Do R&D Tax Credits Work? Evidence from a Panel of Countries 1979–1997", *Journal of Public Economics*, 85(1), 1-31.

Bonnel, R. (2000), *HIV/AIDS: Does it Increase or Decrease Growth in Africa?*, Washington, D.C.: Africa Department, World Bank.

Breman, J., M. Alilio, and A. Mills (2004), "Conquering the Intolerable Burden of Malaria: What's New, What's Needed: A Summary", *American Journal of Tropical Medicine and Hygiene*, 71(2), 1-15.

Bremen, J. (2001), "The Ears of the Hippopotamus: Manifestations, Determinants, and Estimates of the Malaria Burden", *American Journal of Tropical Medicine and Hygiene*, 64(1,2), 1-11.

Buchanan, M. D. and J. Yoon (2000), "Symmetric Tragedies: Commons and Anticommons", *Journal of Law and Economics*, 43(1), 1-13.

Burke, J. (1978), *Connections*, London: MacMillan.

Burpee, C. E. (1999), *Report of Economic Survey*, Washington, D. C.: American Intellectual Property Law Association.

Calabresi, G. and A. D. Melamed (1972), "Property Rules, Liability Rules, and Inalienability: One View of the Cathedral", *Harvard Law Review*, 85(6), 1089-1126.

Callan, B. and I. Gillespie (2007), *Neglected Diseases: The Path to New Medicines*, Nature, September 13, 2007, 449: 164-165.

Case, K. E. and R. C. Fair (1999), *Principles of Economics*, Lebanon, Indiana, USA: Prentice-Hall.

Castro Bernieri, R. (2006), "Intellectual Property Rights in Bilateral Investment Treaties and Access to Medicines: The Case of Latin America", *Journal of World Intellectual Property*, 9(5), 548-572.

Cavusgil, S. T. and E. Sikora (1988), "How Multinationals Can Counter Gray Market Imports", *Columbia Journal of World Business*, 23, 75-85.

Champ, P. and A. Attaran (2002), "Patent Rights and Local Working under the WTO TRIPS Agreement: An Analysis of the U.S.-Brazil Patent Dispute", *Yale Journal of International Law*, 27(2), 365.

Chang, H. F. (1995), "Patent Scope, Antitrust Policy, and Cumulative Innovation", *RAND Journal of Economics*, 26(1), 34-57.

Chard, J. S. and C. J. Mellor (1989), "Intellectual Property Rights and Parallel Imports", *World Economy*, 12(1), 69-83.

Chaudhuri, S., P. K. Goldberg, and P. Jia (2006), "Estimating the Effects of Global Patent Protection in Pharmaceuticals: A Case Study of Quinolones in India", *American Economic Review*, 96(5), 1477-1514.

Chen, Y. and T. Puttitanun (2005), "Intellectual Property Rights and Innovation in Developing Countries", *Journal of Development Economics*, 78(2), 474-493.

Chiang, A. C. (1984), *Fundamental Methods of Mathematical Economics*, New York et al.: McGraw-Hill.

Chien, C. (2003), "Cheap Drugs at What Price to Innovation: Does the Compulsory Licensing of Pharmaceuticals Hurt Innovation?" *Berkeley Technology Law Journal*, 18(3), 853-907.

Chima, R., C. Goodman, and A. Mills (2003), "The Economic Impact of Malaria in Africa: A Critical Review of the Evidence", *Health Policy*, 63(1), 17-36.

Chin, J. C. and G. M. Grossman (1990), "Intellectual Property Rights and North-South Trade" in Jones, R. and A. O. Krueger (ed.), *The Political Economy of International Trade*, 90-107, Oxford: Basil Blackwell.

Chisum, D. S. (2001), *Chisum on Patents: A Treatise on the Law of Patentability, Validity, and Infringement*, San Francisco: Bancroft-Whitney.

Coase, R. H. (1960), "The Problem of Social Cost", *Journal of Law and Economics*, 3, 1-44.

Coase, R. H. (1988), *The Firm, the Market and the Law*, Chicago: University of Chicago Press.

Cockburn, I. and R. Henderson (1988), "Absorptive Capacity, Coauthoring Behavior, and the Organization of Research in Drug Discovery", *Journal of Industrial Economics*, 46(2), 157-182.

Cohen, W. M., R. R. Nelson, and J. P. Walsh (2000), *Protecting Their Intellectual Assets: Appropriability Conditions and Why U.S. Manufacturing Firms Patent (or Not),*, NBER Working Paper No. 7552, Washington, D. C.: National Bureau of Economic Research.

Commission on Intellectual Property Rights (2002), *Integrating Intellectual Property Rights and Development Policy*, Report of the Commission on Intellectual Property Rights, London:

Conley, N. L. (1987), "An Economic Approach to Patent Damages", *American Intellectual Property Law Association Quarterly Journal*, 15, 354-390.

Cooter, R. D. (1982), "Economic Analysis of Punitive Damages", *Southern California Law Review*, 56(1), 79-101.

Cooter, R. D. and H. B. Schäfer (2007), *Law and the Poverty of Nations - Conditions of Legal Reform*, Berkeley Electronic Press, German Working Papers in Law and Economics, Vol. 2007, Article 15, http://www.bepress.com/gwp/default/vol2007/iss2/art15.

Cooter, R. D. and H.-B. Schäfer (2008), *Law and the Poverty of Nations*, To be published: Preliminary version available on: http://works.bepress.com/cgi/viewcontent.cgi?article=1150&context=robert_cooter.

Cooter, R. D. and T. Ulen (2004), *Law and Economics*, Boston: Pearson.

Correa, C. M. (1991), "The Pharmaceutical Industry and Biotechnology: Opportunities and Constraints for Developing Countries", *World Competition*, 15(2), 43-63.

Correa, C. M. (2000a), *Integrating Public Health Concerns into Patent Legislation in Developing Countries*, Geneva: South Centre.

Correa, C. M. (2000b), *Intellectual Property Rights, the WTO and Developing Countries. The TRIPS Agreement and Policy Options*, London, New York: Zed Books.

Correa, C. M. (2002), *Implications of the Doha Declaration on the TRIPS Agreement and Public Health*, Health Economics and Drugs EDM Series No. 12, Geneva: WHO.

Cottier, T. (2003), "TRIPS, the Doha Declaration and Public Health", *Journal of World Intellectual Property*, 6(2), 385-388.

Crampes, C., D. Encaoua, and A. Hollander (2005), *Competition and Intellectual Property Rights in the European Union*, http://idei.fr/doc/wp/2005/crampes.pdf.

Crampes, C., A. Hollander, and C. M. Macdissi (2006), *Bundling under the Threat of Parallel Trade*, https://papyrus.bib.umontreal.ca/dspace/bitstream/1866/558/1/2006-07.pdf.

Crampes, C. and C. Langinier (2002), "Litigation and Settlement in Patent Infringement Cases", *RAND Journal of Economics*, 33(2), 258-274.

Curci, G. and M. Vittori (2004), "Improving Access to Life-Saving Patented Drugs. Between Compulsory Licensing and Differential Pricing", *Journal of World Intellectual Property*, 7(5), 739-760.

Dagan, H. and M. A. Heller (2001), "The Liberal Commons", *Yale Law Journal*, 110(4), 349-623.

Dam, K. W. (1994), "Die ökonomischen Grundlagen des Patentrechts *(The Economic Underpinnings of Patent Law)*" in Ott, C. and H.-B. Schäfer (eds.), *Ökonomische Analyse der rechtlichen Organisation von Innovationen. IV. Travemünder Symposium zur Ökonomischen Analyse des Rechts*, Tübingen: Mohr Siebeck.

Danzon, P. M. (1997), *Pharmaceutical Price Regulation*, Washington, D.C.: American Enterprise Institute Press.

Danzon, P. M. (1998), "The Economics of Parallel Trade", *PharmacoEconomics*, 13(3), 293-304.

Danzon, P. M. and A. Towes (2003), "Differential Pricing for Pharmaceuticals: Reconciling Access, R&D and Patents", *International Journal of Health Care Finance and Economics*, 3(3), 183-205.

Darbà, J. and J. Rovira (1998), "Parallel Imports of Pharmaceuticals in the European Union", *Pharmacoeconomics*, 14(1), 129-136.

Dari-Mattiacci, G. and H.-B. Schäfer (2007), "The Core of Pure Economic Loss", *International Review of Law and Economics*, 27(1), 8-28.

Dasgupta, P. and J. Stiglitz (1980), "Uncertainty, Industrial Structure, and the Speed of R&D", *Bell Journal of Economics*, 11(1), 1-28.

Deardorff, A. V. (1990), "Should Patent Protection Be Extended to All Developing Countries?" *World Economy*, 13(4), 497-507.

Deardorff, A. V. (1992), "Welfare Effects of Global Patent Protection", *Economica*, 59(233), 35-59.

DeBrock, L. M. (1985), "Market Structure, Innovation, and Optimal Patent Life", *Journal of Law & Economics*, 28(1), 223-244.

Delich, V. (2002), "Developing Countries and the Dispute Settlement System" in Hoekman, B. M.A. Mattoo and P. English (eds.), *Development, Trade, and the WTO*, 71-80, Washington, D.C.: World Bank.

Demsetz, H. (1967), "Toward a Theory of Property Rights", *American Economic Review*, 57(2), 347-359.

Demsetz, H. (1998), "Property Rights" in Newman, P. (ed.), *The New Palgrave Dictionary of Economics and the Law*, 144-156, London: Macmillan.

Denicoló, V. (1996), "Patent Races and Optimal Patent Breadth and Length", *Journal of Industrial Economics*, 44(3), 249-265.

Desogus, C. (2008), *Strategic Pricing and Antitrust Issues in the European Pharmaceutical Market: The Case of Dual Pricing. Rotterdam Institute of Law and Economics Working Paper (forthcoming)*, Rotterdam.

DiMasi, J. A., R. W. Hansen, and H. G. Grabowski (1991), "Cost of Innovation in the Pharmaceutical Industry", *Journal of Health Economics*, 10(2), 107-142.

DiMasi, J. A., R. W. Hansen, and H. G. Grabowski (2003), "The Price of Innovation: New Estimates of Drug Development Costs", *Journal of Health Economics*, 22(2), 151-185.

Diwan, I. and D. Rodrik (1991), "Patents, Appropriate Technology, and North-South Trade", *Journal of International Economics*, 30(1-2), 27-47.

Dixon, P. and C. Greenhalgh (2002), *The Economics of Intellectual Property: A Review to Identify Themes for Future Research. Economics Series Working Paper 135*, University of Oxford, Oxford, UK.

Dreier, T. (1996), "TRIPS und die Durchsetzung von Rechten des geistigen Eigentums", *Gewerblicher Rechtsschutz und Urheberrecht, Internationaler Teil*, 45(3), 205-218.

Economist (2008), *Resisting Arrest: Fighting Malaria Drug Resistance*, Economist, May 17, 387(8580): 90-91.

Eger, T., M. Kraft, and P. Weise (1990), "Patents, Innovation, and Imitation: A Game-Theoretic Approach", *Methods of Operations Research*, 63, 57-67.

Eichberger, J. (2004), *Grundzüge der Mikroökonomik (Primer in Microeconomic Theory)*, Tübingen: Mohr Siebeck.

Eisenberg, R. S. (1990), "Patenting the Human Genome", *Emory Law Journal*, 39(3), 721-745.

Eisenberg, R. S. (1996), "Public Research and Private Development: Patents and Technology Transfer in Government-Sponsored Research", *Vanderbilt Law Review*, 82(8), 1663-1727.

Ekelund, R. B. (1970), "Price Discrimination and Product Differentiation in Economic Theory: An Early Analysis", *Quarterly Journal of Economics*, 84(2), 268-278.

El Feki, S. (2005), *Prescription for Change: A Survey of Pharmaceuticals*, The Economist, 375(8431): 1-16.

Encyclopaedia Britannica (1959), *Volume 11*. Chicago, London, Toronto, Encyclopaedia Britannica, Inc.

Epstein, R. A. and B. N. Kuhlik (2004), *Is There a Biomedical Anticommons?*, Regulation, June 1, 2004: 54-58.

Falkman, M. A. (1999), "Metal Cans Still Preserve, Protect and Provide Convenience", *Packing Digest*, 36(12), 64-65.

Farlow, A., D. Light, R. Mahoney, and R. Widdus (2005), *Concerns Regarding the Center for Global Development Report 'Making Markets for Vaccines'*, WHO Commission on Intellectual Property Rights, Innovation and Public Health, http://www.who.int/intellectualproperty/submissions/Vaccines.FarlowLight.pdf.

Feess, E. (2000), *Mikroökonomie (Microeconomics)*, Marburg: Metropolis.

Fink, C. (2005), "Entering the Jungle of Intellectual Property Rights Exhaustion and Parallel Importation" in Fink, C. and K. E. Maskus (eds.), *Intellectual Property and Development: Lessons from Recent Economic Research*, 171-188, World Bank and Oxford University Press.

Ford, S. M. (2000), "Compulsory Licensing Provisions under the TRIPS Agreement: Balancing Pills and Patents", *American University International Law Review*, 15, 941-974.

Friedman, D. (1984), "Efficient Institutions for the Private Enforcement of Law", *Journal of Legal Studies*, 13(2), 379-397.

Friedman, D. D., W. M. Landes, and R. A. Posner (1991), "Some Economics of Trade Secret Law", *Journal of Economic Perspectives*, 5(1), 61-72.

Fudenberg, D., R. Gilbert, J. Stiglitz, and J. Tirole (1983), "Preemption, Leapfrogging, and Competition in Patent Races", *European Economic Review*, 22(1), 3-31.

Fudenberg, D. and J. Tirole (1996), *Game Theory*, MIT Press.

Furubotn, E. G. and S. Pejovich (1972), "Property Rights and Economic Theory: A Survey of Recent Literature", *Journal of Economic Literature*, 10, 1137-1162.

Gallini, N. T. (1984), "Deterrence by Market Sharing: A Strategic Incentive for Licensing", *American Economic Review*, 74(5), 931-941.

Gallini, N. T. (1992), "Patent Policy and Costly Imitation", *RAND Journal of Economics*, 23(1), 52-63.

Gallini, N. T. and A. Hollis (1999), "A Contractual Approach to the Gray Market", *International Review of Law and Economics*, 19(1), 1-21.

Gallini, N. T. and S. Scotchmer (2002), "Intellectual Property: When Is It the Best Incentive System?" *NBER Innovation Policy and the Economy*, 2(1), 51-77.

Gallus, N. (2005), "Parallel Policies on Pharmaceutical Parallel Trade", *International Trade Law & Regulation*, 11(3), 77-83.

Gal-Or, E. (1988), "Oligopolistic Nonlinear Tariffs", *International Journal of Industrial Organization*, 6(2), 199-221.

Ganslandt, M. and K. E. Maskus (2001), *Parallel Imports of Pharmaceutical Products in the European Union*, Research Institute of Industrial Economics Working Paper No. 546, Stockholm: Research Institute of Industrial Economics.

Ganslandt, M. and K. E. Maskus (2004), "Parallel Imports and the Pricing of Pharmaceutical Products: Evidence from the European Union", *Journal of Health Economics*, 23(5), 1035-1057.

Ganslandt, M., K. E. Maskus, and E. V. Wong (2005), "Developing and Distributing Essential Medicines to Poor Countries: The Defend Proposal" in Fink, C. and K. E. Maskus (eds.), *Intellectual Property and Development: Lessons from Recent Economic Research*, 207-223, World Bank and Oxford University Press.

Garrison, C. (2006), *Exceptions to Patent Rights in Developing Countries*, Geneva: UNCTAD - ICTSD Project on IPRs and Sustainable Development, Paper No. 17.

Gervais, D. (2003), *The TRIPS Agreement: Drafting History and Analysis*. London, Sweet Maxwell.

Giaccotto, C., R. E. Santerre, and J. A. Vernon (2005), "Drug Prices and Research and Development Behaviour in the Pharmaceutical Industry", *Journal of Law and Economics*, 48(1), 195-214.

Gilbert, R. and C. Shapiro (1990), "Optimal Patent Length and Breadth", *RAND Journal of Economics*, 21(1), 106-112.

Glennerster, R. and M. Kremer (2001), "A Better Way to Spur Medical Research and Development", *Regulation*, 23(2), 34-39.

Global Alliance for Vaccines and Immunization (2005), *Key European Nations Join UK and France to Commit Nearly US$4 Billion to Expand Child Immunisation in Developing Countries*, Global Alliance for Vaccines and Immunization, http://www.gavialliance.org/media_centre/press_releases/2005_09_09_en_pr_IFFImlaunch.php.

Goldman, M. B., H. E. Leland, and D. S. Sibley (1984), "Optimal Nonuniform Prices", *Review of Economic Studies*, 51(2), 305-319.

Grabowski, H. G. and J. M. Vernon (1994), "Returns to R&D on New Drug Introductions in the 1980s", *Journal of Health Economics*, 13(4), 383-406.

Grabowski, H. G. and J. M. Vernon (2000a), "The Determinants of Pharmaceutical Research and Development Expenditures", *Journal of Evolutionary Economics*, 10(1/2), 201-215.

Grabowski, H. G. and J. M. Vernon (2000b), "The Distribution of Sales Revenue from Pharmaceutical Innovation", *PharmoEconomics*, 18(1), 21-32.

Grabowski, H. G., J. M. Vernon, and J. A. DiMasi (2002), "Returns on Research and Development for 1990s New Drug Introductions", *Pharmacoeconomics*, 20(3), 11-29.

Graham, J. R. (2000), *Prescription Drug Prices in Canada and the United States - Part 2: Why the Difference?*, Public Policy Sources, Occasional Paper 43, Vancouver: Fraser Institute.

Graham, J. R. and B. A. Robson (2000), *Prescription Drug Pricing in Canada and the United States - Part 1: A Comparative Survey*, Public Policy Sources, Occasional Paper 42, Vancouver: Fraser Institute.

Graham, S. J. H., B. H. Hall, D. Harhoff, and D. C. Mowery (2003), "Patent Quality Control: A Comparison of U.S. Patent Re-examinations and European Patent Oppositions" in Cohen, W. M. and S. A. Merrill (eds.), *Patents in the Knowledge-based Economy*, Washington, D.C.: National Academies Press.

Green, J. R. and S. Scotchmer (1995), "On the Division of Profit in Sequential Innovation", *RAND Journal of Economics*, 26(1), 20-33.

Griliches, Z. (1957), " Hybrid Corn: An Exploration in the Economics of Technological Change", *Econometrica*, 25(4), 501-522.

Grinols, E. and H. C. Lin (2006), "Global Patent Protection: Channels of North and South Welfare Gains", *Journal of Economic Dynamics & Control*, 30(2), 205-227.

Grosse Ruse-Khan, H. (2008), "A Pirate of the Caribbean? The Attractions of Suspending TRIPS Obligations", *Journal of International Economic Law*, 11(2), 313–364.

Grossman, G. M. and E. Helpman (1995), "Technology and Trade" in Grossman, G. M. and K. Rogoff (eds.), *The Handbook of International Economics*, 1279-1337, Amsterdam: North-Holland.

Grossman, G. M. and E. L.-C. Lai (2004), "International Protection of Intellectual Property", *American Economic Review*, 94(5), 1635-1653.

Haffner, M. E. (1999), "Orphan Drugs: The United States Experience", *Drug Information Journal*, 33(2), 565-568.

Hall, B. H. (1993), "R&D Tax Policy during the Eighties: Success or Failure?" *Tax Policy and the Economy*, 7, 1-36.

Hall, B. H., A. Jaffe, and M. Trajtenberg (2005), "Market Value and Patent Citations", *RAND Journal of Economics*, 36(1), 16-38.

Hall, B. H. and J. Van Reenen (2000), "How Effective are Fiscal Incentives for R&D? A Review of the Evidence", *Research Policy*, 29, 449-469.

Harberger, A. C. (1954), "Monopoly and Resource Allocation", *American Economic Review*, 44(2), 77-87.

Hardin, G. (1968), "The Tragedy of the Commons", *Science*, 162, 124-148.

Harhoff, D. and M. Reitzig (2004), "Determinants of Opposition against EPO Patent Grants - The Case of Biotechnology and Pharmaceuticals", *International Journal of Industrial Organization*, 22(4), 443-480.

Harhoff, D., F. M. Scherer, and K. Vopel (2003), "Citations, Family Size, Opposition and the Value of Patent Rights", *Research Policy*, 32(8), 1343-1363.

Harris, C. and J. Vickers (1985), "Perfect Equilibrium in a Model of a Race", *Review of Economic Studies*, 52(2), 193-209.

Hausman, J. and J. MacKie-Mason (1988), "Price Discrimination and Patent Policy", *RAND Journal of Economics*, 19(2), 253-265.

Hayami, Y. and V. Ruttan (1971), *Agricultural Development: An International Perspective.*, Baltimore: Johns Hopkins University Press.

Heath, C. (1999), *Parallel Imports and International Trade*, World Intellectual Property Organization Report.

Heller, M. A. (1998), "The Tragedy of the Anticommons: Property in the Transition from Marx to Markets", *Harvard Law Review*, 11(3), 621-688.

Heller, M. A. (1999), "The Boundaries of Private Property", *Yale Law Review*, 108(5), 1163-1223.

Heller, M. A. and R. S. Eisenberg (1998), *Can Patents Deter Innovation? The Anticommons in Biomedical Research*, Science, 280(5364): 698 - 701.

Helpman, E. (1993), "Innovation, Imitation, and Intellectual Property Rights", *Econometrica*, 61(6), 1247-1280.

Hendricks, K. and R. H. Porter (1988), "An Empirical Study of an Auction with Asymmetric Information", *American Economic Review*, 78(5), 865-883.

Hendricks, K., A. Weiss, and C. Wilson (1988), "The War of Attrition in Continuous Time with Complete Information", *International Economic Review*, 29(4), 663-680.

Henkel, J. (1999), *Orphan Drug Law Matures Into Medical Mainstay*, FDA Consumer Magazine, May-June.

Hestermeyer, H. (2007), *Human Rights in the WTO - The Case of TRIPS and Access to Medication*, New York: Oxford University Press.

Hilf, M. and S. Oeter (2005), *WTO-Recht*, Nomos: Baden-Baden.

Hilty, R. M. (2000), "Verbot von Parallelimporten - Heimatschutz oder Schildbürgerstreich? Eine rechtliche Kritik, eine ökonomische Analyse - und ein Regelungsvorschlag zwischen Schwarz und Weiss *(A Legal Critique and Economic Analysis with respect to the Ban on Parallel Imports)*", *sic!*, 3, 231-241.

Hoerger, T. J. (1993), "Two-Part Pricing for Experience Goods in the Presence of Adverse Selection", *International Journal of Industrial Organization*, 11(4), 451-471.

Hollis, A. (2005), *An Efficient Reward System for Pharmaceutical Innovation. Department of Economics, University of Calgary, Institute of Health Economics*, Calgary.

Holmberg, C., H. Kiellberg, and B. Andersson (2003), *Distribution of Pharmaceutical Products in the Nordic Countries. SSE/EFI Working Paper Series in Business Administration.*

Hopenhayn, H., G. Llobet, and M. Mitchell (2006), "Rewarding Sequential Innovators: Prizes, Patents, and Buyouts", *Journal of Political Economy*, 114(6), 1041-1068.

Hunt, R. M. (2004), "Patentability, Industry Structure, and Innovation", *Journal of Industrial Economics*, 52(3), 401-425.

Hunt, R. M. (2006), "When Do More Patents Reduce R&D?" *American Economic Review*, 96(2), 87-91.

IMS Health (2007), *IMS Intelligence.360 Global Pharmaceutical Perspectives 2006*, Norwalk: IMS Health.

International Federation of Pharmaceutical Manufacturers Associations (2004), *Research and Development for Neglected Diseases*. Geneva, International Federation of Pharmaceutical Manufacturers Associations.

Jehoram, H. C. (1996), "International Exhaustion versus Importation Right: A Murky Area of Intellectual Property Law", *Gewerblicher Rechtsschutz und Urheberrecht, Internationaler Teil*, 4(1), 280-284.

Jelovac, I. and C. Bordoy (2005), "Pricing and Welfare Implications of Parallel Imports in the Pharmaceutical Industry", *International Journal of Health Care Finance and Economics*, 5(1), 5-21.

Kamien, M. I. and N. L. Schwartz (1974), "Patent Life and R and D Rivalry", *American Economic Review*, 64(1), 83-187.

Kanavos, P. and J. Costa-i-Font (2005), "Pharmaceutical Parallel Trade in Europe: Stakeholder and Competition Effects", *Economic Policy*, 20(44), 751-798.

Kanavos, P., J. Costa-i-Font, S. Merkur, and M. Gemill (2004), *The Economic Impact of Pharmaceutical Parallel Trade in European Union Member States: A Stakeholder Analysis*, London: Special Research Paper, LSE Health and Social Care.

Kaplow, L. (1984), "The Patent-Antitrust Intersection: A Reappraisal", *Harvard Law Review*, 97(8), 1813-1892.

Kaplow, L. and S. Shavell (1996), "Property Rules versus Liability Rules: An Economic Analysis", *Harvard Law Review*, 109(4), 715-789.

Kaufmann, D., A. Kraay, and M. Mastruzzi (2004), "Governance Matters III: Governance Indicators for 1996, 2000, and 2002", *World Bank Economic Review*, 18(2), 253-287.

Kaufmann, D., A. Kraay, and P. Zoido (1999), *Governance Matters*, World Bank Policy Research Working Paper No. 2196, Washington, D.C.: World Bank.

Kaufmann, D., A. Kraay, and P. Zoido (2002), *Governance Matters II: Updated Indicators for 2000-01*, World Bank Policy Research Paper No. 2772, Washington, D.C.: World Bank.

Kenney, M. (1986), *Biotechnology: The University-Industrial Complex*, New Haven: Yale University Press.

Kettler, H. E. (2002), "Using Intellectual Property Regimes to Meet Global Health R&D Needs", *Journal of World Intellectual Property*, 5(5), 654-683.

Kettler, H. E. and R. Modi (2001), "Building Research and Development Capacity for the Prevention and Cure of Neglected Diseases: The Case of India", *Bulletin of the World Health Organization*, 79, 742-747.

Kitch, E. W. (1977), "The Nature and Function of the Patent System", *Journal of Law and Economics*, 20(2), 265-290.

Kitch, E. W. (1998), "Patents" in Newman, P. (ed.), *The New Palgrave Dictionary of Economics and the Law*, 13-17,

Kitch, E. W. (2003), "Comment on the Tragedy of the Anticommons in Biomedical Research", *Advances in Genetics*, 50, 271-274.

Klemperer, P. (1990), "How Broad Should the Scope of Patent Protection Be?" *RAND Journal of Economics*, 21(1), 113-130.

Kobak, J. B. (2005), "Exhaustion of Intellectual Property Rights and International Trade", *Global Economy Journal*, 5(1), 1-15.

Koopman, G. and T. Straubhaar (2006), "Globalisierung braucht starke Institutionen. Nach dem Doha-Debakel: Zur Notwendigkeit einer WTO-plus", *Internationale Politik (IP)*, 61(9), 6-14.

Kremer, M. (1998), "Patent Buyouts: A Mechanism for Encouraging Innovation", *Quarterly Journal of Economics*, 113(4), 1137-1167.

Kremer, M. (2001a), "Creating Markets for New Vaccines: Part I: Rationale", *NBER Innovation Policy and the Economy*, 1(1), 35-72.

Kremer, M. (2001b), "Creating Markets for New Vaccines: Part II: Design Issues", *NBER Innovation Policy and the Economy*, 1(1), 74-118.

Kremer, M. (2002), "Pharmaceuticals and the Developing World", *Journal of Economic Perspectives*, 16(4), 67-90.

Kremer, M. and R. Glennerster (2000), "A World Bank Vaccine Commitment", *Brookings Institution Policy Brief*, 57, 1-8.

Kremer, M. and R. Glennerster (2004), *Strong Medicine, Creating Incentives for Pharmaceutical Research and Neglected Diseases*, New Jersey: Princeton University Press.

Kremer, M. and J. Leino (2004), "Regional Public Goods and Health in Latin America" in Estevadeordal, A.B. Frantz and R. N. Tam (eds.), *Regional Public Goods:*

From Theory to Practice, 227-242, Washington, D.C.: Inter-American Development Bank.

Kremer, M. and C. M. Snyder (2003), *Why are Drugs more Profitable than Vaccines?*, NBER Working Paper No. 9833, Washington, D. C.: National Bureau of Economic Research.

Kreps, D. M. (1990), *A Course in Microeconomic Theory*, Princeton, NJ: Princeton University Press.

Kreps, D. M. (1994), *Mikroökonomische Theorie*, German edition, Landsberg: Moderne Industrie.

Kreps, D. M. and J. Scheinkman (1983), "Quantity Precommitment and Bertrand Competition Yield Cournot Outcomes", *Bell Journal of Economics*, 14(2), 326-337.

Kuhn, H. W. and S. Nasar (2002), *The Essential John Nash*, Princeton University Press: Princeton, New Jersey.

Kuhn, H. W. and A. W. Tucker (1951), *Nonlinear Programming*, Proceedings of the Second Berkeley Symposium on Mathematical Statistics and Probabilistics, Berkeley, University of California Press.

Lai, E. L.-C. and L. D. Qiu (2003), "The North's Intellectual Property Rights Standard for the South?" *Journal of International Economics*, 59(1), 183-209.

Landes, W. M. and R. A. Posner (1975), "The Private Enforcement of Law", *Journal of Legal Studies*, 4(1), 1-46.

Langinier, C. and G. Moschini (2002), *The Economics of Patents: An Overview, Intellectual Property Rights and Patenting in Animal Breeding and Genetics*, CAB International.

Lanjouw, J. O. (1998), *The Introduction of Pharmaceutical Product Patents in India: "Heartless Exploitation of the Poor and Suffering" ?*, NBER Working Paper No. 6366, Washington, D. C.: National Bureau of Economic Research.

Lanjouw, J. O. (2002a), "A New Global Patent Regime for Diseases: U.S. and International Legal Issues", *Harvard Journal of Law and Technology*, 16(1), 85-124.

Lanjouw, J. O. (2002b), *A Patent Policy Proposal for Global Diseases*, Annual World Bank Conference on Development Economics, World Bank.

Lanjouw, J. O. (2003), "Intellectual Property and the Availability of Pharmaceuticals in Poor Countries", *NBER Innovation Policy and the Economy*, 3(1), 91-129.

Lanjouw, J. O. and I. M. Cockburn (2001), "New Pills for Poor People? Empirical Evidence after GATT", *World Development*, 29(2), 265-289.

Lanjouw, J. O. and J. Lerner (2001), "Tilting the Table? The Predatory Use of Preliminary Injunctions", *Journal of Law & Economics*, 44(2), 573-603.

Lanjouw, J. O. and M. MacLeod (2005), *Pharmaceutical R&D for Low-Income Countries: Global Trends and Participation by Indian Firms*, Economic and Political Weekly, September 24, 2005: 4232-4242.

Lanjouw, J. O. and M. Schankerman (2001), "Characteristics of Patent Litigation: A Window on Competition", *RAND Journal of Economics*, 32(1), 129-151.

Lanjouw, J. O. and M. Schankerman (2002), *Enforcing Intellectual Property Rights: Suits, Settlements and the Explosion in Patent Litigation*. New Haven, Yale University.

Lanjouw, J. O. and M. Schankerman (2004), "Protecting Intellectual Property Rights: Are Small Firms Handicapped?" *Journal of Law and Economics*, 47(1), 45-74.

Layson, S. K. (1994), "Market Opening under Third-Degree Price Discrimination", *Journal of Industrial Economics*, 42(3), 335-340.

Lee, T. and L. Wilde (1980), "Market Structure and Innovation: A Reformulation", *Quarterly Journal of Economics*, 94(2), 429-436.

Lemley, M. A. (2001), "Rational Ignorance at the Patent Office", *Northwestern University Law Review*, 95(4), 1495.

Lerner, J. (1994), "The Importance of Patent Scope: An Empirical Analysis", *RAND Journal of Economics*, 25(2), 319-333.

Lerner, J. and J. Tirole (2004), "Efficient Patent Pools", *American Economic Review*, 94(3), 691-711.

Lévêque, F. and Y. Ménière (2004), *The Economics of Patents and Copyright*, Berkeley Electronic Press, http://www.bepress.com/cgi/viewcontent.cgi?article=1001&context=leveque.

Levin, R. C., A. K. Klevorik, R. R. Nelson, and S. G. Winters (1987), "Appropriating the Returns from Industrial Research and Development", *Brookings Papers on Economic Activity*, 3, 783-831.

Li, C. and K. E. Maskus (2006), "The Impact of Parallel Imports on Investments in Cost-reducing Research and Development", *Journal of International Economics*, 68(2), 443-455.

Lichtenberg, F. R. (1992), *R&D Investments and International Productivity Differences*, NBER Working Paper No. 4161, Washington, D.C.: National Bureau of Economic Research.

Lichtenberg, F. R. and J. Waldfogel (2003), *Does Misery Love Company? Evidence from Pharmaceutical Markets before and after the Orphan Drug Act*, NBER Working Paper No. 9750, Washington, D.C.: National Bureau of Economic Research.

Lister, S. (2005), *Gates Gives Millions to Fund British Fight Against TB and Aids*, The Times, London, June 28.

Lloyd, W. F. (1833), *Two Lectures on the Checks to Population*, Oxford, England: Oxford University Press.

Loury, G. C. (1979), "Market Structure and Innovation", *Quarterly Journal of Economics*, 93(3), 395-410.

Love, J. (2001), *Compulsory Licensing: Models for State Practice in Developing Countries, Access to Medicine and Compliance with the WTO TRIPS Accord: Prepared for the United Nations Development Programme*, Washington, D.C.: Consumer Project on Technology.

Lu, Z. J. and W. S. Comanor (1998), "Strategic Pricing of New Pharmaceuticals", *Review of Economics and Statistics*, 80(1), 108-118.

Luce, R. D. and H. Raiffa (1957), *Games and Decisions: Introduction and Critical Survey*, New York: Wiley.

Macedo, C. (1990), "First-to-File: Is American Adoption of the International Standard in Patent Law Worth the Price?" *American Intellectual Property Law Association Quarterly Journal*, 18, 193-234.

Machlup, F. and E. Penrose (1950), "The Patent Controversy in the Nineteenth Century", *The Journal of Economic History*, 10(1), 1-29.

MacLeod, C. (1988), *Inventing the Industrial Revolution: The English Patent System, 1660-1800*, Cambridge: Cambridge University Press.

Malik, N. N. (2008), "Drug Discovery: Past, Present and Future", *Drug Discovery Today*, 13(21-22), 909-912.

Malueg, D. A. and M. Schwartz (1994), "Parallel Imports, Demand Dispersion, and International Price Discrimination", *Journal of International Economics*, 37(3/4), 167-195.

Mansfield, E. (1964), "Industrial Research and Development Expenditures: Determinants, Prospects, and Relation to Size of Firm and Inventive Output", *Journal of Political Economy*, 72(4), 319-340.

Mansfield, E. (1986), "Patents and Innovation: An Empirical Study", *Management Science*, 32(2), 173-181.

Mansfield, E., J. Rapoport, A. Romeo, E. Villani, S. Wagner, and F. Husic (1977), *The Production and Application of New Industrial Technology*, New York: W. W. Norton.

Mas-Colell, A., M. D. Whinston, and J. R. Green (1995), *Microeconomic Theory*, New York: Oxford University Press.

Maskin, E. and J. Riley (1984), "Monopoly with Incomplete Information", *RAND Journal of Economics*, 15(2), 171-196.

Maskus, K. E. (2000a), *Intellectual Property Rights in the Global Economy*, Washington, D. C.: Institute for International Economics.

Maskus, K. E. (2000b), "Parallel Imports", *World Economy*, 23(9), 1269-1284.

Maskus, K. E. (2001), *Parallel Imports in Pharmaceuticals: Implications for Competition and Prices in Developing Countries*, Geneva: Final Report to the World Intellectual Property Organization.

Maskus, K. E. and Y. Chen (2002), "Parallel Imports in a Model of Vertical Distribution: Theory, Evidence, and Policy", *Pacific Economic Review*, 7(2), 319-334.

Maskus, K. E. and Y. Chen (2004), "Vertical Price Control and Parallel Imports: Theory and Evidence", *Review of International Economics*, 12(4), 551-570.

Maskus, K. E. and Y. Chen (2005), "Parallel Imports in a Model of Vertical Distribution: Theory, Evidence, and Policy" in Maskus, K. E. and C. Fink (eds.), *Intellectual Property and Development, Lessons from Recent Economic Research*, 189-206, World Bank, Oxford University Press.

Maskus, K. E. and M. Ganslandt (2002), "Parallel Trade in Pharmaceutical Products: Implications for Procuring Medicines for Poor Countries" in Granville, B. (ed.), *The Economics of Essential Medicines*, 57-80, London: Royal Institute of International Affairs.

Matteucci, G. and P. Reverberi (2005), "Price Regulation and Public Service Obligations under International Arbitrage", *Journal of Regulatory Economics*, 28(1), 91-113.

Maurer, S. M. (2005), *The Right Tool(s): Designing Cost-Effective Strategies for Neglected Disease Research*, Report to WHO Commission on Intellectual Property Rights, Innovation and Public Health, Geneva: WHO.

Maurer, S. M. (2006), "Choosing the Right Incentive Strategy for Research and Development in Neglected Diseases", *Bulletin of the World Health Organization*, 84(5), 376-381.

Maurer, S. M. and S. Scotchmer (2002), "The Independent Invention Defence in Intellectual Property", *Economica*, 69(276), 535-547.

Maynard Smith, J. (1974), "The Theory of Games and Evolution in Animal Conflicts", *Journal of Theoretical Biology*, 47(1), 209-221.

Maynard Smith, J. (1982), *Evolution and the Theory of Games*, Cambridge University Press.

Mazzoleni, R. and R. R. Nelson (1998), "The Benefits and Costs of Strong Patent Protection: A Contribution to the Current Debate", *Research Policy*, 27(3), 273-284.

McAfee, R. P. and J. McMillan (1987), "Auctions and Bidding", *Journal of Economic Literature*, 25(2), 699-738.

McCalman, P. (2001), "Reaping what You Sow: An Empirical Analysis of International Patent Harmonization", *Journal of International Economics*, 55(1), 161-185.

McCalman, P. (2002), "National Patents, Innovation and International Agreements", *Journal of International Trade and Economic Development*, 11(1), 1-14.

McCalman, P. (2005), "Who Enjoys 'TRIPS' Abroad? An Empirical Analysis of Intellectual Property Rights in the Uruguay Round", *Canadian Journal of Economics*, 38(2), 574-603.

McGee, J. S. (1966), "Patent Exploitation: Some Economic and Legal Problems", *Journal of Law & Economics*, 9, 135-162.

McNeil, D. G. (2008), *Eradicate Malaria? Doubters Fuel Debate*, New York Times, New York, March 4, 2008.

Médecins Sans Frontières (2003), *Act Now to Get Malaria Treatment that Works to Africa*, Geneva: Médecins Sans Frontières.

Menell, P. and S. Scotchmer (2007), "Intellectual Property Law" in Polinsky, A. M. and S. Shavell (eds.), *Handbook of Law and Economics*, 1473-1570, Amsterdam: North-Holland.

Mercurio, B. C. (2004), "TRIPS, Patents, and Access to Life-Saving Drugs in the Developing World", *Marquette Intellectual Property Law Review*, 8(2), 212-250.

Merges, R. P. (1994), "Intellectual Property Rights and Bargaining Breakdown: The Case of Blocking Patents", *Tennessee Law Review*, 62(1), 75-76.

Merges, R. P. and J. F. Duffy (2007), *Patent Law and Policy: Cases and Materials*, New York: LexisNexis.

Merges, R. P. and R. R. Nelson (1990), "On the Complex Economics of Patent Scope", *Columbia Law Review*, 90, 839-916.

Merton, R. (1973), *The Sociology of Science*, Chicago: University of Chicago Press.

Michaelis, M. and T. Bender (2005), "Handelsrelevante Aspekte des geistigen Eigentums" in Hilf, M. and S. Oeter (eds.), *WTO-Recht – Rechtsordnung des Welthandels*, 435, Baden-Baden: Nomos.

Michaelis, M. and H. Jessen (2005), "WTO und Entwicklung" in Hilf, M. and S. Oeter (eds.), *WTO-Recht – Rechtsordnung des Welthandels*, 601-621, Baden-Baden: Nomos.

Michelman, F. I. (1982), "Ethics, Economics, and the Law of Property" in Pennock, J. R. and J. W. Chapman (eds.), *Nomos XXIV: Ethics, Economics and the Law*, 3-40, New York: New York University Press.

Milgrom, P. and R. Weber (1982), "The Value of Information in a Sealed-bid Auction", *Journal of Mathematical Economics*, 10(1), 105-114.

Morantz, A. and R. Sloane (2001), *Vaccine Purchase-Commitment Contract: Legal Strategies for Ensuring Enforceability. Harvard University*, Cambridge, MA.

Morris, J., P. Stevens, and A. van Gelder (2005), *Incentivising Research and Development for the Diseases of Poverty*, International Policy Network Working Papers on Intellectual Property, Innovation and Health, London: International Policy Network.

Morthy, V., M. Good, and A. Hill (2004), "Malaria Vaccine Developments", *Lancet*, 363, 474-481.

Müller-Langer, F. (2007), *A Game Theoretic Analysis of Parallel Trade and the Pricing of Pharmaceutical Products*, Berkeley Electronic Press, German Working Papers in Law and Economics, Vol. 2007, Article 6, http://www.bepress.com/gwp/default/vol2007/iss2/art6.

Müller-Langer, F. (2008a), *An Analysis of the Welfare Effects of Parallel Trade Freedom*, Berkeley Electronic Press, German Working Papers in Law and Economics, Vol. 2008, Article 9, http://www.bepress.com/gwp/default/vol2008/iss1/art965.

Müller-Langer, F. (2008b), "Does Parallel Trade Harm Consumers in Small Markets?" *Croatian Economic Survey*, 11(11), 11-41.

Murray, C. J. L. and A. D. Lopez (1996), *Global Burden of Disease*, Harvard University Press: Cambridge, Massachusetts.

Murray, H. W., J. Pépin, T. B. Nutman, S. L. Hoffman, and A. F. Mahmoud (2001), *Recent Advances: Tropical Medicine*, London: BMJ Publishing.

Mutangadura, G., D. Mukurazita, and H. Jackson (2000), *A Review of Household and Community Responses to the HIV/AIDS Epidemic in the Rural Areas of Sub-Saharan Africa*, Geneva: Joint United Nations Programme on HIV/AIDS.

Nadiri, M. I. (1993), *Innovations and Technological Spillovers*, NBER Working Papers No. 4423, Washington, D. C.: National Bureau of Economic Research.

National Academy of Sciences (1996), *Vaccines Against Malaria: Hope in a Gathering Storm*, Washington, D.C.: National Academy Press.

Nauta, W. (2004), "Ausnahmen vom Erschöpfungsgrundsatz im Markenrecht", *Gewerblicher Rechtsschutz und Urheberrecht, Internationaler Teil*, 12, 994-1001.

NERA, S. J. Berwin & Co., and IFF Research (1999), *The Economic Consequences of the Choice of Regime of Exhaustion in the Area of Trademarks*, Final Report for DG XV of the EC, London: National Economic Research Associates.

Nerkar, A. (2003), "Old is Gold? Value of Temporal Exploration in the Creation of New Knowledge", *Management Science*, 49(2), 211-229.

Nogués, J. (1990), "Patents and Pharmaceutical Drugs: Understanding the Pressures on Developing Countries", *Journal of World Trade*, 24(6), 81-104.

Nordhaus, W. D. (1969), *Invention, Growth and Welfare: A Theoretical Treatment of Technological Change*, Cambridge, MA.: MIT Press.

Nordhaus, W. D. (1972), "The Optimum Life of a Patent: Reply", *American Economic Review*, 62(3), 428-431.

Norman, G. (1999), *The Economics of Price Discrimination*, International Library of Critical Writings in Economics, Edward Elgar: Cheltenham, UK.

O'Donoghue, T., S. Scotchmer, and J.-F. Thisse (1998), "Patent Breadth, Patent Life, and the Pace of Technological Progress", *Journal of Economics & Management Strategy*, 7(1), 1-32.

OECD (1994), *Main Science and Technology Indicators*, Paris: Organisation for Economic Cooperation and Development.

OECD (2000), *Competition and Regulation Issues in the Pharmaceutical Industry*, Paris: Organisation for Economic Cooperation and Development.

OECD (2002), *OECD Health Data 2002: A Comparative Analysis of 30 Countries*, Paris: Organisation for Economic Cooperation and Development.

OECD (2007), *Neglected Diseases: Towards Policies without Borders*, OECD Observer No. 262 July 2007, http://www.oecdobserver.org/news/fullstory.php/aid/2282/Neglected_diseases.html.

Oi, W. Y. (1971), "A Disneyland Dilemma: Two-Part Tariffs for a Mickey Mouse Monopoly", *Quarterly Journal of Economics*, 85(1), 77-96.

Ott, C. and H.-B. Schäfer (1994), *Ökonomische Analyse der rechtlichen Organisation von Innovationen*, IV. Travemünder Symposium zur Ökonomischen Analyse des Rechts, Mohr Siebeck: Tübingen.

Outterson, K. (2004), "Pharmaceutical Arbitrage: Balancing Access and Innovation in International Prescription Drug Markets", *Yale Journal of Health Policy, Law & Ethics*, 5(1), 193-286.

Over, A. M. (1992), *The Macroeconomic Impact of AIDS in Sub-Saharan Africa*, Washington, D.C.: Population, Health and Nutrition Division, Africa Technical Department, World Bank.

Palia, A. P. and C. F. Keown (1991), "Combating Parallel Importing: Views of US Exporters to the Asian-Pacific Region", *International Marketing Review*, 8, 47-56.

Pecorino, P. (2002), "Should the US Allow Prescription Drug Reimports from Canada?" *Journal of Health Economics*, 21(4), 699-708.

Pejovich, S. (1997), *The Economic Foundations of Property Rights*, Lyme, US: Edward Elgar.

Penner, J. E. (1997), *The Idea of Property in Law*, Oxford: Clarendon Press.

Penrose, E. (1973), "International Patenting and the Less-Developed Countries", *Economic Journal*, 83(331), 768-786.

Pharmaceutical Executive (2008), *9th Annual Report on the World's Top 50 Pharmaceutical Companies*, http://pharmexec.findpharma.com/Special+Reports.

PhRMA (2005), *Pharmaceutical Industry Profile 2005: From Laboratory to Patient: Pathways to Biopharmaceutical Innovation*, Washington, D.C.: Pharmaceutical Research and Manufacturers of America.

PhRMA (2008), *Pharmaceutical Industry Profile 2008*, Washington, D.C.: Pharmaceutical Research and Manufacturers of America.

PhRMA (2009), *Pharmaceutical Industry Profile 2009*, Washington, D.C.: Pharmaceutical Research and Manufacturers of America.

Pigou, A. C. (1932), *The Economics of Welfare*, London: Macmillan.

Pindyck, R. S. and D. L. Rubinfeld (2005), *Microeconomics*, New Yersey: Pearson Prentice Hall.

Polinsky, A. M. (1980), "Resolving Nuisance Disputes: The Simple Economics of Injunctive and Damage Remedies", *Stanford Law Review*, 32(6), 1075-1112.

Polinsky, A. M. and S. Shavell (1998), "Punitive Damages: An Economic Analysis", *Harvard Law Review*, 111(4), 869-962.

Primo Braga, C. A. (1989), "The Economics of Intellectual Property Rights and the GATT: A View from the South", *Vanderbilt Journal of Transnational Law*, 22(2), 243-264.

Pugh, T. (2003), *Drugmakers Curb Canadian Outlets - Prescription Tabs Increase for Buyers from the U.S.*, Detroit Free Press, Detroit, September 6, 2003.

Rapp, R. T. and R. P. Rozek (1990), "Benefits and Costs of Intellectual Property Protection in Developing Countries", *Journal of World Trade*, 24, 75-102.

Reiffen, D. and M. R. Ward (2005), "Generic Drug Industry Dynamics", *Review of Economics and Statistics*, 87(1), 37-49.

Reinganum, J. F. (1981), "Dynamic Games of Innovation", *Journal of Economic Theory*, 25(1), 21-41.

Reinganum, J. F. (1982), "A Dynamic Game of R and D: Patent Protection and Competitive Behavior", *Econometrica*, 50(3), 671-688.

Reinganum, J. F. (1984), "Practical Implications of Game Theoretic Models of R&D", *American Economic Review, Papers and Proceedings*, 74(2), 61-66.

Reitzig, M. (2003), "What Determines Patent Value? Insights from the Semiconductor Industry", *Research Policy*, 32(1), 13-26.

REMIT Consultants (1991), *Impediments to Parallel Trade in Pharmaceuticals within the European Community*, Report to DG IV of the European Commission,

Rey, P. (2003), *The Impact of Parallel Imports on Prescription Medicines*. mimeo, IDEI, University of Toulouse.

Rey, P. and J. Venit (2004), "Parallel Trade and Pharmaceuticals: A Policy in Search of Itself", *European Law Review*, 29(2), 153-177.

Richardson, M. (2002), "An Elementary Proposition Concerning Parallel Imports", *Journal of International Economics*, 56(1), 233-245.

Ridder, C. (2004), *Die Bedeutung von Zwangslizenzen im Rahmen des TRIPS-Abkommens*, Heidelberg: Recht und Wirtschaft.

Ridley, R. G. (2002), "Medical Need, Scientific Opportunity and the Drive for Anti-malarial Drugs", *Nature*, 415(6872), 686-693.

Ridley, R. G., E. Win, E. Gutteridge, and L. J. Currat (1999), *Medicines for Malaria Venture: A Case Study of the Establishment of a Public Sector/Private Sector Partnership*, 3rd Global Forum for Health Research, Geneva.

Roberts, K. and M. L. Weitzman (1981), "Funding Criteria for Research, Development, and Exploration Projects", *Econometrica*, 49(5), 1261-1288.

Robinson, J. (1933), *Economics of Imperfect Competition*, London: Macmillan.

Rockefeller Foundation (1997), *The STD Diagnostics Challenge: Rules and Regulations*, New York: Rockefeller Foundation.

Rose, C. M. (2000), "Left Brain, Right Brain and History in the New Law and Economics of Property", *Oregon Law Review*, 79(2), 479-492.

Rott, P. (2002), *Patentrecht und Sozialpolitik unter dem TRIPS-Abkommen*, Baden-Baden: Nomos.

Rozek, R. P. and N. Tully (1999), "The TRIPS Agreement and Access to Health Care", *Journal of World Intellectual Property*, 2(5), 813-819.

Sachs, J. (1999), *Helping the World's Poorest*, Economist, August 14, 352(8132): 17-20.

Sachs, J., M. Kremer, and A. Hamoudi (1999), *The Case for a Vaccine Fund, Center for International Development Policy Proposal*, Cambridge, Mass.: Harvard University.

Samuelson, P. (1999), "Challenges for the World Intellectual Property Organization and the Trade-Related Aspects of Intellectual Property Rights Council in Regulating Intellectual Property Rights in the Information Age", *European Intellectual Property Review*, 21(11), 578-591.

Samuelson, P. A. (1954), "The Pure Theory of Public Expenditure", *Review of Economics and Statistics*, 36(4), 387-389.

Samuelson, P. A. (1955), "Diagrammatic Exposition of a Theory of Public Expenditures", *Review of Economics and Statistics*, 37(4), 350-356.

Schäfer, H.-B. and C. Ott (2004), *The Economic Analysis of Civil Law*, Cheltenham, UK: Edward Elgar.

Schäfer, H.-B. and C. Ott (2005), *Lehrbuch der ökonomischen Analyse des Zivilrechts*, Heidelberg: Springer.

Schankerman, M. and S. Scotchmer (2001), "Damages and Injunctions in Protecting Intellectual Property", *RAND Journal of Economics*, 32(1), 199-220.

Scherer, F. M. (1972), "Nordhaus' Theory of Optimal Patent Life: A Geometric Reinterpretation", *American Economic Review*, 62(3), 422-427.

Scherer, F. M. (1980), *Industrial Market Structure and Economic Performance*, Chicago: Rand McNally.

Scherer, F. M. (1993), "Pricing, Profits, and Technological Progress in the Pharmaceutical Industry", *Journal of Economic Perspectives*, 7(3), 97-115.

Scherer, F. M. (2000), "The Pharmaceutical Industry" in Culyer, A. J. and J. P. Newhouse (eds.), *Handbook of Health Economics*, Elsevier.

Scherer, F. M. (2004), "A Note on Global Welfare in Pharmaceutical Patenting", *World Economy*, 27(7), 1127-1142.

Scherer, F. M. and J. Watal (2001), *Post-TRIPS Options for Access to Patented Medicines in Developing Countries*, Commission for Macroeconomics and Health Working Paper Series Paper No. WG4 : 1, Geneva: World Health Organization.

Scherer, F. M. and J. Watal (2002a), "The Economics of TRIPS Options for Access to Medicines" in Granville, B. (ed.), *The Economics of Essential Medicines*, 32-56, London: Royal Institute of International Affairs.

Scherer, F. M. and J. Watal (2002b), "Post-TRIPS Options for Access to Patented Medicines in Developing Nations", *Journal of International Economic Law*, 5(4), 913-939.

Schmalensee, R. (1981a), "Monopolistic Two-Part Pricing Arrangements", *Bell Journal of Economics*, 12(2), 445-466.

Schmalensee, R. (1981b), "Output and Welfare Implications of Monopolistic Third-Degree Price Discrimination", *American Economic Review*, 71(1), 242-247.

Schmookler, J. (1962), "Changes in Industry and in the State of Knowledge as Determinants of Industrial Invention" in Nelson, R. R. (ed.), *The Rate and Direction of*

Inventive Activity: Economic and Social Factor, Princeton, N. J.: Princeton University Press.

Schmookler, J. (1966), *Innovation and Economic Growth*, Cambridge, Massachusetts: Harvard University Press.

Scholing, E. (2000), *Messung der Bevölkerungsgesundheit in Entwicklungsländern auf der Grundlage eines MIMIC-Modells*, Sozialökonomisches Seminar der Universität Hamburg, http://www1.uni-hamburg.de/iiw/.

Schulz, N., F. Parisi, and B. Depoorter (2002), "Fragmentation in Property: Towards a General Model", *Journal of Institutional and Theoretical Economics*, 158(4), 594-613.

Schwartz, H. F. (2006), *Patent Law and Practice*, Arlington: BNA Books.

Schwartz, M. (1990), "Third-Degree Price Discrimination and Output: Generalizing a Welfare Result", *American Economic Review*, 80(5), 1259-1262.

Scotchmer, S. (2006), *Innovation and Incentives*, Cambridge, Massachusetts: MIT Press.

Scotchmer, S. and J. R. Green (1990), "Novelty and Disclosure in Patent Law", *RAND Journal of Economics*, 21(1), 131-146.

Scott Morton, F. M. (1999), "Entry Decisions in the Generic Pharmaceutical Industry", *RAND Journal of Economics*, 30(3), 412-440.

Scott Morton, F. M. (2000), "Barriers to Entry, Brand Advertising, and Generic Entry in the U.S. Pharmaceutical Industry", *International Journal of Industrial Organization*, 18(7), 1085-1104.

Sell, S. K. (2003), *Private Power, Public Law: The Globalization of Intellectual Property Rights*, Cambridge: Cambridge University Press.

Selten, R. (1965), "Spieltheoretische Behandlung eines Oligopolmodells mit Nachfrageträgheit", *Zeitschrift für die gesamte Staatswissenschaft*, 121(1), 301-324.

Shapiro, C. (2003), "Antitrust Limits to Patent Settlements", *RAND Journal of Economics*, 34(2), 391-411.

Shavell, S. and T. Van Ypersele (2001), "Rewards versus Intellectual Property Rights", *Journal of Law and Economics*, 44(2), 525-547.

Shulman, S. R. and M. Manocchia (1997), "The U.S. Orphan Drug Programme: 1983-1995", *PharmacoEconomics*, 12(3), 312-326.

Silbertson, Z. A. (1998), "Patents" in Eatwell, J.M. Milgate and P. Newman (eds.), *The New Palgrave- A Dictionary of Economics*, 815-816, London: MacMillan.

Sim, L.-L., S.-K. Lum, and L. C. Malone-Lee (2002), "Property Rights, Collective Sales and Government Intervention: Averting a Tragedy of the Anticommons", *Habitat International*, 26(4), 457-470.

Simon, B. (2004), *Pfizer Moves to Try to Stop Drugs From Canada*, New York Times, New York, January 14, 2004.

Slotboom, M. M. (2003), "The Exhaustion of Intellectual Property Rights. Different Approaches in EC and WTO Law", *Journal of World Intellectual Property*, 6(3), 421-440.

Smits, E. (2006), "On Parallel Trade and Preliminary Issues - A Healthy Approach to Competition Law Enforcement?" *Legal Issues of Economic Integration*, 33(1), 61-83.

Sobel, D. (1995), *Longitude*, New York: Walker and Company.

Spence, M. (1977), "Nonlinear Prices and Welfare", *Journal of Public Economics*, 8, 1-18.

Spengler, J. J. (1950), "Vertical Integration and Antitrust Policy", *Journal of Political Economy*, 58(4), 347-352.

Stack, A. J. (1998), "TRIPS, Patent Exhaustion and Parallel Imports", *Journal of World Intellectual Property*, 1(4), 657-689.

Subramanian, A. (1990), "TRIPS and the Paradigm of the GATT: A Tropical, Temperate View", *World Economy*, 13(4), 509-521.

Subramanian, A. (1999), *TRIPS and Developing Countries: The Seattle Round and Beyond*, http://www.tradeobservatory.org/library.cfm?filename=TRIPs_and_Developing_Countries_The_Seattle_Rou.pdf.

Subramanian, A. (2001), "The AIDS Crisis, Differential Pricing of Drugs, and the TRIPS Agreement - Two Proposals", *Journal of World Intellectual Property*, 4(3), 323-336.

Sullivan, M. P. (1988), *Private Contests and Lotteries: Entrants' Rights and Remedies*, American Law Reports, 64 (4), 1021.

Sykes, A. O. (1992), "Constructive Unilateral Threats in International Commercial Relations: The Limit Case for Section 301", *Law and Policy in International Business*, 23, 263-317. Reprinted in: P. C. Mavroidis and A. O. Sykes, eds. (2005). The WTO and International Trade Law / Dispute Settlement. Cheltenham, UK, Edward Elgar.

Sykes, A. O. (2002), "TRIPS, Pharmaceuticals, Developing Countries, and the Doha "Solution"", *Chicago Journal of International Law*, 3(1), 47-68.

Szymanski, S. (1999), *International Exhaustion of Right: Review of the Economic Issues*, London: Intellectual Property Institute.

Szymanski, S. and T. M. Valletti (2005), "Parallel Trade, Price Discrimination, Investment and Price Caps", *Economic Policy*, 20(44), 705-749.

't Hoen, E. (2002), "TRIPS, Pharmaceutical Patents, and the Access to Essential Medicines: A Long Way from Seattle to Doha", *Chicago Journal of International Law*, 3(1), 27-50.

't Hoen, E. (2005), *TRIPS, R&D, and Access to Medicines: A Guide to the Post 2005 World*, Campaign for Access to Essential Medicines, Geneva: Médecins Sans Frontières.

Tandon, P. (1982), "Optimal Patents with Compulsory Licensing", *Journal of Political Economy*, 90(3), 470-486.

Tarr, D. G. (1985), *An Economic Analysis of Grey Market Imports*, Washington, D.C.: U.S. Federal Trade Commission.

Thorpe, P. (2002), *Study on the Implementation of the TRIPS Agreement by Developing Countries. UK Commission on Intellectual Property Rights Study Paper No.7.*

Tirole, J. (1988), *The Theory of Industrial Organization*, Cambridge, Massachusetts: MIT Press.

Tirole, J. (1995), *Industrieökonomik*, München: Oldenbourg.

Trouiller, P., P. Olliaro, E. Torreele, J. Orbinski, R. Laing, and N. Ford (2002), "Drug Development for Neglected Diseases: A Deficient Market and a Public-Health Policy Failure", *Lancet*, 359(9324), 2188-2194.

Trouiller, P., E. Torreele, P. Olliaro, N. White, S. Foster, D. Wirth, and B. Pécoul (2001), "Drugs for Neglected Diseases: A Failure of the Market and a Public Health Failure?" *Tropical Medicine and International Health*, 6(11), 945-951.

Tversky, A. and D. Kahneman (1992), "Advances in Prospect Theory: Cumulative Representation of Uncertainty", *Journal of Risk and Uncertainty*, 5, 297-323.

U.S. House of Representatives (1998), *Prescription Drug Pricing in the 1st Congressional District in Maine: An International Price Comparison*, Minority Staff International Report, Washington, DC: U.S. House of Representatives.

United Nations Development Programme (2001), *Human Development Report 2001, Making New Technologies Work for Human Development*, New York: United Nations Development Programme.

URA (1991), *The DGP Process: URA's New Planning Approach*, Singapore: Urban Redevelopment Authority.

URA (1993), *Heralding a Historical Milestone in Singapore's Planning History*, Singapore: Urban Redevelopment Authority.

Valletti, T. M. (2006), "Differential Pricing, Parallel Trade, and the Incentive to Invest", *Journal of International Economics*, 7(1), 314-324.

Valletti, T. M. and S. Szymanski (2006), "Parallel Trade, International Exhaustion and Intellectual Property Rights: A Welfare Analysis", *Journal of Industrial Economics*, 54(4), 499-526.

Vanneste, S., A. Van Hiel, F. Parisi, and B. Depoorter (2006), "From "Tragedy" to "Disaster": Welfare Effects of Commons and Anticommons Dilemmas", *International Review of Law and Economics*, 26(1), 104-122.

Varian, H. R. (1985), "Price Discrimination and Social Welfare", *American Economic Review*, 75(4), 870-875.

Varian, H. R. (1988), "Price Discrimination" in Schmalensee, R. and R. Willig (eds.), *Handbook of Industrial Organization*, Amsterdam: North-Holland.

Varian, H. R. (1996), *Intermediate Microeconomics: A Modern Approach*, New York: Norton.

Varian, H. R. (1999), *Intermediate Microeconomics: A Modern Approach*, New York: Norton.

Vaughan, V. S. (2001), "Compulsory Licensing of Pharmaceuticals under TRIPS: What Standards of Compensation?" *Hastings International and Comparative Law Review*, 25, 87-110.

Vega-Redondo, F. (2003), *Economics and the Theory of Games*, New York: Cambridge University Press.

Vickrey, W. (1961), "Counterspeculation, Auctions, and Competitive Sealed Tenders", *Journal of Finance*, 16(1), 8-37.

Wagener, H. J., T. Eger, and H. Fritz (2006), *Europäische Integration - Recht und Ökonomie, Geschichte und Politik (European Integration - Law and Economics, History and Politics)*, Munich: Valen.

Waldron, J. (1988), *The Right to Private Property*, Oxford: Clarendon Press.

Walsh, J. P., A. Arora, and W. M. Cohen (2003), "Research Tool Patenting and Licensing and Biomedical Innovation" in Cohen, W. M. and S. Merrill (eds.), *Patents in the Knowledge-based Economy*, Washington, D.C.: National Academies Press.

Watal, J. (1998), "The TRIPS Agreement and Developing Countries: Strong, Weak, or Balanced Protection?" *Journal of World Intellectual Property Protection*, 1(2), 281-307.

Watal, J. (2000), "Pharmaceutical Patents, Prices and Welfare Losses: Policy Options for India under the WTO TRIPS Agreement", *World Economy*, 23(5), 733-752.

Watal, J. (2001), *Intellectual Property Rights in the WTO and Developing Countries*, Den Haag: Kluwer Law International.

Waterson, M. (1990), "The Economics of Product Patents", *American Economic Review*, 80(4), 860-869.

Webber, D. and M. Kremer (2001), "Perspectives on Stimulating Industrial Research and Development for Neglected Infectious Diseases", *Bulletin of the World Health Organization*, 79(8), 735-741.

Weise, P., W. Brandes, T. Eger, and M. Kraft (2005), *Neue Mikroökonomie*, Heidelberg: Physica.

Widdus, R. (2001), "Public-private Partnerships for Health: Their Main Targets, Their Diversity, and Their Future Directions", *Bulletin of the WHO*, 79, 713-20.

Willig, R. D. (1978), "Pareto-superior Nonlinear Outlay Schedules", *Bell Journal of Economics*, 9(1), 56-69.

Wojahn, P. L. (2001/2002), "A Conflict of Rights; Intellectual Property Rights under TRIPS, the Right to Health, and Aids Drugs", *UCLA Journal of International Law and Foreign Affairs*, 6, 463-497.

Word Health Organization and World Trade Organization (2002), "Differential Pricing and the Financing of Essential Drugs" in Granville, B. (ed.), *The Economics of Essential Medicines*, London: Royal Institute of International Affairs.

World Health Organization (2001a), *Macroeconomics and Health: Investing in Health for Economic Development*, Geneva: Report of the Commission on Macroeconomics and Health, WHO.

World Health Organization (2001b), *World Health Report 2001*, Geneva: World Health Organization.

World Health Organization (2002), *Network for Monitoring the Impact of Globalization and TRIPS on Access to Medicines*, Geneva: World Health Organization.

World Health Organization (2003a), *Africa Malaria Report 2003*, Geneva: World Health Organization.

World Health Organization (2003b), *State of the Art of New Vaccines Research & Development Initiative for Vaccine Research*, Geneva: World Health Organization.

World Health Organization (2003c), *World Health Report 2003*, Geneva: World Health Organization.

World Health Organization (2004), *World Health Report 2004*, Geneva: World Health Organization.

World Health Organization (2005), *World Malaria Report 2005*, Geneva: World Health Organization.

World Health Organization (2006), *Public Health, Innovation and Intellectual Property Rights*, Report of the Commission on Intellectual Property Rights, Innovation and Public Health, Geneva: World Health Organization.

World Health Organization (2008a), *Anti-tuberculosis Drug Resistance in the World*, WHO/IUATLD Global Project on Anti-tuberculosis, Geneva: World Health Organization.

World Health Organization (2008b), *The Global Burden of Disease: 2004 Update*, Geneva: World Health Organization.

World Health Organization and World Trade Organization (2002), "Differential Pricing and the Financing of Essential Drugs" in Granville, B. (ed.), *The Economics of Essential Medicines*, London: Royal Institute of International Affairs.

World Trade Organization (2002), *Communication from Brazil on Behalf of the Delegations of Bolivia, Brazil, Cuba, China, Dominican Republic, Ecuador, India, Indonesia, Pakistan, Peru, Sri Lanka, Thailand and Venezuela.* Council for Trade-Related Aspects of Intellectual Property Rights: WTO Doc. IP/C/W/355.

World Trade Organization (2004), *World Trade Report 2004, Exploring the Linkage between the Domestic Policy Environment and International Trade*, Geneva: World Trade Organization.

World Trade Organization (2006), *World Trade Report 2006, Exploring the Links between Subsidies, Trade and the WTO*, Geneva: World Trade Organization.

World Trade Organization and World Health Organization (2002), *WTO Agreement and Public Health*, Joint report by the WHO and WTO, Geneva: World Trade Organization.

Wright, B. D. (1983), "The Economics of Invention Incentives: Patents, Prizes, and Research Contracts", *American Economic Review*, 73(4), 691-707.

Yang, Y. (1998), "Why Do Southern Countries Have Little Incentive to Protect Northern Intellectual Property Rights?" *Canadian Journal of Economics*, 31(4), 800-816.

York Health Economics Consortium (2003), *Benefits to Payers and Patients from Parallel Trade*, University of York.

Yusuf, A. and A. Moncayo von Hase (1992), "Intellectual Property Protection and International Trade: Exhaustion of Rights Revisited", *World Competition*, 16(1), 115-131.

Ziedonis, R. M. (2003), "Patent Litigation in the U.S. Semiconductor Industry" in Cohen, W. M. and S. A. Merrill (ed.), *Patents in the Knowledge-based Economy*, 180-212, Washington, D.C.: National Academy Press.

Zumla, A. and J. M. Grange (2001), "Multidrug Resistance Tuberculosis - Can the Tide be Turned?" *Lancet Infectious Diseases*, 1(3), 199-202.

Zweifel, P. and F. Breyer (1997), *Health Economics*, New York: Oxford University Press.

Index

MIX
Papier aus verantwortungsvollen Quellen
Paper from responsible sources
FSC® C105338
FSC
www.fsc.org

If you have any concerns about our products,
you can contact us on
ProductSafety@springernature.com

In case Publisher is established outside the EU,
the EU authorized representative is:
Springer Nature Customer Service Center GmbH
Europaplatz 3, 69115 Heidelberg, Germany

Printed by Libri Plureos GmbH
in Hamburg, Germany